Land, Labor, and Capital in Modern Yucatán

Land, Labor, & Capital in Modern Yucatán

Essays in Regional History and Political Economy

Edited by Jeffery T. Brannon
and Gilbert M. Joseph

THE UNIVERSITY OF ALABAMA PRESS
TUSCALOOSA AND LONDON

∞

The paper on which this book is printed meets the minimum requirements of American National Standard for Information Science-Permanence of Paper for Printed Library Materials, ANSI Z39.48-1984.

Library of Congress Cataloging-in-Publication Data

Land, labor, and capital in modern Yucatán : essays in regional history and political economy / edited by Jeffery T. Brannon and Gilbert M. Joseph.
p. cm.
Includes bibliographical references and index.
ISBN 0-8173-0555-6 (alk. paper)
1. Yucatán (Mexico : State)—Economic conditions. 2. Yucatán (Mexico : State)—Social conditions. 3. Land, tenure—Mexico—Yucatán (State) History. 5. Plantations—Mexico—Yucatán (State)—History. 6. Mayas—Economic conditions. 7. Mayas—Social conditions. 8. Peasantry—Mexico—Yucatán (State)—History. I. Brannon, Jeffery. II. Joseph, G. M. (Gilbert M.), 1947–
HC137.Y8L36 1991
330.972′65—dc20 90-46746

British Library Cataloguing-in-Publication Data available.

An earlier version of "From Hacienda to Plantation: The Transformation of Santo Domingo Xcuyum," by Allen Wells, was published in *Yucatán's Gilded Age*, copyright 1985 by the University of New Mexico Press. Reprinted with permission.

0-8173-1287-0 (pbk: alk. paper)

Contents

Preface

Interdisciplinary regional studies have been at the forefront of research in Mexican and Latin American history for over a decade, and work on Yucatán has been particularly abundant. Lured, perhaps, by the past glories of ancient Mayan civilization, its conquest by the Spaniards, the fierce resistance of the Maya to their Spanish and, later, Mexican rulers, and finally by the fabled riches of the henequen boom and its dramatic demise in the aftermath of the Mexican Revolution, historians (along with other social scientists) have made important contributions. This recent surge of interest in the Yucatecan past has been notably pronounced for the modern period (c. 1750–1940). Over the past five to ten years, the traditional political and institutional histories of the Caste War, henequen boom, and revolutionary eras have been superseded by an impressive harvest of monographs and articles on regional social and economic themes by an ever-widening circle of Mexican and international scholars.

Each of the ten chapters in this book, by an international cohort of U.S., Mexican, Canadian, and Belizean social scientists, taps new research on the political economy and agrarian history of the region; several suggest new thematic and methodological approaches to the study of Mexico at the subnational level. Adding to the uniqueness of the collection is its mix of contributions by well-established and younger scholars. The result is a perspective on regional historical development that is at once international, interdisciplinary, and intergenerational. The book demonstrates that if, in certain respects, Yucatán developed with a degree of autonomy unmatched elsewhere in Mexico, its historical experience also illuminates broader discussions of capitalist agricultural expansion and forms of peasant resistance, plantation monoculture and obstacles to regional development, and revolutionary mobilization and strategies of social change.

Finally, an effort has been made—both in the introduction by Joseph and more implicitly throughout the book—to grapple with certain neglected themes and conceptual problems that Latin America's "new regional history," despite its early promise and popularity, has been slow to address.

While this book is a testament to several years of collaboration among editors and contributors, other individuals and organizations have lent valuable support at critical stages. The editors' home institutions—the University of Texas at El Paso and the University of North Carolina at Chapel Hill—along with the Universidad Autónoma de Yucatán and the University of Alabama, Tuscaloosa, generously funded the 1987 International Conference on the Historical Development of Yucatán, held in Mérida, that generated initial drafts of most of the chapters and provided their authors a lively forum in which to critique each other's work. We express special gratitude to Malcolm MacDonald, director of The University of Alabama Press, who encouraged the book from its inception and patiently endured the delays that accompany multiauthored projects. Thanks also go to Sue Brannon, who compiled the bibliography, and to Billy Patterson, Jackie Headen, Catalina Macías, and Rosalie Radcliffe, who prepared the final draft of the manuscript.

J. T. B.
G. M. J.

A Brief Chronology

Major Events in Mexico and the Yucatán Peninsula

National		Regional	
1810–1821	Wars of Independence against Spain	**1825–1847**	First legislation by white regional elites to appropriate Mayan land and labor
1821	Independence	**1847**	Caste War of Yucatán breaks out
1856–1857	The liberal reforms and the Constitution of 1857: first national precedents for the breakup of Indian village lands	**1853**	Truce ends hostilities in northwestern Yucatán; rebel Maya continue in revolt in southeastern Quintana Roo
1858–1861	The War of Reform	**1858**	Campeche receives independent statehood
1876–1910	The "Porfiriato," the rule of General Porfirio Díaz	**1878**	Perfection of the McCormick reaper-binder triggers Yucatecan henequen boom (1880–1915) and further appropriation of Mayan village lands and labor
		1901	Defeat of the rebel Maya at Chan Santa Cruz by federal troops
		1902	Designation of Quintana Roo as a federal territory, apart from the State of Yucatán

National

1910 The Mexican Revolution begins with Francisco Madero's armed uprising against Díaz

1913 Madero assassinated; General Victoriano Huerta becomes president

1914 Huerta defeated by Constitutionalist revolutionary coalition; coalition dissolves and war between revolutionary factions commences: Venustiano Carranza's Constitutionalists vs. Pancho Villa's and Emiliano Zapata's Conventionists

1917 Promulgation of new revolutionary constitution

1917–1920 Presidency of Carranza

1920 Carranza assassinated

1920–1924 Presidency of Alvaro Obregón

1923–1924 Rebellion of Adolfo de la Huerta

1924–1928 Presidency of Plutarco Elías Calles

1929 Establishment of the National Revolutionary party

1928–1934 Dictatorship of Calles ("El Maximato")

1934–1940 Presidency of Lázaro Cárdenas

Regional

1902–1915 The "Olegariato," the rule of Governor Olegario Molina and his "Divine Caste"; increasing dependence on U.S. corporate capital

1915 Constitutionalist General Salvador Alvarado's Army of the Southeast invades and conquers Yucatán

1915–1918 Governorship of Alvarado; establishment of the Socialist Party of the Southeast

1922–1924 Reform governorship of socialist Felipe Carrillo Puerto

1924 Assassination of Carrillo Puerto by *delahuertista* forces

1937–1938 *Cardenista* expropriation and *ejidal* distribution of Yucatán's henequen estates

Land, Labor, and Capital in Modern Yucatán

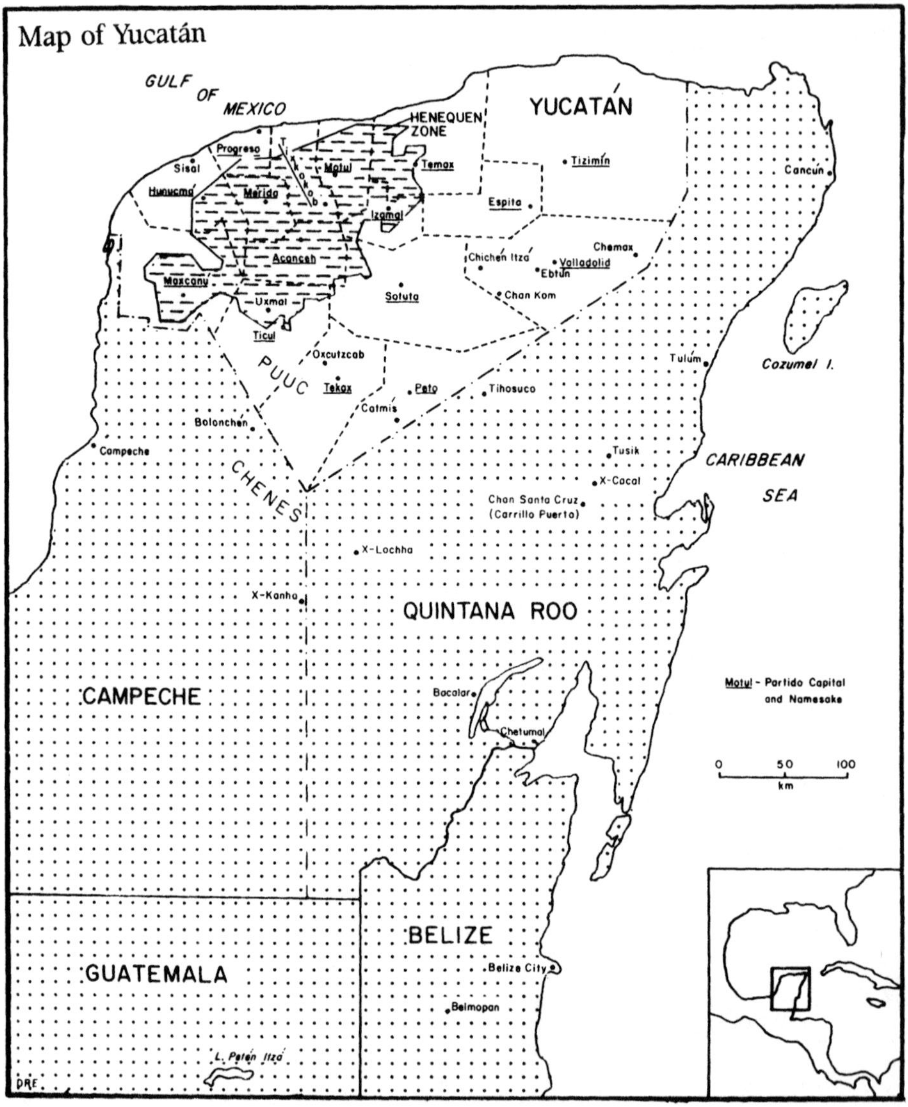

Map 1 The Yucatán Peninsula

1 Introduction: The New Regional Historiography at Mexico's Periphery

GILBERT M. JOSEPH

The Ascendancy of the Regional Approach to Mexican History

In 1986, almost fifteen years after his amiable challenge to fellow professionals to produce "microhistories" of modern Mexico,[1] Luis González could take a certain satisfaction in the state of the new genre. Practitioners were legion, and the value of a regional or subnational approach to Mexican (and Latin American) studies was undisputed. Observed Don Luis: "We no longer have to prove the truth of the tongue-twisting *muchos Mexicos* . . . it is a fundamental truth."[2]

It was not always so. Until about twenty years ago, there was an exaggerated tendency among professional scholars to concentrate almost exclusively on events in the capital and to assume that all meaningful ideas and forces for change ultimately radiated outward from the heartland to the regional peripheries. It was as if professional historians, writing from the Olympian perspective of the Federal District, upheld with other *chilangos* (residents of the national capital) the adage "Fuera de México, todo es Cuautitlán" (beyond Mexico City, every place is Cuautitlán—an obscure rural hamlet). Today, *capitalinos* concur with their professional colleagues based in the provinces and abroad that "the pervasiveness of regionalism in Mexico—the stubbornness and distinctiveness of regional [and local] identities and loyalties and their frequent projection onto the national scene in the form of political conflict—is one of the most important themes in Mexican history."[3] Furthermore, Mexicanists have come to appreciate that the historical trajectories of the nation's regions and localities represent intricate sets of variables, analysis of which includes, but is not exhausted by, linkages with the national metropolis. Commenting recently on the state of Mexican historiography, the eminent chilango scholar Enrique Krauze concluded (with a touch of irony): "Fuera de México, nada es Cuautitlán."[4]

Moreover, the regional experience will continue to preoccupy students of Mexican affairs. In the early 1970s, Luis González alluded compellingly to "the regionalist impulse of our times," a search for identity in the authentic world of local, often rural, traditions in the face of disorienting modernization and stifling centralization.[5] Now, as we move closer to the millennium, at a time when the word *crisis* is used so pervasively that it has come to describe the routine pattern of Mexican life, and critics on both ends of the political spectrum question the capacity of the Institutional Revolutionary party (PRI) to maintain its once-potent legitimizing rationales of modernization and national unity, the regional pull remains undiminished. A variety of social scientists have suggested that Mexico has entered a new, "postmodern" period in which, as one commentator provocatively observes, "the national unity forged by the PRI is unraveling, and the mosaic of civil society can no longer be ordered neatly along 'corporatist' lines. Rather, it is necessary to consult another social and political map, one which expresses Mexico's characteristic fragmentation by region, locality, class, gender, and ethnic group."[6]

Certainly, the current impulse to reform or "democratize" the Mexican system takes the form of pressures being exerted, by increasingly autonomous *regional* economic elites and by opposition political leaders, upon a crisis-ridden central state that, while espousing decentralization, still resists granting substantial recognition and legitimacy to regional oppositions in the electoral arena. It is hardly coincidental that, within this political climate, the new regional history of Mexico is flourishing, demystifying official interpretations and often searching for historical roots and analogies that might inform the political activity of the present.[7]

Not surprisingly, a subnational approach to the Mexican past is congruent with some of the most vital long-term trends within the historical discipline and the larger social science community. By narrowing the aperture, scholars can undertake case studies in which extraordinarily rich and diverse local data shed light on larger historical problems, testing conventional wisdoms and frequently prompting their revision. In a real sense, therefore, we must agree with Wigberto Jiménez Moreno that "without good regional and local history, there can be no good national history."[8]

Microhistorical evidence can also enable historians and other social scientists to bridge the gap between long-running, complex, structural processes of change and the more tangible, textured reality at the local level. In the hands of the French Annalists, searching inquiry into the development of a region or locality over the *longue durée* has raised the possibility of an *histoire totale*, an ambitious tapestry of politics and society, culture and mentality. Such a multidisciplinary regional approach, which draws upon local archives, informants, and traditions, and seeks a closer approximation of the societal whole, necessarily places a greater emphasis on the social history of ordinary people, much neglected by more conventional historians.[9]

The new regional history has been aided by the Mexican central government's evolving commitment to institutional decentralization, which has meant greater support for regional projects and research centers, as well as for upgrading local archives and libraries.[10] Scholarly production has, in turn, boomed: Foreign and Mexican scholars have produced a storehouse of empirical research, particularly abundant for several areas (e.g., Chihuahua, Sonora, San Luis Potosí, Morelos, Tlaxcala, Veracruz, Oaxaca, Chiapas, and, of course, Yucatán).[11]

Conceptual Problems in the New Regional History

For all of its popularity and promise, the regional approach remains fraught with pitfalls and conceptual difficulties. Perhaps most critically, much work in the new genre suffers from a failure to define *region*. Historians rarely make a distinction between regional and local history, and most employ the term *regional history* as a kind of shorthand for all subnational history. To be sure, *region* is a multivalent concept, and a certain amount of conceptual flexibility—as opposed to an a priori definition—may be beneficial.[12] It is sad that, as Eric Van Young has observed, too often " 'regions' turn out to be what any individual researcher happens to be working on at the moment."[13] This lack of definitional precision impedes comparative work, since it is never really clear what variables are being compared from one historical case to another.[14]

Moreover, despite its many virtues, in certain respects the new literature may be missing the forest for the trees, liable to the same charges of parochialism that were once leveled against earlier generations of amateur chroniclers. Such parochialism manifests itself in several ways:

1. Much regional work on Mexico (and other parts of Latin America) has failed fully to explore the complex, interactive relationship between center and periphery. Too often, otherwise reliable and richly detailed

subnational monographs are poorly integrated into larger, regional, national, and international structures and processes. Regional history cannot be insular; indeed, however "regionalist," no region can be viewed as a unique and self-contained social and economic system.[15]

2. Regional specialists must also guard against the danger of their work's becoming compartmentalized chronologically as well as spatially. Although regional history's rich, if disparate, sources lend themselves to longitudinal explorations of local institutions and processes, Mexican regionalists have often hewed rather timidly to sacrosanct national dates and benchmarks (1810, 1910, etc.). They have been too willing to pour their often heterodox regional findings into ready-made periodizations that often tell us more about the ideological process of state-building than about the characteristic history of a particular region. One need not deny the importance of significant national events and conjunctures to appreciate the larger continuities and often-subtle transitions at work in regional historical development.[16]

3. The failure to appreciate the longue durée points up a more general shortcoming in the new regional literature: the slowness with which it has followed up interesting conceptual and methodological leads offered by social historians working from a regional or local perspective in related fields and disciplines. It was precisely here, in the realm of social history, that the regional approach was to have paid the richest dividends. Nevertheless, twenty years after their European counterparts began in earnest to reconstruct the experiences and mentalities of elites and everyday people, Latin American social historians have only begun to scratch the surface of these problems.[17]

4. Finally, the academic regional scholarship on Mexico and Latin America—in the main spearheaded by highly trained North Americans—has occasionally been marked by ethnocentrism and failure critically to examine traditional ideological/methodological biases. (Often this expresses itself in a predilection for elite studies within the context of a larger process of "modernizing" transformation.) These are strong words perhaps, yet to the extent that North American scholars have been reluctant to enter into discourse or collaboration with their Latin American colleagues, their regional investigations have suffered.[18] This "failure to communicate" has been evident on two levels. North American professionals have frequently ignored the venerable amateur tradition of *historia matria*, which is not only redolent with local factual detail but also provides important clues for reconstructing elite social networks and systems of belief.[19] North Americans have also tended to remain aloof from

the current generation of professionals whose Marxist formation diverges markedly from their own, and who, they assume (generally in error), want nothing to do with them. While there have been striking exceptions—for example, the fruitful continuing dialog between North American social historians and their Latin Marxist counterparts on the productive and social relations of circum-Caribbean sugar plantations,[20] and, as we shall see, among historians of modern Yucatán—these collaborations, unfortunately, have been more the exception than the rule.[21]

The New Regional History of Modern Yucatán

Recent historical scholarship on modern Yucatán has been particularly successful in avoiding or minimizing these pitfalls and conceptual difficulties.[22] On the whole, *yucatecólogos* have built a clear understanding of the definitional complexities of regionality into their research designs. On one level, they have examined the leitmotiv of Yucatecan regionalism or sectionalism: the self-conscious political, cultural, and sentimental identification that has historically bound *yucatecos* to the state and peninsula and invariably run counter to the national process of state-building[23] (see, for example, the chapters by Chacón and Konrad).

Yet, on another level, Yucatecanists have appreciated that regions are also economic structures, defined by geographical factors and systems of production and exchange. In this sense, the traditional notion—unfortunately too readily applied in many North American monographs—that politicoadministrative structure governs regionality, that region is congruent with the political borders of a state, is often arbitrary and misleading.[24] As several contributors here demonstrate, rather than speaking of the State of Yucatán as a region, it is often more meaningful to identify a metropolitan northwestern zone of commercial agriculture, centered around the capital city of Mérida, and a vast, peripheral, southeastern zone of peasant production, extending into Quintana Roo and northern Belize (e.g., see the chapters by Güémez, Patch, Cal, Wells, Konrad, and Batt). At yet another level of analysis, both of these "regions" become peripheries—albeit with differing politicoeconomic roles—in the capitalist world system (e.g., see the chapters by Cal, Konrad, and Batt). Thus, the concept of region is multivalent and relational, with the analytic contours of regionality often shaped by the research problem at hand.[25]

This recognition of the necessity and value of multilayered, regional research strategies has produced the beginnings of a bold, new synthesis of Yucatán's past. Transcending parochial and restrictive notions of geography or place, Yucatán's new regional history seeks to integrate locality, region, and nation within the larger framework of western capitalist expansion. Operating within this broader conceptual framework, Yucatecanists can account for characteristic or "exceptional" aspects of the region's historical development without retreating into "localism." Whereas traditional chroniclers—and some professional historians—have been wont to portray Yucatán almost ahistorically as "a world apart" or "another Mexico" with a "strange and exotic" past,[26] recent scholarship has attempted to analyze the complexities of its dynamic participation in the national and world systems.[27]

In the process, Yucatán's new regional historians have questioned conventional interpretations and periodizations, which have pivoted narrowly on the great national political benchmarks—Independence, The Reform, The Revolution. Probing beneath the surface of such official compartmentalizations of history, scholars have explored larger problems of change within the context of long-term structural continuity. As this book illustrates, much attention has been given to evolving relations of land, labor, and capital, and to their impact on socioeconomic, political, and cultural processes and institutions.[28] What has emerged is the foundation for a new periodization of Yucatecan history based upon a sustained analysis of the uneven process of capitalist development in a peripheral, dependent society. This has involved examining the evolution of systems of production and relations between classes, as they are conditioned by the interplay of factors internal and external to Yucatán. It has impelled historians to pursue central themes and problems, such as the evolution of the great estate, mechanisms of social control, and forms of peasant resistance, across longer periods of time, that overlap traditional periodizations (e.g., see the chapters by Patch, Cal, Wells, Konrad, and Batt).[29]

Mexicanists will immediately grasp that this book's thematic organization reflects a significant departure from conventional orderings of Mexico's past. Instead of fitting Yucatecan history into Mexico's three great "revolutionary cycles" (Independence, Reform, Revolution)—a schema into which, I have shown elsewhere, it fits poorly[30]—we have conceived the region's modern past in terms of distinguishing "episodes" in the development of its political economy. It is rather more difficult to attach precise dates to each major politicoeconomic episode than to the conventional political periods. Roughly speaking, however, our schema comprises three historical periods that, collectively, run from about 1750 to 1940: (1) the early expansion of the great estate, which brought with it a range of Mayan responses (c. 1750–1880); (2) the heyday of export monoculture (c. 1880–1915); and (3) the assault that a series of twentieth-century mobilizations—some organized by the state, others emanating from the grass roots—made on the Old Regime centered on export monoculture (c. 1915–1940).[31] (In the concluding chapter, we bring the story of Yucatán's development up to the present and reflect on its broader implications.)

Generally speaking, the new regional history of Yucatán, Mexico, and Latin America as a whole has been more successful in analyzing larger events and their politicoeconomic context from a regional (as opposed to the national) level, than in recreating history at a grass-roots level from the perspective of the participants. As I have suggested, surprisingly little inspiration has been taken from the more established traditions of European or U.S. social history or even from scholarship on other parts of the Third World. Nevertheless, as a new decade begins, significant efforts are being made in the Latin American field to understand the experiences and mentalities of everyday people—perhaps nowhere more so than for Yucatán. Nancy M. Farriss's masterful study, *Maya Society under Colonial Rule* (1984), effectively combined anthropological tools and archival sources to reconstruct the social organization, culture, and ideology that enabled a colonial Mayan peasantry collectively to sustain a way of life.[32] More recently, in *Ambivalent Conquests* (1987), Inga Clendinnen teased out of partisan chronicles by conquistadores and the Maya's own few and fragmentary writings a nuanced interpretation of the earlier period of contact and conquest.[33] Both of these prize-winning books complement Victoria R. Bricker's similarly acclaimed study *The Indian Christ, the Indian King* (1981), which contains a penetrating reconstruction of the Yucatecan Maya's participation in the apocalyptic nineteenth-century Caste War and of the meaning they and their descendants put upon it.[34] Meanwhile, Joseph and Wells are completing a long-term investigation of elite factional politics and its relationship to forms of social action and consciousness among Mayan villagers and peons during the late Porfiriato and early revolutionary years.[35]

This book includes a variety of fresh examinations of elite strategies of appropriation and control, and the responses they elicited from Mayan peasants, Belizean black creoles, and Yucatecan urban workers—the last group almost completely ignored by historians until now (see the chapters by Güémez, Patch, Cal, Wells, Konrad, Batt, and Spenser). These chapters illustrate the steady infusion of conceptual and methodological insights from related fields and disciplines, as well as the array of sources that Yucatecan social historians now count as weapons in their arsenal.[36] Ranging far beyond standard institutional sources and the regional press, the contributors have mined parish registers and notarial archives; searched out land titles, litigation files, agrarian census records, and tax lists; collected oral histories and popular traditions; and gained access to the papers of private estates and multinational corporations. Their efforts have taken them outside the peninsula, to governmental and private collections in Mexico City and Belize, as well as in North America and Europe.

Finally, Yucatán's new regional history has been distinguished by a degree of international, interdisciplinary collaboration that is perhaps unique in Mexican regional studies. This book and the April 1987 conference out of which it was born reflect a climate of collegiality that builds on significant foundations and has particularly flourished in the 1980s.

In the early decades of this century, a cohort of North American and Mexican anthropologists, affiliated with the Carnegie Institution of Washington, presided over a golden age of Mayan studies.[37] Beginning in the early 1970s, the Latin American Studies Program of the University of Alabama, which traditionally has maintained a strong interest in Yucatán, initiated a succession of seminars and conferences on Yucatecan themes, from which several publications have issued.[38] These events in the United States have usually involved the participation of Yucatecan officials and intellectuals, occasionally noted historians. Then, in 1978, the Universidad Autónoma de Yucatán inaugurated in Mérida the Primera Semana de la Historia de Yucatán, assembling a diverse group of amateur and professional scholars from Mexico and abroad, for the purpose of sharing research and cementing collegial ties.[39] In subsequent years, a Second History Week and several more specialized research symposia on themes in agrarian history and political economy, culminating in the 1987 Specialists Conference, have brought Mexican and international scholars together to reflect on and actively debate the state of regional historiography. These gatherings have generated a spate of publications and attracted substantial public and media attention. In fact, they have become a regular feature of the region's cultural life.[40]

The 1987 conference was the most ambitious collaborative effort to date. It promoted lively exchanges between professional and amateur historians, Marxists and non-Marxists, and Mexican and foreign scholars. For several days, participants debated the broad contours and fine points of regional history and political economy, often being forced to question guiding paradigms and tightly held assumptions. Apart from the publications that will appear in both Spanish[41] and English, such intellectual exchange was itself an achievement. This book represents the ripe fruit of seeds sown at that conference.

Part I

The Erosion of Traditional Society: The Early Expansion of Commercial Agriculture and the Mayan Response

The chapters in Part I are unified by a preoccupation with the early expansion of commercial agriculture and the erosion this caused in traditional Mayan society in Yucatán as well as northern Belize. Yet, collectively, the contributions portray more than social deterioration and decline; equally as important, they suggest a broad range of indigenous forms of opposition and adjustment to evolving strategies of white domination. By means of cattle rustling, tax evasion, vagrancy, and flight; through litigation within the system or quiet land incursions outside it; and (as a last, desperate resort) through acts of violent rebellion, local subaltern groups sought to resist, or stategically adapt to, the emerging new order. In the process, these people played an active role in shaping the terms of their oppression; Yucatán's agrarian past can no longer be viewed from the top down, in the fashion of much "imperial" Latin American historiography. Only a reciprocal approach to relations between the Maya and the dominant white society can illuminate structures and mentalities of domination and suggest new sources for addressing these problems.

The chapters in Part I build upon a solid foundation of Howard Cline's and Robert Patch's scholarship on the belated rise of the Yucatecan great estate, and on the more recent work of Yucatecan economic historian Pedro Bracamonte y Sosa. At the 1987 conference, Bracamonte y Sosa shared important research in progress on the development of the hacienda in northwestern Yucatán during the early nineteenth century.[1] Unlike Cline and Patch, who emphasized the estate's "mixed" character (corn and cattle), Bracamonte y Sosa took pains to show that, in the northwest, livestock predominated, with mixed haciendas more characteristic of the area around Campeche and in the southeast of the peninsula.

Bracamonte contended that prosperous *haciendas ganaderas* (livestock estates) increasingly controlled the northwestern Maya's access to subsistence and transformed their traditional notion of property. Indeed, there are important cultural continuities between these early livestock haciendas and the more formidable henequen estates that replaced them later in the century in the northwestern quadrant. More than previous writers had, he underscored the hacienda ganadera's strength as a hegemonic "cultural complex," capable of exercising social control by means of ideological and religious suasion as well as through physical coercion and debt. It is this view of landlords' hegemony in the northwest, reinforced by the region's fragmented agrarian pattern, that Bracamonte y Sosa invokes to explain why northwestern campesinos ultimately did not participate on the rebel side in the 1847 Caste War.

In his contribution to this book, fellow Yucatecan historian Arturo Güémez Pineda rather differently conceives the relationship between domination and the capacity to resist. Drawing on Bracamonte y Sosa's research on the cattle hacienda's encroachment upon surrounding Mayan communities, he recognizes that by 1847 the great majority of the northwestern Maya lived or periodically worked on haciendas. Yet, based on a reading of court records and other government documents, Güémez raises serious questions about the extent of landlords' hegemony and the nature of Mayan resistance. He argues that Mayan villagers deeply felt the loss of common lands and resented the trampling of their milpas by neighboring haciendas' cattle. In this social context, cattle rustling emerged as one of several characteristic forms of northwestern Mayan resistance. Rustling, Güémez contends, enabled campesinos to work an onerous system to their minimum disadvantage, to thwart the expansive claims of white proprietors materially and symbolically. At the same time, it also put meat on the table, providing a margin of subsistence for poor households in times of scarcity. Indeed, not only were political and economic motives both present in the act of rustling, they were likely fused in the perpetrator's consciousness. Güémez's chapter, which is sure to provoke discussion regarding the motivation of such "social bandits," also analyzes the modus operandi of nineteenth-century rustling, exploring its ties to peasant communities and kin groups. Finally, he examines successive attempts by the landlord-dominated state to fashion a mechanism to control what it monochromatically perceived to be deviant, criminal acts.

Güémez challenges the prevailing tendency in Yucatecan, Mexican, and Latin American historiography to conceptualize Indian resistance exclusively in terms of armed conflict and insurgency. He also questions the widely held notion that the campesinos of northwestern Yucatán did not join the Mayan rebels of the southeastern frontier in the Caste War because they were enmeshed in an exploitative, symbiotic relationship with their white masters that rendered them docile, alienated, and unable to mount a response. He is inspired by a more-established social history of crime and banditry, by European scholars such as Hobsbawm, Thompson, and Rudé[2] and, in turn, supports the current trend of comparative work on "everyday forms of resistance" by social scientists working on other Third World peasantries.[3]

Such minimally organized, clandestine forms of resistance do not leave the impressive paper trail that concerted peasant protests and full-blown insurgencies—such as Yucatán's nineteenth-century Caste War—do. Nevertheless, apart from oral tradition (elite and folk variants) and problematic inference from the social context, historians have occasionally been able to mine such "routine" resistance in rich veins of criminal-court testimony. Fortunately for

Güémez and a growing number of other regional scholars, such records exist abundantly for modern Yucatán.[4]

Of course, a broader understanding of Mayan resistance by no means preempts further investigation of the so-called Caste War, regarded by many to be the most militarily successful Indian rebellion in Latin American history. Even today, the Guerra de Castas remains the central historical event in the popular mind, and many yucatecos often assume that when one speaks of the Revolution in Yucatán, one is referring to the great peasant rebellion unleashed in 1847, not the more-recent national upheaval that began in 1910.[5]

Robert Patch's chapter contributes to the literature on the rebellion's agrarian origins; at the same time, he addresses a problem of larger relevance to Latin Americanists: the extent to which the Spanish imperial regime was "decolonized" after independence. Certainly, early nineteenth-century Latin American liberals sought to dismantle what they regarded as a restrictive "feudal" system—or, as Wolf has observed with greater sophistication, to effect the transition from a "tributary" or state-led mode of production to a market-oriented, capitalistic one.[6] Patch relates how, during the Independence era and the subsequent 1821–1847 period, Yucatecan liberals waged a concerted campaign to break up properties vested in colonial corporations such as the church and Indian communities, and to effect their sale like any other commodity. This campaign received powerful support at the federal level in 1856–1857, when legislation, enshrined in a new national Constitution, sanctioned the alienation of village and church lands (see the chapters by Wells, Chacón, and Batt). Given the great significance of this agrarian issue to the social, economic, and political history of modern Latin America, it is unsettling that we have so little empirical data on the timing and scope of land alienations prior to, or during, the consolidation of export-oriented oligarchical regimes—such as the Porfiriato—at the end of the nineteenth century. Patch's work, carefully researched in notarial and state governmental archives, is an illuminating case study.[7]

Patch demonstrates that, although the new generation of liberal elites did not attempt to dispossess the Maya completely, communal landownership was significantly restricted and private ownership dramatically extended in the 1840s. Village lands were limited directly by agrarian decree and indirectly by burdensome taxes on plots worked by the Maya; meantime, everything outside the reduced core of the *ejido* was declared to be *terrenos baldíos*—unoccupied land subject to colonization by private individuals. In point of fact, as the indigenous population continued to grow throughout the period, concentrations of Mayan peasants continued to cultivate a good part of this "unoccupied" land, setting them on a collision course with white elites bent on promoting a land rush. Patch's quantitative analysis of hundreds of previously untapped records of registrations and adjudications of terrenos baldíos reveals some interesting findings regarding the ultimate disposition of Indian village lands. His study also confirms earlier interpretations that the area most affected by the 1840s land rush was the southeastern borderlands, the fertile crescent running from Hopelchén to Valladolid. It was here, where white entrepreneurs were developing a profitable sugar industry and free Mayan villagers had greatest tactical mobility, that the rebellion of 1847 would gain its greatest force.

Patch's account of the Maya's persistent efforts to litigate their agrarian grievances before a newly independent creole regime not disposed to grant them justice complements earlier studies of Indian recourse to more sympathetic colonial courts, by Borah, Gibson, Taylor, Stern, Farriss, and others.[8] At the same time, Patch underscores an emerging consensus that armed insurrection was usually perceived as a terrible and final resort. Rebellion, typically, was chosen when institutional channels had been exhausted, "everyday forms" provided insufficient relief, and the balance of political forces had temporarily shifted in favor of aggrieved local groups.

Of course, as Patch admits, the southeastern Maya had other, nonagrarian grievances that entered into their decision to rebel. Particularly worthy of future investigation is the question of increased clerical fees.[9] Increased prices of sacraments had a profound impact on the Maya, who, as Farriss has shown, used the institution of marriage to shore up political and social status in their communities.

The Caste War quickly devastated southeastern Yucatán's nascent sugar industry. But, as Belizean historian Ángel Cal documents in his chapter, sugarcane cultivation was revived in the northern part of the colony of British Honduras (today Belize), principally because of the efforts of thousands of Yucatecan refugees who arrived between 1847 and 1860. Drawing on extensive research in Belizean and British archives, Cal reconstructs the complex political economy and multiracial society that developed in one of Britain's more remote imperial outposts during the nineteenth century. He demonstrates how an increased flow of British capital into sugar and timber extraction, between about 1850 and 1885, had important consequences for labor relations and patterns of land tenure, and was, in turn, affected by changes in these sectors.

Cal employs the reports of British officials, notarial records, and oral history to address not only the impact that deepening capitalist relations and colonial rule had on the free Maya, but also the reciprocal influence that the Maya exerted on the colonial political economy. Ultimately, northern Belize recapitulated a pattern played out a half-century earlier in southeastern Yucatán, for it was the resistance of free Mayan groups on the cutting edge of capitalist expansion that halted the frontier's advance—at least temporarily. Yet, Cal also documents the other side of the dialectical equation. Over time, Mayan opposition melted away, less the victim of British arms than of an encounter with British commodities and wage labor. He identifies as crucial intermediaries in this proletarianization that segment of the Yucatecan refugee community that used its managerial and entrepreneurial skills to broker the acquisition of Mayan labor for larger, British commercial interests.

Cal narrates the immigrant saga of these Yucatecan petty entrepreneurs in personal detail, highlighting their position as hinge-men in the concentric circles of dependency that characterized northern Belize's insertion into the world economy. Mayan and black creole workers were tied by wage advances to Yucatecan labor contractors, who were, in turn, dependent upon credit, land-leases, and marketing outlets provided by local British companies. Similarly, these Belizean firms were forced to rely upon large amounts of capital advanced by their parent companies and banks, based in England. When, in the face of labor unrest and reduced commodity prices, Belize's enclave economy could no longer convince London of its long-term prospects, British investors withdrew their capital and reduced northern Belize to a colonial backwater.

2 *Everyday Forms of Mayan Resistance: Cattle Rustling in Northwestern Yucatán, 1821–1847*

JOSÉ ARTURO GÜÉMEZ PINEDA

While it has filtered very slowly into the Mexican and Latin American historical literature, some of the best work being done in peasant studies for other parts of the Third World and for Europe concerns alternative forms of protest and the peasant consciousness (*mentalité*) that informs them. Scholars now posit a continuum of peasant (and working-class) resistance, ranging from petty, individual acts focused on the here-and-now to highly organized, durable movements of broad ideological purpose. Certainly, the "noisier events of agrarian history," the peasant jacqueries and full-blown insurgencies (such as Yucatán's nineteenth-century Caste War), which preoccupied the state and left an impressive paper trail, have also riveted the attention of historians. Yet, given the preponderant strength of the state and dominant classes, such revolts invariably ended in defeat, even massacre. Recently, scholars such as James Scott have argued persuasively that less-risky, "quieter forms of resistance," proceeding without overt protest and often with only minimal formal organization, may well have been more successful over the long run in mitigating claims by the powerful on the peasantry.[1]

These everyday forms of resistance, which have been used for centuries by peasants and other relatively powerless groups, include, at a minimum, foot-dragging, dissimulation, and false compliance; somewhat more aggressively, arson and sabotage, poaching, rustling, and theft. Such "small arms fire in the class war"—to use Scott's phrase—makes no headlines and rarely surfaces in official administrative records.[2] Nevertheless, social historians have occasionally been able to tease evidence of these acts out of oral traditions and judicial records, as well as to infer them from a careful examination of the social context.

Criminal-court records are particularly abundant for modern Yucatán and help us to document various "routine" forms of Mayan protest against encroaching commercial agriculture in northwestern Yucatán during the early nineteenth century. Not only did Indian communities use the legal system to fight land usurpation, abuses of authority, high taxes, and unwarranted seizures of people and property;[3] when this avenue failed they transgressed creole interests by mounting land invasions, evading taxes, fleeing, and rustling livestock.[4]

An appreciation of such quiet forms of Mayan protest in the northwestern zone of haciendas before (and after) the Caste War should prompt revision of a variety of tendencies and notions in Yucatecan historiography, most notably the tendency to perceive Indian resistance exclusively in terms of armed conflict, and the notion that the northwestern Indian peasants did not join the Mayan rebels of the southeastern frontier in the Caste War because they were the products of an exploitative, symbiotic relationship with the dominant white society that left them passive, alienated, and incapable of resistance.[5]

Cattle rustling was one form of "routine" resistance in the Mérida district, a jurisdiction that encompassed most of the northwestern part of the peninsula during 1821–1847. Although they have been characterized as docile and alienated, Yucatán's northwestern campesinos did not submit passively to the demands of the creole elite that took up the reins of power following Mexico's independence from Spain. Despite their subordinate condition, the northwestern Maya adopted a variety of attitudes and postures that had an impact on, and served to modify, the regime under which they lived.

Moreover, we should keep in mind that, in addition to these "active" expressions of Mayan resistance, there were other, more deeply rooted modes of cultural resistance to white rule that were not subject to judicial proceedings. Indeed, many of the Maya's customs—their religious practices, their language, and their seeming indifference to work, which nineteenth-century creole writers routinely ascribed to a "rejection of progress"—might well be conceived as part of a broader response to the claims and authority of dominant white rule. Cattle theft was underwritten by a social organization rooted in family and communal ties. While further research must flesh out these networks of kin and community, they clearly suggest something of the climate or "subculture of resistance" that Scott argues is so essential to everyday forms of resistance.[6]

The Structure of Domination

Cattle Raising during the First Half of the Nineteenth Century

At least until 1847, cattle raising was the principal activity of the great majority of haciendas and other rural establishments in the northwestern and central parts of Yucatán. Statistical evidence for 1838 (see Table 2.1) indicates that the *partidos* of Mérida, Camino Real Alto, and Sierra Baja, together with those of Izamal and Beneficios Bajos, contained almost 70 percent of the peninsula's haciendas. The first three partidos, or at least the majority of the pueblos therein, formed the district of Mérida, while the last two formed the district of Izamal. Another statistical report, for 1846, reported that there were 1,388 haciendas in the peninsula; of these, 884 (63 percent) were located in the districts of Mérida and Izamal. Mérida district alone had 446 haciendas (32 percent) distributed among the partidos of Mérida, Ticul, Maxcanú, and Tecoh. By and large, these livestock estates were dedicated to the raising of cattle, horses, and mules.[7]

It has been argued that livestock raising in Yucatán never could have been as productive as in other parts of Latin America, owing to the dryness of the soil, frequent tick infestations, and the depredations of wild animals; nonetheless, nineteenth-century authorities always highlighted cattle raising as one of the most important productive activities of the Yucatecan economy. Based on data for 1834, José María Regil and Alonso Peón estimated that Yucatecan haciendas had about four hundred thousand head of cattle and sixty thousand horses.[8] José Tiburcio Cervera calculated the average estate's herd at three hundred head during the first half of the nineteenth century.[9] The Mérida district, with its 446 haciendas, was the most important cattle-raising region in the peninsula; by the middle of the last century its haciendas ran about 133,800 head.[10]

Although livestock raising was the most important activity on the northwestern haciendas, it was inherently incompatible with developing other agricultural activities. Free-ranging cattle convulsed the economy of the Mayan *milpero*, the small-scale cultivator of corn and other crops. In the face of the destruction that cattle wrought on his milpa, the campesino was forced to enclose his fields, thereby substantially increasing

Yucatecan state militia troops on the southeastern frontier during the final campaign of the Caste War, c. 1900 (Fototeca "Pedro Guerra" de la E.C.A.U.D.Y.)

Decorticating plant on a henequen hacienda in northwestern Yucatán, Porfiriato (Fototeca "Pedro Guerra" de la E.C.A.U.D.Y.)

Raw fiber drying on the patio of a henequen estate, Porfiriato (Fototeca "Pedro Guerra" de la E.C.A.U.D.Y.)

Portrait of an oligarchical family at the height of Yucatán's henequen boom
(Fototeca "Pedro Guerra" de la E.C.A.U.D.Y.)

Portrait of a young elite woman, Mérida, c. 1910 (Fototeca "Pedro Guerra" de la E.C.A.U.D.Y.)

Early twentieth-century promotion for North American Schaefer beer in Mérida (Fototeca "Pedro Guerra" de la E.C.A.U.D.Y.)

General Salvador Alvarado (seated, eighth from the left), Yucatán's revolutionary governor from 1915 to 1918, dines with political supporters in Mérida. (Fototeca "Pedro Guerra" de la E.C.A U.D.Y.)

Assembly of the Socialist Party of the Southeast's resistance league in Temax, 1923 (Archivo General del Estado de Yucatán)

Agraristas in Yaxkukul receive their ejidal grant from Yucatán's Socialist Party of the Southeast, 1930 (Archivo General del Estado)

A family of agrarian beneficiaries on a cattle cooperative in Yaxkukul, 1930 (Archivo General del Estado)

¡Jonrón! Baseball in the Yucatecan countryside, c. 1920s (Fototeca "Pedro Guerra" de la E.C.A.U.D.Y.)

Table 2.1 Ranchos, Haciendas, and Other Rural Properties by Partido

	Municipalities	Haciendas	Ranchos, Huertas, Etc.
Beneficios Altos	1	38	60
Beneficios Bajos	17	215	-
Camino Real Alto	9	65	30
Camino Real Bajo	11	278	-
Campeche	1	6	-
Carmen	2	19	23
Espita	10	102	58
Izamal	17[a]	507	-
Lerma	3	35	-
Mérida	1	103	-
Seibaplaya	4	14	15
Sierra Baja	9	244	15
Valladolid	9	202	196
Totals	104	1,929	434

Source: José Maria Regil y Alonso M. Peón, *Estadistica de Yucatán* (Mexico City, n.p., 1853), pp. 283-288.

Note: a. The municipality of Tekax is not included; the source mistakenly placed it under the partido of Izamal. The twenty haciendas that belonged to it are included in this table under the partido of Sierra Baja, where this municipality was listed a second time in the source. The sum of haciendas presented by Regil and Peón is 1,859, contrasted with my sum of 1,949 based on the same data. I have subtracted the twenty haciendas for Tekax for the reasons mentioned, leaving a total of 1,929 haciendas. The sum total of ranchos, huertas, and othe rural properties is also in error in Regil and Peón's work; they present a figure of 452, whereas my calculations based on the same data result in 434.

the effort required to achieve an adequate crop.[11] Especially in Yucatán, enclosure was difficult since milpas were rotated every two or three years.[12]

Without question, invasions of milpas by livestock, particularly in the northwest quadrant of the peninsula, bred conflict between Mayan campesinos and *hacendados*, and galvanized attempts to prevent creoles from introducing cattle. Such was the case in 1837, when the Indian village of Ucú opposed a request by Felipe Gil for four hundred *mecates* of land to establish a herd. The villagers argued that their fields would be destroyed because the cattle would move closer than the law allowed.[13] There were also cases in which hacendados proceeded against campesinos who squatted near their properties. In 1831, seventeen farmers of the town of Hunucmá were expelled from the vicinity of Hacienda Santa María, whose owner, Doña Manuela Solís, had reported "damage to her cattle." The local judge evicted the campesinos, citing damages they had caused to Santa María and to other estates in the area.[14]

The incompatibility of cattle raising and subsistence agriculture contributed to intensify the nomadism inherent in Yucatecan milpa cultivation—Indian cultivators would build their huts almost anywhere to be near their fields. This practice was addressed in an 1832 decree that sought "to stop the dispersion of the Indians and to encourage them to comply with their civic and religious obligations" (that is, with the payment of taxes and tithes). Those Mayan groups that lived in the hills were declared "illegal and fugitive" and were given one month to join a pueblo, hacienda, or rancho "according to the stipulations of the law."[15] A similar law was passed in 1836, along with others that sought to check the spread of cattle rustling on the haciendas. With these measures hacendados attempted to counter the characteristic dispersion of the Indian population. Clearly, the elite's interests were best served by limiting the autonomy and subsistence of the free Mayan *campesinado*.

Given the labor-intensive nature of production on haciendas, proprietors found it necessary further to rationalize their labor force, and, during the first half of the nineteenth century, work was organized more systematically. There were three types of *sirvientes*, sorted out according to the tasks they performed. One group was engaged in cattle raising; a second labored in crop production; and a third was made up of artisans.[16]

The labor legislation in effect during this period demonstrates that debt obligations were already a generalized practice in the peninsula. It has been stated repeatedly that debts "acquired" by the workers were one of the principal forms whereby hacendados managed to retain them in service.[17] However, an examination of the same legislation also reveals that debts constituted one of the most important motives for workers to abandon their labors. Consequently, hacienda proprietors were compelled repeatedly to use the state's powers to counter the flight of workers that was so detrimental to their interests. Authorities in pueblos, barrios, and haciendas were marshaled to ensure that vagrancy and fugitive-worker laws were effectively implemented. In this manner, the political network set up to control the internal affairs of the pueblos was placed at the service of the hacendado elite.

Cattle Rustling: Mayan Resistance

A search of the documentation for 1821–1847 in the Archivo General del Estado de Yucatán's *Poder Ejecutivo* and *Justicia* sections reveals a panorama of diverse attitudes and strategies that campesinos developed in response to the agrarian policies of the dominant white group, as well as those actions that directly threatened elite interests. Among the various manifestations of Indian "criminality"—which included assault, injury, homicide, arson, theft, and highway robbery—cattle rustling assumed a prominent role throughout the peninsula.

The archive's *Justicia* section contains the records of criminal cases. Among those dealing with cattle rustling, two characteristics stand out: (1) Indians were involved in the largest number of cases, and (2) most of the cases were concentrated in the Mérida district (see Table 2.2). Certainly, there were many more cases than those included in Table 2.2; not all the rustlers were caught nor did all of the cases find their way into the courts (1821 revealed no recorded cases). Moreover, the Archivo General does not have a complete set of the judicial proceedings initiated between 1821 and 1847. Nevertheless, it seems that the data at hand adequately reflect real tendencies.

The large number of Indian cattle rustlers can be explained without a profound knowledge of the nature of criminality during the period. In Yucatecan society, it was the Indian population that suffered most severely the exploitation of the clergy, the hacendados, and the state—all of which eroded the Maya's fragile subsistence base. Grain shortages, epidemics, and wars further aggravated the dismal material condition of the campesinado. Among the court proceedings that involved rustling, hunger is frequently mentioned as the primary cause that impelled the Maya to steal cattle. It is interesting to note that after an epidemic of cholera swept the region in 1833–1834, and privation increased, the incidence of cattle rustling also increased noticeably; in 1835, the number of cases involving Indians accused of cattle theft rose to thirty-four. The same tendency can be associated with the armed conflicts that pitted Centralists against Federalists after 1840, which occurred about the same time that creole elites were mounting a more aggressive land policy against the communal lands of Indian pueblos. As Table 2.2 reveals, the increase in the number of rustling cases from 1841 to 1847 is particularly striking when compared with the years 1822–1840 (with the exception of 1835).

The Maya who cultivated lands on the haciendas—the *luneros* and

Table 2.2 Cattle-rustling Cases in the Five Districts of Yucatán, 1822-1847[a]

	Mérida				Izamal				Valladolid				Tekax				Campeche				Total			
	I[b]	C[c]	I/C[d]	Subtotal	I[b]	C[c]	I/C[d]	Subtotal	I[b]	C[c]	I/C[d]	Subtotal	I[b]	C[c]	I/C[d]	Subtotal	I[b]	C[c]	I/C[d]	Subtotal	I[b]	C[c]	I/C[d]	All Cases
1822						1		1														1		1
1823		1	2	3																		1	2	3
1824	1			1																	1			1
1825	5	4	1	10																	5	4	1	10
1826	1			1																	1			1
1827		2		2																		2		2
1829	1			1		1		1													1	1		2
1832	3			3																	3			3
1833	2	1		3																	2	1		3
1834	4			4																	4			4
1835	19	2	3	24	1			1	1			1	3	1	1	5	6	2		8	30	5	4	39
1836	2	1		3													1			1	3	1		4
1837	1	1		2					1			1			2	2					2	1	2	5

Table 2.2. Continued

	Mérida				Izamal				Valladolid				Tekax				Campeche				Total			
	I[b]	C[c]	I/C[d]	Subtotal	I[b]	C[c]	I/C[d]	Subtotal	I[b]	C[c]	I/C[d]	Subtotal	I[b]	C[c]	I/C[d]	Subtotal	I[b]	C[c]	I/C[d]	Subtotal	I[b]	C[c]	I/C[d]	All Cases
1838	6	1		7	1			1					2	1	1	4	1	1		2	10	3	1	14
1840	2	1		3										1		1					2	2		4
1841		5		5	1	1		2	1			1	2			2		2		2	4	8		12
1842	1	5		6	2	1	2	5	1	1		2		2	1	3	2	2		4	6	11	3	20
1843	14	5		19			1	1	1	2	1	4		1		1	2			2	17	8	2	27
1844	9	7	1	17	1	1		2	2			2	5	1	2	8	3		1	4	20	9	4	33
1845	2	4	2	8	2	3	1	6	3		1	4	5	1	1	7	6	4	3	13	18	12	8	38
1846	3	3	2	8	1	3		4		4		4	3	2		5	2	3	1	6	9	15	3	27
1847	2	2	1	5					1			1	3			3	2	2		4	8	4	1	13
District Totals	78	45	12	135	9	11	4	24	11	7	2	20	23	10	8	41	25	16	5	46	146	89	31	266

Source: Archivo General del Estado de Yucatán, Justicia.

Notes:
a. No cases were reported for 1828, 1830, 1831, or 1839.
b. Cases involving Indians.
c. Cases involving castas (whites and other non-Indians).
d. Cases involving both Indians and castas.

arrendatarios—without question had motives similar to those of the free campesinos for engaging in the "crime" of cattle rustling. During an 1841 court proceeding against Feliciano Balam and José Antonio Chan for the theft of a heifer from Hacienda Hupichén, Balam stated that he had shot the animal because he had confused it with some deer that were threatening his milpa.[18] In another case, brought in 1843 against José Dzib for stealing a heifer from the Canchakan hacienda in the town of Umán's jurisdiction, the public defender, Wenceslao Encalada, argued that Dzib had killed the animal to protect his father-in-law's milpa. Encalada added that if Dzib had consumed the meat it was only because of hunger, grain being in short supply at the time.[19]

Another important motive that contributed to cattle rustling was the Maya's struggle against the hacendados' constant encroachment on Indians' common lands. It is likely that many of the cases described by the creole elite as rustling were, in fact, reprisals following the destruction of milpas by cattle, or the expression of continuing struggles over land rights between hacendados and campesinos. Of course, in their court testimonies, free Mayan defendants rarely cited these reasons as justification for their crimes; it was simply not to their advantage to argue reprisal as the underlying motivation. Hacienda peons were similarly loath to invoke any motive other than hunger, yet it seems clear that, for many, rustling presented an opportunity to avenge a variety of abuses—beatings, overwork, late payment of wages, and confiscation of personal possessions among them.

Not all of the cattle rustlers who figure in the court proceedings were Maya; many had Spanish names but obviously did not belong to the elite. The condition of many of these poor whites, mestizos, or mulattos was likely similar to that of the Maya, although generally these individuals were defined as *castas* to distinguish them from the creole elite.

It is not coincidental that between 1822 and 1847 the largest percentage of cases of cattle rustling was registered in the district of Mérida. Here, the power of the dominant white elite was concentrated. By contrast, the vast majority of the inhabitants of the district's pueblos, haciendas, and ranchos were poor Indians. Finally, the cattle haciendas lay only a short distance from the Indian villages and, in many cases, were also close to the district capital. It is not surprising, therefore, that Mérida's Mayan campesinos should have "hunted" some cattle now and then. But, how did the dominant white group perceive the root causes of rustling? One influential opinion, expressed in 1844 and based on the criminal records for that year, echoed the prevailing elite concerns:

> Among those crimes against property, rustling is without a doubt the most frequent, since those involved in this crime total 41 [73] while all other theft adds up to only 35 [50]. Nor can these violations of the sacred right of property be explained by need, because, with the exception of the years of scarcity, our working class, blessed by the abundance of corn and a frugal way of life, does not suffer the pains of hunger, nor does it bother to save or improve its lot in life, but instead is content to live from one day to the next. Thus, if we are not mistaken, it is opportunity that makes the thief and not the other way around. That is why rustling is so frequent in our midst, when cattle graze unguarded in the vast expanses of the countryside, protected only by a brand and thus subject to the unchecked temptation of others' greed. We must infer, therefore, that neither drastic sentences nor a strict enforcement of the law, often plagued by the difficulty of presenting clear-cut evidence, will diminish the frequency of the crime as much as a more effective effort at vigilance or an increase in public morality.[20]

The elite perception corroborated the reality perceived by the campesino: Free-ranging cattle were indeed an important cause of rustling, but not in the sense that such cattle merely constituted a "temptation" for the "working class." More importantly, rampaging cattle were a constant threat to the milpas; that they ranged freely simply made it easier for Mayan campesinos to steal them.

Characteristics of Mayan Rustling. Cattle rustling was a generalized phenomenon; those who engaged in it came from a variety of social origins. Indian *cuatreros* might be workers from the pueblos or *rancherías*, servants on the haciendas, or inhabitants of the urban barrios of the capital. Of the seventy-eight proceedings analyzed between 1823 and 1847 for the Mérida district in which individuals with Mayan names were involved, it is possible to trace the place of residence in thirty-seven cases. Of these, sixteen were residents of haciendas, fourteen lived in pueblos, three were from barrios, and four came from small holdings or ranchos.

Another characteristic of the Mayan rustlers was their tendency to act in small informal groups. Two or more individuals were involved in fifty-two of the seventy-eight cases. It is also clear that these "bands" were frequently made up of related individuals. Of those cases that involved people with Mayan surnames, at least two with the same surname appear in thirty-two cases (although in only six is a kinship relationship mentioned specifically). A request presented by the association of hacendados to the government in 1836, concerning legal measures to protect against cattle theft, emphasized that the small ranchos that the Indians had established "clandestinely" in the outlying hills were made up of two or three related families and their acquaintances, all of whom set about stealing cattle when the animals wandered into their vicinity.[21]

The fact that Mayan rustlers shared family ties as well as a common rural vocation enabled them to act within a wider territorial radius, to plan actions with greater care, to choose the most opportune, risk-free moments to nab their prey, and to carry out their operations over a longer period of time. In the process, some Mayan rustlers might inflict significant losses on hacendados. One illustrative example is that of José and Gregorio Can who, together with Pablo Uc, Feliciano Che, and José Chan, were processed in 1832 for cattle rustling after a cave located within their pueblo's fields was discovered "full of cattle bones." The investigators assigned to the case determined that the remains were those of "four or more head of cattle."[22]

It was not uncommon for the workers of an hacienda to steal cattle frequently, either from the hacienda they worked on or another nearby. In 1825, for example, Ilario, Cayetano, Juan Pablo, Santiago, and Baltazar May, along with Florentino Chan—all servants of Hacienda Teuitz—were convicted of stealing ten of Teuitz's cattle and rustling steers from nearby Hunxectaman.[23]

Of course, we cannot discount the existence of bands organized exclusively for the purpose of cattle rustling. Even allowing for the characteristic rhetoric of creole judges and officials, which branded all rustlers as outright thieves and criminals, there is substantial evidence to suggest that "professional" bands threatened a variety of haciendas. A request for lands and a watering hole near the pueblos of Bolón and Chocholá, presented in 1827 by Jerónimo Torre, owner of the Sihunchén hacienda, specified that he intended to build a corral and two houses—deemed necessary to protect his cattle from the "numerous thieves" who lived nearby. Although the municipal council of Chocholá rejected the request, arguing that lands under private ownership would be detrimental to the village population, it did acknowledge that "there was no question" the locality was a "warren of thieves," as Torre had described it.[24] The owners of the neighboring Tuquichen and Chablé haciendas, Francisco de la Cámara and Juan José Duarte, supported Torre's request, arguing that they also would be aided to the extent that increased vigilance would reduce the number of thefts they themselves had suffered. They pointed out that they had caught thieves in the area who had been tried previously and sentenced to jail. On the basis of these arguments, the government finally granted Torre the fifty mecates of land he had requested.[25] These cases point to the existence of groups dedicated expressly to stealing cattle. However, such was not the typical characteristic of the Mayan cattle rustler, who was more likely engaged in agricultural tasks in his pueblo and/or on nearby haciendas.

The Indian cuatrero usually killed and skinned the steer on the spot, often in the hacendado's own corrals. Both guns and machetes were employed to finish off the animal, although machetes must have been more common given the high price of firearms; in addition, blades did not make any noise. The carcass was immediately butchered and distributed among the participants. In August 1838, for example, Felipe Dzul and his brothers Concepción and Andrés, together with Manuel Puch, stole a steer from the Cehchán hacienda near the pueblo of Kinchil. Felipe later declared that they had gotten together in his house in the pueblo and afterward had gone out in the country to find a steer. Andrés lassoed the animal and all of them killed, skinned, and quartered it. After splitting up the meat, Concepción took the skin and dumped it in a well near the pueblo.[26]

The Mayan campesino's preference for stealing cattle, independently of the political motivations that might lie behind the deed, had to do with the fact that the meat thus obtained served in most cases to supplement his and his family's diet. Moreover, distributing the carcass among the participants made it much more difficult to trace the evidence, since each Indian could hide his part until it was totally consumed. It was common for the campesinos to bury the stolen meat in clay containers and to cut or burn out the brand mark if they intended to use the skin.[27] By contrast, horse rustling by campesinos was much less frequent, since the horse itself was evidence enough of the crime. Furthermore, horses were used under the close supervision of hacienda cowboys and other trusted personnel.

Cattle rustling must be viewed as a form of Mayan resistance not only because it represented a survival strategy in the face of creole agricultural expansion and appropriation, but also because it constituted a form of social protest. In this sense, rustling mingled economic and political motives in an act that enabled Mayan campesinos to lash out at the claims of the dominant society both materially and symbolically. Not surprisingly, Yucatecan hacendados responded to this affront to their interests. Acting on their own account and with the support of the state, they moved on a variety of fronts to control the incidence of such "lawlessness."

Repression of Rustling. The measures adopted to combat rustling on the haciendas during the first half of the nineteenth century were diverse and began with apprehending and punishing the rustlers. It seems clear that hacendados occasionally dispensed "justice" informally and arbitrarily, but the state also maintained an elaborate network of judicial institutions for the purpose of processing and punishing those who committed crimes against property and persons. Finally, Yucatán's white elites fashioned a battery of legislative and institutional reforms in an attempt to eradicate the "devastating plague" that was cattle theft. These three aspects of social control reinforced each other in what became a long-term struggle pitting creole hacienda proprietors against poor Mayan rustlers who lived in pueblos, ranchos, and haciendas, or came into the countryside from the humble barrios of the regional capital, Mérida.

Campesinos were rarely caught in the act; generally, they were captured as a result of investigations following the discovery of a missing steer or of a skin hidden in the brush, of blood marks on the ground (which frequently led to the suspect), or of an Indian who had some meat or a hide in his possession that he could not explain. Occasionally, perpetrators were captured following testimony by an informer. Such was the case in 1836 with Feliciano, Apolonio, and José Canul, Rafael Chalé, José Caamal, Julián Tut, and Simón and José María Tullín—all residents of Hacienda San Ignacio—who were found out and arrested when the owner of the nearby San Mateo hacienda, Don Matías de la Cámara, discovered that he was missing cattle and set his own personnel on the trail of the thieves.[28]

Another theft committed that year by Juan Santos Pech, José María Chan, José María Iuit, and Antonio Tun was discovered when an overseer, Gregorio Quintal, told his hacendado, Esteban Quintal, that one of his cows had been killed and that the thief had taken only the two hind legs and the back, leaving the rest of the carcass on the spot. The overseer followed the track to a neighboring hacienda, Cansap, where the owner, Doña María Cabrera, told him that she had arrested Pech after he had confessed to the crime and involved the others, who also lived on her hacienda.[29]

The discovery of a skin was frequently the first indication that a theft had been committed. In one case in 1838, the overseer of the Cehchan hacienda, Francisco Caamal, found the hide stuffed into a well and proceeded to investigate. Subsequently, Andrés and Felipe Dzul, inhabitants of the neighboring rancho, and Concepción Dzul, who lived near the well, were arrested and charged with the crime.[30]

Although not as frequent by any means, there were also cases in which rustlers were uncovered by pure coincidence. In 1824, for example, Pedro Espinosa went to collect some money owed to him by Paulino Aké. There was no one at home, but, since the door was open, Espinosa entered and found a basketful of meat on the floor and some more meat on the fire. He then went to the authorities and reported the suspicious situation.[31]

No doubt, the circumstances under which cattle rustlers were discovered were numerous. It is likely that interrogations of suspects or witnesses were often violent and accompanied by forceful searches of homes. Thus, in 1835, José Vidal Ku and Juan Chan were arrested and soundly beaten under orders from Doña Joaquina Pren, the owner of the Haltuchén hacienda, from which they had stolen a steer.[32]

The trusted personnel of the estates—the administrators, overseers, and foremen—played an important role in capturing rustlers, often operating, it appears, under an informal agreement among the hacendados themselves. For example, in 1837, Dionicio Chim and Bonifacio May were arrested by the overseers of the Chunyá and Dzibichaltún haciendas after José Dolores Piña had discovered the remains of a slaughtered steer. Piña alerted the foremen of the two estates, who then opened an investigation leading to the apprehension of the rustlers.[33] This kind of cooperation was particularly frequent among the personnel of neighboring haciendas.

In some cases, the white authorities and inhabitants of the towns intervened. In 1834, for example, Miguel Aguilar, owner of a property in the jurisdiction of Hunucmá, discovered the loss of two of his heifers. Once he had identified the possible culprits, he secured the assistance of fellow whites Feliciano Vargas, Antonio Ceballos, and José Gregorio Solís. Together, they raided the house of José Bernardo and José Agapito Caamal, where they found abundant meat, as well as ropes and sacks reeking of blood. The suspects were promptly apprehended.[34]

The *repúblicas de indígenas* of the Indian villages also intervened in the arrest of suspected cattle rustlers. For example, in 1838, the chief alcalde of the Indian pueblo of Chuburná commissioned three of the villagers to arrest José Ceh who, along with Luis and Juan Ceh, was suspected of stealing a steer from the Yokolá hacienda. In another case in 1835, the cacique of Chuburná, Manuel Ku, discovered a trace of blood that led to the house of one Juan Tomás Tun. The cacique formed a posse with three of his men and raided the house, where they found five hides that belonged to cattle from the Cumpich hacienda. Tun confessed his crime, and he and his accomplices were arrested.[35]

Thus, Mayan rustlers were captured by the trusted employees of the haciendas and, occasionally, by the authorities of the Indian villages as well. Those authorities, of course, had been created by the white elite to handle the internal affairs of the pueblos. Together, hacienda personnel and Indian authorities carried out the most direct, and likely the most effective, campaign against rustlers.

Judicial and Legislative Efforts to Repress the "Crime" of Rustling

Punishment in the Courts

The judicial network constituted a second line of attack against cattle rustlers. The Constitution of 1825 had established that in every *cabecera* there would be at least one judge of first instance,[36] who was responsible for initiating the criminal proceedings in his jurisdiction, while at the same time informing the higher courts of his actions. It was his duty to conduct investigations, interrogate the accused and all witnesses, appoint public defenders, and, ultimately, mete out sentences.[37] However, the judicial network of the region really began with the alcaldes: These were the officials who in most cases initiated judicial proceedings in criminal cases, carrying out the instructions of the judges of first instance or of the higher courts. Moreover, in many cases the alcaldes acted as judges of first instance.

The Constitution of 1825 had determined that the magistrates of second and third instance would reside in the state capital, where they would review all the civil and criminal decisions of the judges of first instance. In 1841, the organization of these tribunals was modified with the creation of the Supreme Court of Justice, a high court made up of three magistrates and one prosecutor, distributed among three chambers. The second and third chambers would alternately review the civil and criminal cases of second instance, which had been initiated in the courts of first instance.[38] Thus, those trials carried out in the first instance were handed up to the second and third instances for review and confirmation, as well as for appeal if the defendant did not agree with the verdict.

In actuality, these state tribunals constituted a repressive network that punished those who violated the norms of a society controlled by a small creole elite in whose interest the law was administered. Mayan rustlers were processed through this judicial mechanism, although it is possible (indeed, highly likely) that there were a variety of cases, which never made it to court, in which irate hacendados took justice into their own hands. At any rate, the court records indicate that, most often, suspects of cattle theft were turned over by their captors to the nearest authority, who commenced regular judicial proceedings. Generally, the captors became the first witnesses for the prosecution, explaining what they knew about the crime and suspects and often presenting the court with some evidence of the theft, usually some remains of the animal.

For example, on December 20, 1825, the cowhands Marcelo Zetina, José Dolores Lara, José Preve, and Juan de Mata Cocom hauled three suspects, Miguel Dzib, Jacinto Aguilar, and Aguilar's daughter Cesaria, before the associate mayor of Mérida, José Cosgaya. The captors stated that they had found in the defendants' houses parts of the heads of two steers and a hide with a brand that identified it as belonging to Hacienda Petha, owned by Andrés de Zepeda.[39] It was most common for the witnesses in such cases to be trusted retainers (*empleados de confianza*) of the affected haciendas or of others in the vicinity, since it was they who generally carried out the initial investigations and arrested the suspects.

Of course, it was very difficult to prove that an individual was a cattle rustler, since evidence of the crime was needed to start a judicial proceeding. For that reason, most of the cases found in the files involved charges that were devastating to the accused. The prima facie evidence, the statements of witnesses, and, in general, the virtual impossibility of mounting an effective self-defense under such circumstances made a confession by the defendant practically inevitable. Furthermore, the accused's statements, translated from the Maya (usually the defendant's only language) into Spanish, were set down in a formulaic fashion that did not permit much detail.

The accused were further hampered by their limited economic resources, so the judge frequently appointed a defense attorney. Unfortunately, there were few people in the state who could adequately perform this duty. Consequently, on April 12, 1824, an order was issued instructing judges to appoint private individuals to function as defenders, without any remuneration other than the satisfaction of having done a good deed by aiding a miserable convict and serving the public good. The same order stipulated that those who refused to serve without a legal excuse would be fined.[40]

This practice adversely affected indigent prisoners—among whom were the numerous Mayan campesinos accused of rustling—since such court-appointed defense attorneys seem most often to have carried out a purely formal, ineffective defense of their clients. In most cases, the defense's case was based on the sworn statements of the accused and witnesses. Occasionally, the defense underscored extenuating circumstances, such as the famines that followed droughts, epidemics, and wars, but it rarely maintained the complete innocence of the accused; rather, defenders argued mitigating factors in an attempt to reduce the sentence.

The prosecutor's role in the proceedings of the higher courts had an important effect on the rustler's fate. In addition to handling the government's case, the prosecutor was also empowered to seek a quick verdict, requesting punishment or leniency.[41] In some cases, he even acted as something of an advocate for the accused. His opinion in rustling cases was therefore particularly important; nevertheless, the final word was always that of the court's magistrates.

A Colonial Antecedent: The Junta de Hacienderos

The third component of the creole campaign against Mayan cattle theft, an elaborate battery of legislative measures and reforms designed to eradicate or at least control the offense, points up the white elite's constant preoccupation with this brand of "routine" resistance during the first half of the nineteenth century. The dominant society's approach to rustling was never rigid; it continually adjusted its tactics, although its efforts were never crowned with notable success.

Rustling and the campaign to eradicate it were not new issues when the creole elite assumed political power at independence. In fact, the colonial regime had already involved itself with the problem. In August 1818, Spanish Governor Miguel Castro y Araoz had arranged for establishing the *Junta de Hacienderos* to combat the "excessive" and "frequent" cases of cattle theft in different parts of the province. Moreover, he had proposed creating a fund to contain that "pernicious crime to society by tracking down those evil individuals who engage in this horrendous practice and handing down the punishments that the law contemplates in these cases."[42]

As a result, in April 1819, the government issued the Reglamento de buen gobierno (ordinance of good government), setting up a fund and a board (the junta) of large estate owners, which would "seek to reduce drastically the incidence of cattle rustling." The decree was circulated in Mérida, Campeche, and various towns of the province, where the king's officials would see to its implementation.[43]

The Reglamento described the steps for forming the junta, as well as for administering the organization's monies. Each cattle hacienda would contribute two pesos a year to cover operating expenses. Furthermore, the proclamation set forth a variety of measures to investigate cattle theft and seek its eradication: More strigent rules were established for the sale and transportation of cattle and the distribution of beef; surveillance of Mayan pueblos would be improved by appointing, in each village, four Indians of good conduct and experience to patrol the surrounding countryside around the clock; finally, bounties and rewards were established for the capture of rustlers and for each head of stolen cattle impounded.[44]

Another provision, which undoubtedly caused much resentment among the Mayan population, placed limits on the possession of firearms —indispensable for hunting the game that complemented the campesino's regular diet. Under the rationale that many of the cattle that were stolen were shot by "hunters," the authorities were empowered to round up all muskets. Each gun was to be returned, with a written permit, "to those of sound mind who would not use this weapon improperly," but no firearm would immediately be returned to "suspicious individuals," whose behavior would be reported to the authorities before a final decision was taken.[45] In fact, the Reglamento established that the damage done to cattle with gunshot would be the collective responsibility of all gun users within the partido, who would have to cover the cost to the owner. It was hoped that this stipulation would serve to promote the "proper use" of firearms.[46]

Further, the Reglamento recognized the indigence of the cattle rustlers and provided that the junta's fund would cover their court costs. Once these convicts had paid their debt to society and were released from jail, they would be turned over to the junta so that their labor could be "sold" and half of their wages discounted to repay the junta for the court costs and earlier expenses involved in their capture.[47]

Creation of the Presidio Correccional

These measures notwithstanding, cattle rustling continued to be a problem after the declaration of independence from Spain. Although this situation is not immediately reflected in the statistical criminal data (see Table 2.2), one piece of information evidences the concerns of the incipient creole elite. In March 1823, the public defenders of the city of Mérida, Juan José Leal and Joaquín García Rejón, presented a plan to the Municipal Council for the creation of a correctional penal facility (presidio correccional) that would provide work for the prisoners. This proposal was approved on July 18, 1823, by the government of the state, the Junta Provisional Gubernativa del Estado. A number of reasons were adduced to justify such a proposal,[48] but its principal objective was "duly to punish cattle thieves, while at the same time requiring them to improve the public roads and streets."[49] It was asserted that such work would redound to the prisoners' social and physical benefit and "serve as a brake on their criminal propensities."[50] The prisoners would be organized in gangs when they went to work on the roads, while their upkeep would be covered by the *peaje* (a tax on the right of transit) and other municipal levies.[51] For the maintenance of the prison, a contribution of two pesos annually was levied on every cattle hacienda; merchants would pay four reales per month.[52]

To implement the project, a *Junta de Caridad* was created on August 3, 1823. Its president was the provincial governor, who would sit with a member of the legislature, a representative of the church, several members of the Mérida city council, and representatives of both the hacendados and the merchant community.[53]

In 1825, a row broke out between members of the city council and the Junta de Caridad over the contributions that were levied on the hacendados and the merchants. The council members wanted to close down the prison and abolish the junta, but they were unsuccessful in their attempt.[54] The prison continued to function at least until 1847, and the prisoners, including the convicted Mayan rustlers, continued to labor on public works. It seems clear that the survival of the prison had more to do with its capacity to provide free labor to the district than to any success it had in rehabilitating rustlers and other prisoners.

The Amparo Centralista

The incidence of cattle rustling in Yucatán rose in 1833–1835, during the cholera plague and its aftermath, which claimed over sixty thousand victims and brought famine to the land.[55] Although Table 2.2 registers only seven cases of rustling during 1833 and 1834, qualitative evidence points to a rather different situation in the countryside. After the civil strife of June and July 1834 between *centralistas* and *federalistas*, Governor Francisco Toro ordered that all muskets be rounded up to avoid "the scandalous practice of rustling that is ruining the haciendas" because so many of the firearms issued to the troops "were later used to shoot cattle."[56]

However, the data for 1835—thirty-nine cases of rustling—suggest that the measure was hardly effective. In April 1836, the Junta de Hacienderos formulated a new proposal requesting greater legal action against rustling. Simply confiscating muskets, while it "improved the situation, did not eliminate the problem entirely." Indeed, the junta observed, the rustlers were also using shotguns—more-modest weapons and more often owned by campesinos—for the same illegal purpose.[57] The hacendados recognized that shotguns could not be confiscated from every campesino: They were private property and might be used legitimately for hunting. Accordingly, the junta decreed a new prohibition on hunting on private property, a measure it considered reasonable and lawful under the circumstances.[58]

The hacendados realized, however, that their measure would have to be backed up with sanctions if it were to prove effective. Consequently, they also mandated the confiscation of infractors' firearms, plus a fine of five pesos for any landowner who consented to accept a stolen steer. In this manner they hoped to stem "the rising tide of criminality."[59]

Moreover, the hacendados proposed that the use of shotguns be forbidden to "men of bad conduct," for such types would be free to rustle unguarded cattle and to commit a variety of other crimes. Estate proprietors insisted that hunting be strictly limited to those issued licenses by the local authorities or by the *amos* of the haciendas.

But most hacendados concurred that even implementing these measures would not definitely resolve the problem of rustling unless they were accompanied by the eradication of the small, dispersed communities of campesinos in the remote hills. As one proprietor put it, "The lessons of experience tell us that these [communities] are nothing but nests of thieves and pits of vice."[60] Such small campesino groups, knitted together by familial and communal ties, moved around at will and stole whatever cattle wandered in their direction. Since these people went largely unpunished, they became accustomed to a life of crime and caused "the hacendados, the real victims of all this immorality, a host of damages."[61]

Consequently, the junta proposed to the government that these dispersed ranchos be destroyed, arguing that such a measure was nothing new; it was congruent with the principal of Spanish colonial law (found in the Recopilación de Indias) that spoke of the need to concentrate the Indian population in towns and villages (*reducciones*). The junta added that such dispersed ranchos had been declared illegal under Article 4 of the decree issued by the provisional government of Yucatán on July 26, 1831, and ratified by the Congress on March 1 of the following year.[62]

The junta went further, requesting that illegally established cattle farms (*sitios de ganado*) also be destroyed, since such operations prejudiced the "legitimate cattle raisers" who managed larger herds. The junta pointed out that through a loophole in the law any outlaw could build himself a house in the *monte* and acquire a couple of cattle to begin his herd. "Using this situation as a cover, he is then able to steal cattle, and if by chance he is discovered with meat in his hands, he merely says that it is one of his cows that he just killed." Thus, the junta maintained, do thefts go unpunished, since crimes are impossible to prove. As a solution, it asked for full implementation of the 1831 decree prohibiting the establishment of cattle herds closer than four leagues from unmarked properties and two leagues from those haciendas with marked boundaries.[63]

Ultimately, all of the requests that the Junta de Hacienderos made of Francisco Toro's government were met by a decree of June 27, 1836, the so-called Amparo Centralista, which limited hunting rights and required the settlement of campesinos in central towns and villages under the terms demanded by the hacendados.[64]

The Yucatecan Law Against Rustling

During the first half of the nineteenth century, reference is frequently made in the court proceedings to the "Siete Partidas" (the seven laws), the medieval Spanish legal code of King Alfonso the Wise. In the case of rustling, Alfonso's code prescribed that those who stole cattle for a living should be put to death, while those who were not habitual offenders should be required to work the king's lands for a certain period of time. The law further specified that those who stole ten sheep, five pigs, four mares or cows, or an equal number of their offspring should die, while those who covered up such crimes should be exiled from the kingdom for ten years.[65]

In fact, the Spanish law was never implemented as specified. Yucatecan judges and legislators considered the death penalty excessive; none of the court proceedings consulted indicate that any rustler received a capital sentence; nor was exile ever contemplated. From 1823 onward, after the creation of the presidio correccional, cattle rustlers were sentenced to forced labor on public works, although this seems to have been intended more for the benefit of the Yucatecan creole elite than as a reflection of King Alfonso's law. In other words, there was really no existing legislation that was adequate to the reality and the circumstances of rustling in Yucatán.

Cattle theft was an endemic crime in the peninsula, but in view of the anachronistic nature of Alfonso's Siete Partidas, Yucatecan judges were forced to hand down sentences based, it seems, on the precedents of previous rustling cases in the local courts. A marked inconsistency in the length of sentences reflects the lack of commonly held standards for punishment. For example, Leonardo Coox, a chronic offender convicted in 1826 for stealing a cow, was sentenced to one year and seven months at hard labor on public works,[66] while in 1829, Francisco Pech and Antonio and Basilio Baas, convicted of stealing one cow from the Mulchechén hacienda, were sentenced to a year and a half in jail. Their accomplice, twenty-year-old Pedro Baas, received only a year in view of his age and the fact that the judge considered him "less malicious" than the others. (Interestingly, Basilio Baas was only eighteen but received a longer sentence because the judge deemed him "full of malice.")[67]

Such subjective considerations, common in the Yucatecan courts, determined the extent of the prisoner's guilt and the severity of his punishment, even though the value of stolen property might be comparable. In fact, sentences invariably hinged on the arguments that both sides presented and not on any law that specified the length and the severity of the jail term.

It was not until 1841 that this shortcoming was addressed, but the primary concern of the lawmakers was to intimidate the cattle rustlers rather than update the penal code. Even though our data for 1841 do not show any appreciable increase in the incidence of rustling (see Table 2.2), Yucatecan elites remained extremely concerned about the problem. In September of that year the secretary general of the state government, Joaquín G. Rejón, referred specifically to rustling in his report to the Congress. He indicated that cattle theft was one of Yucatán's most common and costly crimes, emphasizing that it entailed the greatest losses to the state's inhabitants (read hacendados), most of whom made a livelihood from cattle raising. He added that even though the crime was penalized, rustling continued to spread in a "scandalous" manner. Since the death penalty, although prescribed under Spanish law, was not applied by the government, owing to its severity, Rejón recommended an increase in other forms of punishment that would be put into practice "without hesitation." He believed that the idea of severe punishment and, more importantly, the certainty of its implementation would serve to curtail this "devastating plague."[68]

With the support of the executive branch, the Commission on Judicial Affairs of the State Congress prepared a bill consisting of eight articles, which was subsequently approved by the Chamber of Deputies and the Senate on November 29, 1841.[69] Given that the State of Yucatán had seceded from the Mexican Republic in February 1840, this law against rustling replaced the one in effect for the rest of the country.

The Yucatecan law tied the length of sentences to the value of the stolen cattle, as well as to the circumstances under which the crime was committed (such as repeated offenses and cover-ups). It specified that the theft of a steer or a horse, of four sheep or goats, or of two pigs would carry a sentence of one year in jail. If the theft were greater, one year of jail would be added for each steer or horse, for each four sheep or goats, or for each two pigs. Those who stole a whole herd would receive six years, while second offenses would merit double the punishment meted out to first-timers. Third-time offenders would face quadruple sentences. As a general principle, the new law provided that those who covered up cattle theft or who purchased or received stolen cattle would be subject to one-half of the punishment applied to the rustlers. Finally, the Yucatecan law abolished those stipulations of Alfonso's Partidas that referred to rustling and its punishment.[70]

Following promulgation of the new law, judges in Yucatán tried to adhere to its stipulations when they handed down sentences. For example, when Lorenzo Kantún was tried in 1842 for stealing three horses, he received a sentence of three years at hard labor. His accomplices, Fernando Lugo and Antonio Matú, were sentenced to one and a half years under the same conditions. Similarly, in 1843, campesinos Juan May, Felipe Puch, and Manuel Baak, who had stolen a cow from the Oxtapacab hacienda, were sentenced to one year in prison even though the defense argued that the accused had acted in a moment of great need.[71]

The State of Yucatán was reincorporated into the Mexican Republic in December 1843, and the old Partidas again became, at least formally, the law of the land, setting back legal matters and producing some confusion and inconsistencies in sentencing. Nevertheless, in the majority of cases heard between 1844 and 1847, the provisions of the 1841 law were applied even though no direct reference was made to it. José María Ku was sentenced in 1844 to one year in prison for the theft of a horse. In 1845, Isidro and Ignacio Noh were sentenced to two years in prison for stealing two cows, while Domingo Acosta and Blas Pacheco, who purchased the stolen goods, got one year's imprisonment.[72]

Conclusion

There is no question that the Yucatecan law brought more precision in determining sentences. Nevertheless, it is questionable that its application lessened the incidence of cattle theft, as its framers had hoped. The continuing concern of Yucatecan elites regarding cattle rustling was expressed in May 1844, when the secretary general of the government, Francisco Martínez de Arredondo, issued a circular to the *jefes políticos* of the state's districts. He pointed out that hacendados constantly complained about the frequent and uninterrupted theft of steers and horses from their properties. He recognized that the law specified severe punishment for cattle rustlers, but laws alone were insufficient if not accompanied by vigilance and pursuit of the criminals, or if punishments were not meted out swiftly so as to dissuade violations against property.[73]

Martínez de Arredondo concluded by instructing the jefes políticos and other local authorities to redouble their efforts at vigilance and step up the campaign to track down cattle and horse thieves. He also suggested that stolen animals not be mistreated and that no damage be done to planted fields or agricultural establishments because these also were under the protection of the authorities.[74]

The circular speaks volumes about the indifferent results of the state's multidimensional campaign to eradicate rustling. In no sense had Yucatán's white elite turned the corner in its struggle against the "devastating plague." Of course, the resources of the campesino-rustlers must be taken into consideration here—namely, their mobility, knowledge of the terrain, and, probably most important, their ties of solidarity rooted in the extended family and rural community. Circumstances demanded such solidarity, and only by pondering the notion of a "subculture of resistance" can the persistence of rustling be explained in an environment such as that of the Mérida district, in which the creole elite exercised great sway over the instruments of economic, ideological, and juridical control. Yet, however formidable, such hegemony was not complete, and many writers have exaggerated its influence in denying northwestern Mayan campesinos the capacity to resist in the generation prior to the Caste War.

Because cattle theft on northwestern haciendas was a social phenomenon that affected one of the principal economic activities of the Yucatecan creole elite, they were constantly preoccupied with containing this threat to their property, which came largely, as we have seen, from the Indian population. Independent of the political or economic motivations that pushed the Maya into cattle theft, and that may well have been blurred even in their own consciousness, the incidence of rustling suggests that campesinos were not willing to submit passively to the worsening social conditions that creole agricultural expansion brought upon them. Rather, they were more than capable of carrying out daily acts of resistance that permitted them, in Eric Hobsbawm's words, to work an exploitative system "to their minimum disadvantage."[75]

We are not suggesting here that cattle rustling and other forms of everyday Mayan resistance constituted an organized, highly coordinated movement; quite the contrary. The beauty of such "routine" forms of protest and resistance lies in their ability to proceed clandestinely with little or no formal organization. Their execution requires only a modicum of room to maneuver and a supportive climate within the campesino sphere. Only in such a manner could the northwestern Maya hope to challenge, both economically and figuratively, the interests of the dominant creole society. Given the unequal power of the two groups that characterized the northwest in the period of "peace" prior to the apocalyptic Caste War, it is no exaggeration to suggest that such widespread social phenomenon as cattle rustling, tax evasions, foot-dragging, and flight represented the greater portion of the Maya's struggle. Through such modest, "quiet" acts of avoidance, protest, and resistance to white rule, Mayan campesinos sought to improve their life chances while simultaneouly affirming their distinct interests and identity.

3 *Decolonization, the Agrarian Problem, and the Origins of the Caste War, 1812–1847*

ROBERT W. PATCH

The Caste War of Yucatán was one of the most important Indian uprisings in nineteenth-century Latin America. No single factor can explain a historical phenomenon as complex as a war lasting more than fifty years and resulting in large-scale death and destruction. Certainly one of the most important causes of the Caste War was the agrarian change that threatened to deprive many Indian peasants of the land that they needed to survive both as Indians and as peasants.

It is well known that the Mayan leaders of the rising considered the agrarian problem to be of great importance. It was a major point in the negotiations held in April 1848, in Tzucacab, between the state government and Jacinto Pat, one of the principal Mayan leaders. The resulting Treaty of Tzucacab, which failed to stop hostilities because of the opposition of the other native leader, the more radical Cecilio Chí, contained a clause providing for the rescission of all the recently introduced agrarian laws. At the same time, the government agreed to abolish newly imposed taxes on land cultivated within the Indians' ejidos and on terrenos baldíos. And finally, it was agreed that the villages that had lost land because of the agrarian laws either would have their communal property returned or be indemnified.[1]

As a result of these provisions of the abortive treaty, historians have frequently argued that the agrarian problem is central to an understanding of the Caste War. Justo Sierra O'Reilly, a contemporary of the struggle, noted the importance of the land tenure laws in provoking the uprising.[2] However, later Yucatecan historians overlooked the land question, arguing that the war was essentially the resumption of the age-old conflict between Indians and whites, that is, between cultures and races.[3] Some even maintained that the whole problem was caused by the British, who, it was alleged, provoked the war in order to acquire more of Yucatán to add to their colony, now Belize—a belief widely held today in Yucatán, although contradicted by the evidence.

However, in the 1940s Howard F. Cline rescued Sierra's interpretation from oblivion and made the agrarian problem central to his overall interpretation of the Caste War.[4] Cline argued that the rapid expansion of sugar plantations in the area he called the borderlands (the region south of Tekax and Valladolid) resulted in the sudden invasion of traditional Indian lands by whites. Closely following Sierra's work, Cline analyzed the state's agrarian policy and demonstrated how the acquisition of private property in the borderlands was facilitated by legislation limiting the size of Indian ejidos, allowing for easy purchase of public lands, and rewarding soldiers with land grants (*premios de campaña*) in lieu of wages. As a result, Indian communities found themselves with less land to work at the very moment their population was growing rapidly. The Maya of the borderlands, joined by those of the Chenes region (south of the Puuc) and by the traditionally hostile Indians of the east (the area around Valladolid), rose up against this threat to their way of life and attempted to drive the non-Indians from the peninsula.

Lack of time prevented Cline from preparing his dissertation for publication, but Nelson Reed[5] took up the task and relied entirely on Cline for his interpretation of causation. Also following in Cline's footsteps (and consequently in Sierra's as well) were later studies by Moisés González Navarro, Victoria Bricker, and Marie Lapointe.[6] Fidelio Quintal Martín[7] attempted to take the discussion in a new direction by applying Engels's analysis from *The Peasant War in Germany*. But in practice, Quintal Martín merely fitted old facts into old frameworks and thereby failed to improve upon, or contradict, Cline's and Sierra's work. Their interpretation therefore continues to hold the field in regional historiography.

Howard Cline carried out his research more than forty years ago, when working in local archives was impossible. He had available to him only published sources, a handful of original manuscripts, and the meager holdings relating to Yucatán in the Archivo General de la Nación. Since then the Archivo General del Estado and the Archivo Notarial del Estado have been opened; in addition, more liberal use of the documents belonging to the now-defunct Instituto Yucateco de Antropología e Historia is possible. These primary sources provide us with a much broader perspective on the history of Yucatán and allow for testing the hypotheses of earlier historians. I seek here to employ these newly available sources to reexamine the agrarian problem as a cause of the Caste War. I attempt to clarify, and at times modify, the reigning interpretation and thereby improve our understanding of the history of Yucatán in the nineteenth century.

The Emergence of an Agrarian Program

Of primary importance among the Spanish colonial regime's laws and practices concerning agrarian affairs in America was the Crown's sanctioning of the Indian system of land tenure. Communal ownership was legally recognized, and the Leyes de Indias included various measures designed to maintain the preconquest landholding system. Indians as individuals were not permitted to sell property belonging to the group as a whole; only the officially sanctioned—theoretically representative—village government could alienate property, and then only if it received permission from the Spanish authorities. Moreover, properties that Spaniards wanted to establish had to be at least two leagues away from the village, in order to protect the villagers' milpas from the colonists' livestock.[8]

At the same time, important restrictions were imposed on Spanish-owned property, in accordance with the essentially medieval attitudes of sixteenth-century Spaniards toward private property. Land was not to be thrown open to indiscriminate colonization. Rather, the principle of *tierras realengas* (Crown lands) was introduced; colonization required legal permission, and land grants were given only for the general welfare—to provide such needed consumer goods as meat and grains—and were contingent upon the recipient's occupation and use of the land.[9] Finally, entailed estates (*mayorazgos* or *vínculos*) were permitted under certain circumstances, and mortmain (*manos muertas*) was also tolerated, thereby protecting the church as a property-owning institution.[10]

To be sure, a large part of this legislation, like many of the Leyes de Indias, was a dead letter even in the sixteenth century and became even more flagrantly violated as time went on. The principle of *composición* (the regularization of land titles through the payment of a fee) in practice permitted landowners to legalize squatting and even outright theft. Indians could be tricked into selling land; caciques could be bribed to allege that land was unneeded; and government officials entrusted with the protection of Indian interests were frequently corrupt. The result was that a large quantity of what had once been Indian property was occupied by Spaniards who established farms, ranches, plantations, and haciendas. Nevertheless, Spanish laws did have some effect, for both church and state benefited from the survival of a tribute-paying, dependent peasantry. Also, in many cases Spaniards simply had no reason completely to dispossess the Indians. At the end of the colonial period a majority of Indians in Latin America lived in independent villages that continued to own significant quantities of communal land.

This situation changed dramatically in the nineteenth century. Even before creoles gained control over the former colonies, Spanish liberals had begun to institute new laws designed to eliminate the antiquated principles of the ancien régime and to modernize the property-holding system. When the Spanish liberals wrote the Constitution of Cádiz (1812), they included provisions recommending that communal property be divided among the heads of families. Also, they tried to make it easier to colonize unused lands, which now began to be called baldíos. Finally, after authorizing the establishment of *ayuntamientos* run by non-Indians in the large villages, the Constitution permitted the sale of municipal property to raise the revenues needed for local government. Clearly, the Constitution of Cádiz was an important transitional step between the old colonial regime and the independent, liberal states of nineteenth-century Latin America.[11]

Of course, that Constitution was in effect only briefly in America, in 1813–1814 and 1820–1821. This hardly mattered; in Yucatán, liberal ideas had already taken root before the emergence of the reform program in Spain. In the latter part of the eighteenth century Yucatán experienced growing commercial relations with the outside world. At the same time, its political ties with Spain were strengthened. Enlightenment ideas from abroad entered the peninsula and were sometimes accepted with great enthusiasm; of course, these were almost always the ideas of the Spanish, not the French, Enlightenment. But, on the matter of agrarian problems, the intellectual environment in Spain was by no means conservative in outlook: people such as Campomanes and, above all, Jovellanos called for genuine agrarian change in order to modernize and improve the rural economy.[12]

By the first decade of the nineteenth century there existed in Yucatán a small but significant group of liberal thinkers. They called themselves the *sanjuanistas*, for their regular meeting place in Mérida was the Hermita de San Juan.[13] When the crisis of the Bourbon monarchy began in 1808, these people became politically active and enthusiastically embraced the Constitution of Cádiz in 1813. When the Diputación Provincial convened shortly thereafter, liberals, for the first time, had the opportunity officially to consider changing the agrarian structure. The free colonization of terrenos baldíos was brought up, and the right of the municipalities to alienate property was also recommended.[14] Ferdinand VII's coup d'état of 1814 put an end to these projects, and though the Constitution came back into effect in 1820 as a result of Riego's liberal coup, Yucatán's adherence to the Plan de Iguala in the following year definitively ended the province's ties to Spain's constitutional order. Nevertheless, the ephemeral character of the Constitution of Cádiz does not diminish its significance as a transitional step in the destruction of the colonial regime.

The next step was taken shortly after the collapse of the Mexican Empire of Iturbide. On December 2, 1825, the state Congress passed a new Law of Colonization, which facilitated the acquisition of terrenos baldíos as private property. This was done to attract foreign immigrants as well as to colonize the allegedly unused state lands.[15] Nevertheless, in the first years after independence there was no mad rush to acquire public lands. Despite liberal ideas, Yucatán was still run by moderate or conservative men representing the interests of the old, colonial, commercial and landowning elites, who favored neither rapid change nor the acquisition of terrenos baldíos by anyone but themselves. For the moment, they had no need to gain possession of huge quantities of land. In the 1820s and 1830s, therefore, the interests of the old elite were protected by cautious interpretations of the Colonization Law, which at times was even suspended.[16]

Several factors eventually intervened: First, the expansion of the sugar and logwood industries in the southern part of the state and near the Belizean frontier could no longer be contained. It became more difficult for the old elite to control the interests that favored a less restrictive agrarian policy. Moreover, many powerful landowners wanted to join in the colonization process, either to benefit from the profits generated by sugar or logwood in the frontier areas or to extend their control over the rural population around their maize and cattle–producing haciendas in the northern part of the peninsula. Finally, the political situation shifted dramatically, for increased conflict between Centralists and Federalists at both the regional and national levels threatened to bankrupt the state treasury. The political leaders had to find new sources of public revenue; the easiest solution was to exploit the possibilities offered by the terrenos baldíos.[17]

Beginning in the 1840s, changes were made in agrarian policy. On April 5, 1841, the Federalist state government passed a new colonization law.[18] Village communal lands—which at this time began to be called ejidos—were limited in extent to one league in each direction of the compass from the center of the pueblo, or four square leagues. Smaller Indian settlements, called ranchos or rancherías, would have ejidos of only one square league. Everything outside the core of communal land not having a legitimate owner was declared to be baldíos and as such subject to lawful colonization by private individuals. In practice, this law would begin to dispossess the peasantry.

The new agrarian policy was further developed with the law of August 26, 1842,[19] which provided baldío land grants of one-quarter league to soldiers who had served in the campaign against the Centralists. This permitted the state government to pursue its policies without having to pay the soldiers in money. The need for revenue was so great that the government implemented a forced loan—euphemistically termed a *contribución patriótica*—and paid its creditors with no-interest bonds to be redeemed in the future. Since the government knew that it would not be able to repay these loans in cash, it again resorted to the public lands to secure its revenue: a law of November 17, 1843, permitted using government bonds in lieu of cash to purchase terrenos baldíos.[20] This law gave real value to the bonds but, along with the other measures, had the effect of unleashing a veritable land rush.

From the peasants' point of view, it might have seemed that the situation could hardly get worse, but it soon did: On October 18, 1844, yet another law imposed a tax of one real for every ten mecates (0.4 hectares) of milpa being worked, whether in the ejido or on the so-called baldíos; in addition, it required that villagers pay for the surveying necessary to delineate the ejidos and distinguish them from the baldíos.[21]

Indians, Land Tenure, and the New Agrarian Policy

The changes that the liberals introduced after independence were, in effect, a decolonization, for the goal was to destroy the colonial regime's institutions. At the same time, the new agrarian policy was designed to bring progress to Yucatán by introducing modern capitalism, a system in which property rights are less restricted and land, in fact, a commodity. The greater economic liberty, it was thought, would allow people to put resources to work more effectively and thus contribute to the general welfare.[22]

In practice, the new ideas were based on long-standing creole conceptions regarding the Maya. The new agrarian policy reflected the apparently unanimous agreement of people of Hispanic culture that the Indians were intellectually and technologically backward. Justo Sierra O'Reilly, for example, believed that the Maya could not possibly be descended from the people who had constructed the ancient ruins that were beginning to attract foreigners' attention; he continued to believe this even after John Lloyd Stephens and others had made a good case to the contrary.[23] Moreover, Sierra considered Mayan agricultural techniques to be "filled with the most grave consequences" because the peasants left untilled huge quantities of land and based their agrarian system on the "damaging" concept of communal ownership.[24] Importantly, Sierra was the dominant intellectual figure in nineteenth-century Yucatán. In the 1840s he served as a judge in land disputes between Indians and creoles; he was a defender of the state's agrarian policy, which he declared to be "a measure that in our judgment is and has been a saving grace that is most essential to the entire country and is both useful and beneficial, especially to the native race."[25] It was with such attitudes that the agrarian policy developed.

Modern science is much less harsh on Mayan technology; in fact, it is now well accepted that in the absence of fertilizer, slash-and-burn agriculture is by no means an inefficient system for producing grains. Mayan agriculture was a rational and efficient system of production and was not, as many creoles believed, a waste of resources.[26] In practice, the new agrarian policy soon ran up against the harsh reality of Mayan traditional technology and culture.

Nancy Farriss has analyzed the interplay of ecology, technology, and society in colonial Yucatán. She emphasizes the existence of strong centrifugal tendencies toward the growing dispersion of settlements as well as the countervailing centripetal forces leading to integration and cohesion.[27] Yucatán's thin soil dictates a low ratio of cultivated to fallow areas—usually on the order of one to five and frequently as low as one to ten—to allow land to lie fallow long enough for nutrients to cycle. This means that the quantity of land required to maintain a given human unit of production is greater than is the case in ecological conditions permitting more rapid replanting of the fallow. In Yucatán, as communities grow, more land is put into cultivation, and peasants have to walk farther to get to their milpas. Eventually, it becomes practical for the milperos to establish temporary dwellings closer to the lands being worked, or even to establish new villages. The new settlements could be satellites of the original ones, or communities of colonists occupying land in new areas removed from the parent settlement.

This dispersion, which could be stimulated even more by peasants' desire to escape from the demands placed upon them by political and religious authorities, was partially offset by the forces of integration and cohesion. Before the conquest, the frequent warfare among the Mayan states undoubtedly made it dangerous at times to be far from one's home community and thus exposed to enemy slave-raiding expeditions. Cultural activities and kinship ties may have discouraged outmigration in some cases. Also, commerce led naturally to the development of economic interests favoring the cohesion of communities located along trade routes. Finally, the political power of the native elite may have made dispersion more difficult.

In the colonial period these centripetal forces were strengthened at first, for the Franciscans, backed by the power of the state, carried out the policy of reducción, the forced relocation of smaller settlements into the major villages of the parishes. But eventually, the centrifugal elements reasserted themselves, for the weakened political and ideological authority of the native elite made it more difficult to control the Indians. Moreover, by the late sixteenth century the power and prestige of the church had declined somewhat, and the ecclesiastical establishment never recovered the influence that the first two generations of priests had exercised. Finally, the power of the state diminished, especially in the last century of Habsburg rule, and though the Bourbon monarchs succeeded in strengthening administration during the latter part of the eighteenth century, the government by that time had abandoned its policy of trying to control the Indians' settlement pattern. For all these reasons, little stood in the way of emigration or dispersion. The bonds of local community were snapping. Since there was no longer danger of raids from hostile neighbors, the Maya gradually returned to a settlement pattern characterized not only by the official villages but also by a large number of dispersed hamlets and other unauthorized communities.[28]

By the time of independence, the forces of disintegration were stronger than at any time since the Post-Classic era. In the 1780s the church had begun the destruction of the Indian *cofradías* that, controlled by the villagers, had been an important element of community cohesion.[29] Their demise meant a further weakening of the prestige of the native elite that had managed them. Moreover, the church itself was in a period of crisis. The abolition of tithes and religious tribute in the 1830s reduced the already low clerical morale. To make up for lost revenue, priests began to increase substantially their fees for performing the sacraments. Tensions between clerics and Indians were therefore increasing, and this contributed to the outbreak of the Caste War. In short, religion as an integrating force was being weakened.[30]

The new agrarian program was thus being effected when there were few countervailing centripetal forces to check the dispersion of the Indian population or prevent the formation of new villages by emigrants. The government in fact was informed of the situation in the countryside before the policy of agrarian change was intensified in the 1840s, having requested local officials to report on population, settlement, and availability of land. In 1838 the *juez de paz* of Tepich had reported to his superiors that "more than two-thirds of the Indians who make up this pueblo are to be found living out in the bush, at distances of four, six, ten, fifteen, and twenty leagues [from the village], one house after another as far as the sea, trying to hide their persons as well as their idolatry and to avoid paying their civil and religious taxes." This justice of the peace had been informed by the parish priest that the Indians were carrying out their own burial ceremonies, while their authorized village was nothing but empty houses and streets overgrown with weeds. Since the natives had no shame and feared only the whip, he continued, the whip ought to be used more freely: "With it I have no doubt that they will return to order and subordination" for, in the past, when whipping was permitted, Indians had obeyed their authorities. Finally, the juez reported that the government's efforts to encourage people to return to their villages by promising them several years of tax relief were not working.[31]

The prefect of Tekax confirmed that this was indeed the situation in the southern part of the peninsula, and he called attention to "the scandalous emigration of the Indians of the Partido of Tihosuco." The measures taken to restrain the peoples' movement, he reported, had thus far been ineffective, and he counseled the implementation of stronger ones "to avoid [the current excesses] and at least neutralize the most notable damages that that wandering way of life by necessity produces for the social order."[32]

In the borderlands, unauthorized settlements could most easily proliferate, for it was an open frontier stretching all the way to Belize and the Petén. When construction began on a road to connect Champotón, Campeche, with Bacalar, it was found that the region was not unpopulated, as had been thought. The engineers reported finding numerous rancherías scattered throughout the bush. The people lived as independent farmers, free from civil taxes and religious charges, which the Indians resisted with "implacable hatred."[33] The government therefore found it necessary to appoint a special commissioner with orders "to discover the occult settlements in the wilds of the south" of the state.[34] It was at this time that it introduced the program of temporary tax relief to encourage the Indians to accept civil authority. Yet, little progress was made in bringing these free souls under government control. In 1844 the region's part-time tax collector complained that his job was almost impossible to carry out because the so-called taxpayers were "settled in little hamlets scattered throughout the bush," and the lack of decent roads meant that he had to dedicate practically all of his time to wandering in the wilds in search of them.[35]

The borderlands was not the only area in which the Indian population lived in dispersed and uncontrollable settlements. Even in the more stable regions, government officials reported that some Indians were living outside their authorized pueblos. In 1837 the owner of an hacienda near Maxcanú complained that in that part of the state there were many unauthorized settlements that "serve only as a place of asylum for the exercise of conduct offensive to society." She requested that these hamlets be destroyed and that the inhabitants be made to live in the official pueblos. The government agreed and ordered the Indians to reside in the authorized villages "so that, being under the direct vigilance of the civil and ecclesiastical authorities, they will carry out their civic duties and be useful to society."[36]

The dispersed settlement pattern became more common the farther one went from the state capital of Mérida. Documents originating from the Temax area are so detailed on this matter that they deserve special attention. Indeed, one such document, a letter submitted by the subprefect of Temax, Don José Castellanos, on July 18, 1837, is one of the most descriptive reports ever submitted by a government official in Yucatán about the settlement pattern of the Maya.[37] Asked by the governor's office to report about "the extremely abundant number of people dispersed in small settlements," Castellanos explained that in his partido there were three kinds of ranchos. The first of these were long-established, small hamlets, earlier referred to as satellite communities, that were located close to the villages; in them resided Indian families of milperos, with their own houses, domestic animals, and livestock. The inhabitants never broke their ties to the original community and regularly carried out their civic duties. The second kind of rancho, Castellanos continued, were privately owned holdings founded to carry out agricultural production. Since the people performing the labor were Indians who lived permanently on the farms, these properties were similar to the first kind of rancho. The difference was that the farms were owned by non-Indians who through their *mayordomos* provided the communities with de facto government.

A threat to the social and political order, wrote Subprefect Castellanos, was presented only by the third kind of rancho, namely, the unauthorized settlements free from civil and religious control. They were formed in two stages. First, the milperos established temporary residences in order to be near their fields; and then the women and children arrived. Their residence, in practice, signaled the creation of a self-sufficient community. Once this second stage had been reached, wrote Castellanos, the inhabitants devoted themselves "to a truly savage life," while the authorized villages became "almost like deserts and the houses closed up and abandoned." When their agricultural labor was done, these people passed their time in "true idleness." Moreover, "the drunkenness, obscene living, adultery, robbery, and quarrels that often lead to murder and all classes of crimes repudiated by civilized nations are committed without the least shame and with the greatest scandal."

These evils were clearly bad for the state, but their solution was not easy, wrote Castellanos, because the laws ordering the elimination of these ranchos had proved unenforceable. Lawmakers did not understand that it was almost impossible for all the peasants to live in the villages and work on lands a great distance from their homes. In short, Subprefect Castellanos was pointing out what many had noted before and since, namely, that ecology and traditional agricultural technology tended to disperse the rural population. In his partido alone, Castellanos reported the existence of 157 ranchos.

This natural tendency toward large-scale emigration was exacerbated by another factor: flight to thinly populated areas during times of famine. This had occurred frequently in colonial and, presumably, pre-Hispanic, Yucatán. It persisted after independence because grain shortages continued to occur throughout a large part of the nineteenth century. Famines on the scale of those of 1726/27 and 1770 through 1772 did not take place. But bad harvests in 1834/35 and 1842/43 provoked severe food shortages and instances of starvation, as well as concomitant social dislocation, dispersal, and flight to the frontier.[38] In one case, it was reported that Indians from Bolonchenticul, Campeche, had fled all the way to Central America because of the scarcity of food in 1842/43.[39]

In sum, the politicians were clearly mistaken in declaring that all lands outside the newly defined village ejidos, and not already privately owned, were baldíos and therefore colonizable. To be sure, there were some areas that were thinly populated, and therefore it was possible at times to carry out colonization without disrupting Mayan society. This was especially true in the eastern and southern extremities of the state. In fact, the Maya themselves were continually colonizing lands in the south and apparently had little, if any, conflict with people already there. This helps explain why it was possible for some non-Indians to do the same. For example, in 1840 a land grant north of the border with Belize was made to a resident of Bacalar named Matías Estévez, who wanted the land to cut mahogany and logwood. Estévez had already been occupying the land for six years and had sixty employees working for him at the time of his request for title. The government, after studying the matter and considering the report submitted by the ayuntamiento of Bacalar, confirmed Estévez's possession of more than six square leagues on the north bank of the Río Hondo.[40] Almost at the same time, the government approved a grant of more than two square leagues to another resident of Bacalar named Francisco Vásquez, who had been occupying the land for four years and was already producing sugarcane and maize.[41] In neither case does it seem that colonization was seriously interfering with Mayan agriculture.

The same was probably true in the case of several grants made further inland. In 1837 Francisco Buenfil requested legal title to land that he had occupied five years before in the jurisdiction of Tihosuco, beyond the village's ejidos. Reports by the *junta municipal* and the jefe político of Tihosuco confirmed the veracity of Buenfil's statements and added that the claimant had made improvements on the site, including digging a well, building houses and corrals, and planting fruit trees. The local authorities recommended that Buenfil be granted legal title.[42] Similarly, after carefully considering the reports of the jefe político and alcaldes of Peto, as well as the assessment by the land survey officer, the government in 1845 confirmed title to land claimed by a *vecino* of Peto named Pablo José Arceo, who was already producing sugarcane at the site. Arceo's estate even had resident sirvientes who were cultivating maize and other subsistence crops in addition to their *cañaverales* (cane fields).[43]

The relative ease with which land could be acquired when no one was likely to object strongly soon brought foreigners into the colonization process. This is not surprising, for, as we have seen, one of the goals of the colonization laws was to attract foreign immigrants. (Nevertheless, judging by the small number of foreigners appearing in the documents, the government's policy in this area seems to have failed.) Land on the southwestern side of Cozumel was claimed by George Fisher, Nathaniel Hoyt, and George Wheelwright in 1842.[44] The documents do not inform us as to these men's nationality (although, judging by their names, we may presume them to be either British or North Americans), nor do they explain what these three intended to do with their beachfront property on Cozumel. On the other hand, an 1845 grant made to foreigners, namely, to "Mr. Vaughan Cristi y Compañía" of Belize, states that the land requested along the Río Hondo was to be used to cut mahogany.[45]

No one protested these grants because there seemed to be unused land in these thinly populated areas, but in the more heavily populated central and northwestern areas, colonizable—truly unused—land was scarce or nonexistent. The subprefect of Sotuta reported to the government in no uncertain terms: "The lands in the jurisdiction of this partido belong to the ejidos of the villages or to private owners, there being a total lack of any that could be colonized."[46] The subprefect of Motul's report was also clear and to the point: "I can assure you, Sir," he wrote to his immediate superior, "that in this partido colonizable lands do not exist, unless by that term one is referring to the cultivated fields that every village has, or to the same lands which the villages have possessed without interruption since the time when the Laws of Spain were in effect."[47] Subprefect José Castellanos reported from Temax that in his partido all the land was in fact occupied and used, although the long period of fallow made it appear that the contrary was true.[48] In 1840 an official from Ichmul informed his superiors that in no part of the partido were there lands suitable for colonization.[49]

Thus far, reports by other local officials have not been found. But, if there was no land available for colonization in Ichmul, Sotuta, Motul, and Temax, it is certain that there was none in many of the other partidos, especially those closer to Mérida.

Despite this information, the government went ahead with its colonization program and limited the village ejidos to four square leagues, thereby defining all other land not privately owned to be suitable for colonization. This caused immediate problems for many villages, for it was frequently the case that a large part of the land a league or less in distance from the pueblo—in other words, within the four square leagues designated as the ejido—was in fact private property and thus could not be used by the villagers. Hampolol, Campeche, was reported to be in this condition as early as 1822.[50] Other villages in Campeche—Champotón and Pich, for example—were reported to be without any common lands even before the colonization laws went into effect.[51] Once colonization was well under way, after 1840, a flood of documentation poured into the state capital, confirming that in many cases private individuals had long before established properties so close to the pueblos as to be less than a league from the center of town.

Extant documentation does not permit an analysis of each village's situation, but it does allow us to conclude that many pueblos were going to be left with severely truncated ejidos unless more land were made available to them beyond the limitations established by the colonization laws.[52] Moreover, some villages were suddenly limited to only one square league (or less, depending on the presence of haciendas). This was because the law stated that settlements of rancho or ranchería status would have only one quarter the ejido of a full-fledged pueblo. Yet, many such settlements were much larger than official pueblos. For example, Rancho Nohcacab (near Peto) had more than a thousand inhabitants, yet it was to be limited to an ejido of only one square league. Therefore, Nohcacab (and presumably several other settlements that were called ranchos according to traditional nomenclature) quickly appealed to be raised to pueblo status in order to be entitled to a larger ejido.[53]

Some villages may have succeeded in mitigating the effects of the new laws, but the overall impact of the agrarian policy was to deny Indians access to land. The terrenos baldíos, far from being uncultivated, were frequently an integral part of the milpa economy. According to the laws, the villagers would no longer have the right to use them. To make matters worse, the agrarian program was being implemented at a time when many villages were already feeling the effects of a growing land shortage. Local officials' reports in the 1830s and 1840s that there was no unused land in their jurisdictions were echoed by several village and municipal government reports, sometimes even before the promulgation in 1841 of the laws limiting the size of ejidos. Other pueblos requested that no terrenos baldíos be converted to private ownership because those lands were needed by the peasants. Finally, villages were in conflict over land, suggesting a greater awareness of the need to hold onto or expand the resources available to peasants.[54]

The impact of the new land policy was intensified by the growing determination of hacendados to expand their holdings. Usually, they were guided by purely economic motives, but sometimes social and political factors were also involved in expansion. Many proprietors realized, for example, that greater control of land meant greater control over the rural population. Laying claim to sites occupied by real or alleged cattle thieves was one way of solving the problem of theft.[55] It could also kill two birds with one stone, as is revealed by the case of a vecino of Dzitbalché, Campeche, named Don José Teodoro Rodríguez, who laid claim to land occupied by squatters who allegedly were cattle thieves. Rodríguez stated that his principal objective was to stop the theft of his cattle, but he also pointed out that the thieves had begun "to introduce disorder among the resident servants [i.e., debt peons] of my above-mentioned hacienda by selling *aguardiente* [cane alcohol] and by the bad example that they demonstrate, demanding the almost complete abandonment of service."[56]

Indians sometimes complained about this implication of increased social control. In 1837, for example, the village of Kinchil (near Hunucmá, in northwestern Yucatán), locked in a land dispute with hacendados, pointed out that the alienation of terrenos baldíos should be permitted in theory but not in practice if, at the same time, the villages did not possess their rightful common lands as had been prescribed by the Leyes de Indias: "For if the village of Kinchil has more inhabitants than before; if from its ejidos the inhabitants take their firewood, charcoal, and other things necessary for life; if there is not enough land for the village's crops of the grain necessary for its sustenance, is it not clear that the purpose of private owners in having the terrenos baldíos sold is to annihilate the villagers, or at least enslave them, making them feudatories of the buyers?" Kinchil's complaint drew attention to the harsh reality of rural life in Yucatán: Hacendados would have more power if they controlled more resources, and if, in turn, the villagers were left without enough land to support themselves.[57]

The government's requirement that Indians have their ejidos surveyed in order to distinguish common lands from supposedly colonizable terrenos baldíos, was still another problem. It cost the pueblos a considerable sum of money to pay professional surveyors; indeed, many villages found it difficult or impossible to defray the expense. As the alcalde of Huhí notified the government in Mérida: "In a small village like this one, which has neither commerce nor capitalists . . . it is difficult to find anything to tax in order to pay the indispensable costs of the measurement that must be carried out." Therefore, he attempted to raise the money by imposing a tax of one-half real for every mecate of first-year milpa planted on terrenos baldíos[58] (which in itself was proof that the baldíos were being used by milperos and were not uncultivated). The ayuntamiento of Baca introduced a simple head tax of one real per adult male to raise funds.[59] The small village of Xcupilcacab (near Hopelchén, Campeche) imposed a progressive head tax to pay for the survey: each adult male Indian paid one and one-half reales, "los vecinos pobres" (poor non-Indians) paid three reales each, and "los demás" (all others) were required to contribute at the rate of three pesos.[60] Kinchil attempted to raise the necessary revenue by instituting a complex plan combining a four-real head tax with imposts on milpas, liquor, pigs, slaughtered cattle, henequen fishing nets, mules, and shoe soles.[61]

Sometimes, tax revenues were still insufficient to pay for the survey, and other measures had to be taken. The jefe político of Motul reported that the village of Yaxkukul had no commerce to tax and, when the head tax that he had imposed failed to raise enough funds, ordered that several plots of land within the village be sold to raise money. Even that was not enough, so the jefe finally ordered the sale of communal lands to defray the costs.[62] Tekax also had to sell communal property to pay for the survey.[63] The alcalde of Buctzotz (near Temax) reported that in his village "there is nothing whatsoever that could possibly be taxed to pay for the indispensable expenses of the measurement that must be carried out." He therefore requested permission for the villagers themselves to do most of the labor in order to cut down on the costs that a professional survey would entail.[64] While the documentation is by no means complete, it seems fairly clear that for the villages of Yucatán, the need to pay for the surveying of their ejidos placed a considerable financial burden on the peasants. Ironically, in some cases it even entailed the loss of land through sales in order that more land would be lost through surveys. In short, the state's agrarian policy was far from being "useful and beneficial, especially to the native race," as Justo Sierra O'Reilly and other liberal thinkers had imagined.

The Land Rush

In the twenty-five years after independence, Yucatán's ruling elite gradually dismantled the colonial regime. The politicians did not attempt to dispossess the Maya completely, but the prevailing ideas about the Indians' so-called backwardness required a new regime that would restrict communal landownership, extend private property, and make land a commodity to be bought and sold like any other item of commerce. The result was agrarian change, slow at first, but eventually quite rapid. Large quantities of property began to be claimed by private individuals either as lands suitable for colonization or as rewards for military service.

Unfortunately, the documentation is not complete enough to permit a thorough study of this process. Nevertheless, there are two sources that can be used to gain at least some insight into the impact of the government's policy: (1) the 528 adjudications of terrenos baldíos found in the notarial records for the years 1843–1847;[65] and (2) the 465 entries in the government's Registry of Claims of Terrenos Baldíos.[66] The latter seems at first glance to be an excellent source, but further examination reveals that the registry has numerous defects, diminishing its overall value. A comparison of its entries with the adjudications in the notarial records demonstrates that the vast majority of the grants that were eventually legalized by notaries were not included in the Registry of Claims. In part this was because almost one-half of the notarial adjudications were premios de campaña, none of which were included in the registry. But even leaving aside the premios and concentrating just on the sales of terrenos baldíos, less than 30 percent of the notarized purchases were ever registered. Moreover, the registry seems to have been haphazardly kept.[67] Whoever made the entries failed to note the quantity of land claimed in ninety cases, failed to give the location in seven, and on one occasion even failed to record the name of the claimant. Over 20 percent of the entries, therefore, have at least one notable defect. Even when the pertinent information was recorded, there was a notable lack of precision: practically all entries include only rough estimates of the quantity of land being claimed. A comparison with the notarial adjudications reveals that very rarely was a grant exactly one-quarter, one-half, or one full league, as was almost always the case in the registry.

The adjudications, on the other hand, are characterized by the usual precision of notarial documents evident since early in the colonial period. In no case did the notaries neglect to record the name of the claimant or the quantity of land being granted. In fact, on a few occasions the notaries were too precise: In eleven cases the documents specify the location of the grant in terms not of nearby and known villages, but of haciendas that can no longer be identified. But, since this occurs in only two percent of the adjudications, the notarial documents are clearly a better source than are the entries in the Registry of Claims and, moreover, are practically the only source for the study of the premios de campaña. Still, since the registry does contain a large number of usable cases, the best course to follow seems to be that of somehow combining both sources in order to get the largest possible sample for analysis.

A summary of the usable data contained in the registry is given in Table 3.1.[68] Individuals received 349 grants of roughly identifiable size totaling more than 211 square leagues, or approximately 370,000 hectares. If the ninety other grants, of unspecified quantity, were of average size, then approximately 466,000 hectares of terrenos baldíos would have been given to private individuals, according to the registry. Most affected was the region referred to by Howard Cline as the borderlands, namely, the Prefecture of Peto, wherein almost one-third of the terrenos baldíos converted to private property were to be found.

Not included in Table 3.1 are eight additional grants that represent an interesting, although minor, dimension to the process of land coloniza-

Table 3.1 Terrenos Baldíos Claimed According to the State's *Registry of Claims*, 1844-1847

Political Jurisdiction	Quantity of Land Claimed (in Leagues)	Approximate Equivalent in Hectares	Percentage of Total
Campeche, Ciudad del Carmen, and Seibaplaya	3.00	5,269	1.4
Hopelchén	15.25	26,786	7.2
Hecelchakán	10.25	18,004	4.9
Mérida	15.65	27,484	7.4
Maxcanú	10.75	18,882	5.1
Tecoh	6.63	11,637	3.1
Izamal	6.50	11,417	3.1
Motul	5.00	8,782	2.4
Temax	2.00	3,513	0.1
Valladolid	6.00	10,539	2.8
Tizimín	12.50	21,956	5.9
Espita	9.25	16,247	4.4
Tekax	10.00	17,565	4.7
Ticul	11.25	19,760	5.3
Sotuta	19.00	33,373	9.0
Peto	64.37	113,072	30.5
Bacalar	1.00	1,756	0.5
Location not given	2.75	4,830	1.3

Source: Registro de anotaciones de las denuncias de terrenos baldíos, consecuente del Art.° 1° del acuerdo de la Exma. Asamblea departamental de 5 de Diciembre de 1844 (Manuscript in the Special Collection, Biblioteca Crescencio Carrillo y Ancona, Mérida.)

Note: Twenty percent of all entries did not include the quantity of land being claimed and, therefore, are not in the table.

tion. These claims were filed by the Indian village governments of Kinchil, Nunkiní, Sitilpech, and Tixcancal, by the ayuntamiento of Tecoh, and by people identified only as Indians or as residents of Indian ranchos. These are instances of group efforts by peasants to counteract the restrictions on the size of ejidos by laying claim to baldíos and thereby expanding their landholdings. Of course, the laws were designed to diminish, in practice, the villages' holdings, but the lawmakers apparently left open a loophole by failing to rule out land grants to corporate entities. (The federal Constitution of 1857 would not repeat this error.) Some villagers thus succeeded in getting around the spirit of the law, but since there were only eight cases of such claims by groups, the overwhelming impact was in the opposite direction, that is, the reduction of common lands.

In Table 3.2, the data contained in the notarial records are summarized. A comparison of Tables 3.1 and 3.2 reveals an important difference: In relative terms, although Peto was still the area most affected by the conversion of terrenos baldíos to private property, several other jurisdictions were almost equally affected. The reason for this is made clear by the information contained in the column labeled "Premios de Campaña": Such grants were distributed overwhelmingly in the thinly populated partidos of Tizimín, Temax, and Espita, which together contained over two-thirds of all the land granted to veterans. This statistic offsets the relative weight of the terrenos baldíos sold in the Peto area.

To get a better insight into the effects of the state's agrarian policy, it is best to combine the data from both the registry and the notarial adjudications and remove all possible cases of overlapping data that would result in double counting.[69] This is done in Table 3.3. At a minimum, the state sold or granted over 425 square leagues of land, or approximately 746,800 hectares. In fact, the figure was higher, for Table 3.3 does not include the ninety grants of unspecified size found in the registry. Assuming that these ninety were of average size, over 840,000 hectares were affected. In any case, since neither of the sources used is complete, it is certain that at least eight hundred thousand hectares of terrenos baldíos were converted to private property in the years 1843–1847.

A close analysis of the combined data reveals that the areas most affected by the agrarian policy were in fact those that were relatively thinly populated, namely, Peto, Tizimín, Hopelchén, Espita, the eastern part of Temax, and Bacalar. On the other hand, "relatively thinly populated" does not mean that there was no one there. In fact, certain areas within these jurisdictions contained significant concentrations of Indians who had never been as thoroughly colonized by the Spaniards as had those of

Table 3.2 Terrenos Baldíos Adjudicated in Notarial Records, 1843-1847

Political Jurisdiction	Purchases			Premios de Campaña			Total		
	Leagues	Hectares	Percentage	Leagues	Hectares	Percentage	Leagues	Hectares	Percentage
Campeche, Ciudad del Carmen, and Seibaplaya	0.27	476	0.1	-	-	-	0.27	476	0.1
Hopelchén	26.08	45,813	13.9	5.25	9,221	7.1	31.33	55,034	12.0
Hecelchakán	13.85	24,328	7.4	0.25	439	0.3	14.10	24,767	5.4
Mérida	7.93	13,927	4.2	0.75	1,317	1.0	8.68	15,244	3.3
Maxcanú	21.27	37,356	11.3	0.66	1,164	0.9	21.93	38,520	8.4
Tecoh	2.02	3,548	1.1	-	-	-	2.02	3,548	0.8
Izamal	1.86	3,336	0.9	1.13	1,989	1.5	2.99	5,256	1.1
Motul	2.31	4,059	1.2	2.01	3,536	2.7	4.32	7,595	1.7
Temax	15.46	27,154	8.2	16.44	28,871	22.3	31.90	56,025	12.2
Valladolid	5.23	9,182	2.8	1.25	2,196	1.7	6.48	11,377	2.5
Tizimín	12.17	21,379	6.5	25.10	44,091	34.0	37.27	65,470	14.2
Espita	20.54	36,073	10.9	8.34	14,656	11.3	28.88	50,729	11.0

Table 3.2. Continued

Political Jurisdiction	Purchases			Premios de Campaña			Total		
	Leagues	Hectares	Percentage	Leagues	Hectares	Percentage	Leagues	Hectares	Percentage
Tekax	2.09	3,677	1.10	2.00	3,507	2.7	4.09	7,184	1.6
Ticul	0.09	174	0.05	2.25	3,952	3.0	2.35	4,126	0.9
Sotuta	9.15	16,071	4.90	4.90	8.606	6.6	14.05	24,677	5.4
Peto	38.01	66,766	20.20	2.70	4,744	3.7	40.71	71,509	15.5
Bacalar	4.25	7,465	2.30	-	-	-	4.25	7,465	1.6
Location not given	5.47	9,614	2.90	0.74	1,305	1.0	6.22	10,919	2.4
Total	188.07	330,330		73.78	129,594		261.85	459,923	

Source: Archivo Notarial del Estado de Yucatán, Notarías de Manuel Barbosa, Francisco del Río, Pedro José Canto, José Dolores Roche, Antonio Patrón, Joaquín María Mendoza, and Manuel González, 1843-1847.

Table 3.3 Claims and Adjudications of Terrenos Baldíos, 1843-1847

Political Jurisdiction	Total Claims and Adjudications			Items Possibly in Both Sources	Net Total		
	Leagues	Hectares	Percentage	Leagues	Leagues	Hectares	Percentage
Campeche, Ciudad del Carmen, and Seibaplaya	3.27	5,746	0.1	-	3.27	5,746	0.8
Hopelchén	46.58	81,820	9.8	5.87	40.71	71,508	9.6
Hecelchakán	24.35	42,771	5.1	9.38	14.97	26,294	3.5
Mérida	24.33	42,728	5.1	4.34	19.98	35,097	4.7
Maxcanú	32.68	57,402	6.9	8.41	24.27	42,629	5.7
Tecoh	8.64	15,184	1.8	0.78	7.87	13,816	1.8
Izamal	9.49	16,673	2.0	0.28	9.21	16,176	2.2
Motul	9.32	16,377	2.0	-	9.32	16,377	2.2
Temax	33.90	59,538	7.2	-	33.90	59,538	8.0
Valladolid	12.48	21,916	2.6	1.00	11.48	20,160	2.7
Tizimín	49.77	87,426	10.5	2.25	47.52	83,467	11.2
Espita	38.13	66,976	8.1	1.50	36.64	64,350	8.6

Table 3.3. Continued

Political Jurisdiction	Total Claims and Adjudications			Items Possibly in Both Sources	Net Total		
	Leagues	Hectares	Percentage	Leagues	Leagues	Hectares	Percentage
Tekax	14.09	24,749	3.0	-	14.09	24,749	3.3
Ticul	13.60	23,886	2.9	-	13.60	23,886	3.2
Sotuta	33.05	58,050	7.0	2.41	30.64	53,817	7.2
Peto	105.09	184,581	22.2	10.41	94.67	166,290	22.3
Bacalar	5.25	9,221	1.1	-	5.25	9,921	1.2
Location not given	8.97	15,750	1.9	1.18	7.79	13,682	1.8
Total	473.00	830,795		47.82	425.18	746,801	

<u>Sources</u>: Registro de anotaciones de las denuncias de terrenos baldíos, consecuente del Art.° 1° del acuerdo de la Exma. Asamblea Departamental de 5 de Diciembre de 1844 (Manuscript in the Special Collection, Biblioteca Crescencio Carillo y Ancona, Mérida); and Archivo Notarial del Estado de Yucatán, Notarías de Manuel Barbosa, Francisco del Río, Pedro José Canto, José Dolores Roche, Antonio Patrón, Joaquín María Mendoza, and Manuel González, 1843-1847.

other regions of the peninsula. If an analysis is made of the areas in which the Indian rebellion of 1847 was most determined—Peto, Hopelchén, Sotuta, Tekax, and Valladolid—one discovers that about 45 percent of all terrenos baldíos converted to private property were precisely in these jurisdictions. This is statistical confirmation of Howard Cline's interpretation of the Caste War.

On the other hand, the data also demonstrate the need for some revision of Cline's thesis. First, although the borderlands was the single area most affected by the government's policy, other regions were by no means isolated from the state-imposed agrarian change. Almost one-fourth of the terrenos baldíos alienated were located in the heavily populated northwest (the prefectures and subprefectures of Maxcanú, Mérida, Hecelchakán, Ticul, Motul, Izamal, and Tecoh). Since the contemporary government reports state that there were few, if any, genuinely unused lands in these jurisdictions, the agrarian change must have been painful indeed for their growing Indian populations.

Second, the data do not suggest much of a land rush in the Campeche area. It might be objected that the notarial records of Mérida are misleading on this matter because they contain few documents relating to Campeche, which after all had its own notaries. The same might be said regarding Valladolid, yet this district is clearly well represented in the Mérida records. This is true because practically all the people requesting adjudications were either paying with government bonds from the contribución patriótica or were requesting land grants as veterans; in both cases confirmation and certification by the governor's office and by the state treasury were necessary. In practice it was easier to have all this "red tape" carried out in Mérida. Moreover, as far as we know there was only one Registry of Claims, and that fact also required the claimant to be present in the state capital. The government's procedures therefore tended to ensure that most official claims and adjudications of terrenos baldíos were carried out in Mérida. Consequently, the records probably do not significantly undercount claims made in Campeche. In any case, *campechanos* with logwood interests did not need title to the state lands; these people only wanted to cut down the trees, then move on to another site. They were already doing this without the need to register claims, pay for measurement, purchase land, and pay taxes. In short, the sources' suggestion that the state's laws regarding terrenos baldíos had little impact in Campeche is probably accurate. The rush to cut logwood went on independently of the new agrarian policy.

Third, the data reveal that the state's program of paying veterans with land grants in lieu of money may not have been unsound and probably did not contribute in a major way to the outbreak of the Caste War. As already noted, most of these premios de campaña were given out in the subprefectures of Tizimín, Espita, and the eastern part of Temax—areas of sparse population and weak Indian cultural presence. The Maya who rebelled in 1847 found scant support in this region.

But, before one concludes that the policy of rewarding common soldiers with land might have created a class of small independent farmers—a genuine goal of Mexican liberalism in the nineteenth century—a careful study of what happened to these premios de campaña must be made. An impressionistic survey of the documents suggests that many recipients may have been front men for the interests of the landowning elite. In some cases, the soldiers granted these premios immediately sold them to large landowners. A good example is that of a grant of over four thousand hectares made to nine veterans in early 1847. The land in question was in the Muna area, just to the west of Hacienda Uxmal. In practice, four officers and four enlisted men had ceded their rights to Colonel Don José Cosgaya, who thus claimed one-quarter league as his own premio and the rest in his capacity as beneficiary of the other eight men. The land grant was duly adjudicated. On the next day, Cosgaya sold it for eight hundred pesos to Don Felipe Peón, owner of a nearby hacienda and member of one of the great landowning families of Yucatán.[70] (His cousin, Don Simón Peón, who figures prominently in Stephens's account of travels in Yucatán, was the owner of Uxmal.) In several other cases veterans similarly sold their land immediately upon receiving it.

Information contained in the notarial records also strongly suggests that the land policy, far from accomplishing its goal of stimulating the emergence of a class of small farmers, would have worked to strengthen the existing elite had the Caste War not put an end to the land rush. Most of the time the notaries carefully distinguished between people who were referred to as *don* and those called *ciudadano* (citizen). This was a status distinction, a holdover from the late colonial era, when all white people were called *don* and everyone else had nothing at all before their names. After independence, people of nonelite and nonwhite status began to be called citizens. In the 1840s the term *don* continued to mark a status distinction between its bearer and the "citizens," for this was a time before the "inflation of honors" had resulted in the use of *don* and *señor* for everyone, as is now the custom. In short, the distinctions made by the notaries provide us with useful data.

In practice, people of elite status received no less than two-thirds of the terrenos baldíos adjudicated by the notaries, although they made up only 45 percent of the total recipients. Even this statistic may understate the importance of the dones, for most of the land given to common ciudadanos was in the form of premios de campaña, some of which, as we have seen, passed immediately into the hands of the elite. If these grants to veterans are left out of the sample and only outright purchases of terrenos baldíos are considered, then the elite, comprising 74 percent of the purchasers, bought up 82 percent of the lands being converted to private property.[71] Moreover, as will be recalled, two-thirds of the premios de campaña were in the jurisdictions of Tizimín, Espita, and eastern Temax, areas of very thin soil and not very plentiful rainfall. The nonelite tended to get the worst land, while the dones acquired the more fertile areas in the south. No matter how one looks at it, the social group most favored by the state's land policy was the Yucatecan elite.

On the other hand, there is a significant number of cases of nonelite participation in the acquisition of terrenos baldíos. This suggests that class and caste lines were not perfectly drawn, and that the social system was not as rigidly organized as is sometimes assumed. Ten purchasers of land, including a priest, had Mayan surnames. In Yucatán in the 1840s, society considered people with Mayan names to be Indians, although in this case the ten men must have learned the ways of the dominant society.

Those who had learned best were the caciques; at least two appear in the registry claiming terrenos baldíos. One of these was no less a personage than Jacinto Pat, cacique of Tihosuco and one of the two most important leaders of the Mayan rebellion. On August 10, 1846, Pat laid claim to one-half league of land close to his own village.[72] Perhaps because he belonged at least partially to the Hispanic world, as his land claim reveals, he was the less radical of the two principal rebel Mayan leaders. It was Jacinto Pat, not Cecilio Chí, who tried to negotiate an end to the Caste War in the peace talks held at Tzucacab. Perhaps it was also for this reason that Cecilio Chí quickly moved to sabotage those negotiations. There are similar examples from the colonial era of caciques acquiring private property and participating in the non-Indian sphere of economic activity. Consequently, there is nothing to indicate that any substantial change in the social structure had taken place in Yucatán since the late eighteenth century.

Several other characteristics of colonial society were plainly evident in the decade before the Caste War. The clergy continued to play an economic role out of proportion to its numbers: More than 10 percent of all sales of terrenos baldíos were adjudicated in favor of priests, while clergymen made up less than 1 percent of the total population. At the same time, women played a very restricted role in the landowning economy. Only thirteen women appear in the notarial records as purchasers and were adjudicated only 4 percent of the land. In the registry sample, only fifteen of 360 claimants are female.

Thus, in practice, the state's progressive agrarian policy was implemented along traditional lines. It was designed to stimulate economic growth by making it easier for entrepreneurs to acquire the land necessary for development. This in fact was accomplished, as our statistics demonstrate, but it also resulted in a struggle for land between whites and Indians, a struggle that in its earliest phases was carried out in the traditional manner, that is, in the courts. Only later did the conflict become a violent rebellion.

The Struggle for Land and the Coming of the Caste War

One of the most characteristic features of Spanish colonialism was the elaborate institutions created to dispense justice to everyone. Since the king perceived the special vulnerability of the native population in America, he provided a special court to protect its interests.[73] It goes without saying that justice was not always dispensed; nevertheless, the bureaucrats staffing these courts had to represent the interests of the Crown at least minimally. Law suits involving Indians did not always end in their defeat, since often the interests of the creoles conflicted with those of the king. If the political constellation of forces was right, judges or governors might well decide against the members of local Hispanic society. Indians soon learned to play by the rules of the new system imposed on them by the Spaniards and took their cases to court with such frequency that they were often reputed to be excessively litigious.

Although after independence the special courts were abolished, the Indians—if Yucatán is in any way representative—lost none of their willingness to take their creole opponents to court. On the other hand, political institutions now no longer represented the interests of a distant monarch but those of a new creole ruling elite. Undoubtedly, this diminished the Indians' chances of success in legal disputes.

The rich and powerful frequently succeeded in getting the law interpreted in their favor despite the opposition of native people. Such was the case in a conflict between Doña María del Carmen Quijano and the Indians who had established an unauthorized rancho near her hacienda in the Hoctún area. In 1843 she laid formal claim to the land to annex it to her hacienda and eventually succeeded in getting the government to expel the Indian residents.[74] In the same year, the village of Maxcanú attempted to prevent Don Lorenzo Peón from acquiring some terrenos baldíos, claiming that the villagers needed the land for their milpas. The judge in the case, Don Justo Sierra O'Reilly, decided in favor of Peón, because the land in question was not in the village ejido and therefore was legally a terreno baldío. Moreover, Sierra wrote, Peón's claim antedated that made by the village and took legal precedence. The Indians then complained that they had not been able to claim the land before Peón had, because they had not been informed of the new agrarian laws—promulgated in Castilian but not translated into Maya. The judge, however, responded that the villages always had someone who knew Castilian and therefore the Indians had no excuse for being ignorant of the law.[75] The villages of Hunucmá and Calkiní also lost legal disputes in which they attempted to maintain control over land that had been recently defined as alienable terrenos baldíos.[76] Although the documentation is far from complete, we may presume that many other villages were losers in similar legal battles.

Apparently, some Indians perceived that the best way to prevent outsiders from acquiring the terrenos baldíos needed by the villagers was to make formal claim to them before anyone else did. This helps explain the already cited cases of such claims by villages, found in the Registry of Claims. Several more examples were discovered in the government's archives.[77] The practical result of carrying out this formality was to give the village's claim precedence over any made later by an individual and to strengthen its case if the conflict ended up in court.

The legal odds may have been against the Indians in the struggle for land, but shrewd legal and political maneuvering by a village sometimes produced success. For example, in 1837 the pueblo of Kinchil, which had so eloquently argued that local hacendados were trying to enslave the peasants, convinced an investigating commission's judges of the validity of its case in a struggle with a local landowner. The judges finally recommended that Kinchil maintain possession of the lands in question, and that persons wishing to claim terrenos baldíos be given lands that were genuinely unused.[78] Legal decisions in favor of the Maya were also handed down in cases involving the villages of Dzoncauich and Tecoh.[79]

One of the most interesting cases of a pueblo successfully defending its land is that of Pocmuch, Campeche. In April 1845, this village found itself in two separate disputes with creoles over terrenos baldíos that the villagers considered to be part of their traditional communal lands. In the area north of the village, Don Pablo José Reyes was attempting to acquire one full league of land contiguous to his hacienda, which was located between Pocmuch and Hecelchakán. Reyes stated that he wanted to expand his hacienda in order to cultivate more maize. When the government investigated his claim, the República de Indígenas of Pocmuch produced an old map, which revealed that the land was outside the village's ejido. Nevertheless, the juez de paz of the pueblo stated that the villagers needed the land for their own subsistence, and when the jefe político of the partido agreed with that assessment, the governor ruled against Reyes.[80]

Even as this case was pending, Don Cristóbal Espínola was invading Pocmuch's lands to the west by laying claim to a large part of Isla Jaina. Espínola had already established a fishing enterprise on the island and wanted agricultural land to grow cotton and maize, which he understood could be produced on Jaina "in abundance and of good quality." The government ordered the usual investigation. The juez de paz reported that the village's right to Jaina had been recognized "since time immemorial," for "besides the right of possession, which the village has maintained since even before the conquest, [Pocmuch's claim] is attested by its documents, which are preserved in its possession along with a corresponding map more than two centuries old." Proper surveying had been carried out, he went on, and the results had been ratified by various "captains general or intendants," who had granted Jaina to Pocmuch as a *real merced.* After receiving this report, the governor again decided for the village.[81] Here, then, was a pueblo that knew its history, knew its rights, and knew enough to preserve its documents.[82]

Pocmuch and other villages won their legal disputes in part because the local juez de paz and jefe político took the Indians' side in the case. The pueblo of Ucú (just to the northwest of Mérida) was also fortunate in this respect. In 1837, when the villagers opposed Felipe Gil's efforts to acquire some terrenos baldíos to establish a cattle ranch, they too were supported by the juez de paz. Moreover, the case provides a clue as to why a local official might choose to side with the Indian villagers. In rendering his decision, the governor noted that Gil's pretensions were also opposed by the cattle ranchers in the area, for their properties would be damaged by the establishment of another ranch so close to their own.[83] Thus, although the laws were designed to bring large quantities of supposedly unused land into use, in practice not all members of creole society were in agreement with the indiscriminate colonization of terrenos baldíos.

The land rush had unleashed a fierce competition to gain possession of a piece of the so-called public domain, leading sometimes to violence among whites. Government officials soon found that they had to deal with a substantial quantity of litigation.[84] To make matters worse, some Indians joined in the land rush by becoming private owners, inevitably getting them involved in legal disputes.[85] The government's offices were deluged with the problems of implementing the new agrarian laws. What had appeared on paper to be easy to accomplish was proving difficult to manage in practice.

As Indians and whites fought with each other and among themselves, the government came to realize that changes in agrarian policy were necessary. As early as 1844, Governor Santiago Méndez had pointed out to the state legislature that the villages should be allowed to keep "land that they cultivate," whether or not it was within the newly defined ejidos.[86] In short, the governor was aware that the new laws did not take into consideration the reality of the agrarian system.

Political instability prevented any immediate change in the direction of policy, and it was soon too late to do anything to remedy its effects. Indications emerged that the Mayan villages were seething with discontent. As early as 1841, a minor uprising took place in Acanceh (south of Mérida), where the cacique led the villagers in a disorderly protest against the sale of terrenos baldíos. Eventually, the Indians marched on the state capital to present their demands before the governor.[87] Two years later, the Indians of Rancho Yalkuk (an auxiliary hamlet of Sacalum, near Muna) rebelled against the government's newly imposed taxes on milpas. They drove out the tax collectors, beating them with clubs and pelting them with stones, all the while screaming that they would not pay. The collectors barely succeeded in escaping with their lives.[88] Two years later, yet another minor rebellion broke out in Huhí, again over the taxes on milpas.[89]

The most portentous of these small uprisings took place in Teabo in April 1843. The gathering of more than eighty Indians in that village was considered by the militia commander of nearby Maní to be such an ominous development that he called up several companies of reservists. The interim jefe político of Ticul then informed the governor of the matter and, in a panicky letter, reported that these uprisings, "although isolated, and apparently directed against particular individuals, are in reality the general outbreak of a caste war [*guerra de castas*], with the extermination of all white people being the long-desired goal of the Indians."[90] (This was apparently the first time that the phrase *guerra de castas* was used in Yucatán.) The Caste War did not break out for another four years. Nevertheless, relations between Indians and whites must have been very bad indeed for local officials to respond as they did, and this was not even in an area in which the Caste War would be strongly supported by the local Indians. A major rising was clearly at hand.

The Caste War differed from earlier Mayan uprisings in one important way. During colonial times the Indians had always faced the severe handicap of being poorly armed. This would not be the case in 1847. During the political strife of the 1840s, the competing factions, desperate for support, had begun to arm the people to serve as the rank and file of their forces. Eventually, so many arms had been distributed, with even more available from gunrunners in Belize, that the uprising actually had a chance for success. Many Indians took that chance.

Conclusion

A major cause of the Caste War was the rapid agrarian change implemented by the state government after independence. The conversion of at least eight hundred thousand hectares of land to private property must have represented a grave threat to the Mayan way of life, probably the greatest threat since the conquest some three centuries before. The historical evidence therefore supports the interpretation put forth by Howard F. Cline.

Not all Indians chose to join the rebellion. Just as the political strife characteristic of the pre-Hispanic Maya had aided the conquistadores by making possible a Romanesque strategy of "divide and rule," so too did the regional differences evident in the 1840s lead to varying responses to this new threat. The historical evidence suggests that the danger was real even in the areas that did not support the uprising. Here, it must be concluded that Cline's analysis, although clarifying the nature of the economic differences among regions, cannot explain the causes of political and social divergence. In effect, Cline tended to see all rural Indians as either peasants or peons; he did not consult the sources that would have allowed him to go beyond the Hispanic society's understanding of the Maya and to see the important political, social, and cultural factors that at times united, but at other times divided, the Yucatecan Maya.

The agrarian factor has been emphasized here as a cause of the Caste War, but more research needs to be done before the relative importance of all the factors can be better understood. For example, the breakdown of church finances after independence, and the resulting need to raise the price of the sacraments, had a major impact on the Maya, oriented as they were to the careful use of matrimony to maintain political power and social status within the community. Clerical fees were so important that, like the agrarian laws, they were included among the negotiating points of the Treaty of Tzucacab. Yet, no one has thus far attempted to examine systematically the significance of the disruption of native religious practices, even though this factor's importance in other cases of social upheaval, most notably the popular counterrevolution unleashed by the French Revolution, is well known.

At the same time, comparative studies of other regions of Mesoamerica must be carried out in order to distinguish between a historical process common to many areas and the developments that were unique to Yucatán. In other words, we need to know more about the timing and scope of land alienations taking place in other regions in the period between independence and the great liberal reforms carried out in the late nineteenth century. Only with this expanded knowledge will it be possible to place the apparently unique events in Yucatán into a broader historical context.

Nevertheless, the research carried out up to the present demonstrates that the agrarian problem was certainly one of the major causes of the Caste War. The war was the result of both demographic growth and, perhaps more importantly, the implementation of a liberal agrarian program by the state government. The people who carried out those policies may genuinely have believed that the new laws favored the common good. But, despite such liberal sentiments, the new agrarian policy was for the most part simply one more step in the dispossession of the Maya, one more step in the creole's occupation of the soil. What was different was the nature of the Indian response.

4 Capital-Labor Relations on a Colonial Frontier: Nineteenth-Century Northern Belize

ÁNGEL E. CAL

The British industrial revolution increased the demand for raw materials from the empire's overseas territories. Growing quantities of *moscavado* sugar, tobacco, cotton, and dyewoods were supplied by the British Caribbean. Outside investment, dependent on an acceptable climate of business confidence, was required to secure these products. Levels of investment were determined not only by market conditions, but also by capital-labor relations, which in turn were influenced by labor-control mechanisms, availability of resources, wages, and interclass relations.

Regardless of the ethnicity of the laboring population, the cash economy turned workers, in varying degrees, into dependent laborers and consumers. On the eastern coast of Central America, African slaves and Indians had labored in timber camps since at least the eighteenth century. Although slaves had little choice but to work for their masters, they soon learned how to acquire meager amounts of cash to temper their dismal working conditions. To obtain Indian labor in these areas, the English, unlike the Spanish, immediately resorted to the cash economy, a tactic facilitated by the historically hostile relations between the natives and Spaniards, attributable in no small measure to Iberian methods of Indian exploitation.

British investments gave rise to far-reaching transformations of what were essentially subsistence economies on the periphery. In Belize, increased investments, particularly after the middle of the nineteenth century, were accompanied by changes in land tenure, land use, and capital-labor relations.

Foreign interest in the area's resources had antecedents stretching back to the sixteenth century. What helped stimulate it after the middle of the nineteenth century, besides the boosted demand for raw materials, was the air of business confidence associated with the construction of an interoceanic canal in Central America and the completion in 1855 of a transisthmian railroad in Panama: Both were regional manifestations of the expansion of capitalism into the periphery.[1] In Belize, the influx of a relatively large Mayan and mestizo population, refugees of the Caste War of Yucatán, proved to be a further attraction for British capital.[2]

To assess the impact of increased investments in this frontier area, we focus on the northern 3,350 square miles of colonial British Honduras, now the independent country of Belize. Clearly, before the arrival of English investors, the sixteenth- and early seventeenth-century Spanish conquest and attempted colonization had had critical demographic and other effects that can only be summarized here; similarly, important eighteenth-century developments that had repercussions on the economy can only be outlined. More attention will be given here to pre-1850 conditions, particularly the ways in which the local economy was affected by interethnic relations and labor conditions. Finally, we will examine the changes ushered in by increased economic activity in the second half of the nineteenth century.

Three tiers of dependency resulted from the increased economic activity after 1850: one between workers and employers; another between the small-scale refugee entrepreneurs from Yucatán and the local British companies; and the third between these British companies and externally based mercantile and banking firms. Most Belizean black creoles and a few Mayan and mestizo workers became dependent on wage advances—the cornerstone of capital-labor relations in Belize. Refugee entrepreneurs, in turn, became dependent on the local British companies for land-leases and credit, and for the marketing of their produce. Finally, locally based British firms relied on the large sums advanced by their directors in England.

Workers' dependence on wages for subsistence was directly linked to land tenure and land use. The British abolition of slavery in 1833 and the end of apprenticeship in 1838 (when ex-slaves were no longer legally bound to work for their ex-masters) did not result in timber camps being abandoned, as whites had feared. Land prices, local legislation, and, more importantly, the proletarianization of the woodcutters saw to that. A few Mayan and mestizo workers who were caught up in the advance-wage system were also peonized (proletarianized), but the majority of the Caste War refugees never completely abandoned subsistence farming and are categorized here as peasant-peons. At the end of the scale were

Map 4.1 Northern Belize and the Mayan Frontier, 1860

the traditionalist Maya who depended almost exclusively on farming and gathering for their subsistence. However, as investments increased in northern Belize, the relative size of the three categories—peasant, peasant-peon, and peon—changed, as land became more expensive and wage labor became more available.

The raw-material boom did not last long. Beginning in the mid-1870s, the growth rate of investments began to slacken. By 1885, external credit had practically dried up. The local economy seemed to have gone through a full cycle with the withdrawal of British capital from commercial agriculture. How do we account for such fluctuations in the flow of foreign capital to a peripheral area of the British Empire? What effects did the increased economic activity have on local socioeconomic structures such as capital-labor relations, land tenure, and land use? Why did foreign capital fail to lay the foundations for self-sustained development in areas such as northern Belize?

Northern Belize Before the Caste War

Political Struggle, 1545–1847

The Spanish attempt to colonize Belize in the sixteenth century and first half of the seventeenth failed for several reasons. The Yucatán Peninsula as a whole did not attract many conquistadores. Native resistance was more effective there than in central Mexico, in part because of the several, relatively autonomous ministates against whom the Europeans had to contend.[3] More importantly, unlike other parts of New Spain, Yucatán had no valuable minerals. Its main attraction lay in its abundant, tribute-paying population. This, however, did not apply to the southeastern portion of the peninsula, which had apparently suffered a very dramatic population decline.[4]

Even so, Mayan resistance in Belize was prolonged and not effectively subdued. Although the Maya were outwardly accommodating with respect to the building of *visita* churches,[5] they were far less receptive to the larger idea of Spanish suzerainty. In 1641, the Belizean natives literally kicked out the Franciscan friars and, amid insults, challenged the Iberians: "Let the governor come; let the king come; let the Spaniards come. We are here to fight them."[6] The widespread revolt of 1638 sought to undermine Spanish domination both through apostasy and the abandonment by natives of established visita villages. Bringing these *sublevados* back to the firm grip of "civilization" was both expensive and difficult.

The Spanish Crown apparently encouraged its subjects to undertake *entradas* with the expectation of royal favor, but in northern Belize, such expeditions were largely unsuccessful.[7]

The arrival of the English in the 1650s[8] added another dimension to the equation of colonization. Fearful of a potential Anglo-Mayan alliance aimed against Spanish rule and aware of the potential use of the Indians as a cheap labor pool, Spanish authorities based in Yucatán and Guatemala sought, not entirely successfully, to relocate the Maya.[9] The descendants of those who escaped the entradas, when joined by Mayan refugees from Yucatán, would challenge the presence of the English in Belize, particularly during the nineteenth century.

Starting around 1650, the English began operating in the area surrounding the mouth of the principal rivers of northern Belize, but neither their numbers nor their exclusive attention to logwood placed much pressure on Mayan territory until about the 1770s.[10] Logwood grows best in freshwater swamps that are not suitable for milpa farming; its shoots grow from the stump and mature in twelve to fifteen years.[11] One might thus infer, at least with respect to the use of the area's resources, that there was initially little conflict of interest between the two groups. This inference might be too simplistic. Since little is know about the Belizean Maya's demography, settlement patterns, political structure, and trade networks during this period,[12] definitive statements are hazardous. Moreover, if British raids for Mayan women and male slaves, reported in the Bay of Campeche, were duplicated in Belize,[13] some friction likely arose.

Leaving speculation aside, documentary evidence of the clash between the Maya and the British coincides with the switch from logwood to mahogany extraction in the 1770s. Unlike logwood, mahogany grows best in the limestone ridges of northern Belize. Mahogany stands were located further inland, on land most suitable for milpa farming. Moreover, the treaties of Paris (1763) and Versailles (1783), and the Convention of London (1786), while regularizing the presence of the British in Belize, also required them to withdraw from the other areas they occupied, particularly on the eastern coasts of Nicaragua and Honduras. Traffic on the rivers and streams of Belize increased with the introduction of more slaves, woodcutters, and capital to increase the profitability of British activities. Land-extensive mahogany extraction and land-extensive milpa farming would inevitably clash as the British started to encroach on Mayan-held territory.

References to "numerous tribes of hostile Indians" became more frequent in the late eighteenth century.[14] *Bravos* were described as going "without clothing of any kind," and, armed with bows and arrows, "they not infrequently committed the most sanguinary murders." Woodcutters had to request military protection for their gangs working in the forests.[15] By the beginning of the nineteenth century, despite the bravos' occasional forays, the British had expanded their boundaries of operation to the Río Bravo. For the next three decades this river was regarded as the de facto British northwestern boundary.

Contact with the British was disastrous for the Belizean Maya because of epidemics. Yellow fever raged in the British Settlement in 1803 and returned in 1830.[16] An undated report, most likely from the early 1840s, refers to "intermittent fevers" as endemic to the settlement.[17] The Maya's general susceptibility to European diseases must have caused considerable havoc within their villages.

The introduction of wage labor reinforced the negative biological effects of closer contact with British settlers. With Mexico hopelessly embroiled in internal political strife and at war over Texas, the local British authorities declared the Blue Creek, not the Río Bravo, the British Settlement's northern boundary.[18] A canal project connecting Booth's River and the Bravo was said to have cost £10,000 "and many Indian lives."[19] Wage labor began to drive a wedge between those Maya who would not compromise with the English presence and those who welcomed the opportunity of temporary work in the timber camps. A new chapter of intense Anglo-Mayan conflict opened after 1847 over control of northwest Belize. The Maya would eventually lose their land, but the local British firms would find it impossible to develop it as anticipated.

Economy, c. 1700–1847

The British were not interested in land per se in Belize. Plantation agriculture, which required investment of a fixed, permanent nature, was clearly out of the question, given the Spanish zeal to expel them from the area and the hostile posture of the natives. Only products that yielded high profits, while not requiring extensive fixed investment, could justify the high risks involved in exploitation. Interest initially settled on logwood.

The switch to mahogany extraction, which was sanctioned by the Convention of London of 1786, introduced the prospect of a land-extensive and capital-intensive industry. Mahogany trees are very large (one cut by Charles Craig weighed fifteen tons)[20] and had to be transported by water.

Because the entire commercial economy revolved around the timber industry, there was no incentive for the local British elite to construct public roads; the rivers were regarded as adequate public highways, and trucking paths and secondary streams connected the timber works to the major waterways. However, the larger firms with better access to capital sought to improve their capacity to extract timber by extending their network of private pathways and, in some cases, by dredging or opening canals.[21]

The process of acquiring land was based on the eighteenth-century "location system," sanctioned by Sir William Burnaby in 1765. Under this system, a woodcutter located an unoccupied "spot of logwood," built his hut, and claimed the area within a thousand yards of each side of his camp, "with the course of the River or Creek on both sides." The size of the logwood works was thus scaled to the area that an individual could operate alone or with a few workers. No woodcutter was allowed to claim more than one works on the same stream, but the law was silent on the sale of such works.[22]

The expensive outlay required to operate a mahogany works virtually excluded individual proprietors from the industry. The first response of the woodcutters to this dilemma was to form partnerships: One partner operated the business in Belize while the other, usually a merchant in England, looked after credit and marketing.[23] But even so, only those with good access to capital survived in the business. As early as 1787, an indignant superintendent complained that some "fifteen men, through fictitious Collusive Copartnerships," controlled "at least twelve-fifteenths of all the Mahogany works."[24] This pattern of land concentration continued in the nineteenth century.

The profitability of the large tracts of land with rich mahogany stands and logwood groves depended upon the availability of cheap labor. African slaves, because of their cost, became a prominent investment feature only in the early eighteenth century. This development was significant in that it marked the change from the transitory nature of the British presence to one of more permanence. Although a detailed analysis of slavery in Belize is beyond the scope of this chapter, the institution's major impact on nineteenth-century capital-labor relations warrants some discussion.

It is significant that the British did not resort to enslaving the Maya, who were the most readily available labor force. They, like the Spaniards who had formerly held the Maya of southeastern Yucatán under *encomienda*, learned that the natives could not easily be controlled in an area familiar to them. Instead, the British resorted to African slaves, who by 1803 made up 75 percent of the territory's population of about four thousand.[25]

The skilled and semiskilled job requirements of the mahogany industry, and the sheer physical demands of the job, determined the characteristics of the slaves purchased by the British. There was, for example, very little need for female slaves since timber work was regarded as a man's job. Buyers preferred tall, stocky men who could justify their purchase price by their work in the forests. This inevitably helped to improve conditions in the camps; there was no question of the slaves' capability to overpower a foreman who behaved tyranically.

For the slaves, who often carried machetes and firearms and worked alone in the forest, freedom through desertion was only a few paces away. Of course, the jungle, like the ocean, need not be an ally, but there is indirect evidence to suggest that runaways constituted a problem for the British.[26] Desertion served as a safety valve for those slaves who otherwise would have rebelled or gotten into difficulties with the foremen. For obvious reasons, the whip was used little in the forest. Foremen usually reported recalcitrant slaves, who were then punished in Belize Town where the whites had the advantage of a nearby militia. Still, there were cases of grave injustice, as the revolt of 1820 testified.[27]

Because workdays often extended into the night to take advantage of the coolness of the evenings, slaves were compensated with a free day on Saturday or were paid for work done on that day. Although the day's pay was little (three-quarter pence for unskilled labor),[28] its effect was significant. Skilled slaves, particularly, could eventually save enough to purchase their freedom or become consumers of items not normally included in their rations. On the other hand, those who preferred not to work for the master on Saturdays often planted a small plot of provision crops. At the end of the cutting season or at Christmastime, they could bring home some produce or sell it. A spirit of self-reliance fostered by this practice helps to account for the establishment of the small Belizean creole peasant villages that cropped up along the riverbanks after the end of apprenticeship in 1838, when all ex-slaves were freed from the obligation to work for their ex-masters.

But, what accounts for the persistence of Belizean creole labor in the timber camps after emancipation? Two reasons may be suggested: a lack of access to land and the advance-wage system.

Crown lands in the interior were completely inaccessible, while those along the rivers were owned by British companies. Further, the eighteenth-century mode of free land acquisition, the location system, was abolished by royal proclamation in 1817.[29] And, precisely coinciding with the end of apprenticeship, the local elite sponsored legislation ending the system of Crown land grants, replacing it with the sale of such lands at £1 an acre,[30] a price far beyond the resources of most ex-slaves.

Despite these obstacles, many Belizean creoles opted to squat on private lands along the riverbanks. Why the timber companies tolerated this arrangement is not altogether clear, but peasant farmers did supply the local markets with some food crops, and, more importantly, they represented a reservoir of labor for the timber industry. Further investigation should clarify why the British companies tolerated some but not other squatters and why more urban-based Belizean creoles did not resort to squatting.

The contractual system of labor also promoted Belizean creole proletarianization. Both the employee and the employer (or his agent) appeared before the police magistrate to sign a labor contract, which stipulated length of service, wage rate, rations, and, in some cases, conditions of work. Absence from work, for any reason, resulted in loss of the day's pay and a fine for the consumption of rations already provided. Disobedience, damage to the employer's property, and the like were punishable by the police magistrate through fines or imprisonment.

The contract, signed by the usually illiterate worker with his "X," legally bound him to his employer for the stipulated length of time, normally the cutting season. Part of the season's wages was advanced, half in cash and half in goods. The goods were priced above their retail value and often included items of little use to the worker, who, therefore, frequently resold them at a fraction of the original prices. In the forest, workers invariably ran out of food provisions. Employers obliged by advancing these goods from their commissaries, but again at a hefty markup. At the end of the season, workers received the balance, if any, of their wages. Often the amount in their favor was not enough to clear their accounts, particularly in light of the additional debts incurred by their dependents in Belize Town. But, even when workers balanced their accounts, they needed to go back to the timber camps as there were very few jobs available elsewhere.[31]

Unlike the hacendados of Yucatán, Belizean businessmen generally limited the maximum credit advanced to their workers to the equivalent of a season's wages. Sensitive about the interest rates charged on their accounts with financial firms in England, Belize-based capitalists avoided tying up too many assets in promised labor. Moreover, with fluctuations in timber prices, employers preferred the flexibility of being able to determine the size of their labor force at the beginning of the cutting season, when, with the advice of their associates in England, they could better project short-run profit margins. So, when mahogany prices declined, workers who were inclined to be less docile and submissive could easily find themselves cut off.

Despite their precautions, Belizean firms sometimes had to deal with workers' running away without completing the terms of their contract. This problem was essentially related to labor demand. When demand for mahogany was high, as it was in the 1840s, employers enticed workers away from rival camps, despite the tacit understanding on the desirability of discouraging runaways.[32]

From the worker's point of view, running away was a decisive step. Belizean creoles found it difficult to make a transition from an urban, British colonial setting to a rural, predominantly Mayan one. More importantly, workers seldom questioned the legitimacy of their debt. Even if they did, there was little they could do about it as solidarity among them was practically nonexistent; the isolated and widely dispersed locations of the timber camps worked against cohesion. So, when workers ran away, it was more often as a result of committing a felony than because of debt.[33]

Toward the middle of the nineteenth century the timber industry had become big business. The capital required to establish and operate a mahogany firm far surpassed what an individual woodcutter could afford. Much to their regret, individual proprietors and, later, partnerships mortgaged their timber operations beyond recovery, enabling financial and mercantile houses based in the mother country to become the new owners of Belize's natural resources. Many of the former operators migrated, while others obtained management posts with the firms that had bought them out. Some turned to supplying the new owners with logwood, an industry still marginally viable and requiring much less capital.

The coming of the Caste War refugees reinforced the Belizean economy's extreme pattern of dependency on foreign capital and the international market.

Changes in Land Tenure and Land Use After 1847

A new phase in the economy of northern Belize began in 1847 with the arrival of the whites, mestizos, and Maya who were fleeing the ravages of the Caste War then raging in Yucatán. As at least most of them were willing to enter into temporary working arrangements, the size of the regional labor force increased substantially. Even the traditionalists among the refugee (and local) Maya, although maintaining a considerable degree of aloofness, frequently sought temporary employment in the timber camps or small plantations.[34] The estimated refugee population was four thousand in 1850;[35] according to the 1861 census, it had increased to about fourteen thousand, with the Maya accounting for 33.3 percent of the total, mestizos for 57.1, and white Yucatecans for 9.6 percent. Equally important was the fact that most of the immigrants needed land to subsist. Some of the better-off among them wished to lease lands to extract logwood or to establish small ranchos for the production of cash crops. Others, with experience in Yucatán's timber industry, sought management posts with local British firms.[36]

Initial tenure agreements based on sharecropping were soon deemed inadequate by the refugees. For example, James Welsh, manager of the Corozal estate, charged his tenants one-third of their product as rent.[37] Good business contacts enabled some of the refugee farmers to sell their maize in Belize Town, but, clearly, the small domestic market was not conducive to commercial farming.

A handful of the most wealthy refugees, such as the Orio family, bought small tracts of land to establish their own timber works,[38] but most leased tracts. British companies preferred to lease rather than to sell land, but they could not always avoid selling when their need for cash was urgent. In the past, speculation had been the principle that guided many business decisions. Low-priced timber works, entirely depleted of exportable trees, were bought to be resold when new timber matured. Now, for the first time in the territory's postconquest history, the price of land was significantly affected by its agricultural potential.

Land values were also affected by the high rental prices of house plots. Throughout the last half of the nineteenth and even past the middle of the twentieth century, most of the towns and villages of northern Belize were located on private land, compelling all but a few of the better-off inhabitants to pay rent for their house lots. The Belize Estate and Produce Company, for example, owned twelve of the approximately sixteen villages of the Orange Walk district, together with practically all of the surrounding milpa land.[39] Naturally, with the increase in refugee population, the demand for house plot rentals and land-leases for subsistence and commercial farming pushed up real estate values.

Much of the land that the British occupied at the beginning of the nineteenth century had been obtained gratis under the location system. The number of land disputes generated under this system and the signs of the impending extinction of Spanish authority in the region might have prompted the change to the more orderly and selective system of Crown grants in 1817. But, as we have seen, Crown grants were replaced in 1838 by a purchasing system intended to check the development of a landowning peasantry.

Still, land claims and disputes persisted. A Board of Commissioners, representing the territory's landed elite, was established in the early nineteenth century to regularize the relocation of logwood and mahogany works.[40] However, few estates could be clearly demarcated. The coming of the refugees and the resulting increase in real estate values only exacerbated an already confused situation. In an unprecedented step, local government authorities went so far as to imprison John Hodge, general manager of the British Honduras Company, for matters related to a long-standing land dispute. Company officials in London fired off a strongly worded protest, and Hodge was quickly released,[41] but the altercation contributed to the speedy enactment of Belizean legislation equivalent to the old, Spanish colonial composición. Under the Honduras Land Titles Act of 1861, the local government offered legal title to British subjects holding quiet possession of lands in Belize.[42] Naturally, this prompted a number of fresh disputes and even a few fraudulent claims. After the dust had settled, over two-thirds of the choice agricultural lands had been registered as private property, and four British companies had emerged as proprietors of about 90 percent of the privately owned land.[43]

The increase in land prices in the mid-nineteenth century and the land concentration schemes devised by the territory's elite relegated most of the Yucatecan refugees to the status of dependent peasant-peons, most of whom rented land for their milpas and/or worked the lands leased by the small refugee entrepreneurs. A milpa of one hundred mecates (about nine acres) returned between $7 and $11 to the landlord.[44]

There is little doubt that by the time most of the refugees came to Belize, they had already been exposed to the monetary economy of southern Yucatán.[45] In Belize, the major cabeceras provided a full array of imported merchandise, some of which found its way into the refugees' villages. The prestige value and prices of imported goods proved too competitive for locally produced counterparts.[46] Of course, these manufactured goods had to be purchased with cash, which suited the small entrepreneurs as well as the British landowners who rented land, marketed most of Belize's export produce, and supplied the small entrepreneurs with credit. The economy of the metropolitan power from which most of the goods came, and to whose markets the raw materials went, was none the worse for this arrangement. Space does not allow an analysis of other sociocultural variables that contributed to reinforce the status of most of the refugees as landless peasant-peons.[47]

The nature of milpa farming also worked against the emergence of a landowning peasantry in northern Belize. Calculating on the basis of a one hundred–mecate plot, the average size of a new milpa, a peasant would need to buy about four hundred mecates (thirty-six acres) to subsist more or less permanently. The technology at his disposal enabled him to use a plot continuously for only two or three years; it then had to remain fallow for about eight years.[48] Using a conservative Crown price of $5 an acre, the peasant would need about $180 to buy enough milpa land for subsistence. Average monthly wages at this time were $8 plus rations.

Land investments also placed certain limitations on the milpero's options. Peasants often sought thickly wooded land for their milpas, and, when their sons grew old enough to do a man's task, the size of the family plot was increased accordingly.[49] Given the volatile conditions that prevailed in northern Belize in the second half of the nineteenth century, such a large investment could be wasted if the peasant had to move.

Although a handful of refugee entrepreneurs did become small landowners, the evidence suggests that there were deliberate schemes to prevent the emergence of an independent peasantry in northern Belize. There was the issue of the use of land that was technically Mexican, but under the control of the rebel Maya: Refugees settling along the banks of the Río Hondo often farmed these lands to avoid paying rent to British landlords. However, both the Santa Cruz Maya (at war with the Yucatecan government) and the Icaiche Maya (at war with the Santa Cruz Maya) demanded rent from the *ciudadanos de la banda inglesa* (residents of British-held territory).[50] There were two problems with this arrangement. Unable to pay their rent in advance, milperos sometimes defaulted on their commitment after the harvest; regarding their residence under the British flag as adequate protection, they ignored repeated warnings to settle their accounts. The Río Hondo notwithstanding, rebel Maya sometimes came in pursuit of the "rent-dodgers," throwing the whole area into panic and disrupting the all-important business of timber extraction as well as the fledgling sugarcane industry. The second problem was more straightforward: the loss of potential rental income suffered by the land companies.

Consequently, the British elite turned to the local legislature for help. Termed an "Act for Better Securing the Peace of the Frontier," the 1868 law prohibited non-British residents from renting land in Mayan-held territory.[51] An earlier law (1855) had summarily restricted alien property rights to twenty-one years,[52] unequivocally asserting the preference of the British elite for tenants and laborers. And, modeling their 1862 anti-squatting legislation on the Jamaican equivalent, the local legislature made trespassing on private property and the unauthorized destruction of timber a felony punishable by a fine.[53] Finally, for those aliens who might have considered applying for a land grant, the attorney general reminded the lieutenant governor that refugees did not qualify.[54]

Labor Conditions

The Belizean system of advance-wage or peonage labor, as we have seen, was well established before 1847. Although it secured, in the case of the proletarianized Belizean creoles and a few Mayan-mestizo workers, a relatively tractable labor force, the system did not measure up to the expectations of Belizean capitalists. Its coercive powers were very real, but peasant-peons could and did turn to milpa farming for most of their subsistence needs. Wages, therefore, were slightly higher in Belize than in southern Yucatán.[55]

In Belize, the formal system of advance-wage labor was both a form of labor control and an incentive to attract workers. As practiced among the Yucatecan refugee entrepreneurs, cash and goods were advanced to prospective "servants" with the usual 20 to 25 percent markup.[56] Rum, an item high in demand, likely facilitated these transactions for seasonal work; seasonal labor was particularly critical to the Yucatecan refugee entrepreneurs, who lacked the capital to operate on a scale whereby workers might be employed year-round.

Mayan peasant-peons had a greater capacity to resist the exploitative employer-employee relationship than did the proletarianized Belizean creole and Mayan-mestizo workers who were more strictly peons. This capacity was directly related to the availability of land, settled either upon the payment of rent or by squatting. In addition, the Maya had learned the political value of organized violence, or the threat thereof, during the Caste War. Thus, the Yucatecan conflict seems to have worked against the Belizean system of peonage labor, but, as we shall see, the war also limited the options open to Mayan and mestizo workers.

Because of their long experience in controlling Belizean creole labor, the British preferred them over the potentially troublesome Mayan-mestizos.[57] Nonetheless, the latter became a significant component of the northern Belizean labor force. Instead of dealing directly with Mayan-mestizo workers, the British typically relied on refugee entrepreneurs as middlemen. Sometimes, however, even these Yucatecan entrepreneurs miscalculated in their dealings with the Maya. A case in point was the employment of the San Pedro Maya. These Icaiche Maya immigrated into Belize as a group with their structure of government intact.[58] When the employer's agents tried to impose their work regulations on the Maya, the agents were required to comply with village rules. When they refused, they were tied up all night in the village prison. Embittered, entrepreneur Florencio de la Vega instigated British military action against the villagers. The plan backfired when the British were humiliated in the Battle of San Pedro in 1866.[59]

The relative control of the employer was less attributable to the advance-wage system of labor than to the sociopolitical conditions prevailing in the region. Informants of the village of San Antonio, Río Hondo, for example, referred to the days of "slavery" when Manuel Jesús Castillo required all villagers to work for him.[60] Why did employers such as Castillo get away with this imposition? The political climate in southeastern Yucatán provides one possible explanation. An Icaiche runaway, for example, would not be welcomed among the Santa Cruz because the two groups were at war. Neither could he easily return to Santa Clara, the Icaiche capital, having deserted the native army to go to Belize. Going westward placed him in Guatemalan territory where local officials might press him into a labor gang. Escape to another village in northern Belize was not impossible, especially under an assumed name, but only a few resorted to this unpopular strategy;[61] moreover, employers or their agents, in constant communication with one another, were likely to find out his whereabouts. Escape into the jungle was yet another possibility: Footpaths in the Icaiche forest connected the Belizean frontier area with settled parts of Campeche and beyond.[62] This alternative, however, meant virtual exile.

Moreover, one needs to compare the attractiveness of northern Belize as a refugee's destination point with other areas in the region. The frontierlike economy of northern Belize provided the peasant-peon with not only a relatively safer place of residence but also with a marginally better opportunity for subsistence through the rental of milpa plots, supplemented by wage labor in the timber and sugarcane industries. On the other hand, southern Yucatán, from which most refugees originated, had been entirely disrupted by the Caste War. Wage labor and markets for surplus provision crops were almost nonexistent. In addition, continued fighting between the Santa Cruz rebels and Yucatecan government forces rendered the entire unpopulated area a no-man's-land. Labor conditions on the henequen plantations of northwestern Yucatán were at least as harsh as those in Belize, while wages were less attractive. Moreover, milpa land was far less accessible in northern Yucatán.[63]

Because the attractiveness of Belize lay in the availability of both wage labor and "safe" milpa land, it is not surprising that most refugees sought seasonal wage labor. The fact that the labor season did not always coincide with milpa work (when it did, one of the sons could be spared from the milpa) enabled most of the residents of northern Belize to limit their dependency on the cash economy.

Proletarianized workers or peons, trapped in the advance-wage system, were not as fortunate as the milperos. Indebted, they did not have time for their own milpa. As permanent workers, they had to subsist on an average wage of $8 per month plus rations.[64] For their part, employers felt that since their servant-workers subsisted from their granaries, lived on their land, and resided in their farmhouses, they were entitled to absolute obedience from these *mozos*. Not surprisingly, refugee Yucatecan entrepreneurs characteristically resorted to practices imported from Yucatán to "discipline" their predominantly Mayan-mestizo peons.

To their credit, the British authorities would not condone arbitrary justice,[65] both on principle and because of the statement the abused Maya were making about the issue in the Caste War of Yucatán. This is not to say that the British favored the servants over the masters. Beginning in 1850, enforcement of the Masters & Servants Ordinances was assigned to the resident magistrate of the northern district. That the full weight of the law was thrown in favor of the employers is corroborated by the data in Table 4.1, which indicate that the incidence of legal action taken by employers against workers increased dramatically between 1855 and 1869, precisely the period when investments in the area peaked.

Yucatecan employers were not the sole abusers of peonage; the British elite persuaded the local government to finance an immigration scheme, and, in July 1865, 474 workers arrived from China, preceded by 129 from Barbados.[66] Ultimately, however, the scheme failed. Inhumane treatment of the immigrants resulted in revolt and in the mass flight of 150 Chinese to the rebel Maya, who refused to hand them back. Over a hundred of the remaining Chinese died within two years of their arrival. As for the Afro-Caribbean workers, their conditions were not much better, but their plight seldom gained the attention of the authorities.[67]

In addition to dealing with the vicissitudes of labor, capitalists in northern Belize faced the problem of dwindling timber supplies. The forest reserves of the northwest seemed to be the answer. The resulting struggle between the Maya and the British would contribute to the demise of sug-

Table 4.1 Corozal Magistrate's Court Hearings, 1855-1869

	Offenses[a]						
	Against Masters & Servants Act	Percentage Total	Against Persons	Percentage Total	Against Property	Percentage Total	Total
1855	3	5.7	27	50.9	3	5.7	53
1857	10	12.2	33	40.2	1	1.2	82
1860	29	25.0	26	36.2	1	0.9	116
1863	75	55.9	42	31.3	6	4.5	134
1869	281	100.0	-	-	-	-	281

Sources: For 1855-1863, see Archives of Belize, Annual Report of District Magistrates in R.s. 54, 58, 79, and 84; for 1869 figures, see Nigel Bolland, "Labour Conditions in Belize: The Century After 1838," *Belcast Journal of Belizean Affairs* 1 (1984):48-54.

Note: a. Not all offenses are listed here.

arcane production and reduced levels of investment in the timber industry later on in the century.

British Capital in a Frontier Economy

The 1855 legislation limiting alien property rights was prompted by the local British elite's desire to control the potential growth of a refugee landowning class. Such a development would have produced undesirable competition in the mahogany industry and even in sugarcane. The British elite's objective was realized for the most part, not as a result of enforcing the law, but because of the small entrepreneur's chronic need for working capital.

Most Yucatecan refugee entrepreneurs first turned to logwood extraction to accumulate enough capital to lease land and purchase basic sugar-processing equipment. When their credit ratings had been established, they sought additional capital from local British firms to expand their operations. Of course, creditors obtained adequate compensation for this service. In addition to paying interest, tenants usually signed away their rights to their cane fields and any improvements thereon; and, since sugar and rum were generally marketed through the land company or its business associate, the credit advanced was reasonably protected.

Interestingly, a handful of native Mayan entrepreneurs also tried their hand at logwood extraction, including a most unusual woman, Micaila Mai of Cocos. At her death in 1854, Señora Mai had an account of $3,500 with the predecessors of the British Honduras Company and another $300 with a commercial firm.[68] There was a brief spurt of Mayan entrepreneurship in the cotton industry as well. The U.S. Civil War stimulated a sudden increase in demand for raw cotton. As the Yucatecan Maya were no strangers to cotton production, some were attracted to its commercial possibilities. The more cautious of them planted the cash crop along with maize, while a few, such as Juan José Cal, undertook more ambitious projects. Backed with credit extended by the British Honduras Company, Cal employed the men of sixteen families to produce at Jesús María, now Yo Creek.[69] This type of evidence suggests that there was not a *necessary* relationship between ethnicity and class in mid-nineteenth-century northern Belize. Mestizos and white Yucatecans were fairly well represented in the peasant-peon category. The criteria for entrepreneurship clearly had more to do with access to land, capital, and credit, and the ability to manage labor. When market conditions were favorable, a few of the more successful peasant-peons could and did become small-scale entrepreneurs. In years of poor returns, however, mini-capitalists often could not clear their accounts and consequently had to sign away their property if they had not already done so. Under these circumstances, most of the small entrepreneurs could not afford to keep more land than they could personally use.

Refugee investments in sugarcane soon persuaded British capitalists of the industry's viability. Simple *trapiche* technology imported from Yucatán showed them the way. Beginning in the late 1850s, the British turned to sugar and rum production as an important supplement to their declining timber reserves. The introduction of steam equipment sharply increased output; by 1861, sugar exports began to figure prominently in export statistics (see Table 4.2). The British had access to the best lands, could obtain credit from their parent companies in England, and, if necessary, transfer Belizean creole workers from their timber camps to their sugarcane plantations. The marketing infrastructure that serviced the timber industry could, with some slight modifications, be applied to sugarcane. The same ships that brought manufactured goods to Belize and Central America and took on mahogany and logwood could also carry barrels of sugar and rum to the British market.

Table 4.2 Belizean Sugar Exports, 1861-1887[a]

	Exports (in Tons)	Value (in BH Dollars)
1861	160	18,400
1862	734	84,180
1863	1,563	179,745
1864	2,773	318,895
1865	2,279	262,085
1878	1,736	199,640
1879	2,202	253,230
1880	2,807	322,805
1881	1,931	222,065
1882	2,572	295,780
1883	2,023	232,645
1884	2,391	155,415
1885	1,679	109,135
1886	479	31,135
1887	659	42,835

Sources: Archives of Belize: For 1858 figures, see Note from Treasury, R. 63, June 22, 1859; for 1861-1865, see Austin to Sheldon, R. 72, March 12, 1867; for 1868, see Lt. Gov. to Gov. of Jamaica, R. 98, March 3, 1869; for 1878-1887, see. L. Bristowe and P. Wright, *The Handbook of British Honduras for 1888-1889* (Edinburgh and London: William Blackwood and Sons, 1890).

Note: a. Figures for 1866-1877 are not available.

Increased British investments in sugarcane made it more difficult for refugee entrepreneurs to survive in the business. Interest rates rose, and, to compete for labor, refugees had to rely on the more expensive advance-wage system. Also, since distribution for the domestic and export markets was controlled by the British land or mercantile companies, the small producer had to consign his crop through his competitors while simultaneously hoping to obtain credit from them.

Even the local British government weighed in, exacting its share of the fruits of the refugee entrepreneur's labor. Increased spending incurred in defending the frontier could not be offset by custom duties alone. In 1856, legislation imposed an excise tax of fifty cents per hundredweight of sugar and twenty-five cents per gallon of rum, with a possible $500 fine for inaccurately reported acreage returns.[70] When the cost of containing the Icaiche spiraled in the mid-1860s, the impost was doubled. This was a steep increase, considering that the average price of sugar in the domestic market was $5 per hundredweight.[71] Equally exasperating to the refugee rancheros was the fact that mahogany and logwood were exempt from the new round of taxation.

Ironically, the advance wages that tied peons to their Yucatecan employers paralleled the outstanding debts that tied the small entrepreneurs to British landowners. Administration and probate records demonstrate the extent of the entrepreneurs' indebtedness. Inevitably, British companies adsorbed most of the refugee entrepreneurs' estates, suggesting that in some instances creditors continued funding small entrepreneurs merely to prevent them from defaulting.[72]

To the Yucatecan refugees, their short-lived prosperity appeared to be a hoax practiced on them by the British companies. In effect, British capital had used their managerial skills the better to exploit the area's Mayan-mestizo labor. This perception seems borne out by the fact that Yucatecan employers seldom owned the land. Moreover, their equipment was heavily mortgaged on account of the cash and provisions advanced for their day-to-day operations.

The British land and mercantile companies exploiting the natural and human resources of northern Belize were themselves not exempt from the problems associated with operating in a frontier area. Political instability frequently disrupted timber cutting and sugarcane production. The volume of exports from Belize was small relative to the world market. A primitive communications infrastructure, increasing labor costs, and declining timber reserves made investments very risky.

No sooner had the British decided to increase their level of investments in the sugar industry than the political instability of the area took a turn for the worse. The expansion of the economy prompted British capital to move into territory claimed by the traditionalist Icaiche. The Icaiche–San Pedro Maya subsequently advanced their claims to the northwest based on treaties signed in the eighteenth and nineteenth centuries, causing a British retreat in 1868.[73]

With the benefit of hindsight, it is easy to point out the major economic obstacles that British capitalists faced in northern Belize. Long accustomed to the use of slave labor and the natural infrastructure of the rivers, they were not inclined to invest in more efficient equipment and a more reliable communications network. Except for the increased use of gunpowder, most of the work of cutting, trucking, and squaring of logs was done manually until late in the nineteenth century. In the sugarcane industry, most of the Yucatecan entrepreneurs employed small, animal-driven mills and simple processing equipment. Their scale of operation would not have allowed for more sophisticated equipment even assuming that they could have afforded it. British investments in steam technology were beset by a host of problems, not the least of which included the Anglo-Mayan struggle for northwestern Belize. The Icaiche occupation of Corozal Town in 1870 left much of the season's sugarcane unharvested as the entire population fled. The Icaiche Mayan raid on Orange Walk in 1872, and the British military response to these incursions, wrought similar havoc on the steam-mill operators of Indian Church, Tower Hill, and Caledonia.[74]

To make matters worse, local companies had no control over the amount of credit they could obtain from financial firms in the mother country. Agents on the other side of the Atlantic did not always appreciate the conditions under which local companies had to operate. John Carmichael, for example, often could not harvest all of the season's sugarcane crop for lack of adequate supplies, his appeals to Vaughan & Company notwithstanding.[75] Neither could overseas firms appreciate that, unlike timber, which could be floated to the coast, sugarcane required a network of cart roads connecting the fields to the mill. The construction and upkeep of these roads and bridges constituted a heavy outlay of capital.

The coup de grace was the decline of sugar prices on the international market, from an average of twenty-three shillings in the 1870s to thirteen shillings six pence per hundredweight in 1884.[76] With an increased scale of production, better infrastructure, and more efficient technology, the British in Belize might have weathered the storm, as did some estates in other sugar-producing areas.[77] But, overseas creditors were not convinced. As available investment capital dwindled, the small entrepreneurs were the first to go. Sharp reductions in land-leases and in demand for goods and provisions followed. These shock waves were too much for Belize's fragile economy. By the turn of the century, British capital had been restricted almost exclusively to timber extraction, while a handful of small entrepreneurs continued producing sugar and rum for the domestic market.

Conclusion

Not all of the major economic changes that accompanied the influx of capital and labor to northern Belize in the second half of the nineteenth century were structural changes. British capital and management had been involved, at least since the early eighteenth century, in exploiting the region's resources, relying mostly on slave and, later, Belizean creole labor. Where labor was concerned, the most prominent feature after 1847 was the appearance of a large peasant-peon sector. The creation of this class can be attributed to several factors, including the local elite's deliberate policy of discouraging the development of an autonomous landowning peasantry; land concentration and the peculiarities of milpa farming worked in favor of that policy. Given the limited amount of capital and the risks involved in investing in frontier areas, it could be argued that peasant-peon labor was the most appropriate type for the local economy. As peasants, the refugees rented land from the British companies, and, as peons, they provided seasonal wage labor in timber camps and small sugarcane plantations.

Additionally, the prestige value and competitive prices of imported manufactured goods, and the need to pay land rent in cash, were strong incentives that attracted peasant-peons to seasonal wage labor. The disappearance of the traditionalist Belizean Maya and the sharp reduction in the number of neighboring groups of traditionalist natives were hastened particularly by the growth of the peasant-peon sector.

The long-established advance-wage system of Belizean labor, as modified by Yucatecan practices, was meant both to attract and to control workers. Its record was mixed. Workers found it difficult to abscond after entering into labor contracts; however, this can be attributed more to the sociopolitical conditions prevailing in the region as a result of the Caste War than to the system itself. Unlike proletarianized workers, peasant-peons had access to milpa land. Moreover, the negative British attitude toward Mayan labor and the chronic shortage of capital restricted the rate of proletarianization, although more workers were trapped in the system as the level of investments increased. All in all, contrary to the expectations of foreign firms, Mayan peasant-peon labor turned out to be less reliable and more expensive than that of imported indentured servants.

Unwilling and unable directly to exploit the labor of the refugee population, British firms turned to Yucatecan entrepreneurs. This was evident in the fact that most small-scale entrepreneurs were not the real owners of land and capital, nor did they have any leverage on domestic and external marketing networks or on local policy-making. Even so, the Yucatecan entrepreneurs sought to expand their operations. Evidence indicates that they tried to obtain as much credit from the local British firms as possible. In many cases, local creditors carried "managers" who were disastrously indebted.

British capital faced another serious obstacle in northern Belize: the hostile posture of the traditionalist Maya who wished to halt the advance of the colonial frontier or at the very least to share in the wealth of the region's resources. This posture left the Belizean economy vulnerable to constant work stoppages, as the British military found it almost impossible to defeat the natives. Mayan opposition, however, gradually melted away, not because of the effectiveness of British arms, but because of the attractiveness of wage labor. Nevertheless, the Anglo-Mayan frontier remained unstable throughout the nineteenth century, a factor that seriously affected the attitude of overseas financial and mercantile firms whose continued confidence in the viability of the timber and sugar industries was absolutely essential if these ventures were to withstand the shocks of the competitive, fluctuating international market.

In the late nineteenth century, the dynamic relationship among the various social and economic sectors of northern Belize ultimately undermined investors' confidence. Access to the area's physical, financial, and human resources involved the various sectors in open competition. The traditionalist Maya eventually disappeared within the peasant-peon class, but not before they had seriously disrupted the business of timber extraction and sugarcane production. The peasant-peons wished to use the land for subsistence farming, but this did not sit well with the British firms and small-scale entrepreneurs who were in need of a cheap and reliable labor force. The Yucatecan entrepreneurs wished to expand their logwood and sugarcane operations but had to compete with the very firms that wished to keep them as more-efficient managers of foreign capital.

A continuing relationship among the various socioeconomic sectors was predicated on the benefits each perceived it would derive from participating in the local economy; nevertheless, the perception and behavior of external firms was paramount, since they supplied the working capital. The region lacked the capacity to generate, locally, the capital required to confront the exigencies of the international market. As a peripheral enclave economy, the region had to convince the external sector of its continued viability. Unfortunately, northern Belize could not do this in the late nineteenth century, and, consequently, capital was withdrawn from the area.

Part II

Forging the New Order: Commercial Agriculture and Export Dependency

Part II examines the intensification of commercial agriculture and external dependency, which occurred dramatically in northwestern Yucatán during the final third of the nineteenth century but proceeded more gradually in Quintana Roo. Together, Wells's and Konrad's chapters support the recognition in modern Latin American historiography that, despite its flaws, the dependency perspective has some explanatory power for the late nineteenth and early twentieth centuries.[1] During this era—in which several Mexicanists identify the onset of a "new imperialism"[2]—agrarian capitalism and significant, enclave-based, extractive ventures took hold in Yucatán, Quintana Roo, and other parts of Mexico, and there was a pronounced redirection of production, social relations, and political life. Throughout the long and stable dictatorship of General Porfirio Díaz (the thirty-four-year regime known as the Porfiriato), the national government, local oligarchies, and foreign interests collaborated to drive economic growth and "progress," invariably at the expense of local majorities and established social traditions.

The northwestern quadrant of the Yucatán Peninsula—the broader locus of historian Allen Wells's microhistory of the Santo Domingo Xcuyum estate—was thoroughly transformed by the requirements of North American mechanized agriculture and governed by its fluctuating rhythms during the Porfiriato. Unlike the sugar industry on the ravaged southeastern frontier, the nascent northwestern henequen fiber industry had suffered only temporarily during the Caste War and ultimately had benefited from the conflict. Once the northwest had been cleared of rebels, a significant number of Mayan refugees from the war-torn southeast opted for the food and security that northwestern estates offered them as newly recruited peons. Thus, when the invention in 1878 of a mechanical knotting device for the McCormick reaper-binder began to revolutionize the North American grain industry and geometrically expand demand for binder twine, the northwestern estates were in a position to take advantage of the expanding hard-fiber market.[3]

The production of henequen increased furiously throughout the Díaz era: Annual exports rose from forty thousand to more than six hundred thousand bales of raw fiber. Wells details how, by the turn of the century, the grazing cows and green cornfields of the northwest's former, colonial-style haciendas had been replaced by endless, rectilinear rows of bluish-gray spines and the brisk, factorylike pace of the modern plantation. Mérida was no longer the dingy, muddy, overgrown village it had been before the Caste War. Now the republic's "White City," it was immaculate and modern, a fitting seat for Yucatán's newly minted henequen millionaires.

Elsewhere, Wells and other scholars have explored the external linkages of northwestern Yucatán's monocrop economy, debating the terms and consequences of the International Harvester Company's increasing involvement in the henequen industry.[4] More recently, in collaboration with Gilbert Joseph, Wells has examined the internal structure of domination on northwestern fiber estates and reconstructed a neglected history of adaptive resistance by hacienda peons.[5] Here, Wells focuses on the evolution of the henequen estate as a unit of production. Informed by an extensive comparative literature on Caribbean plantation agriculture, Wells argues that the Porfirian henequen estate was essentially a hybrid institution, suspended in its transition from hacienda to plantation, and exhibiting characteristics of both ideal types (in this regard, also see the chapter by Batt). Using notarial archives and a wealth of private papers for Santo Domingo Xcuyum and other properties, Wells probes the implications of the fiber estate's hybrid status in the areas of agricultural technology, the acquisition and utilization of land and labor, and the hacendado's mentality as entrepreneur. His thesis invites further comparison with other Latin American agrarian societies that afford access to comparably rich bodies of documentation.

As Canadian ethnohistorian Herman Konrad demonstrates in his contribution, it took longer to forge the new order on Quintana Roo's tropical-forest frontier. In 1901, the Porfirian principles of "peace and progress" were bestowed, at bayonet point by an invading force of *federales* supported by state militiamen, upon the *cruzob* Maya—the die-hard rebel faction that had never capitulated in the nineteenth-century Caste War. Yet, as was the case in northern Belize, new economic dependencies (and diseases), more than military defeat, undermined traditional patterns of autonomy and subsistence,[6] ultimately drawing the frontier Maya into an expanding network of capitalist relations based on chicle and timber extraction.

Konrad reveals that, ironically, the former military chiefs of the cruzob resistance were often in the vanguard of this proletarianization and political reintegration. Striking bargains with government bureaucrats and private capitalists alike, they frequently ended up as petty despots and entrepreneurs. As labor contractors and chicle producers, they mediated the consolidation of an infrastructure of dependency that eroded the very cruzob identity and social organization that they had previously defended. Here, Konrad's analysis (like Cal's discussion of Yucatecan refugee entrepreneurs) is consonant with recent efforts by anthropologists and historians of Latin America to explore the linkages between local and external spheres, and between the state and society.[7] An increasing emphasis on "collaborators" and "compradores," caciques and caudillos, "brokers" and "hinge-men" in recent Yucatecan historical studies reflects the current trend and promises a continuing infusion of anthropological (and other social science) methods into the historical literature.[8]

In the resulting equation of frontier dependency, Konrad argues that the only clear-cut winners were foreigners. As in nineteenth-century northern Belize and in northwestern Yucatán during the late Porfiriato, control over Quintana Roo's export staples increasingly passed into the hands of large foreign investors. By the outbreak of the revolution, Mexican entrepreneurs played only a supporting role in the exploitation of forest products. Subsequently (following World War I), North American corporations gradually supplanted British firms, but Quintana Roo and its inhabitants realized little gain throughout. Foreigners successfully resisted government export taxes, preferred British Belize as an entrepôt, and garnered a 600 percent markup on each quintal (one hundred pounds) of chicle between bush camp and sale in New York.

Konrad's chapter, based on a multinational array of archival, statistical, and oral sources, is a pioneering effort to portray Quintana Roo's early territorial history on a broad canvas. He explains the transformation of the frontier political economy by examining the dynamic interplay of local, regional, national, and international interests and forces.[9] Through it all, the reader cannot help but reflect that while chicle and timber are no longer important export staples, and the territory has now achieved statehood, Quintana Roo is again very much a frontier—for deluxe domestic and international tourism—during a new phase in its capitalist development.

5 From Hacienda to Plantation: The Transformation of Santo Domingo Xcuyum

ALLEN WELLS

Defining Haciendas and Plantations

The development of commercial agriculture in Latin America transformed how large landholders and peasants lived off the land. Buoyed by increasing demand for export staples from the industrialized world, the agrarian sector underwent a modernization that altered the landscape, economic structure, and social relations of production throughout the diverse regions of rural Latin America.[1] Students of agrarian history agree that the emergence of commercial agriculture in the last decades of the nineteenth century was an uneven process that had a variety of effects on preexisting agrarian societies.[2] Endogenous factors such as ecology, demographic patterns, ethnicity, and land tenure all played a role in shaping the evolutionary path that a rural society followed.

Unfortunately, diversity and unevenness have complicated the formulation of analytical frameworks to interpret such key agrarian institutions as the hacienda and the plantation. In a seminal article written over three decades ago, Eric Wolf and Sidney Mintz attempted rigorously to define these two landed estates. An hacienda, they maintained, is "an agricultural estate operated by a dominant landowner . . . and a dependent labor force, organized to supply a small-scale market by means of scarce capital in which the factors of production are employed not only for capital accumulation but also to support the status aspirations of the owner." On the other hand, they defined a plantation as "an agricultural estate operated by dominant owners (usually organized into a corporation) and a dependent labor force organized to supply a large-scale market by means of abundant capital, in which the factors of production are employed primarily to further capital accumulation without reference to the status needs of owners."[3] Although this typology no doubt simplifies complex institutions, it points up key differences in property ownership, capitalization, markets, and the desire for conspicuous consumption by landowners. Magnus Mörner has suggested that Wolf and Mintz's formulations "are only two extremes on a continuum, variations of the same phenomenon."[4]

Undoubtedly, the anthropologists had certain Mesoamerican rural societies in mind when they constructed their typology.[5] Indeed, the modern Caribbean sugar complex clearly illustrates the plantation type. The tradition-bound sugar industry underwent a thorough transformation during the last decades of the nineteenth century, stemming from technological improvements, international competition, changes in consumption patterns and labor practices, and the penetration of the international financial establishment. The end result of this process was an agroindustrial complex that exemplified the principal characteristics of Wolf and Mintz's plantation type: corporate ownership; ample capitalization; a variegated yet dependent labor force, organized to supply a distant yet substantial market; and an emphasis on profit maximization.[6]

If the late nineteenth-century cane-sugar estate dovetails nicely with the social organization of Wolf and Mintz's plantation, other large landholdings throughout Latin America lie somewhere along the continuum between the traditional, self-reliant hacienda and the modern corporate enterprise. The definitions begin to blur—as Wolf and Mintz predicted they would—when we get down to empirical cases and find characteristics of one type interwoven with the other. For example, qualitative differences between primarily "status-conscious" haciendas and those that were profit-oriented were not so clear-cut in many "modernizing" agrarian societies. Conversely, plantation owners in the Caribbean did not abandon their ostentatious style of living—witness the taste for high fashion and frivolity that many continued to indulge even after the transition to corporate enterprise. Furthermore, some hacendados played an active role in the day-to-day running of the estates, while others lived in the city, visiting their properties only occasionally and leaving management to hired administrators. Finally, although absentee ownership was an integral feature of some sugar-plantation societies prior to modernization, at other times and in other regions, the "hands-on" corporate mentality postulated by Wolf and Mintz was more characteristic.[7]

The problem becomes even more complicated when labor relations are examined. Wolf and Mintz contended that the poorly capitalized hacienda "must thus bind labor by means other than money wages."[8] Such coercive techniques as naked force and debt were coupled with more subtle, indirect methods such as parceling out subsistence plots and "[institutionalizing] personal relationships between employer and employee"[9] to secure an at least outwardly compliant labor force. Traditional social relations of production, such as debt peonage, are contrasted with those of the plantation, which often took advantage of a free (or relatively free) labor market and paid cash wages. Unlike the hacendado, the corporate-plantation manager did not have to rely on debt or cultivate a paternalistic relationship. Even this apparently clean distinction, however, is found wanting when specific cases are examined. Many plantation societies had labor regimens that were highly differentiated and exhibited employer-worker practices that harkened back to traditional institutional patterns. In Yucatán, for example, rural proletarianization occurred in fits and starts as hacendados consciously employed a heterogeneous work force, combining indebted Mayan peons with neighboring villagers and a smaller number of ethnic and linguistic strangers—Yaqui deportees, indentured Asian immigrants, and central Mexican *enganchados*. The result was a labor system that in some ways resembled a rural proletariat but continued to embody many of the characteristics of the paternalistic hacienda.

Notwithstanding these variations on the heuristic model, Wolf and Mintz's analytical construct serves a useful purpose in drawing attention to the gradual, uneven process by which such traditional institutions as the hacienda evolved into capitalist enterprises. Typically, haciendas lost their self-reliance and came to resemble capitalist estates in the kind of markets they served, the changing aspirations of their owners, and the proletarianization of their work force. Slave plantations, on the other hand, were invariably transformed into modern corporate enterprises. Rarely, however, did regions that featured traditional haciendas develop into export-oriented monocultural societies.[10] Yucatán's transformation from self-sufficient cattle and maize haciendas in the nineteenth century to modern henequen estates seems to illustrate a unique path that rural Latin American society followed on the road to agrarian capitalism.[11]

While the henequen estate may have physically resembled a modern commercial plantation—with modern machinery, narrow-gauge tramways, and land-intensive cultivation of the staple crop—familial ownership, management, and mentalité continued to imbue the institution with characteristics of the pre-henequen hacienda. Emblematic of a rural society in the midst of a complex transition, the henequen estate is best viewed as a hybrid that illustrates some of the traits of its predecessor but reflects inevitable adjustments in land, technology, labor, and infrastructure. Moreover, it appears that the emergence of a full-fledged plantation society was inhibited by lingering vestiges of the earlier institution, particularly by the way in which hacendados confronted their labor problems.[12]

Yucatán's incipient henequen planters also faced serious management difficulties. Because of significant price fluctuations, which the industry experienced even during its Porfirian boom years, Yucatán's henequen estates were in a continuous state of tension and flux that constantly challenged the adaptive skills of their proprietors. Capitalization of the syncretic henequen estate, although relatively abundant in comparison with that available to its predecessor, still was problematic, owing to volatile price fluctuations; and even though agricultural joint-stock companies did surface from time to time during the boom (*auge*), the great majority of large landed estates fell under the rubric of family ownership rather than corporate management. Yucatecan elite families during the auge followed in the footsteps of their forebears, entertaining lavish status aspirations that inhibited profit maximization.[13]

The Porfirian henequen estate, then, represents a fusion of modernizing influences, wrought by the rapidly expanding export trade, and the legacy of Yucatán's socioeconomic past. To illustrate this hybrid plantation society and to trace the transformation from self-reliant haciendas to agrocommercial enterprises, this chapter concentrates on the evolution of one hacienda, Santo Domingo Xcuyum, over a 150-year period.[14]

The Henequen Boom

The growth of mechanized agriculture in North America and Europe during the nineteenth century stimulated the demand for henequen fiber, grown principally in the semiarid, rocky, northwest of Yucatán. At first, henequen was used to manufacture cordage and rigging, but, after 1880, North American farmers, demanding inexpensive twine to bind sheaves of wheat, turned to Yucatán's henequen industry to provide it. By 1900, more than 85 percent of North American binder twine was manufactured with Yucatecan fiber.

Sleepy cattle haciendas were gradually replaced by busy, commercial henequen estates.[15] The young henequen fields were enclosed by stone fences that partitioned the countryside and delineated estate boundaries while keeping the declining cattle herds from trampling the rows of spiny, green agaves. Campesinos, who previously had grown their milpas on village and hacienda lands, now worked in the estate's machine house or cut *pencas* (leaves) in the sun-drenched fields. Workers stoked boilers, rasped leaves to separate the fibers, cleared land for future cultivation, and tended to the every want and need of the fibrous plant.

Fundamental changes in the predominant agricultural unit of production—the hacienda—enabled local henequen producers to meet rising world demand. The emergence of Santo Domingo Xcuyum during the boom reflects all of these modifications. Located in the heart of the *zona henequenera*, in Conkal *municipio*—fifteen kilometers northeast of Mérida—Xcuyum was one of the largest and most productive Yucatecan haciendas. Managed by Don Eulalio Casares during the Porfiriato, Xcuyum had its share of ups and downs, mirroring the tenuous nature of the monocrop economy. Casares's ability to procure capital, to negotiate with

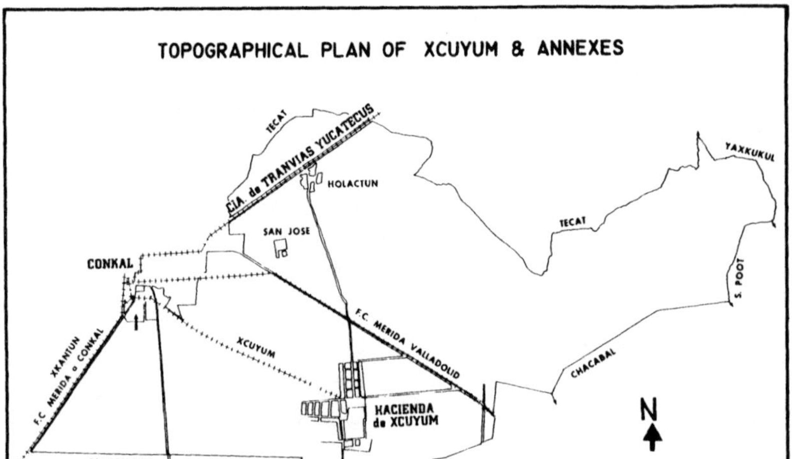

Map 5.1 *Source:* Personal Papers of Juan Peón Ancona

neighboring landlords, to obtain sorely needed labor, and to survive a perilous financial panic during the 1890s shows the versatility of hacendados during this period of sustained economic growth. The fact that most haciendas were not as successful as Xcuyum confirms that wealth, land, and status were not, in and of themselves, a guarantee of success. To operate a successful henequen estate, henequeneros had to expand the hacienda's physical boundaries, gradually replace livestock with henequen, import improved fiber-processing technology, secure reliable railway connections, bolster their labor force, and persevere through unpredictable fluctuations in international fiber prices that plunged the regional economy into alternating fits of inflation and recession. The manner in which Casares coped with difficult territorial, financial, and labor questions offers insights into the day-to-day operation of the Yucatecan henequen estate.

Xcuyum Before Henequen

During the first centuries of Spanish colonization, local elites for the most part operated cattle ranches in the northwestern portion of Yucatán. In the eighteenth and early nineteenth centuries, increasing population pressures, insufficient rains, and devastating plagues destroyed corn crops and forced starving peasants to forsake their independent existence to join the growing hacienda community. The hacendado, who obtained corn regularly through the judicious rental of his land to local villagers, enticed nearby residents by offering a continuous supply of grains.[16]

Within the boundaries of these cattle and maize haciendas, a complex social organization grew up: An extended family of sorts emerged from the overlapping of living and working areas of a large group of dependent laborers. Theoretically, a resident servant was free to come and go, but, in practice, he was confined to the estate by the institution of debt peonage. In return for workers' immobility, hacendados and peons established a patron-client relationship combining protection, direction, and mutual duties and responsibilities.[17] The local landed elite kept the framework intact by relying heavily on the notion of "security." As Stanley and Barbara Stein note, "above all, [the hacienda] held the promise of continuity through the preservation of status from generation to generation."[18]

Xcuyum—which in Mayan means a tree that grows on top of the hill—typified Wolf and Mintz's model.[19] The earliest extant records, dating back to 1769, corroborate this picture of a self-sufficient estate catering to limited local markets. Owned and operated by the Conde de Miraflores, Sebastián Calderón, one of the more prominent aristocrats of Yucatecan society, the Xcuyum of 1769 consisted of nothing more than a main house, a few corrals, livestock, animal-driven water pumps, and housing for an unspecified number of resident peons. Like many local estates, a portion of Xcuyum was rented to tenants, who, in turn, gave the landlord a share of their crop; this served to supplement the main source of revenue, cattle raising. Henequen, although native to Yucatán, was not exploited commercially during the colonial era. Xcuyum did, however, produce henequen on an extremely small scale for a variety of purposes, including making ropes, sacks, and hammocks.[20]

It was not until the 1830s that these land-use patterns began to change as Xcuyum and other northwestern haciendas began gradually to diversify.[21] Hacendados added rows of henequen to take advantage of a recently opened market. At first, fiber production served only to complement the livestock and grain economy, providing a sorely needed cash flow. Agave cultivation was limited by the absence of a mechanical rasper or decorticator; time-consuming and wasteful manual rasping argued against large-scale production.[22]

Following the trend set by innovative entrepreneurs, Xcuyum's owner, Manuel Casares de las Llanes, began to cultivate henequen during the late 1830s. Casares, who had purchased the estate on March 9, 1836, for nearly nine thousand pesos, had emigrated to Yucatán from Spain, Cuba, and New York City. After successful ventures in the import-export trade and in education, he decided to invest his earnings in agriculture. When he purchased Xcuyum, the hacienda consisted of Xcuyum proper and annexes San José, Xcancay, and Koben. The three annexes offered Casares a degree of flexibility in grazing his livestock herds, since each tract had its own water supply and corrals.[23]

Expansion

Casares and other hacendados soon came to realize that if large-scale monocrop cultivation was to become a reality, additional land and labor had to be procured. Henequen was harvested throughout the year, requiring a permanent labor supply. Although technological advances would increase production capabilities, the henequen industry would not require a skilled work force. Rather, a large and mobile group of laborers was needed to work in all phases of production. The demand for a permanent work force increased the value of local labor. Planters were forced to buy out neighboring small property holders (*pequeños propie-*

tarios) in order to snare prospective workers. With one act, they expanded their estates and secured a dependable workers' contingent. This was a gradual process. The expansion of the Yucatecan plantation and the concomitant creation of a large, mobile labor pool began in the second half of the eighteenth century and continued throughout the nineteenth.[24]

Casares de las Llanes systematically began to push out the boundaries of his estate in the 1840s. By purchasing lands that bordered his, Casares, while not adding properties of considerable size, was creating a solid base for the future expansion of Xcuyum. By 1856 the Casares family fortune was valued at 7,300 pesos (see Tables 5.1 and 5.2).[25]

Jorge Ignacio Rubio Mañé, in a short biographical sketch of the Casares family, characterized Manuel as an industrious man dedicated to the growth of his hacienda. In addition to expanding henequen production and fostering livestock herds, Manuel invested considerable time and effort in setting up a cottage industry at Xcuyum, in which women and chil-

Table 5.1 Expansion of Xcuyum, 1836-1856[a]

Property	Previous Owner	Purchase Date	Price (in Pesos)	Location
San Antonio Holactun	José González	1846	?	Annex to Xcuyum
Unspecified	Silvestre Rivas	1836	25	In Conkal
Unspecified	Lorenzo Camal	1845	12	East of Conkal
Unspecified	Santiago Aguilar	1845	13	East of Conkal
Unspecified	Santiago Aguilar	1845	12	East of Conkal
Unspecified	Casimiro Citoc	1846	10	On road to Yaxkukul
Unspecified	Timoteo Camal	1850	15	East of Conkal
Unspecified	Melchor Tacu	1850	15	Hacienda Kuman

Source: Peón Ancona papers.

Note: a. In all but one of the properties mentioned, the surface area of the lands purchased was not specified. San Antonio Holactun, the sole exception, was stipulated as being two hundred mecates.

Table 5.2 Property of Manuel Casares de las Llanes, 1856

		Value (in Pesos)
Xcuyum (with annexes San José, Xcancay, Koben, San Antonio Holactun) 500 head of cattle, 70 horses and mules; unspecified number of salaried servants; 1 administrator; 3 overseers; 4 cowboys; 2 work-gang chiefs; 1 bookkeeper; and 40 day workers		7,500
Xkantun 70 head of cattle; rows of henequen; one-quarter league of land; and unspecified number of workers		1,000
Chaczinkin 120 head of cattle; rows of henequen; one-quarter league of land; and unspecified number of workers		1,500
House in Mérida (Calle de Iturbide, Cuartel 1, Manzana 2; downtown area: 28 by 28 meters)		2,500
Subtotal:		12,500
Outstanding Debts		
Mortgage on Xcuyum *(capellania* Father Julian Cepeda), at 5% interest	3,000	
Mortgage on Koben, nearby nunnery, at 5% interest	200	
Mortgage on house in Mérida *(capellania* Manuel Jesús Pérez)	200	
Unspecified creditor	1,800	
Subtotal	5,200	
Net Worth		7,300

Source: Peón Ancona papers.

dren manufactured henequen sacks and hammocks.[26] An 1879 census found 111 women and children employed as sack-makers.[27] This early attempt to diversify the henequen industry supplemented the growing raw-fiber production on the estate.

When Manuel Casares de las Llanes passed away in 1864, leaving the management of the properties to his wife Bruna Galera y Encalada, Xcuyum was in a position to take advantage of the ensuing boom in henequen cultivation. The Casares family doggedly continued to expand the estate by purchasing adjoining tracts, clearing land, and planting rows of the spiny agave. Although Bruna Galera y Encalada had legal title to

Xcuyum, by 1870 the actual direction of the estate was left to two sons, David and Eulalio. The sons' determination to expand the hacienda, and to mirror the growth of similar large landholdings throughout the northwestern henequen zone during the boom, is clearly demonstrated in Table 5.3.

The Casares family purchased many of these properties during bust cycles of the unstable monocrop economy. The 1884–1887 period was a notable example of a cyclical downturn in the world market price of henequen. Pequeños propietarios fell on hard times when prices declined and reluctantly had to sell out. Eulalio Casares purchased several properties at deep discounts during this period as the expansion of Xcuyum continued unabated.

Table 5.3 Xcuyum Expansion, 1856-1893

Property	Previous Owner	Purchase Date	Price (in Pesos)	Location
Unspecified	Conrado Zapata	1857	?	On Mocochá road
San Luis Pech	María Aguilar	1863	?	Sitpach
Unspecified	Ramón Madera	1866	35	Conkal
San Francisco Yaxché	Ramón López	1875	?	Sitpach
Unspecified	Ramón Madera	1877	35	Conkal
San Lázaro Copó	Manuel A. Pérez	1886	100	Conkal
Public land grant	Federal government	1887	?	Yaxkukul
Unspecified	Pool	1887	?	Yaxkukul
Quinta Atenas	Bibiano Aguilar	1887	175	Conkal
Yuyumal	María Pech	1888	10	Yaxkukul
San Roman	Marcelo Pérez	1893	?	Conkal
Ejidal lotes	Various	1888-1893	Various	Conkal, Mocochá, Sitpach, Yaxkukul

Source: Peón Ancona papers, except ejidal lotes, which are from the personal papers of Carlos Peniche Escalante and Archivo Notarial del Estado de Yucatán, passim.

In addition to buying out nearby pequeños propietarios, the Casares family also utilized favorable government land policies to their benefit. A dispute between neighboring property owners and a nearby village gave Eulalio the opportunity to secure a 512-hectare public land grant. Under Mexican law, residents could file a claim with the secretary of development (*fomento*) to petition vacant public lands. Casares's actions were similar to the attempts of other opportunistic land speculators and property owners to expand their holdings throughout the zona henequenera. His case deserves discussion because it sheds light on the potential for land aggrandizement in Porfirian Yucatán.

Juan Bautista Contreras, a Yaxkukul resident, originally petitioned the federal government for a 910-hectare land grant in early 1886. A preliminary survey of the property aroused protest from three neighboring landowners—Hacienda Chacabal owner Daniel Peniche, residents of the village of Yaxkukul, and Casares—all of whom claimed that the terreno baldío infringed on their own properties. The residents of Yaxkukul went so far as to file a grievance with the court to contest the Bautista Contreras survey. The petitioner, who evidently had limited resources, went to Casares and offered to cede his rights to the baldío in exchange for a cash settlement. Casares, who had the means to pay for litigation as well as for a second survey demanded by the local justice of the peace, paid off Bautista Contreras and split the 910 hectares with fellow hacendado Daniel Peniche. The Chacabal owner bought four hundred hectares from Casares, leaving Xcuyum's owner with 512 hectares. The secretary of development approved the land grant a year later. The incident typifies the manner in which Casares was able to increase his landholdings, first by taking advantage of pequeños propietarios and village leaders, and then successfully negotiating with neighboring landlords.[28]

Another means of land aggrandizement directly involved Eulalio Casares with neighboring villages. Casares took advantage of the 1856 reform law that provided for the breakup of village common lands. Ejidos were to be divided among village heads of family, each to receive a small dotation. Casares wasted no time in buying up plots from individual heads of family; less than eight months after the secretary of development had approved the breakup of village lands in the town of Conkal, Casares paid forty-two townspeople five pesos each for their nine-hectare dotations. In this manner, Xcuyum acquired nearly four hundred hectares of Conkal property at a minimal expenditure (see Table 5.4). Similarly, Eulalio purchased ejido lots from all of the surrounding villages, with the exception of Yaxkukul, gobbling up twelve lots in Cholul, eleven in Mocochá, and four in Sitpach.[29]

Table 5.4 Casares's Purchases of Conkal Lots,[a] 1890

Lot No.	Purchased from	Occupation
1	Rudecindo Martín	Carpenter
2	Francisco J. Pérez	?
4	Santiago Pérez	Worker
5	Pedro Pablo Pérez	Merchant
6	Justo Canché	Field hand
8	Teodocia Pérez	Housewife
9	Vicenta Chim	Housewife
11	Petrona Cen	Housewife
12	Francisco Rivas	Field hand
13	Cornelia Quijano	Domestic
14	Bacilio Matú	?
15	Anastasio Pérez	Carpenter
16	Ramón Aguilar	Merchant
17	Augustina de P. Aguilar	?
18	Daniel Acosta	Carpenter
19	Emeterno Victora	?
20	Julian Chi	Field hand
21	Pedro Pech	Field hand
22	Pedro Chi	Field hand
23	Tranquilino Argaez	?
24	Santos Mences	Carpenter
25	Antonio Balam	?
26	Baltazara Quijano	?
27	Eulalia Angula	Housewife
29	Nasaria Aguilar	Domestic
30	Rodolfo Pérez	?
31	Cacilada Zapata	Housewife
32	Ricardo Zapata	?
33	Antonio Canché	Field hand
34	María Buenaventura	Housewife
35	Manuel Martín	?
38	Sacarias Canché	Housewife
40	María Bibiano Camal	Housewife
42	Justa Tep	Housewife
43	Ysac Pérez	Merchant
44	Esaltación Argaez	Housewife
45	Demetrio Rivas	Field hand
46	Antonio Chim	Field hand
47	Ysidora Zapata	Housewife
48	Samuel Quijano	Field hand
49	Esteban Chan	Field hand
50	Fernando Pool	?

Source: Personal papers of Carlos Peniche Escalante, "Título de Ejidos," Conkal, 1889-1890.

Note: a. Size of lots: 9 hectares, 44 aras, 2 centiaras; awarded by federal government on June 8, 1889; dates of purchase: October 19 and 23, 1889, February 19 and 22, 1890.

By the end of the Porfiriato, Xcuyum encompassed 3,512 hectares, having effectively doubled its size in less than a century. To finalize and demarcate the new, enlarged boundaries of Xcuyum, Casares engaged in trade (*permuta*) with neighboring hacendados. For example, in 1890 he delineated his southern boundary with the Monchac proprietor, Leandro León Ayala, by giving his neighbor 378 hectares of *anexa* San Francisco Yaxché in exchange for 307 hectares of Hacienda Monchac. In the same year, Casares surveyed Xcuyum's western boundaries and then squared off his property lines with Esteban Andrade, owner of Xkantun, by trading twelve of the ejidal *lotes* of Cholul and a twenty-hectare parcel for nearly four thousand mecates of Xkantun property. A year later, Casares made a similar arrangement with neighboring Hacienda Dzonot. These permutas completed Xcuyum's final demarcations during the Porfiriato; each neighbor, in effect, tacitly recognized through careful negotiations his own boundaries as well as those of Xcuyum.[30]

Casares's expansion of Xcuyum was not an isolated happenstance. Throughout the henequen zone, landed estates experienced similar transformations, acquiring adjoining tracts of land owned by pequeños propietarios and taking advantage of nearby villagers. Sometimes, violence accompanied disputes between property owners and *ejidatarios*.[31] In general, however, the emergence of the large landed estate met with little resistance in the henequen zone, as hacendados, with the support of local authorities, utilized state and federal laws to their advantage; small proprietors were oftentimes powerless to object.[32]

Emergence of the Plantation

If accumulating land was not exceptionally difficult, transforming the self-reliant hacienda to a profitable commercial plantation required some ingenious problem solving. Although by 1855 Yucatecan entrepreneurs were firmly convinced that the future of the regional economy lay in henequen monoculture, they had to await technological advances in the processing sector to increase production capabilities and enable supply to approach demand. Prior to the invention of a mechanical decorticator (*desfibradora*), or rasper, in 1855 to extract the fiber from the henequen leaves, time-consuming hand tools were used.[33] Labor-intensive implements not only limited production, but wasted fiber as well.

After several failures by U.S. inventors, two Yucatecans, working independently, built manually operated machines that scraped off the pulp by means of a "large fly wheel with strong blunt knives attached to its periphery."[34] These early scrapers, first marketed in 1856, cleaned only one thousand leaves in a ten-hour period. As the industry grew, however, refinements in the desfibradora and the introduction of the steam engine in 1861 gradually increased production capabilities. Motivated by the growing trade and by the state government's attempts to stimulate advances in machine productivity and safety, Yucatecan inventors had decorticators made to specifications in the United States.[35] By 1900 automatic Prieto machines, such as the one in operation on Xcuyum, cleaned 150,000 leaves within a ten-hour period, a far cry from the earlier output.[36]

Rasping machines had to be installed on nearly all large henequen haciendas because the fiber must be processed within twenty-four hours after harvesting the leaves; otherwise, it tends to dry out, inhibiting proper processing of the penca. This idiosyncrasy of the henequen crop ruled out the possibility of centralized processing facilities and forced planters to combine the agricultural and industrial facets of production in the same area. As early as 1879, Xcuyum employed the most powerful machinery in Tixkokob partido: a twelve-horsepower steam engine with four rasping wheels. Less than five years later, in an attempt to increase productivity, the Casares family doubled the number of rasping wheels to eight. By 1895 Xcuyum boasted a mammoth, fifty-five-horsepower, U.S.-manufactured Corliss steam engine (and a twelve-horsepower English engine as a backup) with two independently operating rasping machines, one Prieto and one Villamor; the value of Xcuyum's machine house alone, excluding tramway equipment, exceeded fifteen thousand pesos. The self-reliant hacienda had witnessed a gradual evolution as proprietors intent on maximizing profit, and oriented toward the foreign market, equipped their estates with the latest technology available.[37]

Yucatán's transportation revolution followed the modernization of the processing sector. Not until the industry was firmly established in the 1880s did hacendados begin to lay a network of Decauville narrow-gauge rails to transport the leaves from field to rasping machine and from processing house to nearby railhead. Before the introduction of trams to the countryside, henequeneros had been forced to rely on more costly and traditional means of transport, such as the mule train. Casares began laying Decauville rails throughout Xcuyum in 1889, completing a four-kilometer tramway two years later. The tram, valued at nearly twenty thousand pesos, connected the center (*casco*) of the hacienda with the nearest railway station, in Conkal. The line was equipped with one passenger car, one baggage car, five platforms, and the mules necessary to pull the rolling stock. This revolution in transportation reduced transaction costs and enlarged productive capacities.[38]

Eulalio Casares was also instrumental in completing the infrastructural link that directly tied Xcuyum to the port city of Progreso. The Mérida-Valladolid railway company owned by General Francisco Cantón was, like many fledgling Yucatecan railway concessions, experiencing capitalization problems during the early 1880s. With work on the Mérida-Conkal-Progreso branch stalled in 1885, Cantón went to local merchants and hacendados to appeal for a loan to help the company resume construction. Casares, along with many local planters and Méridan merchants involved in the profitable henequen trade, agreed to loan Cantón over 170,000 pesos to complete the branch. The mortgage agreement demonstrates the way in which Yucatecan commercial interests and landowners aided in the growth of the peninsular transportation system, especially as it served their own best interests.[39]

The mortgage represented a cooperative venture by local elites who understood the strategic importance of the railroad for the continued expansion of the henequen industry (see Table 5.5). Although many of the creditors did not own haciendas located directly on the intended railway route, as was Casares's Xcuyum, many of them stood to gain from the eventual completion of the Mérida-Valladolid railroad. For example, the *señores* Peón de Regil, Pedro Leál Gamboa, and Manuel Espinosa Rendón all owned properties in Tixkokob partido that would receive service as soon as the Mérida-Conkal-Progreso branch was terminated. The line would also serve to reduce transportation costs of hacendados in Motul and Temax, such as Roque J. Campos, Palma y Hermano, and Ignacio Peón.[40] Like many of his neighbors, Casares grasped the significance of the completion of the railway and agreed to extend Cantón the needed capital to finish the branch. Terms of the contract illustrate Cantón's precarious financial position.

1. Cantón promised not to alter railway rates on corn and henequen, the two principal commodities to be shipped by rail, for the duration of the mortgage.
2. Cantón could not pursue a second mortgage for more than fifty thousand pesos for the duration of the mortgage agreement.
3. Fifty percent of the railway's cargo earnings were earmarked for mortgage payments.
4. Investors would receive a 50 percent discount on shipping expenses up to a specified amount. Creditors were to pay half in cash and half in the form of a note. A rider permitted a reduction in the rebate from 50 to 20 percent should competition ap-

Table 5.5 1885 Mérida-Valladolid Railway Mortgage

Creditor	Occupation[a]	Amount Loaned (in Pesos)	Owned[b] property near route
Marcos Duarte Ruela	m/p	26,124.74	No
Bernilo Cámara	m/p	8,650.37	No
Manuel Dondé y Cía[c]	m	16,077.37	No
Leandro León Ayala	p	9,649.57	Yes
José María Ponce	m/p	21,913.91	No
Eulalio Casares	p	6,596.75	Yes
Nicanor Ancona	m/p	25,588.08	Yes
Ceferino Montforte	p	5,464.00	No
Ybarra y Cía, Sucs.[d]	m	5,024.54	No
José Font	m	5,024.54	No
Pedro Leal Gamboa	p	5,024.54	Yes
Carlos Peón Machado	p/m	4,850.00	No
José Rafael de Regil	m	5,000.00	No
Ignacio Peón	p	3,000.00	Yes
Palma y Hermano	m/p	3,169.73	Yes
Francisco Martínez de Arredondo	m	2,735.00	No
José E. Cámara Peón	p	2,648.00	Yes
Manuel Pasos Gutiérrez	p	1,205.00	Yes
Roque J. Campos	p	2,000.00	Yes
Acevedo y Sandoval	m/p	1,500.00	Yes
Sres. Peón de Regil	p/m	1,000.00	Yes
Crescencio Terrorio Z.	p	1,000.00	Yes
Manuel Espinosa Rendón	p	1,000.00	Yes
Pedro Peón Contreras	m/p	1,000.00	No
Juan José Herrera	p	1,000.00	Yes
Juan J. Sansores	p	850.00	Yes
Servula Conde de Peniche	p	500.00	Yes
Manuel Martínez de Arredondo	p	500.00	Yes
Leonido Kuyoc	p	500.00	Yes
	Total	170,596.23	

Source: Archivo Notarial del Estado de Yucatán, Oficio no. 5, José Patrón Zavlegui, vol. 40, 31 de Diciembre de 1885, pp. 1122-1134.

Notes:
a. Merchant (m), planter (p). In cases where there is more than one occupation, I have placed the borrower's principal means of livelihood first.
b. Owned property column includes those who stood to prosper by the eventual completion of the Mérida-Conkal-Progreso branch.
c. Cía (compañia).
d. Sucs. (sucesores).

pear (which did in fact occur with the completion of the Mérida-Izamal line in 1890).

5. The mortgage carried a 12 percent annual interest rate.[41]

Despite its prejudicial conditions, Cantón signed the agreement with the thirty investors on December 31, 1885. Although the third condition in the contract insisted that 50 percent of the railway's cargo earnings were to be earmarked for mortgage payments, Cantón did not repay Casares's share (6,596.75 pesos) until 1897. Nevertheless, for eleven years Casares enjoyed a privileged status based on the contract's first and fourth conditions. Besides demonstrating the upper hand that henequen entrepreneurs held vis-à-vis capital-starved railway promoters, the agreement also illustrates the significant role that merchants and planters played in the creation of the henequen zone's infrastructural network.[42]

Given the radical transformation in the transport and industrial sectors, which sparked the growth of the commercial plantation, cultivation techniques employed by administrators and overseers surprisingly did not change significantly throughout the nineteenth century. A patient approach was advised by a henequen plantation administrator (*encargado*) named José I. Rivas Font. In a manual written in 1906, Rivas outlined the painstaking preparations required for the proper cultivation of the agave: Land had to be surveyed in July; all trees felled and bushes chopped during August; the fields were to be left until March or April of the dry season, at which time they were burned to clear all remaining vegetation; and the land was to be squared off and surveyed, with suckers planted in May and June. The suckers, which had been grafted from healthy plants (*matas*) and placed in a nursery for almost two years (until they were forty-two centimeters high), were then transplanted to the henequen field (*henequenal* or *plantel*) and propped up by stones placed around the trunks. Each worker was charged with planting three hundred suckers daily, in rows at least five and a half feet apart. As the young matas grew, weeding (*chapeo*) was recommended three times yearly, but as the plants matured the chapeo requirements diminished. New plants would not produce for six to seven years and were said to be *en cultivo.* From the seventh to tenth years a few leaves would be sufficiently long to warrant cutting; in the tenth year the foreman was to mark leaves ready for harvesting with white paint. The plant, which was now in *mateo,* was deemed to be mature when the leaf was at right angles to the stock or trunk. As Rivas Font noted, "when the leaf is thus placed the fiber has reached its maximum tensile strength and the wise hacendado will harvest his product."[43] After ten years the mata was in *plena explotación,* all leaves being long enough to harvest. Harvest occurred three times a year, with each plant producing eight to fifteen leaves per cutting. The plant lasted for twenty years, after which productivity dwindled and it was declared *en decadencia*. Ultimately, a ten-meter flower stalk would rise, which indicated the plant's death.[44]

Plantation administrators who employed this rather straightforward approach to henequen cultivation began to clear large blocks of land in anticipation of growing world demand. Production increased from twenty-five thousand mecates in 1880 to over 150,000 mecates in 1905, reflecting the impressive expansion in cultivation throughout the henequen zone.[45]

By 1895 Casares's Xcuyum was producing more than three hundred bales of high-grade fiber a month.[46] The high-grade fiber, a product of Casares's careful management of the henequenales and of the plantation's sophisticated machinery, brought Xcuyum's owner one-half to one cent more than the current market price for fiber. Over the course of the twenty-four months for which data is available, from January 1892 to December 1893, Xcuyum averaged 332 bales of fiber a month, with a high of 529 in June 1893.[47] By 1914 Casares had increased production to more than six hundred bales a month, making Xcuyum one of the largest henequen-producing haciendas in the state.[48]

In addition to other improvements, Casares compartmentalized Xcuyum into separate henequen planteles, all of them at varying stages of development. Even the anexas of Holactun, San José, and San Francisco Yaxché, all formerly cattle ranches, were largely given over to henequen cultivation (see Table 5.6). In 1895 nearly half of Xcuyum was dedicated to the intensive cultivation of fiber. The rest of the hacienda's property was relegated to transport infrastructure, the processing sector, uncleared forests to fuel the machine-house boilers, a garden patch, sundry corrals for livestock, and lands awaiting development.

The hub of Xcuyum was the casco, where the main house (*casa principal*), machine house, chapel, corrals, *tienda de raya*, and workers' huts were located. The most imposing structure on the casco was the machine house where the steam engines, boilers, decorticators, and hydraulic press were installed. Behind the machine house were wires strung from posts across an open field, where the processed fiber was hung out to dry. To the right of the machine house was the casa principal, which was used by the owner on his infrequent visits to the hacienda. The casa was composed of three large rooms with a kitchen, bathroom, porch, and chapel adjoining the main structure. A horse-driven waterwheel, seven corrals, a vegetable garden, and a fruit orchard—reputed to be the envy of the entire henequen zone—lay just behind the casa. The hacienda store, which

Table 5.6 Xcuyum's Henequen Planteles, 1895

	Stage	Mecates	Worth per Mecate (in Pesos)	Total Value (in Pesos)
On Xcuyum				
Nahuat	Old[a]	950	3.00	2,850.00
Xlapak	Old	750	3.00	2,250.00
Koben *antiquo*	Old	700	4.00	2,800.00
Koben *viejc*	Old	550	3.00	1,650.00
Koben *nuevo*	Mature	425	8.00	3,400.00
Quijano	Mature	1,750	10.00	17,500.00
Santa Cruz	2 years	236	3.00	708.00
San Bruno	2 years	241	3.00	723.00
Santa Raquel	1 year	1,800	3.00	5,400.00
Road to Conkal	Old	425	2.50	1,062.50
Naranjo	Old	1,100	2.50	2,750.00
Los Fukes	Old	1,050	4.00	4,200.00
Santo Domingo	Mature	1,000	8.00	8,000.00
Road to Chí	Mature	219	9.00	1,971.00
Santa María	Mature	3,725	8.00	29,800.00
Santa Maria *chica*	1 year	231	2.50	577.50
Road to Yaxché	Old	645	2.50	1,612.50
Loeza	Mature	1,500	8.00	12,000.00
Moca	Mature	390	8.00	3,120.00
Annex Holactun				
San Antonio	Old	490	2.50	1,225.00
Holactun	1 year	650	2.50	1,625.00
San Román	Old	725	5.00	3,625.00
Annex San José				
San José	Old	930	4.00	3,720.00
Annex Atenas				
Unnamed	Mature	500	7.00	3,500.00
Annex San Francisco Yaxché				
Santa Rosa	Old	915	2.00	1,830.00
Alamo	Old	580	2.00	1,160.00
Ramon	Old	460	4.00	1,840.00
Other Planteles on Xcuyum				
El Semillero	Old	700	4.00	2,800.00
San Manuel	2 years	180	3.00	540.00
		Total 23,817[b]	5.06[c]	Total 124,239.50

Source: Peón Ancona papers, and Archivo General del Estado de Yucatán, Justicia, Remate de Hacienda Xcuyum, 1895.

Notes:
a. Old refers to fields described as "en decadencia"; mature to those in "plena explotacion."
b. 23,817 mecates is 9,526.8 hectares or 23,531.2 acres.
c. Average worth per mecate.

stood directly across from the casa, was a separate building with two rooms, one for storage purposes and the other a small office for bookkeeping and transactions. Records do not indicate a separate building for a jail, something that was commonly found on most haciendas. Finally, eighty huts rimmed the casco. Constructed in the typical Mayan style, the huts had stone and mortar (*cal y canto*) walls and palm-thatched roofs. Each had its own garden plot of beehives, corn, and chile peppers, with space set aside for livestock.[49] (Interestingly, the casco of Santo Domingo Xcuyum is still in working order, although it is quite run down. While the casa principal is not in use, the machine house and service buildings are currently used by the local ejido).

Determining the size of Xcuyum's labor force is not an easy task. An 1879 census listed 303 inhabitants (69 field workers) on the hacienda's lands. An 1895 account found 1 administrator, 1 overseer, 10 cowboys, and 122 indebted servants. If the 1879 figure for field workers is accepted as reasonably accurate, Xcuyum's henequen work force grew from 69 to 122 in sixteen years. This would correspond to the physical expansion of the estate and the clearing and planting of new planteles. Although these figures must be accepted with some caution, since district prefects were notoriously unreliable census takers, the growth of Xcuyum's labor force was indisputable.[50]

Like all Yucatecan hacendados, Casares used the institution of debt peonage to ensure a permanent, dependable work force.[51] The field hand (*jornalero*) had two running debts, the *chichán cuenta* and the *no hoch cuenta*. The former was a small debt for daily purchases and weekly wages, while the latter was a large account (accrued when funds were advanced for marriages and fiestas, for example) from which a servant rarely extricated himself. Hacendados kept detailed records of the no hoch cuenta, and the books of henequen zone estates trace the spiraling debts of peons over a period of time.[52] A paucity of data prevents us from determining how many servants actually worked off what they owed. Nevertheless, those who remained tied to the estate found their debts constantly increasing.[53]

World market demand, high henequen prices, debts, and poor wages all conspired to prevent jornaleros from extricating themselves from debt. Although the average wage in Yucatán increased from twenty centavos a day in 1870 to one peso a day in 1910,[54] inflation more than counterbalanced periodic increments. Friedrich Katz estimates that real wages declined 20 percent throughout Mexico during Porfirio Díaz's rule.[55] In Yucatán, monocrop cultivation necessitated the importation of large quantities of foreign and Mexican foodstuffs, driving up the cost of basic commodities and diminishing purchasing power even further. A Ministry of Development circular in 1902 stated that food prices in Yucatán were well above the national average.[56] Specifically, Yucatán's meat, beans, and corn prices greatly exceeded the average, particularly after the 1898 boom in henequen prices. These increases, naturally, were passed along to the resident peon through the tienda de raya.

In Table 5.7, the manner in which Casares was able to ensure an immobile work force is demonstrated: Peons were tied to the hacienda through the debt mechanism, and the store provided the means to increase that debt. In terms of convenience, the store offered a wide variety of items, including food, unfinished cloth, household goods, munitions and gunpowder for hunting, and last—but by no means least in popularity—liquor. Conceivably, the peon never had to leave the inner sanctum of the hacienda. Unfortunately, data is lacking on the tienda's daily prices; we can only speculate as to whether Casares intended to obtain a supplementary profit from the store or if the tienda acted solely as a means of increasing the debts of the resident peons.

Yucatecan hacendados always bemoaned chronic labor shortages and began as early as 1881 to look outside the peninsula for additional sources of labor. The policy of importing indentured workers, euphemistically called "colonization," continued throughout the boom, with local elites desperately trying to meet expanding labor requirements. Casares was one henequenero who was determined to supplement his work force with Asian indentured servants. In 1901, in conjunction with several other hacendados, Casares signed a contract with a Mexico City agent, Francisco Cacho Alonzo, for twenty Asian field workers between the ages of twenty and thirty-five. The terms of the contract specified that Cacho Alonzo had three months to bring the workers to Yucatán. Casares and the other interested planters had to deposit twenty pesos per worker in the account of Olegario Molina y Cía, the *casa exportadora* handling the transportation arrangements. Casares also had to pay an extra amount for one foreman who would act as liaison between the hacendado and the newly indentured servants. The wages specified in the agreement were representative of prevailing wages paid to local Mayan henequen workers. The Asian servants signed a contract for a period of two years from the time they arrived in Progreso; if they left before the requisite period ended, they had to repay the expense of their passage across the Pacific.[57]

Encouraged by the results of his first venture into "colonization," Casares participated in 1902 as a board member of a state government–sponsored Agricultural Colonization Committee. The group, formed at the behest of Governor Olegario Molina, was determined to organize a

Table 5.7 Inventory of Xcuyum's Tienda de Raya, 1895

Liquor			
97	bottles of *anis amargo* (licorice-flavored alcohol)		
22	bottles of *habanero* (sugar-based alcohol)		
24	bottles of beer		
Household items			
18	beeswax candles	2	pounds of gunpowder
500	cast or molded candles	1	piece of narrow cloth
52	sperm candles	4	handkerchiefs
30	packs of matches	4	dozen buttons
60	packs of cigarettes	1	box of explosives
18	pounds of munitions	15	*coas* (tool used for cutting henequen leaves)
1	piece of crude cloth	14	empty containers
1	piece of "cotin" cloth	22	packages of needles
2	pounds of starch	25	bottles of oil
4	axes		
1	box of soap		
	Misc. items: knives, forks, bleach, thread, etc.		
Food			
20	pounds coffee	375	pounds *manteca* (animal lard)
45	pounds sugar	9	pounds chocolate
25	pounds rice	200	pounds salt
10	pounds raisins	900	pounds beans
5	pounds Spanish peppers	5	pounds Tabascan peppers
100	pounds Escurre peppers	2	pounds *achiote* (local spice)
1	pound anise	2	cans of oysters
11	cans sardines	32	bottles of honey
100	cloves of garlic	28	*almudes*[a] corn
14	limes	4	*almudes*[a] chile *bobo*
2,500	*bizcochos* (biscuits)	1	pound cumin
4	ounces cloves	2	pounds noodles
5	pounds of ground coffee		

Source: Peón Ancona papers, and Archivo General del Estado de Yucatán, Justicia, Remate de Hacienda Santo Domingo Xcuyum, 1895.

Note: a. An almud is equivalent to 4.625 liters.

large-scale migration. Planters had to pay 375 pesos per family, with discounts available if an order was placed for more than six hundred families. Henequeneros had to pay 10 percent of the workers' passage in advance and the rest on their arrival in Progreso. The committee was responsible for fulfilling several contracts, but the number of indentured servants never quite met expectations. Casares did have several Chinese,

Korean, and Japanese families on Xcuyum.[58] Despite numerous attempts to increase the labor force through colonization, however, the local Maya always made up the overwhelming majority on henequen estates throughout the Porfiriato.

Profits were, of course, vital to the success of any henequen estate, and one of the most impressive features of the henequen economy was the ability of planters to reap substantial earnings from small expenditures. The *Boletín de Estadística*, which compiled the mandatory production costs (and which prided itself on being a reliable source of statistical data), estimated a net profit of 12,600.74 pesos for one thousand mecates over the twenty-three-year life span of a henequen plantel. Based on its determination that 8,879.26 pesos were required for initial operating expenses (for clearing, planting, machinery costs, management overhead, and interest), the statistical gazette deduced through simple cost-accounting methods that a Yucatecan henequenero could expect a 9 percent return on his investment. If we were to include minimal costs for land, food, medicine, and transport, the profit would be reduced. Even when henequen prices dipped as low as three cents a pound, however, planters could be assured a small return on their investments.[59] In the midst of the 1907–1908 panic, Rodulfo G. Cantón, a prominent merchant and railway builder, told a *Mexican Herald* correspondent that despite the low price of henequen, "[fiber production] is still profitable."[60] When low fiber prices, however, coincided with the henequeneros' inability to repay past-due loans, even paltry labor costs and burgeoning demand could not rescue some from bankruptcy.

The Hacendado Mentality

When given the choice of selling at a low price or withholding production to drive up prices, assured profits invariably prompted planters to choose the former option. Every organized attempt to hold henequen off the market ended in failure.[61] Whatever the world market price, henequeneros cultivated and processed their fiber. Eulalio Casares was no exception. In 1894, in the midst of a serious recession in the world fiber market, the young entrepreneur started the cultivation of plantel Santa Raquel. Eighteen hundred mecates of henequen were planted in the face of scandalously low prices. Similarly, during another lull in henequen prices in 1887, Casares's workers increased the size of Santo Domingo and Road to Chí fields (to one thousand and 219 mecates, respectively).[62] The expansion of Xcuyum continued unabated, regardless of the economic climate, precisely because Casares, like his fellow henequeneros, faced with a seven-year lag between planting and first harvest, could predict neither future prices nor world market demand. Trapped by monoculture and with few realistic options for diversification in the dry, calcareous northwestern district, henequeneros remained tied—for better or for worse—to the uncertain monocrop during the auge.

When Casares did realize substantial profits during the boom years, he lavished large sums of money on the physical appearance of the hacienda and his villa in Mérida. Fond of giving large parties on weekends for the *gente decente* of Méridan society, Casares, affectionately known to his friends as Don Boxol (meaning "little black one" in Mayan), hosted extravagant celebrations in the casa principal of the hacienda. One such event in 1893 was reported in the local newspapers as a cause célèbre: Casares figuratively rolled out the red carpet for several visiting North American newspapermen, going so far as to buy a special, passenger tramcar to usher the members of the entourage from Conkal railway station to the casco.[63] The ostensible reason for the North Americans' visit was to view Casares's advanced machine house. The published description of the tour indicated Casares's careful attention to detail and the impressive layout of the hacienda: "The locomotive passed along the country road under a green arch by a thick mass of branches and expressive *ramón* trees adorned with Mexican banners . . . passed the magnificent [machine house], where the Villamor and Prieto machines were working . . . passed the garden where they admired the most beautiful orange grove in the country."[64] The fête was not an isolated instance, for Casares often entertained dignitaries at Xcuyum.[65] His attitude that "no expense is too great" was typical of the henequen elite, who spent enormous sums on ostentatious carriages, ornate homes in Mérida, and frequent trips abroad.

Although Eulalio remained a bachelor, "marrying himself" instead to the management of Xcuyum, his brothers and sisters integrated themselves into the close-knit henequen oligarchy. The Porfirian generation of the Casares family married with the most prominent and successful families in the state: David married a Cámara; Aurora, a Guerra; Cleta and Gordiana married Peóns; and Donata wed a Regil.[66] All these families were genuine members of the oligarchy—propertied, well-to-do, politically motivated, patrons of the arts. Within one generation, the Casares family had demonstrated the potential for social mobility within the ruling elite.

The ability of such families as the Casareses to join the local elite did not guarantee permanent success in the regional economy. The Casares family ultimately suffered from the malady that afflicted many adventurous Yucatecan investors—an almost religious belief that the henequen economy would survive the short-term bust cycles and enjoy lasting success. Local oligarchs frittered away profits earned from henequen production through conspicuous consumption and poor investments. Henequeneros and local merchants connected with the industry had to contend with the demanding rhythms of the monocrop economy. They reinvested profits in attendant service industries tied to the trade, borrowing heavily on the future of the unstable commodity. Agroentrepreneurs also formed joint-stock companies and speculated in real estate, stocks, and even mortgage credits on the assumption that earnings derived from the fiber trade would eventually supersede any short-term losses. In a sense, the entrepreneur gambled that tomorrow's profits would pay for today's risky investments and ostentatious living.[67] Eulalio Casares would eventually fall prey to alarming trends in the regional economy and file for bankruptcy in 1895.

Bankruptcy and Resurrection

Casares epitomizes the henequen entrepreneur who critically overextended himself at an inopportune time and watched helplessly as the inexorable decline of the world market price of henequen coincided with past-due mortgage payments and late promissory notes. His ability to extricate himself from steadily mounting debts through a strong kinship network attests to the presence of a close-knit familial oligarchy that helped its struggling relatives survive the lean years. A close look at the circumstances surrounding Casares's bankruptcy and his subsequent financial resurrection confirms two recurring phenomena that characterized Yucatán during this Gilded Age: the inability of local investors to predict the future of henequen prices; and the existence of a tight web of family ties among the local oligarchy, all of whom realized only too well that their own spurious investments might just as easily falter.

The crisis of 1894–1897, which led to the dissolution of many prominent henequen merchants as well as affecting henequeneros such as Casares, was not unique. The henequen economy alternately peaked and crashed with startling irregularity as a result of unpredictable price oscillations. A similar panic in 1874–1876 had caused the state government to step in and artificially support henequen prices.[68] The crisis of the mid-1890s was of an even more serious nature because it led to the bankruptcy of one of the peninsula's leading export houses, Manuel Dondé y

Compañía.[69] Shaken by the unexpected failure of one of the cornerstones of the trade and afflicted by a severe scarcity of mortgage capital caused by the decline of fiber prices, many creditors began to demand repayment of outstanding mortgages and loans. Casares's position was not unlike that of many hacendados who had accumulated debts and lacked the wherewithal to meet their commitments.

Eulalio's financial problems began when, in 1889/90, the New York City–based National Cordage Company's attempt to corner the market caused henequen prices to soar to a high of six cents per pound.[70] A chain reaction resulted, generating additional capital, stimulating real estate values, and provoking an influx of manufactured goods, staple commodities, and luxury items. Artificially high real estate assessments fueled inflation and colored the hacendados' business mentality as they borrowed while investment capital was available. Casares spent an enormous amount to construct a tramway (1889–1891), to improve his machine house (installing a sophisticated Prieto rasping machine and his powerful Corliss steam engine), and to clear and plant more than 3,300 mecates of new henequen planteles during the three years immediately preceding the bust (see Table 5.6).[71] He opened lines of credit with the three major casas exportadoras—Henry W. Peabody and Company, Olegario Molina y Compañía, and the Escalante house—which agreed to advance Casares investment capital in exchange for Xcuyum's fiber. With his only asset promised, Casares turned to local financial institutions that were more than willing to provide additional monies. He opened running accounts with all three peninsular banks: the Banco Yucateco; Banco Mercantil de Yucatán; and the Banco Nacional's branch office in Mérida.[72]

By 1894 fiber prices had fallen from six cents per pound to less than three cents, despite attempts by local planters to withhold production and thereby stimulate prices. With his fiber promised at uncomfortably low prices and his debts coming due, Casares turned to his family in an attempt to escape financial ruin. On December 10, 1893, he secured a mortgage of forty-five thousand pesos on Xcuyum from his sisters, Cleta, Donata, and Gordiana. At the same time, he obtained a mortgage of sixty thousand pesos from prominent hacendada Loreto Peón y Peón. Casares would have to make first installments totaling sixteen thousand pesos on the mortgages within one year from the date of the loans. These sums were not sufficient, however, and on April 4, 1894, Casares again had to turn to his family to secure two mortgages of twenty thousand pesos, one from his brother-in-law Alonso Regil y Peón (married to Donata), and another from his sister Raquel.

By the fall of 1894 the situation had not improved. The price of henequen had not rallied, and Casares, who had mortgaged Xcuyum for 145,000 pesos in order to stave off his mounting debts, could not pay the first mortgage installments (see Table 5.8). On October 17, 1894, Loreto Peón y Peón asked for her first payment of ten thousand pesos. Quickly, Casares gave his power of attorney to Alonso Regil y Peón, a prominent merchant and large landowner. This was the beginning of a series of actions by the Casares family to insure that Xcuyum, if lost, would eventually be returned to Eulalio. Alonso filed a mortgage suit (*juicio hipotecario*) against Casares and Xcuyum on November 2, 1894. A tentative date was set for the auction of the estate on November 28 of that year.[73]

Problems with compiling a detailed inventory of Xcuyum delayed the auction until July 13, 1895. Two entrepreneurs appeared to be seriously interested in the hacienda: Joaquín Peón, Loreto's younger brother and one of the most powerful hacendados in Yucatán; and Pedro Peón Contreras, a distant relation of Loreto and Joaquín and, more importantly, Alonso Regil y Peón's son-in-law. The hacienda, which was judiciously assessed (considering the depressed economy) at 220,000 pesos, first drew a bid from Peón Contreras at only two-thirds of its valuation (see Table 5.9).

A counteroffer by Joaquín Peón before Judge Ángel Castillo Manzanilla pushed the bidding over 147,000 pesos. Peón Contreras bid again, increasing the purchase price by a paltry ten pesos. Judge Castillo Manzanilla called a half-hour recess to enable the two contestants to hammer out their differences. When the auction resumed, no further offers were

Table 5.8 Xcuyum Mortgages, 1893-1894

	Creditor	Relationship	Interest Rate (Percent)	Amount (in Pesos)
December 10, 1893	Cleta Casares de Peón	Sister	6	18,000
December 10, 1893	Donata Casares de Regil	Sister	6	18,000
December 10, 1893	Gordiana Casares de Peón	Sister	6	9,000
December 10, 1893	Loreto Peón y Peón	No relation	10	60,000
April 4, 1894	Alonso Regil y Peón	In-law	10	20,000
April 4, 1894	Raquel Casares y G.	Sister	6	20,000
			Total	145,000

Source: Peón Ancona papers.

Table 5.9 Xcuyum Inventory, 1895

	Assessed Value (in Pesos)
Land (physical plant of Hacienda Xcuyum, machine house, *casa principal,* corrals, hacienda store, garden, and annexes	50,000.00
Planteles of henequen on Xcuyum and annexes	120,639.50
Machine house equipment	15,740.00
Decauville tramway, rails, and rolling stock	20,500.00
Livestock on Xcuyum and annexes	492.97
Tienda de raya inventory	12,114.00
Miscellaneous household items, chapel, etc.	704.25
Total	220,190.72

Source: Peón Ancona papers, and Archivo General del Estado de Yucatán, Justicia, Remate de Hacienda Xcuyum, 1895.

made. The judge recognized the last offer, by Pedro Peón Contreras, before the recess as the winning bid and awarded him Xcuyum. In a surprising development, Joaquín Peón, the defeated contestant, acted as guarantor for Peón Contreras, assuring the State of Yucatán the purchase price of 147,303.81 pesos.[74]

It soon became apparent why Peón Contreras had been so determined to secure Xcuyum. Four months to the day after it had been awarded to him, Peón Contreras sold the hacienda to his father-in-law Alonso Regil y Peón for a mere 105,000 pesos (notarized at this smaller amount for tax purposes), less than half the estate's assessed value. Regil y Peón, married to Eulalio's sister Donata, obviously had engineered the complex dealings from the outset.[75]

Xcuyum's auction created quite a stir in Mérida. Several smaller creditors were enraged that the estate had been appraised and sold at such deflated prices. A juicio hipotecario, filed by creditor Dolores de la Guerra de Mendoza against Regil y Peón and the other Casares relatives, claimed that the auction was illegal because the appraisal had failed to include the debts of Xcuyum's 122 servants. The lower valuation meant a lower sale price, which in turn meant that the proceeds of the auction would compensate only the largest lien-holders (i.e., the Casares family and Loreto Peón y Peón). In his brief, Nestor Rubio Alpuche, Guerra de Mendoza's lawyer, noted that Article 2030 of the state's Civil Code stipulated that peons' debts be included in a property's inventory: "In Yucatán, loose teams of peons do not exist. . . . A hacienda that does not have persons obligated by personal contract . . . is not worth anything."[76] The issues raised in the mortgage suit were echoed by Gregorio Torre, a local hacendado who, as *síndico del concurso*, was acting as receiver or provisional administrator of Casares's bankrupt estate. Torre, like Guerra de Mendoza, was furious that the debts were not included in the inventory. The receiver, whose responsibilities included payment of outstanding debts, collection of rents due the debtor, and the administration of Casares's expenses for goods, claimed that the peons' debts were legitimately part of the inventory of the hacienda and should be accountable. Regil y Peón countered that Torre, as síndico, was responsible and that the debts did not have to be included, asserting that "the servants are free men."[77] The judge, Leopoldo Cantón Frexas, supported Regil y Peón's contention despite the fact that many inventories regularly included peons' debts in their accounting. Xcuyum's auction and subsequent sale to Regil y Peón were upheld in the courts.[78]

The legal wrangle was aired in the press when *El Crédito del Estado*, an ephemeral Méridan paper dedicated to watchdogging questionable credit practices, took up the cause of the beleaguered creditors and lambasted the courts and the Casares family for their shady dealings. The paper charged that Judge Cantón Frexas was a personal friend and political ally of the family, and that they, fortuitously aided by the judge, had concocted the entire charade to pay themselves back in full while depriving other lenders of what was rightfully theirs.[79]

Regil y Peón managed the estate until his death in 1897. After one year, his wife Donata completed the complex maneuver by returning the hacienda to brother Eulalio for 110,000 pesos, including a generous mortgage of thirty-six thousand pesos with the sale. After squandering his family inheritance, Casares was able through intrafamilial negotiations to reacquire the hacienda within a scant three years.[80] After 1898, Eulalio did manage to avoid serious financial difficulty; however, he was forced to take out a mortgage of sixty-five thousand pesos on Xcuyum in 1908 during another lull in henequen prices. Eulalio survived and held on to Xcuyum until the federal government mandated the breakup of large estates in Yucatán in 1937.

The lengthy bankruptcy proceedings illustrate the resourcefulness of local elites and their reliance on kinship ties to circumvent the dangerous boom-and-bust cycle in the henequen economy. Brother David Casares experienced similar difficulties with his estate Kancabchén, escaping unscathed thanks to the assistance of another in-law, Dionisia Cámara.[81]

Although Eulalio Casares managed to retain Xcuyum, he did not curb his desire to participate in a variety of joint-stock companies and complementary activities. Determined to circumvent total reliance on Xcuyum's henequen production, he dabbled in the import-export trade, joining General Francisco Cantón's commissions house. However, his investments in this area never amounted to more than a supplementary means of income. Most of Casares's time and money went into expanding the productive capacities of Xcuyum. By 1914 Xcuyum was producing double the number of bales pressed in the early 1890s.[82]

Conclusion

Like many Yucatecan planters, Casares was happily tied to henequen production during the boom. While all planters clearly saw the dangers of monoculture, they were reluctant to diversify. Henequen had created their economic empire, and they were determined to ride the unpredictable price fluctuations. Hacendados modernized their estates to increase production, but they could not or did not desire to erase all vestiges of the pre-henequen hacienda. Large sums of money were lavished on fulfilling the "status aspirations" of the landed oligarchy. Much of the capital earned from henequen production was also wasted on uniformly poor investments in the joint-stock market. Landowners continued to rely on such traditional labor practices as debt peonage and the tienda de raya to inhibit mobility and ensure a dependent-labor regime.

The result was an estate geared to modern commercial operations but lacking a farsighted and sophisticated ownership and management class that could complete the transformation. Xcuyum, our model for all of Yucatán's large henequen estates, was a hybrid—neither a true hacienda nor a true plantation—that exhibited characteristics of both institutions. Given the rapid rise of the henequen boom, a complete break from its traditional past was impossible.

Unlike the Caribbean sugar industry, which utilized new technologies to separate the agricultural and industrial sectors during the late nineteenth century and thereby increased productivity and efficiency, the Yucatecan henequen industry failed substantively to change the means and factors of production. As a result, henequen monoculture, which had enjoyed truly halcyon days during the second half of the nineteenth century and the first decades of the present century, entered a period of prolonged decline. Although there are many reasons for the collapse of the regional fiber economy, the unwillingness of Yucatecan elites to modernize the industry and its fundamental unit of production, the henequen estate, goes a long way toward explaining why Yucatán's henequen trade proved unable to overcome burgeoning foreign competition after World War I.[83]

6 Capitalism on the Tropical-Forest Frontier: Quintana Roo, 1880s to 1930

HERMAN W. KONRAD

The role of foreign capital in the Porfirian strategy of Mexican industrialization had far-reaching consequences in the tropical-forest regions of Quintana Roo. Although presently Mexico's newest tourist frontier, from about 1880 to 1930 this area was new ground for foreign capitalism. As a largely unexplored region with remote indigenous settlements, it also represented a frontier in the conventional sense of the term.[1] Yet, depending upon the point of reference, Quintana Roo's significance varied considerably. For nearby Mérida, it was hostile but desirable, and ultimately unobtainable. For London, however, it represented a distant, attractive, even friendly region. Twice, in fact—in 1867 and 1885—Quintana Roo's Mayan inhabitants had offered to become a formal part of the British colonial empire; and twice London had rejected the offers because they potentially compromised British economic interests in other parts of Mexico. Mérida, on the other hand, had spent half a century attempting actually to control the territory that, since the Spanish conquest, it had claimed as its geopolitical legacy. Thus, when in 1901 General Ignacio Bravo's troops finally achieved what would become a permanent national presence in Quintana Roo, *meridanos* celebrated joyously and promised Yucatecan citizenship to Bravo; but their joy was to be short-lived. Within a year the central government removed the new territory from Mérida's jurisdiction.[2]

If Mérida, Mexico City, and London represented, respectively, the regional, national, and international forces in Quintana Roo's political economy, the key local actors in this developmental drama were the cruzob Maya. Their successful occupation of the area as a base from which to continue their struggle for independence presented the primary obstacle for outside access to its bountiful tropical-forest resources. The transformation of Quintana Roo's frontier involved an interplay of clearly identifiable interests: The local Maya's primary concern was survival and autonomy; Mérida, and to a lesser extent Campeche, wished to incorporate lost territories; Mexico City focused on a national development project and the resolution of regional separatist tendencies. The foreign capitalist stake, on the other hand, was direct access to Quintana Roo's export staples. For roughly fifty years, the only clear-cut winners were the foreign capitalist interests. Those who lost the most were the local Maya. Although immediate regional and federal economic and political objectives were largely frustrated, the changes that took place did establish conditions that were ultimately advantageous to long-term interests at both these levels.

The Geohistorical Context

Activities in the east of the Yucatán Peninsula must be seen within their historical and geopolitical contexts. This area, considered by all but the local Maya to be a frontier in the late nineteenth century, had in pre-Hispanic times sustained dense populations.[3] Although the tropical-forest habitat had proved to be rich in resources long before the arrival of the Europeans in the sixteenth century, they had promptly depopulated and deserted it. Henceforth, it became an enclave of security for those Maya who rejected colonial Spanish and, later, Mexican domination.[4]

A primary reason for neglect of this region was the importance of the Gulf of Mexico in colonial times. Once the Aztec Empire had fallen into Cortés's grasp, the gulf became the primary access route to the treasures of New Spain. The importance of the highly protected Seville-Havana-Veracruz shipping route condemned the peninsula's Caribbean side to virtual abandonment. Spain's New World competitors, notably the English, took advantage of these circumstances to establish their own commercial and political presence. In the eighteenth century, English interests moved from Jamaica to Belize, from whence they penetrated northward in the nineteenth century. The English provided a commercial-military-political counterweight to Spanish and, later, Mexican influence.[5]

Control of offshore islands and inland bays has always been the key factor in access to, and sway over, the Caribbean region. The Caribbean coastal seas were important trade routes for preconquest Maya[6] and the initial point of entry for the Spanish invasion of the peninsula.[7] Maritime accessibility was a fundamental reason why major overland access routes from the west were not built before the mid-twentieth century. The narrow-gauge railways built earlier in the century extended from fifty-kilometer interior points, providing access to the coast.[8] Because there are no rivers from Cabo Catoche to the Río Hondo (now the international border between Mexico and Belize), control of the Hondo was crucial for access to the southern interior of Quintana Roo. Nevertheless, the storms and periodic hurricanes that caused countless wrecks on offshore reefs were (and remain) the primary maritime obstacle to access to Quintana Roo, which suffers more hurricanes than does any other location in the Caribbean.[9]

The rich marine resources of the coastal area, although exploited earlier by the Maya,[10] did not attract Yucatecan or Mexican fishing interests until the 1960s. At roughly the same time, commercial exploitation of coastal natural resources—such as magnificent beaches, coral reefs, and clear waters, consistently pleasant temperatures, and considerable sunshine—became important.[11] During the previous one hundred years, however, it was Quintana Roo's land-based resources that were important. The entire region, apart from patches of savanna, consisted of tropical forests with a wide variety of hardwoods and cabinet woods, and a rich fauna. Despite the myth of impenetrable jungles—endlessly repeated by those uninformed about vegetation densities under the canopy of a tropical forest[12]—the movement of persons and goods in the region has never presented serious logistical problems.[13] Quintana Roo's human populations have always been either an obstacle to, or a facilitator of, access to forest resources.

The tropical forest had proved a positive resource for the dense Mayan population that lived in the area before the arrival of Europeans.[14] As a geographical zone (or ecological niche) in the early sixteenth century, the region was only a frontier in that it bordered on other Mayan provinces.[15] By the 1560s, the religious and military zeal of the conquerors had decimated the Mayan population, creating a colonial Yucatecan frontier zone,[16] which became a place of refuge for those Maya wishing to escape the conquest society's demands and impositions. The only colonial settlement of note was Salamanca de Bacalar, on the shores of the lake of the same name.[17] By the mid-nineteenth century, the partido of Bacalar, already linked economically to the English colony to the south, had a population of 7,601.[18] The so-called Caste War resulted in the abandonment of Bacalar, the reestablishment of a Yucatecan settlement on Cozumel, and the occupation of the area by the war's survivors.[19] These independent, or cruzob, Maya had a population of 85,091 in 1850.[20] They consolidated a hostile frontier between themselves and the western part of the peninsula, maintained commercial ties with the English colony, and established politicoreligious structures around their devotion to the Holy Cross. By the 1860s, their numbers had declined to approximately thirty-five to forty thousand; the most important cruzob settlements were located in the Chan Santa Cruz area.[21] Reliable demographic data, unfortunately, are not extant, although it is estimated that no more than ten thousand cruzob remained by the end of the nineteenth century.[22] They controlled the tropical-forest zone, while small enclaves under Yucatecan jurisdiction existed off the eastern coast on Isla de las Mujeres, on Cozumel, and on the northern perimeter of the peninsula. Thus, commercial access to Quintana Roo was via maritime routes, or overland, from the south.

Southern Capitalist Penetrations

The geopolitical history of Quintana Roo had created conditions favoring non-Mexican commercial access to its tropical-forest wealth. London's financial interests had earlier established a flourishing logwood and cabinet-wood business in Belize.[23] Easy access to the Quintana Rooan coasts resulted in a northern expansion of logwood extraction by the mid-nineteenth century. A progression toward mahogany and other woods, once logwood declined as a commercial product, was a natural development, and, by the early 1890s, chicle (the resin of the *chicozapote* tree) became a viable commercial activity.[24] Belize-based extraction of forest products from Quintana Roo and the Guatemalan Petén is clearly revealed in the export data recorded in the annual *Bluebook* summaries of British Honduran economic activities.[25]

Data in Tables 6.1 and 6.2 indicate a gradual increase in the importance of forest products, from slightly over 60 percent of the value of all exports in 1886 to roughly 80 percent by the end of the nineteenth century. Between 1886 and 1900, the average of forest products as a percentage of the value of the colony's exports was 68.2. In Table 6.1, we see that, overall, 29.3 percent of exports came from noncolonial sources. As these were essentially forest products, this means that over 40 percent of the registered forest exports came from outside the colony. To what ex-

Table 6.1 British Honduran Exports and Values, 1886-1900[a]

	Total Value (in BH Dollars)[b]	Colonial Sources	Percentage	Noncolonial Sources	Percentage	Forest Product Percentage of Total
1886	1,400,234	1,040,591	74.3	359,643	25.7	62.4
1889	2,155,554	1,437,443	66.7	718,111	33.3	55.2
1890	1,866,099	1,310,737	70.2	555,362	29.8	64.7
1891	1,909,903	1,446,707	75.7	463,223	24.3	63.3
1892	1,741,235	1,163,457	66.8	571,778	33.2	58.5
1893	2,135,117	1,493,510	69.9	641,607	30.1	67.7
1894	2,549,583	1,440,102	56.5	1,109,391	43.5	62.1
1895	1,281,969	770,638	60.1	511,331	39.9	69.8
1897	1,404,387	1,094,964	77.9	309,423	22.1	81.4
1898	1,282,593	955,264	74.5	327,329	25.5	81.1
1899	1,278,617	1,018,444	79.6	260,173	20.4	79.1
1900	1,300,565	977,160	75.1	323,405	24.9	72.9

Source: Archives of Belize, *Bluebooks*, 1886-1900.

Notes: a. Data are not available for 1887, 1888, and 1896.
b. The BH dollar, up to 1894, was valued at 9.5 per English pound, after which it was valued at 4 dollars per pound.

tent these products came from Mexico is not indicated. In the case of logwood, however, practically all noncolonial sources would have originated in that country;[26] there is a marked increase, from 3.8 percent of the total value of logwood exports in 1886, to 31.8 percent in 1895. In merely a decade (1886–1895), noncolonial sources for cedar rose to 100 percent, for rubber to 89 percent, and for chicle to 72 percent.[27] Such increases clearly reflected greater commercial activity north and west of the Río Hondo, as the colony's resources became depleted. The lack of accurate

Table 6.2 Selected British Honduran Exports and Relative Percentage,[a] 1886-1900[b]

	Hides/Skins	Cedar	Mahogany	Logwood	Rubber	Chicle	Sugar
1886	0.4	-	26.4	32.6	4.1	-	4.40
1889	0.2	-	16.8	37.5	0.9	-	2.70
1890	0.2	0.5	19.4	43.5	1.3	-	1.30
1891	0.2	0.5	21.9	40.0	0.8	0.1	0.90
1892	0.2	0.2	22.4	35.4	0.4	0.1	0.30
1893	0.1	0.3	24.8	41.9	0.3	0.3	0.40
1894	0.1	0.3	15.9	44.8	0.4	0.7	0.03
1895	0.2	0.2	11.8	54.6	0.5	2.7	0.01
1897	-	0.9	28.6	47.8	0.4	3.7	0.02
1898	0.3	1.2	36.7	38.9	1.5	2.8	0.01
1899	0.2	2.0	29.6	43.0	2.4	2.6	0.20
1900	0.3	1.4	33.7	34.1	1.0	2.6	0.10

Source: Archives of Belize, *Bluebooks*, 1886-1900.

Notes: a. Percentages have been rounded off to nearest tenth of a percent, except in the last column which was rounded off to nearest hundredth of a percent.
b. No data are available for 1887, 1888, and 1896.

monitoring capacities to determine colonial versus noncolonial sources of forest products suggests that even those exports officially listed as being from British Honduras may have had other origins.[28]

The export figures also reveal international linkages and sources of capital for the acquisition of forest staples. Although the United Kingdom and the United States were the primary destinations for Belizean products, they were also being sold to Canada, France, the Netherlands, Italy, Germany, and Russia. Occasionally, they were shipped to Cuba and Mexico.[29] Access to Quintana Roo's products was possible because of half a century of English support of the cruzob cause, or what Marie Lapointe has called a policy of "benevolent neutrality,"[30] but London was also anxious to maintain good relations with Mexico City in order to gain access to the area through contacts and arrangements in Mérida and the national capital.[31]

British investment in Mexico, as well as in Latin America in general, dates back to the early postindependence period.[32] Participation in communications infrastructure, particularly railroads, increased dramatically throughout the nineteenth century.[33] By the mid-1880s, Mexico's external debt to England was 23 million pounds, indicating heavy British investment and a willingness on the part of the Porfirian government to grant attractive concessions.[34] Thus, expansion into Quintana Roo by English capital also had its parallels in other areas. Belize-based companies had their woodcutters working as far north as Tulum as early as 1886, but formal concessions from Mexico City took on greater importance in the 1890s. In 1892, London's capitalists established the Mexican Exploration Company to extract forest products in coastal areas bordering the Bay of Chetumal, and extending as far north as the Bay of Ascensión. This company declared bankruptcy three years later, and another company, represented by J. E. Plummer, who was based in Belize, took over the concession in 1896.[35] That same year, yet another enterprise, the East Coast of Yucatan Colonization Company, was formed in Mexico City. It was financed by the Bank of London and Mexico and took over an 1889 concession, previously held by the Mérida-based Faustino Martínez y Compañía. The Martínez company held concessionary rights to 673,850 hectares of forest land, stretching from Cabo Catoche southward almost to Belize. The English acquisition established an alternative point of access into Quintana Roo, apart from the harbor facilities located in Yucatán's principal port, Progreso.[36]

These concessions positioned English capital to exploit virtually the entire eastern seaboard of the peninsula. The willingness of the Mexican government to grant them was a by-product of the 1893 Mexico–British Honduras boundary settlement, known as the Mariscal–St. John Treaty. It divided the Bay of Chetumal and established the Río Hondo as the international boundary. In effect, this guaranteed both parties access to the interior via this strategic waterway but, in fact, proved to be more advantageous for English commercial interests. With the treaty and the official concessions, the English confirmed, through Mexico City, the access they had previously enjoyed by virtue of good relations with the cruzob.[37] At the same time, the new arrangements made the cruzob expendable, setting the stage for the Mexican attempt to resolve definitively their problems with the rebel Maya. Pressure could now be applied to curtail the flow of arms and munitions from Belize, upon which the cruzob depended.[38] The Mexican government was now in a position to open a southern front of attack on the cruzob and to pursue a military pacification of the frontier area.[39]

Western and Northern Capitalist Penetrations

Yucatecan interior access to Quintana Roo had been blocked by the cruzob since the mid-nineteenth century. Yucatecan governors could and did mount periodic military expeditions that had the capacity to penetrate into the heart of cruzob territory, but with the inevitable response of counterraids and pillaging of Yucatecan towns and villages.[40] Under such conditions, the eastern interior of the peninsula remained unsafe for any significant geographic expansion of the regional economy beyond the increasingly prosperous henequen zone. Interior towns, such as Peto, Valladolid, and Tizimín, would remain economically stagnant (despite their prosperity prior to the Caste War) until the cruzob problem could be resolved.

This did not mean that the Yucatecans were not interested in expanding economic influence toward the eastern frontier. What was clearly lacking for interior development was a communications and transportation infrastructure. The alternative to the relatively small boats that plied the shallow waters along the northern coasts of the peninsula were railroads, which arrived in Yucatán somewhat later than they did in central Mexico. Initially, rail transportation was concentrated in the henequen zone.[41] The Mérida-Progreso line was inaugurated in 1881, and a line connecting Mérida to Izamal was finished in 1890. Although concessions for railroads to Peto and Valladolid were granted as early as 1878 and 1880, respectively, the lines were not placed in service until the first decade of the twentieth century. Service to Tizimín was finally established in 1913.

Leading businessmen in Mérida, however, were interested in connecting the eastern interior to the west by rail. In 1897 the federal government granted a concession to extend the Peto railroad all the way to the Belizean border. With a capital of 1.25 million pesos, work was started on this project in 1900 but abandoned in 1902 after the completion of only fourteen kilometers.[42] Plans for lines from Valladolid to the Caribbean coast and from the Bay of Ascención to the Río Hondo were also proposed, but both projects died in the planning stages.[43] Other plans for railroads from Yucatán into Quintana Roo proliferated before World War II, but they remained just that, plans.

Such schemes need to be seen, not in terms of failures actually to build railroads into Quintana Roo, but rather as indicators of a willingness to invest capital to gain access to the region's resources. Other expressions of the same interest were the concessions acquired by wealthy Yucatecans and other Mexican businessmen with good connections in Mexico City. For example, two of the principals in the frustrated Peto-Belize railroad scheme, Olegario Molina and Rafael Peón, acquired concessions to exploit six hundred thousand hectares of Quintana Roo.[44] Five other Mexican entrepreneurs received concessions for an additional 1.7 million hectares.[45] The railroad projects were, in fact, complementary to these federal forest-exploitation concessions.

The Yucatecan capitalists had more success using the north coast of the peninsula as a point of entry into Quintana Roo. One of Mérida's prominent businessmen, Ramón Ancona Bolio, organized a company in 1876 called the Compañía del Cuyo y Anexas.[46] Initially, he attracted German financial backing interested in the coastal dyewood trade. This support was lost in 1897, when chemical dyes took on greater importance in Germany. The company was then sold to a group of Mérida-based commercial houses, which put up capital to continue operations. This proved to be the most successful of the Yucatecan enterprises in Quintana Roo prior to the end of the nineteenth century. An administrative company town was built at El Cuyo, with warehouses, piers, a narrow-gauge railroad extending 110 kilometers, a telephone system covering 180 kilometers, residences, and a series of satellite estates along the northern coast and inland.[47]

The Compañía del Cuyo y Anexas was a multifaceted commercial venture. Although the working capital was Yucatecan in origin and derived from the henequen boom, El Cuyo drew upon international sources (in Cuba, British Honduras, and the United States) for technical and administrative personnel and labor. The company had up to fifteen hundred employees engaged in a wide variety of activities. The early emphasis on logwood was soon replaced by the extraction of cabinet woods and chicle. Plantation crops such as sugar, rubber, vanilla, and tobacco were also introduced. Livestock was brought to the area to take advantage of good pasture lands, and salt was extracted in considerable quantities from the coastal salt pans.[48] El Cuyo's strategic location, in a part of Quintana Roo not occupied by the cruzob and suited to a variety of agrarian pursuits, was a key factor in its early successes. Its failure and eventual bankruptcy were caused in part by an economic recession in 1906/07 that affected Yucatecan shareholders.[49] Such an ambitious plan to expand capital investment eastward, based on models of success from the henequen sector, proved to be premature. Eventually, Mexican lending institutions took over the company's assets.[50]

The Porfirian Principles—"Peace and Progress"

The late nineteenth-century encirclement of cruzob territory by national and international capitalist ventures represented the early stages of frontier incorporation. This was a direct by-product of the federal government's overall strategy of national development, guided by the principles put forward by a group of planners known as the *científicos*.[51] They decided to broaden the country's narrow economic base, which depended heavily upon the export of precious metals, by promoting agricultural and forestry exports. Such a project was to be stimulated by foreign capital investment, which, in turn, hinged on three essential preconditions: (1) a communications and transportation infrastructure; (2) financial institutions and conditions favorable for foreign investors; and (3) the maintenance of political stability in areas rich in natural resources. Quintana Roo's projected development, before the twentieth century, reflected the principles put forward by the technocrats of the day, the científicos.[52]

The question of political stability, however, remained unresolved. In northern Mexico, where the same national plan was being implemented, the army had been employed to overcome the Yaqui's and Mayo's resistance to the conversion of traditional lands to mechanized agriculture.[53] Successful generals in these campaigns, such as Ignacio Bravo, might now be dispatched to Yucatán to "pacify" the cruzob.[54] In Quintana Roo, only the English, through Belizean agents and companies, had anything resembling peaceful commercial relations with the rebel Maya. The need to resolve the cruzob issue was heightened because national and foreign forest-extraction concerns, previously based in lowland areas along the Gulf of Mexico, now sought access to the interior frontier.[55] Lumbering companies in Veracruz, for example, were already expanding their operations south into Tabasco and Campeche.[56] U.S. demand for chicle, rooted in the new craze for chewing gum, was also increasing. With the depletion of Veracruzan forests as a raw-material source, Quintana Roo, with its extensive stands of the chicozapote tree, became more important. Markets for cedar and mahogany were also expanding while previous areas of exploitation were becoming depleted.[57] As early as 1894, the Díaz government had taken steps to pass comprehensive legislation regulating the exploitation of forest products in all *bosques*, terrenos baldíos, and *nacionales*.[58] Such legislation would become the basis for concessions and the exploitation of Quintana Roo's forests. Since Yucatecan governments had been notoriously unsuccessful in conquering the cruzob, the federal government took control.

The military campaign, portrayed in the literature as a bloody and protracted struggle, was little more than a continuation of ongoing development projects, although now with the army's active participation.[59] Steps were taken to strengthen communications facilities along the eastern coast of the peninsula. A small naval force was deployed, using Cozumel and the Bay of Chetumal as strategic points of operation. Since, as a condition for signing the Mariscal–St. John boundary treaty, the British had agreed to prevent armaments from reaching the cruzob via Belize, the new naval presence along this border helped to ensure compliance. At the same time, it provided logistical support for eastern and southern military activities and put pressure upon cruzob-held territory.[60] The main military push, however, would come from the west, with the support of Yucatecan militiamen and laborers, via the existing transport and communications infrastructures. The official campaign began in 1898, with the patrolling by an armed, naval customs vessel along the Río Hondo. In 1899 General Bravo arrived in Yucatán with federal infantry and cavalry to begin inland operations.[61]

Bravo's primary strategic objective was to capture the cruzob political and religious capital, Chan Santa Cruz (now Felipe Carrillo Puerto).[62] Peto, about to be linked to Mérida by railroad, became the point of departure for the advance into Quintana Roo's forests. In effect, Bravo supervised the clearing of a right-of-way for the extension of rail and telegraph lines to Chan Santa Cruz. The federal army battalions' primary task was to protect the work gangs, and their superior armaments (repeating rifles, machine guns, and field artillery) were more than adequate to prevent any effective military response by the cruzob. Between December 1899 and May 1901—that is, the time it took to reach and occupy the cruzob shrine-settlement—official reports referred to twenty-five "battles," but these were really skirmishes. Bravo dutifully cabled the results of each fight to Mexico City, sending copies to the governor of Yucatán. His reports indicated the loss of fourteen soldiers, with another forty wounded. En route, twelve cruzob were killed, an unknown number were wounded, and one was captured, along with eleven guns and three machetes.[63] Seldom has a "great" military victory, as this was celebrated joyously in Mérida and less spontaneously in Mexico City, been built on such modest military feats.

This does not mean there were no significant losses in these unequal confrontations. Malnutrition, fever, dysentery, and other illnesses took a far greater toll on both sides than did combat.[64] General Bravo's successful campaign revealed the cruzob's inability to halt a militarily backed commercial penetration into their territory. For the cruzob, as for other indigenous tribes throughout the Americas, "progress," represented by the steam-driven iron horse protected by guns, proved to be irreversible. After it came a variety of capital-driven enterprises. The spikes of commercial development, as it were, were being driven into the heart of cruzob territory. As in so many other areas, the local society was reduced to fighting a rearguard action, in this case a guerrilla insurgency that lasted for a quarter of a century.[65] Cruzob psychological resistance, on the other hand, would endure longer.[66]

Dividing the Spoils and Reaping the Profits, 1901–1912

Having driven the cruzob from their capital and shrine, the next step was to make the area safe for the commercial extraction of forest products. Access to the interior from the south was quickly achieved by opening an overland route from Bacalar to Santa Cruz, establishing coastal port facilities at Vigia Chico and Xcalac, and building a narrow-gauge railroad between Vigia Chico and Santa Cruz.[67] Farther to the north, Puerto Morelos, the offshore islands of Cozumel and Mujeres, and other points along the Caribbean coast were either provided with communications infrastructures or plans were made to do so. General Bravo was instructed to rebuild the now-deserted Chan Santa Cruz settlement and establish it as the area's official administrative center. The federal government would "repopulate" Quintana Roo as quickly as possible with cities, towns, and colonists—to bring the "civilized life" to the region.[68] Federal reconquest of the territory, the members of the national Chamber of Deputies were informed, required, "today more than ever, the opening of roads, the construction of railroads, telegraphs, telephones, wharves, and a multitude of other material works, in addition to administrative policies that apply pressure to repopulate those regions, attracting sane and industrious elements that will colonize in order to ensure its future."[69] The most effective manner of accomplishing such objectives would be to administer the area directly from Mexico City.

Although the Yucatecans complained bitterly about losing Quintana Roo, Porfirio Díaz never had any doubts about creating a federal territory.[70] The official steps were taken in November 1902, but the plan to do so undoubtedly predated General Bravo's campaign. By annexing half of the territory claimed by the regionalist states of Campeche and Yucatán, the central government could, at the same time, resolve some outstanding political issues, enhance the centralization of power, and integrate a troublesome frontier area. In fact, during the territory's history—with few exceptions and as a deliberate policy—important administrative posts were never given either to yucatecos or campechanos.[71] And though the territory became something of a "political football" in terms of competing federal and state economic interests,[72] such conflicts had little bearing upon general patterns of economic development. As its price for having "officially" reconquered Quintana Roo, the federal government would play the role of economic and political referee. That stance, first formulated during the Porfiriato, survived the revolution and essentially remained in force until the territory became a state in 1974.

Immediately after Bravo's capture of Chan Santa Cruz (briefly renamed Santa Cruz de Bravo in his honor), Yucatecan authorities planned to offer special concessions to promote settlement.[73] Easy and inexpensive access to land, monetary concessions, and freedom from the unpopular obligation to serve in the civil guard were the incentives proposed. The federal authorities who took over political jurisdiction in late 1902 offered a similar program.[74] To further colonization of the region, Admiral José María de la Vega, who was named jefe político when Bravo returned temporarily to Mexico City, suggested establishing military or penal colonies. Apart from Cozumel and Isla de las Mujeres, however, the territory had attracted only an artificial population of merchants and workers' families along the Río Hondo and the Bay of Chetumal by the end of 1903.[75] The continuing threat posed by cruzob guerrilla activities, and the dangers of malaria, yellow fever, and tuberculosis, were sufficient disincentives for any type of spontaneous colonization from the western parts of the Yucatán Peninsula.

De la Vega did succeed in linking the new territorial capital with the Caribbean coast to the east, Bacalar and the Bay of Chetumal to the south, and Peto to the west. With roads, telegraph lines, and a railroad line protected by the military, the new capital was now open for business,[76] but it was Ignacio Bravo, who returned as territorial governor in 1903 and remained until 1912, who placed Santa Cruz on a real commercial footing. With the army supplying protection and labor—convicts and political prisoners were used at Bravo's discretion—the general set himself up as the regional caudillo. During this period Quintana Roo gained a reputation, popularized both in the Mexican media and by foreign writers such as John Kenneth Turner, as an unhealthy, vice-ridden, convict colony.[77] This was not the kind of reputation that attracted settlers or investors, short of granting them special rights and privileges. Bravo, however, managed to earn a considerable personal profit.[78]

During the military campaign against the cruzob, most economic activities in the territory were halted. In 1903, official sources indicated a total territorial population, including military personnel and surviving cruzob, of 12,504.[79] Soon thereafter, however, the economy rebounded as the territory was rapidly parceled out to individuals and companies intent on extracting forest products. During 1902 to 1905, the *Diario Oficial* published details about eleven concessions, encompassing 3,456,857 hectares, granted to six Mexican, three Belizean, and two Yucatecan parties.[80] Belizean data (see Table 6.3) clearly shows a subsequent increase in the export of chicle, cedar, and mahogany from noncolonial sources. Although caution must be exercised in interpreting these figures because of accounting irregularities in official colonial sources, they do indicate greatly increased activity in Quintana Roo.

During Bravo's tenure as territorial caudillo, the majority of active concessionaries were either Belize-based or controlled by English-colony interests. Rafael Peón's (Yucatecan) concession, for example, was actually being exploited by J. E. Plummer, representing the interests of C. C. Mangel and Brothers. Other major players in the territory included the Stanford Manufacturing Company (U.S.), the Belize Export and Limited Company, and the Compañía Chiclera y Maderera Mexicana (both English), all operating out of British Honduras.[81] Mexican customs and consular officials complained repeatedly about their inability to halt the thriving contraband trade between Quintana Roo and the English colony. Their documentation of border activities, at the same time, indicates that a steady stream of Belizean *chicleros* and woodcutters, frequently accompanied by their families, were arriving in the territory.[82] These workers, plus merchants, shopkeepers, and laborers who were employed by the federal military in the construction and maintenance of federal projects, became an important part of the pioneer populations of the port of Xcalac, and of the settlements around the Bay of Chetumal and along the Río Hondo.[83]

The developments in central and southern Quintana Roo, with the active participation of the federal military forces, were producing great immediate benefits for foreign capitalists.[84] While English interests in London intensified their commercial activities, the U.S. chicle companies

Table 6.3 British Honduran Forest Products Exports and Sources, 1901-1913 (in Thousands)

	Logwood (in Pounds)		Cedar (in Feet)		Mahogany (in Feet)		Chicle (in Pounds)	
	Colony	Other	Colony	Other	Colony	Other	Colony	Other
1901	(19.6)[b]		(421.3)[b]		(6,489.9)[b]		136.3	-
1902	12.4	2.7	363.2	73.1	5,851.6	192.2	249.6	3.2
1903	12.4	1.8	673.1	69.4	8,675.3	683.5	293.3	116.2
1905	6.9	2.6	378.7	37.1	8,022.0	1,993.8	523.2	993.7
1908	5.3	0.4	413.0	323.6	9,957.5	4,440.8	775.6	1,035.2
1909	6.1	0.1	511.3	425.4	6,860.5	3,813.3	724.9	1,470.5
1910	3.6	-	455.3	255.9	6,725.6	3,449.9	529.4	2,261.5
1911	3.2	-	358.4	1,185.5	7,611.6	5,408.9	762.2	2,451.2
1912	3.1	0.5	585.7	2,068.1	7,577.6	8,422.4	930.0	2,379.3
1913	2.8	-	426.3	903.9	9,439.4	5,534.1	1,008.9	2,154.1

Source: Archives of Belize, *Bluebooks*, 1901-1913.

Notes: a. No data are available for 1904, 1906, and 1907.
b. No breakdown regarding sources is available.

also took advantage of this open door to Quintana Roo. In the latter case, participation remained indirect for a time, through Belizean agents and the Chicle Development Company, established in English territory. Mexican benefits, in terms of tariff and tax collections, remained minimal, but there was a beginning of a series of settlements on the Mexican side of the border with Belize, which engaged in agriculture and commerce as well as forestry.

Farther to the north, in areas not directly affected by cruzob resistance, the foreign presence also intensified. Here, we find the deterioration of the Cuyo y Anexas venture and the emergence of the Bank of London and Mexico as a dominating commercial force. Both ventures were linked more firmly to Yucatecan ports, particularly Progreso, from which forest products were exported. Although probably the best-planned and organized operation in the area, the Compañía del Cuyo y Anexas failed to attract sufficient capital for long-term survival.[85] Before 1910, over four hundred Cuyo y Anexas employees were shipping out five hundred tons of logwood, 150,000–170,000 pounds of chicle, plus railway ties, construction lumber, and cabinet woods. Profits during 1907–1910 came to almost one hundred thousand pesos per year, but costs soared because of overly ambitious sugarcane and rubber plantations, heavy investment in port facilities and railroads, and the impact of a 1909 storm. Despite the venture's estimated potential to produce a million pesos in annual revenue,[86] El Cuyo was forced into receivership in 1910.[87]

An evaluation of the enterprise was made by the Bank of London and Mexico, whose report included the following summary:

> There is an area of over 200,000 hectares, valued at a fourth part of the official tariff for Government lands [1 peso per hectare].
>
> The quality of these lands is unsurpassed, as they are suited for the cultivation of cane, all kinds of grain, rubber in certain portions, henequen or sisal fiber, coconuts, and for other agricultural purposes in general. There is an abundance of construction timber, cedar, logwood, zapote for chicle . . . [88]

When sold in public auction in 1910, the estate was acquired by a group of Mexican banks (the Banco Nacional de México, the Banco Central de México, the Banco de Yucatán, and the Banco Peninsular) for 219,753 pesos.[89] El Cuyo's potential was never realized, and even today the ruins of its buildings, wharves, and sugar mill remain as evidence of the high risk involved in capitalist ventures in frontier Quintana Roo at the beginning of the twentieth century.[90]

The Bank of London and Mexico's investment of 2,043,799 pesos for a property it purchased in March 1910 was much more profitable.[91] It acquired 689,588 hectares and the existing installations of the Mexican Compañía Colonizadora y Exploradora de la Costa Oriental de Yucatán, which, prior to 1904, had been the East Coast of Yucatan Colonization Company.[92] In its early stages this project had diversified production goals similar to those of Cuyo y Anexas, but its most profitable activity was chicle production. As early as 1902, a million kilos of chicle were exported from Progreso, 90 percent of which came from the East Coast company.[93] The Bank of London and Mexico was the major producer of chicle from the northern half of Quintana Roo until the mid-1930s. Its control of a vast area, virtually unaffected by cruzob guerrilla activities, promoted an effective monopoly. The bank's base of operation was Santa María (now Leona Vicario), located roughly fifty kilometers inland from Puerto Morelos. A labor force of up to two thousand workers came from Cuba, Belize, Puerto Rico, and Mexico. Although some Yucatecan workers were involved, the majority of Mexicans came from Veracruz, via the port of Tuxpan, and were usually referred to as *tuxpeños*. According to the bank's concessionary contract, it was obligated to establish colonists in the territory.[94] As was the case with the other holders of large concessions, this clause was largely ignored; the bank did, however, create specialized transport and communications systems. Its main base, as well as the larger holdings, became known as the Colonia Santa María.

The patterns established during General Bravo's tenure in Quintana Roo show an increasing concentration of commercial activities under foreign control, a reliance on imported seasonal labor, the development of infrastructures related to forest-staple extraction, and a decreasing involvement by Mexican capitalists. To the extent that Quintana Roo's forest products were now reaching foreign markets, the Porfirian strategy of development might be judged successful.[95] Such activities, however, were taking place largely because of the presence of federal military forces. Moreover, the attempt to use the territorial capital, Santa Cruz, as a base for attracting a significant civilian population was not a success. Although General Bravo, with his draconian tactics, did manage to create a settlement of four thousand people, he did so at the expense of basic liberties.[96] The claim that he had successfully penetrated cruzob territory only to become a prisoner within it has some validity.[97] Between 1909 and 1912 the cruzob, after a decade of retreat and demoralization, began to mount systematic attacks upon military convoys, railway and telegraph installations, and commercial traffic. Contrary to official claims, the interior of the territory was neither peaceful nor safe for capitalist development.[98]

The Impact of the Mexican Revolution

Despite the fall of the Díaz government in 1911, it was not until 1912 that General Bravo was forced to leave Quintana Roo. With his departure, Santa Cruz effectively ceased to be the commercial and political capital of the territory, but it would be as late as 1915, with the arrival of General Salvador Alvarado in Yucatán, that the Mexican Revolution finally reached the tropical forests.[99] A series of peaceful meetings of cruzob leaders with territorial and Yucatecan officials established a political arrangement between traditional enemies.[100] These meetings had an antecedent: A five-man cruzob delegation had met earlier in Mexico City with President Madero, who had promised them control over their lands.[101]

Now, contrary to the "scorched-earth" tactics of the Bravo era, both regional and federal authorities employed positive stimuli to attract the cruzob to the new economic and political realities. Their delegations were treated with pomp and circumstance, and promised agricultural supplies, tools, clothes, and medical assistance.[102] The northern cruzob, led by Juan Bautista Vega, even began to show signs of accommodation by tolerating and participating in the chicle production carried out by the Bank of London and Mexico.[103]

Amid this new spirit of cooperation, Alvarado and Mexico City decided to return the shrine-capital of Santa Cruz to the cruzob.[104] Clearly, the attempt to administer the territory from its inland center had been unsuccessful. The Bay of Chetumal, it was decided, provided a much better logistical position from which to govern Quintana Roo and to control the contraband trade via Belize. The abandonment of Santa Cruz and establishment of Payo Obispo as territorial capital in 1915 was timely, as a 1916 hurricane effectively destroyed most of the infrastructure built by the federal government along the eastern coast of the peninsula.[105] By the time the cruzob reoccupied Santa Cruz in 1917, it already was badly deteriorated. Initially, the cruzob vandalized the existing facilities, which symbolized their forced and unwanted ties with the rest of Mexico. Before long, however, Santa Cruz was playing an important role in the cruzob's active participation in regional economic development.[106]

When Alvarado came to the peninsula as military commander of both Quintana Roo and Yucatán, he took steps to instigate massive economic reforms. Recent studies by James Carey and Gilbert Joseph provide excellent coverage of his Yucatecan activities.[107] However, Alvarado's attempts to transform economic structures in Quintana Roo produced few long-term results. He canceled numerous concessions of holders who had failed to live up to the terms of their contracts, and he endeavered to introduce a new system of more numerous, smaller concessions, larger tariff duties, and better payments for forest workers.[108] The activities of the Bank of London and Mexico, which had been allowed to function as a virtually autonomous domain under General Bravo, received different attention from Alvarado. Fiscal irregularities and a bank administrator's apparent involvement in counterrevolutionary activity was sufficient cause to cancel the concession, the administration of which was temporarily given over to commercial houses in Cozumel.[109] Attempts were also made to have all concession-holders build and maintain roads. By August 1917, there were twenty-nine recognized concessions in Quintana Roo. In practice, however, most were controlled by the large foreign companies,[110] which could and did appeal directly to higher authority in Mexico

City when their interests were threatened. Meanwhile, they bought off local officials.[111] All in all, most of Alvarado's reforms proved to be unenforceable.

International events exerted a stronger impact on the development of Quintana Roo. With the start of World War I, global demand and prices for forest products increased dramatically. When the United States entered the conflict, demand for chicle accelerated, in part because of the U.S. Department of Defense's policy of adding chewing gum to soldiers' rations. Indeed, by 1916, 10 million North Americans had become addicts of the chewing habit.[112] Major U.S. companies such as Adams and Wrigleys began to replace the London-financed companies as the principal capitalists in Quintana Roo, setting up acquisition subsidiaries—the Mexican Exploitation Company and the Chicle Development Company—that operated in both Belize and Mexico.[113] Even the Mexican consul in British Honduras was accused of getting into the act, taking advantage of his position to "exploit the national forest . . . to satisfy personal ambitions . . . and to become a capitalist in short order."[114] With prices and demand booming, regional attempts to force foreign companies to comply with tariff and export regulations proved totally ineffective.

The production systems of these U.S. and British companies were largely derived from lumbering activities developed earlier in the nineteenth century: Production was carried out by concession-holders or, more commonly, by regional subcontractors working for them. The foreign companies provided the necessary capital to cover transportation expenses and the start-up costs of the actual producers. This involved considerable sums that had to cover roughly one-half of the seasonal cost of supplies, food, labor, and administration. High risks were also involved; acts of nature, such as droughts and hurricanes—the 1916 hurricane practically wiped out production—or acts of war by the cruzob could seriously affect production and profits.[115]

The organization of production consisted of a series of hierarchically linked centers. The subsidiaries of the gum manufacturers connected the foreign producer and the area of primary material. These entities established overall administrative and supply centers located at points of export, for example, at Belize City, Cozumel, Santa María, Progreso, and Isla del Carmen, Campeche. Regional centers in the zones of production, known as *centrales*, linked the administrative and supply centers with forest production. Each central serviced a large number of bush camps called *hatos*, the base from which the chicleros worked. The tapping season coincided with the June-to-February rainy season, during which the chicozapote latex becomes accessible. The chicleros were recruited by means of advances (*enganches*) in their home communities in Veracruz and the peninsula—communities to which they returned in the off-season. They were paid according to the amounts individually produced. Cash advances, plus the cost of clothes, food, and supplies drawn from company stores, were deducted from workers' earnings at season's end. In practice, the production system included debt-credit manipulations, the tienda de raya, and other labor-control mechanisms that were seldom advantageous for the chicleros.[116]

The chicle boom affected the regional economics of the entire peninsula. World War I also increased exports of lumber, henequen, and other raw materials throughout Mexico; González Pacheco has detailed activities in the lowland Chiapas and Tabasco forests.[117] What was taking place in Quintana Roo was merely a reflection of a larger pattern that saw foreign capital playing an increased role in the tropical forests of lowland Mesoamerica. At the local level there were protests against this intrusion. In June 1916, the Mexican consul in Belize argued against granting privileges and concessions, since "these companies are made up of foreign capitalists, despite the fact that one of them has pompously called itself the Mexican Chicle and Lumber Company."[118] And the Mexican vice-consul in Corozal claimed that the Belize Export Company "is the one that actually monopolizes the work of exploiting chicle in Quintana Roo."[119]

The amount of chicle and other forest products exported from Belize between 1914 and 1920 is shown in Table 6.4. What percentage of these totals actually came from Quintana Roo cannot be precisely determined. Indeed, a later official report stated that "in the archives of the offices of the Territory there are no precise data to form a complete picture of its economic life, from its creation until the year 1917."[120] Comparing the Belizean data with 1918–1920 Quintana Rooan information on exports to the English colony, however, reveals that 28 percent of mahogany and 10.5 percent of chicle exports came from Quintana Roo.[121] It is a rather safe assumption, in view of known activities and official complaints by Mexican consular officials, that much more territorial chicle was leaving via Belizean ports than was officially recognized. In addition, the Belizean totals must be read with caution and compared with import data from ports of entry in North America and Europe. Total chicle production in Quintana Roo for 1919 was officially registered as slightly over a million kilos.[122]

The year 1919 was also significant in terms of cruzob involvement in the chicle industry. Francisco May, the most important cruzob military and political leader, played a key role in orchestrating the conversion of

Table 6.4 British Honduran Chicle and Lumber Exports, 1914-1920[a]

	Chicle (in Pounds)	Mahogany (in Feet)	Cedar (in Feet)	Logwood (in Pounds)
1914	3,461,809	13,858,327	921,386	1,750
1915	3,467,696	6,907,123	542,513	1,927
1917	2,266,621	9,933,269	776,806	5,260
1918	2,667,784	9,341,991	892,237	-
1919	3,543,764	9,648,700	704,697	2,776
1920	3,690,641	9,773,150	674,485	1,570

Source: Archives of Belize, *Bluebooks,* 1914-1920.

Notes: a. No data are available for 1916.

the cruzob local economy from a subsistence base to chicle production.[123] In negotiating the return of Chan Santa Cruz to Mayan control, General Octaviano Solís invited May to accompany him to Mexico City. May and selected members of his general staff were taken to the federal capital to meet President Carranza in January. The group stayed for three months, were given plane rides, shown the might of the federal army, and showered with gifts and compliments. The intention was to convince these former guerrilla fighters to return to the territory as participants in the federal government's plan of economic development. Indeed, May went back to Santa Cruz a changed man, aided by official recognition of his military rank of general, a life pension, and promises of a wide range of services and assistance from the federal authorities.[124]

Although Francisco May was led to believe that he and his followers would have direct control of much of the area previously occupied by the cruzob, it was in fact granted as a concession to a Señor Ramoneda, an agent for an English company operating out of Belize.[125] But, immediate assistance was supplied to reconstruct the railway between Vigia Chico and Chan Santa Cruz; the concession for this operation was also held by Ramoneda. May eventually gained control of the railway and the region around Santa Cruz, after a protracted political tug-of-war with Mexican officials and Ramoneda, yet he remained almost totally dependent upon

Yucatecan and Mexican administrative and technical assistance. Despite such obstacles, the cruzob chief quickly became the area's main contractor and chicle producer and, as quickly, took on some of the less-savory aspects of the previous entrepreneurial occupant of Santa Cruz, General Ignacio Bravo.[126]

In retrospect, the first two decades of the twentieth century saw the dramatic transformation of Quintana Roo. Unfortunately, Mexican sources of economic data on the region are both scanty and incomplete, a deficiency that increases the importance of Belizean data as a window through which territorial trends can be viewed. Although the federal government's original plans of incorporation of the territory by means of direct Mexican participation in economic development proved unrealistic, the federal presence did become firmly entrenched. Thanks to the activities of the army, General Bravo initially was able to isolate the resisting cruzob and then create a personal fiefdom. However, capitalist penetration and exportation of agrarian resources was due principally to the generous concessions granted to foreign interests. The advent of World War I stimulated these activities, but attempts to reap national benefits through tariffs and taxes, and to create roads and railroads linking the territory to Yucatán and Campeche were unsuccessful.[127] In the end, the traditional regional economic linkages to Belize remained and were strengthened, although the establishment of Payo Obispo as the administrative capital would have important long-term consequences.

Broader Participation and "Business as Usual," 1920–1930

May's conversion and the cruzob's entry into chicle production accomplished what half a century of Yucatecan effort and two decades of federal endeavor had failed to achieve: the reintegration of the cruzob into the national economic and political sphere of influence. Quite apart from May's co-optation, cruzob leaders saw chicle production as a means of acquiring cash to buy arms and munitions with which to continue their struggle for independence. As Anglo-Mexican political arrangements had cut off the traditional Belizean supply of armaments, and English lumbering interests no longer paid rent directly to the cruzob, chicle revenue offered alternatives. Despite the federal military presence and new political arrangements with the Mexican government, the cruzob remained ideologically opposed to the transformations that were taking place. The cruzob leaders had not anticipated that in getting involved in production for the international economy, the Maya's own subsistence economy—milpa, complemented by hunting and gathering—would be seriously affected. The repercussions would have a significant impact upon the theocratic-military and social structures they had built around the worship of the Holy Cross.[128]

This basic internal contradiction in cruzob culture had no positive solutions. On the one hand, chicle production created disposable cash resources that were concentrated in the hands of chiefs such as Francisco May in Santa Cruz and Juan Bautista Vega in Chumpon. On the other hand, economic integration through large-scale involvement in production undercut the military rationale for acquiring monetary assets: Gathering chicle and guerrilla fighting were almost mutually exclusive activities. Increasingly, the chiefs found themselves with hoards of gold coins, no army of forest warriors, and no good reason to purchase great quantities of armaments. Furthermore, the manner in which this new quandary was resolved had disintegrative consequences.

The chiefs, in becoming capitalist producers, also became petty despots. Their behavior heightened internal tensions between the new cruzob shrine-villages clustered at Xcacal Guardia, Chan Cah Veracruz, and Chumpon, and the former sacred center of Santa Cruz. Moreover, there was now a real threat to performance of religious guard duties and milpa activities, since the chicle-gathering season conflicted with fulfillment of these traditional functions. The arrival of outside merchants with luxury consumer goods, as well as large numbers of nonlocal chicleros, introduced new dependencies and diseases. The overall result was a weakened and fragmented cruzob society, rapidly losing its ideological foundations while becoming increasingly dominated by an economic system that provided few meaningful alternatives.[129]

A description in the regional press of cruzob conditions at the end of the decade (December 1929) summed up the dubious benefits of direct engagement in frontier capitalism: The Maya were living in remote, miserable villages of ten to twelve pole-and-thatch huts, each with a church, a few fruit trees, and a well; the people no longer trusted their chiefs, who had become privileged chicle exploiters or contractors and whose land claims were designed to rent areas for chicle extraction; the old theocratic discipline had disappeared; each June there was an invasion of up to eight thousand chicleros who had three hundred to eight hundred pesos to spend at the end of the season, with negative cultural consequences for the Maya; finally, outside goods brought into the area by merchants consisted mostly of canned food and contraband liquor. The contemporary description was quite accurate, reflecting what indigenous groups throughout the Americas typically experienced while tasting the first fruits of international extraction activities: namely, a serious decline in health conditions and social cohesion.[130]

The chicle produced by the cruzob found its way to Chicago through the efforts of Robert Turton, a Belizean mulatto business tycoon who acted as intermediary for the Wrigley Company.[131] Of the eight new concessions for chicle production granted in the 1920s, Turton controlled seven, either directly or through agents dependent upon his financing.[132] The degree to which the English colony continued to dominate Quintana Roo's economic activities, particularly in the central and southern regions, was clearly reflected in an official 1926 forestry complaint, directed to the Mexican president from Payo Obispo. The Mexicans claimed that the territory "was actually a financial liability for the Mexican government and a very profitable business for the English because it was, in fact, a subsidiary of Belize."[133] In reality, U.S. capital had largely supplanted that of the London-based interests.

In the 1920s, chicle was the territory's most important export staple. The figures in Table 6.5 indicate that, on the average, Quintana Roo's chicle accounted for about 40 percent of the national total. The fluctuations of the territory's share suggest the unevenness of production from season to season and within different areas. In terms of value, territorial production reached a high of 4.8 million pesos in 1929 but averaged slightly less than 3 million pesos per year over the decade. During the eleven seasons covered in Table 6.5, the total value was 31.5 million pesos.[134] This represented a great deal of wealth, but little of it directly benefited Quintana Roo. Rather, capital flowed into the areas supplying the labor, equipment, and services necessary for chicle extraction. The Belizean colony, the adjacent peninsular states (Campeche and Yucatán), and Veracruz provided most of the chicleros' supplies and contractors. Of course, the income received by cruzob chicleros also quickly left the territory through purchases of new consumer goods or, as happened with caudillos such as Francisco May and Bautista Vega, was hoarded, even hidden, as personal treasure.[135]

In the northern regions of Quintana Roo there was greater regional participation in chicle production. During the 1920s, there were at least fifteen Yucatecan contractors working in the territory, in addition to a Señor Ancona who was exploiting the area formerly held by the Cuyo y Anexas enterprise. This chicle, as well as much of the production of the Bank of London and Mexico, which regained access to its holdings in the early 1920s, was exported via the Yucatecan port of Progreso.[136]

Territorial officials faced chronic financial problems, despite the substantial economic activity. In 1920–1925, annual federal deficits in the

Table 6.5 Quintana Roo Chicle Production Compared With Regional and National Trends[a]

	Campeche	Yucatán	Quintana Roo	National[b] Exports	Territorial[c] Percentage	Price per Kilogram (in Pesos)
1919/20	1,997,316	174,712	1,028,300	2,865,417	35.9	2.547
1920/21	2,004,896	162,127	1,065,049	2,110,376	50.5	1.990
1921/22	1,114,315	180,106	1,791,541	3,101,398	57.7	1.793
1922/23	1,864,876	183,414	1,169,145	3,154,425	37.1	1.742
1923/24	906,890	187,315	1,365,692	1,872,697	72.9	1.676
1924/25	1,504,611	197,432	1,319,467	4,412,774	39.9	1.789[d]
1925/26	1,671,796	102,222	1,574,025	4,548,997	34.6	1.899
1926/27	976,314	123,342	1,675,204	4,369,541	38.3	1.961
1927/28	2,212,034	99,789	1,879,810	4,932,730	38.1	2.010
1928/29	987,516	213,965	2,390,926	5,090,525	46.9	1.984
1929/30	2,006,178	135,342	1,133,958	4,779,042	23.7	1.872

Source: L. G. Jiménez M., *El Chicle: Su explotación forestal e industrial* (Mexico City: Imprenta Manuel Casas, 1951), pp. 78-98.

Notes:
a. Production is measured in kilograms.
b. This represents exports rather than total production, which also took place in Chiapas, Tabasco, and Veracruz.
c. Quintana Roo's percentage is calculated from national exports rather than total national production, as it was directly exported.
d. The source gives this figure as 7.789, which is most probably an error.

territory approximated 1 million pesos.[137] The costs of supporting the military presence and building and maintaining federal institutions and infrastructures were high, while income from tariffs and taxes was minimal. A principal reason for the low government revenue was large-scale evasion of tariffs and duties, through bribes to officials and the flourishing contraband trade of unregistered exports. Contractors, on the other hand, expected to make an annual profit of 30 percent on their investments.[138] According to financial data available to Mexican officials in 1927,[139] the Bank of London and Mexico had earned five hundred thousand pesos from its concession while paying a paltry nineteen thousand in duties and taxes. During the same year, the Wrigley Company netted 30 million dollars after taxes. Quintana Roo's governor estimated that 50 percent of territorial chicle entered Belize as contraband. At the time, a quintal of chicle was valued at U.S. $90 to $96 in New York; intermediaries in Belize sold it for $43, while concession-holders paid their subcontractors $27 for the same quintal. The chiclero, on the other hand, received $15 for producing that quintal.[140]

Yet, regional and federal attempts to capture a larger share of what amounted to a 600 percent markup between bush camp and eventual destination met with firm resistance. When the territorial governor decided to impose, and the federal government approved, a 4 percent export tax on chicle leaving Quintana Roo, the reaction was swift and forceful.[141] Mexico City officials, including the president, received a barrage of complaints from producers and concession-holders. Foreign interests from New York and Chicago, through their Mexico City agent, put their case in the following terms: Their clients, the manufacturers, purchased 90 percent of territorial chicle production, which represented 70 percent of territorial income. An additional 25 percent of income was derived from lumbering activities by the same foreign interests. Foreign companies were, in fact, the source of whatever income entered the territory. If the government did not remove this additional tax burden, the chicle producers "would surely abandon the area and go to other chicle-producing regions."[142] The result would be an annual loss of 4 million pesos of economic activity. It was a take-it-or-leave-it demand, and when the government initially refused to back down, the concession-holders refused to pay the tax, stopped exporting via territorial ports, and increased contraband exports. Quintana Roo's governor was soon forced to request a lowering of the tax he had originally proposed, in view of the lack of territorial income to cover essential services.[143] Foreign investors clearly held the upper hand in setting the terms of their involvement in regional economic development.

The attempts to lower federal subsidies to the territory had some success by the end of the decade. Expenses for 1930 were projected at 467,000 pesos, with revenues put at 183,000 pesos. The deficit, although less than that of a decade earlier, remained substantial, as did the inability of territorial officials to collect tax and tariff revenues. And, Quintana Roo still lacked colonists; the population had increased by less than six thousand persons since the beginning of the century.[144] Although ambitious projects abounded—to build roads and railways, to grant land titles to individual cruzob families, and to create chicle-producing cooperatives—they remained largely on paper. The territorial governor's report fairly summed up conditions at the end of the decade:

> The colonization of the territory, which is one of the bases for its progress, cannot be attained for lack of communications. The territory does not have them other than with Belize, the English colony, and all the benefits of commerce and of production, overall, go to the said colony. There is no one who dares to colonize if he has no means of getting out his products, nor facilities to communicate with the rest of the country.
>
> The only legal sources of revenue are chicle and lumber production . . . contraband activities by nationals and foreigners continue . . . roads do not exist . . . the Indians have been isolated from their chiefs, who have been converted into capitalists.[145]

Conclusion

Throughout the last two decades of the nineteenth century and first three decades of the twentieth, the tropical-forest areas of Quintana Roo remained a frontier for both Mexico and foreign capital investors. Although Mexican federal authorities expended substantial effort, at great human and financial cost, to integrate the area into the national economy, both the Porfirians and successive revolutionary regimes achieved only limited and contradictory results. Forced pacification of the cruzob and severance of the territory from the political influence of regional separatist states was accomplished. A federal presence, with its institutions, was also established. In this sense, the original intentions of laying a basis for national integration of the frontier were achieved.

Economic integration, however, proved to be a much more difficult undertaking. During his period of governance, General Bravo ran part of the territory as a personal fiefdom, while English commercial activities continued unabated throughout much of Quintana Roo. Such activities continued, as well, during and after the Mexican Revolution. This linkage to London-based capitalists underwent a shift with the emergence of chicle as the primary forest product. New York- and Chicago-based chewing-gum manufacturers, stimulated by wartime demands for their products, gradually replaced the English as the principal investors. The influence of North Americans on the region, as well as their ability to shape Mexico's federal forest-extraction policies, proved to be greater than had been that of London. As U.S. firms, like their British counterparts, used the English colony as a point of entry and port of exit for export staples, Belize benefited economically to a greater extent than did Quintana Roo.

Within the territory of Quintana Roo, as in many resource-rich frontiers of the same period, clearly defined processes of development can be detected. The main trends may be summarized as follows:

1. Commercial outposts, directly linked to metropolitan centers of economic and industrial expansion, developed.
2. Local indigenous populations suffered systematic assault and subjugation by both commercial enticements and military force. The arrival of a well-equipped, modern army forced the cruzob to retreat into scattered guerrilla bands, assailed by federal military might and by introduced diseases. When the cruzob lost the capacity to regain traditionally held lands, they were offered the option of participating in the new economic order, but transition to the capitalist mode of production was accompanied by increased internal dissension and a breakdown of social systems. The co-opted chiefs became petty capitalists, while the rest of the population suffered the consequences of deteriorated living conditions and sense of identity.
3. Outpost settlements of colonists were implanted, a process only initiated during the period under discussion; its realization came later.
4. Available natural resources were exploited in a fashion regulated only by international demand and the price for primary products (lumber, chicle). Mexican agencies had neither the capacity nor the political will to regulate production so as to conserve the resource base. Massive deforestation and rearticulation of ecological habitat were clearly established during the period. The consequences, already recognized by forestry officials at the time, would become more evident later.
5. The frontier aspect of the region was eliminated with the large-scale entry of agricultural and other settlements of national origin. This process was barely started during the period under discussion; it became a reality only after World War II. At present, much of Quintana Roo has been settled and deforested. Neither chicle nor lumber are important commercial activities today.

With the emergence of Cancún and other Caribbean resort facilities during the 1970s, Quintana Roo has again become something of a national and international frontier. But, far from being a tropical-forest frontier, it is a high-priced tourist frontier, increasingly attractive to foreign seekers of sun, sea, sand, and new sensations, but inaccessible to the majority of Mexicans. Notwithstanding a repetition of old patterns, Quintana Roo has entered a new phase of capitalist development.

Part III

Revolutionary Challenges to the Plantation Regime

Part III refines our understanding of the Mexican Revolution in the State of Yucatán, particularly of the much-heralded first decade of revolutionary involvement (1915–1924), when Yucatán was acknowledged to be a social laboratory for the revolution. Although an abundant (and partisan) narrative history exists for this pivotal decade, much of its social and agrarian history remains to be written.[1] The chapters by Ramón Chacón, Rosemary Batt, and Daniela Spenser make diverse contributions to Yucatán's "new revolutionary historiography." Although each author brings a different methodological approach to, and focuses on a different sector or aspect of, the local revolutionary process, collectively they achieve an underlying unity: They shed light on the assault that a series of revolutionary mobilizations—some directed by the state, others emerging from the grass roots of civil society—made on the Old Regime centered around henequen monoculture.

Part III evokes the "exceptional" nature of Yucatán's revolution under the active leadership (1915–1918) of a reform-minded, populist caudillo, General Salvador Alvarado, and a more militantly socialist governor, Felipe Carrillo Puerto (in office 1922–1924). In large part because of Yucatán's geographical isolation and the entrenched position of the plantocracy, it took five years for the Mexican Revolution to reach the peninsula, and only then because of the preponderant might of General Alvarado's eight thousand–man Constitutionalist Army of the Southeast. Once on the scene, the revolution was less violent and probably more radical in its first decade than it was elsewhere in Mexico. Nevertheless, as our contributors reveal, embedded in the characteristic Yucatecan case are important implications for understanding the larger revolutionary process, especially as it pertains to such central problems as export dependency and regional development; the politics of agrarian reform; the relationship between revolutionary ideology and practice; Mexican revolutionary corporatism and its antecedents; the dynamics of mass mobilization and cross-class coalitions; and the adaptability and mentality of elite establishments in the face of revolutionary transformation.

Historian Ramón Chacón focuses on the least-understood component of Alvarado's social agenda: agrarian reform. Chacón agrees with authors of other recent studies that the general's revolutionary project represented an effective blend of bourgeois reform in social areas and pragmatism in the political sphere.[2] He demonstrates how, in the face of unremitting opposition by President Venustiano Carranza's conservative federal government, Alvarado still shrewdly managed to implement a species of land reform that addressed several of the region's most pressing agrarian needs. Tapping his extensive research in the little-used executive and agrarian records of the Archivo General del Estado, as well as a study of the caudillo's career and writings, Chacón first analyzes Yucatán's concentrated structure of landholding during the late Porfiriato, then suggests how Alvarado's formation in the Mexican north predisposed a particular agrarian policy to combat such inequity. Finally, Chacón teases out the strained federal-state negotiations over land reform, making sense of a variety of seemingly disconnected, partial measures that together constituted Alvarado's pragmatic response to Carranza's opposition.

Chacón reveals that thousands of campesinos requested milpa plots, and Alvarado compelled hacendados temporarily to allocate parcels to them. While these stop-gap measures, which provided land to hundreds of cultivators and transformed thousands of others into sharecroppers, never touched lands cultivated in henequen, Chacón argues that they helped to feed a hungry population, relieved mounting social tensions, and generated mobilization upon which Carrillo Puerto and later revolutionary regimes would build. In the process, Chacón raises larger questions about the role that center-periphery tensions played in the phasing of revolutionary-era reforms and, more broadly, about the parameters of social change under transitional "populist" regimes.

While scholars such as Chacón have mapped out the programs put forward by the Socialist Party of the Southeast (PSS), first under Alvarado and, subsequently, under Carrillo Puerto, much less emphasis has been given to gauging the impact that such programs actually registered at the local level, especially outside the dominant henequen zone. Anthropologist Rosemary Batt uses local tax, census, and agrarian records, as well as interviews, to create a microhistory of Espita, a municipality on the eastern fringes of the henequen zone. She assesses the consequences that Alvarado's liberation of hacienda peons and Carrillo Puerto's land distribution had for the local planter-elite's labor supply and patterns of investment and production.

On one level, her Espita study graphically demonstrates the difference between moderate *alvaradista* reform and the bolder *carrillista* attempt at a socialist transition. By and large, Alvarado's "bourgeois revolution" came and went, and local hacendados continued to control the town council and to hold onto (and in some cases even expand) their estates and businesses. Planters' monopolization of land left most former peons with little choice but to continue working for their former masters after "liberation."

The situation changed dramatically as the revolution veered to the left under Carrillo Puerto. Espita's freed peons gained strength through the local PSS resistance league and applied for a communal land grant under Carrillo's new agrarian reform law. Land distribution would prove the undoing of Espita's small, mixed henequen-and-sugar estates. With the formation of the ejido, labor supply was suddenly dictated by the campesinos' priorities rather than those of the hacendados. It was no coincidence, therefore, that *espiteño* planters embraced the nationwide de la Huerta rebellion that toppled Carrillo Puerto early in 1924. Even so, by 1930 all but several of the municipality's estates had ceased to function.

The early demise of the network of estates in peripheral Espita appears to be atypical. The bulk of agrarian reform in Yucatán did not occur until the massive 1937 cardenista expropriations.[3] Up until that time, the majority of the zona henequenera's planters had avoided expropriation largely by making the case that their agroindustrial units were indispensable to the stability of an ailing monocrop economy caught in the throes of a bust. Batt argues that such was not the case for the smaller, less-productive mixed producers in the east, who became expendable when Carrillo Puerto's political goal of building mass support in the countryside outweighed economic considerations.

Beyond its contribution to Yucatecan revolutionary historiography, Batt's microstudy of the rise and fall of a local bourgeoisie outside the dominant henequen zone has broader implications for regional scholars. Her chapter should shatter former notions that such peripheral areas were insignificant to Yucatán's social history and political economy. Examining such marginal areas as Espita raises issues that do not ordinarily arise in studying the dominant sector of a dependent regional economy: for example, the limits to capitalist expansion created by economy, demography, and culture; the economic and political articulations between marginal and metropolitan areas; and the different forms that interclass and intraclass relations can take in peripheral areas. Cast as it is in the broader context of regional, national, and global political economy, Batt's microhistory reinforces themes in our two other studies of the peninsula's periphery, by Cal and Konrad, and suggests new problems for comparative study.

Whereas revolutionary politics in Yucatán have been examined extensively from the perspective of agrarian mobilization and the threat it posed to wealthy hacendados (for example, Paoli and Montalvo's, and Joseph's monographs,[4] as well as Chacón's and Batt's chapters in this book), little attention has been given to Yucatán's small but militant urban labor force. The stevedores and railroad and transport workers who spearheaded the regional labor movement have been treated peripherally when they have been treated at all. Sadly, this reflects a long-running trend in Latin American historiography as a whole. Workers have not received the attention they deserve largely because historians have not always known where to find them. Conditioned by an appreciation of capitalist development in the core regions of the world system, scholars have sought workers in the industrial sector—typically late to materialize in Latin America—while neglecting their pivotal role in the nationally strategic export sector. Recently, Charles Bergquist's provocative comparative examination of export workers in four South American nations has gone some way to remedy this deficiency, but Latin American labor history remains an underdeveloped field.[5]

Daniela Spenser's contribution addresses most centrally the reluctance of Yucatán's urban labor movement to embrace the leadership and policies of Carrillo Puerto's PSS, seemingly its natural ally, in the early 1920s. Some Marxist writers have argued reflexively, without adducing proper evidence, that urban workers' opposition to the carrillista regime was largely instigated by the capitalist class.[6] Other historians speculate that Carrillo Puerto's patronage of the rural masses in difficult economic times excluded (and rankled) urban labor.[7] Ultimately, it appears that urban workers were implicated in the conspiracy that resulted in the Socialist party governor's execution by insurgent delahuertista troops early in 1924. At any rate, urban labor's opposition to socialism in Yucatán warrants serious investigation and remains something of a skeleton in the closet of Yucatecan history.

Drawing upon previously unused PSS documents in the state's archives and other repositories and on materials in the U.S. National Archives, as well as on rare *folletería* and working-class newspapers located in Mexico and Europe, Spenser centers her interpretation of labor's stormy relationship with the PSS on a structural and conjunctural analysis of the region's political economy. She also undertakes to examine urban labor's ideology. Although Carrillo Puerto's predecessor in the State Palace, Salvador Alvarado, was more moderate, he presided over a period of booming fiber prices that enabled him to get on better with the urban *sindicatos*. Carrillo Puerto, on the other hand, governed as prices plummeted after World War I. While his government might distribute land to the campesinos, it had little to give the workers; moreover, Spenser argues that urban labor's anarchosyndicalist roots and bread-and-butter mentality put it on a collision course with the PSS's redistributive, top-down agenda.

Spenser's chapter is an exploratory effort, raising significant issues for future investigation, rather than the final word on labor's role in Yucatecan revolutionary politics. Although she ventures only provisional answers to some of the questions she poses, she contributes to the growing comparative literature reassessing labor's place in Latin American social and political history.

7 *Salvador Alvarado and Agrarian Reform in Yucatán, 1915–1918: Federal Obstruction of Regional Social Change*

RAMÓN D. CHACÓN

The years 1910–1920 witnessed the ascendancy of leaders, both regional and national, with different ideologies of what the Mexican Revolution should achieve. Moderates such as Francisco I. Madero and Venustiano Carranza, for example, believed the revolution should assume an evolutionary course with respect to social reforms, especially land reform, and regarded political changes as the panacea for most of the nation's problems. Other leaders with radical leanings, such as Emiliano Zapata and Salvador Alvarado, maintained that the land question was the country's major social ill and that, therefore, the revolution should initiate reforms to resolve it.

On occasions, conflict developed when a regional chief was more radical in his approach to social reform than was his conservative superior, the president of Mexico. Salvador Alvarado, governor of Yucatán (1915–1918), encountered such a situation in his dealings with President Carranza. The purpose here is to examine Governor Alvarado's efforts to implement land reform in Yucatán and to see how these efforts were thwarted by a conservative federal government that sought to centralize authority.

Monopolization of Land in Yucatán, 1880–1910

The reform laws of the Benito Juárez government, which were incorporated into the Constitution of 1857, set the precedent for the demise of

Yucatán's Indian ejidos. Years later, agrarian laws enacted between 1883 and 1910 created a latifundio system in Yucatán as they did in other parts of Mexico.[1] The Mexican government viewed such agrarian reform laws, which forced the Indians to subdivide their communal lands among heads of family, as progressive acts that would eliminate the backward communal-village system and produce industrious, individualistic farmers working in a free enterprise system.[2] In Yucatán, as in other parts of the republic, little was accomplished toward the subdivision of ejidos until Porfirio Díaz's rule (1876–1911); under the dictator, the breakup of ejidos in Sonora and Yucatán was a particularly important feature of government policy. In those states, Indian rebellions had held the authorities at bay, and the Díaz government decided that accelerating the division of village landholdings would "pacify" the areas.[3] Thus, in Yucatán, during 1879–1912, no less than sixty-six ejidos totaling 134,000 hectares were subdivided into twelve thousand individual plots averaging eleven hectares each.[4]

The growth of henequen haciendas in Yucatán was especially instrumental in the loss of ejido lands. During 1883–1907, for example, the number of henequen bales exported increased from 202,805 to 611,845. The increase in production reflected the expansion of henequen cultivation, which increased from four hundred thousand mecates in 1869 to 2.5 million mecates by 1893.[5] As the demand for fiber increased, particularly in the United States, it became a common practice for neighboring hacendados to encroach on village lands. In the words of the Yucatecan historian Antonio Betancourt Pérez, "the henequen plantations expanded, absorbing the periphery of numerous towns and villages and erasing houses, streets, fences, and ground-plots."[6]

Once the ejidos were divided, the planters, whether through outright confiscation or through purchase, obtained ownership of most of the individual plots. Numerous Indians soon found themselves totally dispossessed of lands that had been held by their forefathers for generations. The district of Izamal offers an example of how village lands were absorbed by henequen plantations during 1880–1910. In 1903, at the town of Tepekán, ejido lands were divided among 194 heads of family. By 1908, 174 of them had sold their plots to henequeneros. In 1905, the communal lands of the town of Hoctún were distributed among 221 Indians; 63 of them maintained ownership of their plots, but 158 sold them to planters shortly thereafter. The same system of land transfer continued throughout the district during the first decade of the twentieth century.[7]

A similar pattern developed in other districts. For example, in Dzilám González, in the department of Temax, the individual plots that had once formed the ejido of that community were sold to the henequenero Atilano Torres, owner of Hacienda Yaxché.[8] In like manner, following distribution into individual plots in 1909, the peasants from the villages of Hoydzonot and Suma lost their ejido lands in sales to Alfredo Novelo, proprietor of the henequen plantation San Nicolás. According to a government report, in addition to purchasing plots, Novelo also "stole approximately 1,250 mecates of Hoydzonot's communal lands by alleging his right to all the ejidos of that village and prohibiting the residents from working those lands. For that reason the villagers are forced by necessity to rent lands from Hacienda Xiat in the municipio of Cansahcab."[9] In 1915, Patricio Sabido, counselor to the Comisión Local Agraria, reported that the residents of the town of Tixkokob had lost their lands, holdings that apparently had been incorporated in 1906 into the henequenales of Hacienda San Antonio, owned by the firm Peón de Regil y Hermanos.[10]

Yucatecan planters also extended their realms through applying the colonization legislation of 1883 and 1894. Under those laws, provisions were made whereby private companies, often controlled by Díaz's political favorites, surveyed, subdivided, and settled terrenos baldíos.[11] The surveying companies were awarded one-third of the public lands outright and were given the privilege of purchasing additional lands at reduced prices. Indian villages unable to establish legal claims to their communal lands were particularly vulnerable and often dispossessed. *La Revista de Mérida* reported in 1909 that Esteban Rejón García, administrator of Olegario Molina's properties, registered a claim and obtained in the name of his employer 2,179 hectares. This area, claimed as baldío land, contained pueblos and two ranchos owned by Laureano Briseño and Rafael Aguilar. On behalf of the new claimant, the jefe político of Tizimín gave the occupants two months to vacate their properties.[12] At Tixcancal, thirty Indians were accused of conspiring to rebel against the government for resisting the takeover of their lands, which had been claimed as public land. In 1907, forty families from the village of Kancabchén, in the department of Maxcanú, were dispossessed on the pretext that their lands were baldíos.

Between 1867 and 1910, close to one-fourth of baldío land—or lands claimed to be baldíos in Yucatán—fell into the hands of a few speculators.[13] Thus, Yucatán followed the trend of *latifundismo* that characterized Mexico during the Porfirian era: The local planter class, representing 0.25 percent of the rural population, owned more than 97 percent of the land, while 96.4 percent of the population was landless.[14]

However, in certain respects Yucatán's landholding system represented a unique form of latifundio. Because of the state's monocultural economy, based on henequen, which had developed into one of Mexico's most successful enterprises late in the Porfiriato, hundreds of henequen haciendas appeared. By 1910 Yucatán had 1,170 plantations distributed among 193 planters, more haciendas per capita than any other state in the republic.[15] This pattern was due to the peculiar requirement of henequen production that planters own more than one tract of land: In addition to the area under cultivation in a given district, the planter needed uncultivated or only partially cultivated properties containing monte in order to provide fuel to generate steam power for the rasping machines that processed the fiber. The restriction of henequen planting largely to the henequen zone, and the demand for fuel, resulted in the growth of numerous specialized monte-land haciendas; thus, the average size of individual properties in Yucatán was considerably smaller—ranging between one thousand and two thousand hectares—than the national average of three thousand hectares.[16]

Salvador Alvarado and Federal Obstruction of Yucatán's Agrarian Reform

Despite the outbreak of the 1910 revolution, the years 1911–1914 witnessed little change in Yucatán. Various factors—geographical isolation, counterrevolutionary movements, lack of revolutionary leadership—caused the revolution largely to bypass Yucatán, and, as a consequence, the state maintained its prerevolutionary socioeconomic structures. Following a local counterrevolutionary movement headed by Abel Ortiz Argumedo against the Venustiano Carranza regime, the first chief (Carranza) ordered General Salvador Alvarado, in February 1915, to defeat the insurgents, to reestablish control over the state, and to install social, political, and economic reforms in accordance with carrancista guidelines. On March 19 of that year, following the defeat of Ortiz Argumedo's forces, Alvarado entered Mérida and assumed the governorship of Yucatán.

Compared to the other officers who had been sent by the Constitutionalists[17] to govern Yucatán, Alvarado had most impressive credentials. He was born in 1880 at Potam, Sonora, where his father owned a small printing shop. As a young man, Alvarado was employed in a drugstore in Guaymas and later owned a small store in Cananea, center of the foreign-owned Greene Cooper Company. In 1906, he enlisted in the ranks of the radical Partido Liberal Mexicano (PLM, or Mexican Liberal party) headed by Ricardo Flores Magón. At the outbreak of the revolution against Díaz in 1910, Alvarado joined the cause of Francisco Madero's Partido Antirreeleccionista. A year later, he held the rank of major in the army of General Juan G. Cabral. His leadership qualities and military expertise impressed his superiors, and, after defeating enemy forces in a major battle at Guaymas on July 17, 1914, he was promoted to brigadier general. Following the defeat of the Victoriano Huerta regime, Alvarado was transferred to Mexico City and served as its military commander, a key post. He remained there until the outbreak of the Ortiz Argumedo rising.[18]

The historian Frank Tannenbaum—who wrote that the Mexican Revolution was anonymous, that no great intellectuals prescribed its program, formulated its doctrine, or outlined its objectives—considered Salvador Alvarado a major exception to that generalization. According to Tannenbaum, Alvarado came the closest to formulating a bonafide program for the revolution:

> Salvador Alvarado, the energetic governor and soldier, whose coming to Yucatán was like a cyclone that destroyed a feudalism rooted deep in the soil, Salvador Alvarado, who abolished slavery in Yucatán, boasts of having issued more than a thousand decrees and laws. He, perhaps more than any Mexican who took an active part in the Revolution, attempted to formulate its program. But no Mexican intellectual would admit that Alvarado was an intellectual or that he formulated the program of the Revolution.[19]

Although his contemporaries viewed Alvarado as a radical socialist and bolshevik, his brand of socialism was non-Marxist in its orientation. Indeed, he was a proponent of state capitalism, whereby the government regulated the economy so as to guarantee benefits to all sectors of society. Alvarado was a developmentalist who sought to eliminate precapitalist structures while actively promoting development through state intervention in the economy and governmental regulation of class conflict. His social reforms, including agrarian reform, must be viewed within that context.[20]

The development of Alvarado's ideology, manifested in the political, economic, and social reforms he introduced, originated from his experience with corrupt government at Potam, Sonora, as well as from his ties to the PLM. He was also influenced by the works of U.S. economist and land reformer Henry George, and to a lesser degree by utopian socialists Robert Owen, Comte de Saint Simon, and Charles Fourier.[21] George's single-tax theory—to tax only land as a means of collecting public revenues and ending the wastefulness of land monopoly and speculation—

appears to have had an impact on Alvarado's land taxation and agrarian reform policies.[22] The writings of Scottish advocate of capitalism Samuel Smiles represented, however, the greatest influence. Alvarado was an avid reader of Smiles, whose works espoused the basic Victorian values associated with the "gospel of work," and who was a proponent of material progress based on individual enterprise.[23]

Alvarado's ideology was shaped not only by his reading of Flores Magón and the utopian socialists but also by the practical requirements of the populist government he was forging in Yucatán to implement his revolutionary reforms. Latin American populist movements, such as the one spearheaded by Alvarado, traditionally have been multiclass, structurally hierarchical and authoritarian, and, typically, based on personalistic relationships between caudillos and dependent followers. Populist regimes have gained power by replacing traditional political elites whose right to rule has been seriously eroded by mass political movements.[24] As a reform-minded, populist caudillo ruling at a time when the Mexican government had just begun its transition to a more-institutionalized revolutionary state, Alvarado realized that it was essential to control the old oligarchy and to establish a strong alliance with the working classes. According to the Mexican historian Francisco José Paoli, Alvarado was able to dominate the workers and develop a program of populist reform because he had "military power, a developed political vision based on the kind of program needed to modernize society, and an integrated ideology that would attract the working class of Yucatán."[25] The development of a caudillo-led, populist regime in Yucatán entailed not only the political mobilization of the rural and urban working classes, but also reforms in the areas of land, labor, and education to benefit these particular groups.

Alvarado's dedication to work and his serious attitude toward life and the revolution left a deep impression on Martín Luis Guzmán, who, in the company of generals Eduardo Hay and Miguel Alessio Robles, visited the Sonoran chief at Guaymas in 1914. Guzmán wrote:

> Many traits of Alvarado's character warranted respect: his passionate eagerness to learn, his sincerity, his sober attitude toward life. . . . A quip interpolated by Hay in connection with the battle of Santa María elicited no response from him until the joke had been repeated twice. The point was that neither laughter nor smile entered into the scheme of his thinking except as something pointless, or having no other purpose than to waste time that could be more usefully employed. He felt that the work underlying the revolutionary effort was of such magnitude that it did not permit of wast-

ing a moment or a thought; the slightest detail called for wholehearted attention, the most sober approach.[26]

When given the opportunity, Alvarado consciously attempted to make his administration a model of what the revolution could and should accomplish. He sought ways to inculcate in the minds of the people, particularly the working classes, the notion that all their recent socioeconomic advances originated from the revolution, which they should therefore cherish. According to James Linn Rodgers, the U.S. consul general at Havana, Cuba, Alvarado had informed him that "he was giving to Yucatán a government which could be accepted as an example of how the Constitutionalist Party in Mexico would generally redeem its promises to the poor."[27] Alvarado wrote to Carranza that his government would not only serve as a model, giving prestige and moral support to constitutionalism, it would also create a feeling of "solidarity among the people of this state and the rest of the republic . . . who before were victims of the greed and arbitrariness of ignorant, criminal rulers and military chiefs."[28]

As a division general and a governor during a preconstitutional period, Salvador Alvarado had tremendous extralegal powers. In large part because of his military prowess, he was able to control to a large extent the regional social, political, and economic institutions. His efforts encountered little opposition during his administration. Throughout his military rule, when constitutional laws and guidelines were lacking, revolutionary change came from above. Salvador Alvarado became, with certain limitations, the major interpreter of the revolution in Yucatán.[29] Although his rule was marked by the militarization of Yucatán, the new governor deeply mistrusted the military and intensely disliked corruption in government.[30] The revolution, according to Alvarado, was not "war, disaster, executions, nor conflagration. But, war, disaster, executions, and conflagration are, unfortunately, the indispensable means of carrying out the reforms that our cause proposes."[31] Alvarado as a developmentalist perceived the revolution as a movement that would bring not only political and social change but also a stable climate to assure economic development.[32]

Although Alvarado's achievements in political, economic, and social reform were noteworthy compared to those of other Mexican revolutionary leaders, he has remained a relatively obscure caudillo. Despite this lack of recognition, several scholars have written that he best personified what the revolution should have achieved in the area of social reform.[33] They contend that he was largely responsible for introducing social reforms that revolutionized Yucatecan society. Jesús Silva Herzog, who lauded Alvarado's achievements, wrote that "during the Salvador Alvarado and Felipe Carrillo Puerto administrations, Yucatán was without a doubt the most progressive state in Mexico. It was the only state that came close to installing a socialist regime."[34]

Alvarado's social reform platform, which gained him his reputation as a reformer, may be divided into two major categories.[35] First, there were reforms he considered to be secondary and attributed primarily to his puritanic moral values (for example, the decrees against gambling, bullfights, cockfights, prostitution, and the sale of alcohol). A notable exception were his efforts aimed toward improving the condition of Yucatecan women. Second, there were the principal reforms that addressed major social problems of the working classes—land, labor, and education.

In Yucatán as in other parts of Mexico, revolutionary leaders who were committed to social reform viewed the agrarian question as the nation's most pressing social problem, one that required drastic measures to resolve. But, because of internecine warfare, economic dislocation, and conservative leadership, little had been achieved during the period 1911–1914. However, in November 1914, the *villista* and *zapatista* armies, which had rebelled against Carranza, forced the Constitutionalist Army from Mexico City and established control over a large section of the country. The first chief was short of manpower and needed to enlist new recruits from society's rank and file to undertake a military campaign against the rebels. His recruitment efforts proved unsuccessful, and, in desperation, he decided that a public pronouncement to initiate land and labor reform would attract support from the working classes. With that objective foremost in his mind, Carranza promulgated two decrees. That of December 12, 1914, promised to improve the living conditions of the workers. Then, on January 6, 1915, a law was published that defined an agrarian platform that he promised to implement in the future.[36]

Carranza's agrarian law is a legal landmark in the nation's history. Land reform in Mexico (particularly prior to 1920) has been based on the first chief's decree, along with Article 27 of the 1917 Constitution.[37] However, during Alvarado's governorship, neither measure succeeded in seriously addressing the agrarian problem. The January 6 decree was limited in its objectives; moreover, the agrarian problem was compounded by Carranza's decision, shortly after the decree's promulgation, not to enforce it; nor did he implement Article 27. As a consequence, land reform came to a virtual standstill.

It is not an overstatement to say that Carranza's land law represented an emergency measure, a political ploy, avowedly provisional in scope.

Although the decree's major purpose was the restoration of village lands, only those settlements that were officially recognized as having lost their ejidos could petition for restitution. This stipulation alone automatically excluded a large sector of the landless populace, among them thousands of workers (former landholders) residing on haciendas. The agrarian law included four major provisions: (1) It declared null and void the alienation of ejidos that had transpired because of the enforcement of the Juárez agrarian law of 1856, by the illegal acts of surveying companies, or through force; (2) villages, pueblos, and rancherías (recognized as within the *categoría política*) whose lands had been confiscated, and which needed land, were the only settlements that could petition for their restoration; (3) communities petitioning for lands were obligated to show that they needed them, to prove their previous ownership, and to show that they had been dispossessed of the lands in question; and (4) landowners were given the right to have legal recourse to courts against the actions of the government. This recourse would be achieved through the *amparo*, or injunction, which proprietors would use, whenever threatened by the law, to delay agrarian reform or to make it ineffective through protracted legal battles.[38]

Thus, Alvarado had to contend not only with the agrarian law's limitations but also, more importantly, with Carranza's conservative stance on agrarian matters. Alvarado's own views on the land question appear to have been typical of the "Men of the North"—Villa, Obregón, and Calles; *norteño* leaders from Coahuila, Chihuahua, and Sonora, who lived on the periphery of Indian Mexico. *Tierra y libertad* (land and liberty) meant for them the right of each Mexican to own in fee simple a plot of land; they were somewhat less committed to communal landownership, which had always been more characteristic of central and southern Mexico.[39]

Alvarado wrote that throughout Mexico a group of *latifundistas* had taken lands illegally and established a pseudo-aristocracy. He made a distinction between unproductive and productive large-scale ownership of land; haciendas that exploited only a fraction of their acreage were, he argued, unproductive and should be subdivided. But, he also asserted that a general policy of subdividing large-scale holdings into small farms should be avoided because it would result in a decline in crop production and consequently cause financial problems. Alvarado stated that "large-scale ownership of land should be permitted if the lands were being farmed and if it concerned important crops such as henequen . . . that required large sections of land for efficient production."[40]

Alvarado's administration distributed lands provisionally—especially through a pseudo-sharecropping system that proved beneficial to the campesinos. In several cases, Alvarado also distributed ejidos to those villages that had lost them to neighboring haciendas; individual plots were subdivided among landless campesinos in other settlements. Of these policies, the first would become the most important, as the Carranza government, which was far less radical than that of Alvarado, systematically thwarted direct forms of agrarian reform in the peninsula.

In Yucatán, as in other parts of Mexico during 1915–1917, the January 6 decree represented the only legal guideline that Constitutionalist governors might use to institute agrarian reform. Alvarado did not waver in the face of Carranza's reluctance to address land reform. As early as June 1915, without federal guidelines to follow, Alvarado began to lay the groundwork for an agrarian reform program in Yucatán, with the expectation that in the future the first chief would enforce the January 6 decree nationally. During the first six months of the Alvarado administration, the state spent more than five hundred thousand pesos in surveying lands, studying land titles, and laying the foundations for agrarian reform. In a report to Carranza, Alvarado wrote that as a consequence of the land reform carried out during this period, in which hundreds of campesinos obtained lands provisionally, maize production was greater and food shortages less than in previous years.[41] Alvarado's measures were impressive considering that the federal government had not enforced the agrarian law; nor had any other state, with the exception of Morelos, seriously attempted to deal with the problem.

Alvarado's commitment to land reform can be gleaned from several government decisions. A report dated July 29, 1915, from Patricio Sabido, the legal adviser to the State Agrarian Commission, to its director, Ramón Guerrera Jiménez, suggests the government's concern to resolve the historical problem of land monopolization. Sabido studied the land titles of Hacienda San Antonio y Anexas, located in the municipio of Tixkokob and owned by the Peón de Regil family. He concluded that the communal lands belonging to the town of Tixkokob had been confiscated by the Peón de Regil family and that those lands should be returned to the villagers, even though the town could not establish its legal foundation. "[The engineer in charge of land distribution] should notify the proprietors involved to vacate the lands even though they have the original title of ownership. In all cases it should be explained that the welfare of the community is more important than personal gain."[42]

Similar cases were studied by the State Agrarian Commission. On several occasions, where evidence indicated that planters had encroached on village lands, the ejidos were returned provisionally to the dispossessed settlements. Before the end of 1915, the commission had distributed lands on a provisional basis among the following villages and towns: San José, Sanahcat, Umán, and Progreso.[43] At Umán, for example, the commission declared null and void the 1908 subdivision of the village's ejido into individual plots, which were later incorporated by neighboring haciendas; it also forced the planters who had confiscated the ejido plots to distribute land among village residents. According to the commission:

> The purchase [and confiscation] of Umán's community lands by the neighboring planters are void. Those ejido lands that are within the environs of plantation henequen fields will remain for now under the hacendados' control. As compensation, the planters are required to distribute to the village of Umán lands that are located near the ejido. These lands must be acceptable to the residents and suitable for the cultivation of crops, the pasturage of animals, and the felling of timber. The planters must give to the village two mecates of land for each mecate confiscated from the ejido. The village will take possession of these lands on a provisional basis.[44]

Yucatán's agrarian reform plan had been largely a reaction to emergency situations before December 3, 1915, when Alvarado decided to make his agrarian decisions official by promulgating a state land law. The December 3 decree represented Alvarado's attempt to institute permanent, full-scale land reform by using Carranza's January 6 agrarian law as a guideline, even though it had not been enforced by the first chief. With its issuance, the Comisión Local Agraria began to devote its activities exclusively to distributing lands among the villages.

Alvarado recognized the shortcomings of Carranza's agrarian law and therefore included in his land law two key provisions that responded to the needs of landless peasants and addressed local conditions: (1) the decree contained a measure that called for the subdivision of haciendas that had confiscated ejidos even if the land in question were planted with henequen; and (2) whereas the January 6 agrarian law limited land reform only to those officially recognized communities that had lost their ejidos, Alvarado's decree promised land to all settlements, including the thousands of landless laborers residing on the plantations.[45]

Shortly after Yucatán had enacted its agrarian law and had begun to establish a land reform plan, the federal Ministry of Interior requested information from Alvarado concerning the state's agrarian policies. In response to the inquiry, dated January 11, 1916, Modesto Rolland, the president of the State Agrarian Commission and Alvarado's chief adviser on agrarian matters, outlined what had been achieved. He stated that Yucatán's land reform program represented a momentous undertaking and suggested that it be a model for the rest of the nation.[46]

The first chief rejected Rolland's proposal and, on January 19, 1916, circumvented land reform by prohibiting the implementation of Alvarado's agrarian law. Carranza, in a letter to Alvarado, argued that his January 6 decree referred "exclusively to the restitution of ejido lands taken from villages and did not include returning lands that are not part of the ejidos, which constitutes another aspect of the agrarian problem in which the chief executive has not enacted legislation."[47] Furthermore, the first chief maintained that the law was federal in scope; consequently, state authorities could neither alter its provisions nor enforce them. State officials, Carranza warned, should also abstain from dealing with the matter of water rights or national forest lands since they were under the auspices of the Secretariat of Development, Colonization, and Industry. In fact, although the central government allowed Yucatán to continue with preliminary investigations to initiate agrarian reform in the future, it ordered that the distribution of land be postponed indefinitely.[48]

Alvarado continued to press the first chief on the matter, sending Rolland to Querétaro to explain his policies and to obtain permission for Yucatán to establish an agrarian reform plan. In a lengthy telegram to Carranza, which preceded Rolland's visit, Alvarado explained the importance of the agrarian problem and the urgency for the first chief to resolve it in behalf of Yucatán's two hundred thousand dispossessed Indians: "The oppression and injustice suffered by the Indians is notorious, and the landholders have offered them bribes and unsuitable land for farming as compensation to escape the government's measures." He added, "The Indians are suffering great hardships because of inadequate landholdings, having to leave their jobs and traveling considerable distances to plant a few liters of grain."[49]

Alvarado also tried to convince Carranza that great political advantage could be gained by winning the Indians to the Constitutionalist cause through land reform. Alvarado maintained that in order to "revolutionize" Yucatán, the government must organize the Indians and gain their support, and that this could best be achieved through land redistribution. He alleged that "by returning the lands to the natives, we bind them to the nation and the revolutionary undertaking."[50]

Alvarado urged Carranza to consider his agrarian plan, to study his program for social change and the legislation initiated in behalf of the working classes in Yucatán. He maintained that each decree enacted to institute social reform represented an effort on his part to interpret the needs of the people and to fulfil the goals of the revolution. He tried to appease Carranza by stating that he would amend any legislation the first chief found undesirable: "However, I implore you to permit me to test the social reform laws for a period of time and study their operation in Yucatán." "I urge you," he continued, "to give the necessary attention to the state's agrarian question because, in addition to resolving an important regional problem, the investigation that you will undertake in Yucatán may help you to lay the groundwork for the definite resolution of this vital issue at the national level."[51] Carranza rejected Alvarado's proposals and once again obstructed agrarian reform in Yucatán.

Two years later, in his *Actuación revolucionaria,* Alvarado expressed regret that he had been unable to fulfil his duty and establish full-scale agrarian reform in Yucatán. Alvarado refused to attack the first chief at this point for obstructing land reform, as he still maintained a political alliance with the Constitutionalist regime when the monograph appeared. Alvarado wrote, however, that "actions beyond my control . . . prevented my discharging that mandate of the revolution."[52]

In *The Whole Truth About Mexico,* Francisco Bulnes, a journalist and a former Porfirian politician, attempted to explain Carranza's "actions" and why agrarian reform was discouraged in Yucatán. According to Bulnes, the U.S. government, acting on behalf of the henequeneros, exerted political pressure on Carranza to prevent Alvarado from initiating land distribution. Bulnes wrote that the henequeneros, failing to convince, first, Alvarado and, then, Carranza not to rescind the governor's land law, sent a commission to Washington, which obtained from Secretary of State Robert Lansing the "promise that the Alvarado decree would be nullified by Carranza. The commission also had a conference in the United States with . . . Luis Cabrera, the First Chief's Secretary of Treasury, who at the instance of Mr. Lansing . . . obtained from Carranza a special decree nullifying all the sacred, socialistic, vindicating work begun by General Alvarado." Bulnes concluded that, in this way, "Mr. Lansing . . . forced Carranza to restore the old order in Yucatan."[53]

Thus far, available historical sources do not support the thesis that the U.S. government forced Carranza to intervene in Yucatán's revolutionary experiment. Rather, the evidence indicates that the first chief acted (with or without foreign influence) to obstruct Alvarado's agrarian reform program for ideological reasons.[54]

Despite Carranza's opposition, Yucatán continued with plans to establish an agrarian program. In 1916–1917, the State Agrarian Commission adopted a policy of distributing lands provisionally without the guidance of a national agrarian law. As late as April 1917, the Alvarado administration hoped that the first chief might reconsider and allow Yucatán to implement a regional agrarian reform plan by issuing a new state land law.[55] The federal government, however, also rejected this proposal. The Carranza administration stated that it would not authorize the commission to implement legislation regarding federal affairs. The central government viewed Yucatán's land reform policies as unconstitutional because they usurped the authority of the nation's legislative branch.[56] This attitude forced Carlos Baz, the director of the State Agrarian Commission, and Alvarado to realize the futility of trying to organize a state-level agrarian reform plan. Nevertheless, under their leadership, the commission began to compile a number of bylaws, which, while they lacked the official standing to initiate full-scale land reform, did not contradict any existing legislation and might serve as guidelines for the State Agrarian Commission's policies.[57]

The central government's decisions did not entirely circumvent land reform in Yucatán. Since mid-1915 Alvarado had adopted an alternative, short-range, emergency plan to meet the immediate needs of landless agricultural workers, a measure that gained even more importance after Carranza's rulings. This federally sanctioned program consisted initially of temporary distribution of privately owned lands among rural workers to achieve two principal objectives: (1) to distribute lands promptly among landless peasants in order to help supplement their dietary needs and sources of income; and (2) to help increase the state's agricultural production by cultivating crops, especially maize and beans, which were being imported at great cost.

Under this plan, the requirements for obtaining land during 1915–1916 were relatively simple. In each municipio the government compiled a list of resident planters and the amount of land that each owned. A percentage of each planter's landholdings were distributed free of charge among landless jornaleros who had petitioned for land to plant milpa. Landless peons thus could easily obtain small plots designated as "fertile land," ranging in size from twenty-five to fifty mecates.[58]

But, by 1917, with increasing requests for land from workers, the government included several provisions that sought to protect the hacendados by preventing the campesinos from misusing their landholdings. Alvarado instructed military commanders to take lands away from those recipients who had misused or not worked their plots. Some, for example, had cut trees to sell for firewood and lumber instead of cultivating crops. The government adopted these measures because the misuse of land not only hurt the hacendados' productivity by reducing monte-land, but also obstructed the government's policies to institute henequen valorization and agricultural diversification. Furthermore, to force campesinos to farm rather than exploit the land's timber resources, and to compensate planters for distributing their lands, the government required all land recipients to give 5 percent of their crops as payment to the landowners from whom they had obtained plots.[59]

Frequently, hacendados' charges that campesinos receiving plots used them to extract firewood to sell were simply tactics to obstruct the government's policies. The large majority of the laborers who received land obeyed the law and cultivated the traditional milpa. The demand for wood fuel, however, had resulted in a situation whereby some campesinos used their newly acquired lands solely to collect wood that they sold to planters, towns, and railway operators for cash. Workers affiliated with the Guillermo Prieto Union from the village of Muna, for example, refused to accept lands alloted to them because they were unsuitable for firewood production.[60]

There were also instances of landowners who refused to comply with the government's policies to subdivide their holdings. Where planters had sufficient uncultivated lands to distribute but declined to subdivide them voluntarily, landless jornaleros who petitioned for land had two alternatives. They could, with government backing, take possession by force; or government officials, without the landowner's consent, could subdivide land among those who had requested plots.[61] The Alvarado administration, for instance, ordered Luis D. Molina, an uncooperative henequenero, to reach an agreement with the local officials of Tekantó regarding the amount of land he should allot to the campesinos; otherwise, "the government will distribute the lands without your permission."[62]

The administration's land policy was not without other serious impediments. The government faced a grave dilemma because it needed monte-land to carry out its land reform plan; yet, the availability of uncultivated lands was essential to maintain the expansion and productivity of the henequen plantations. On the one hand, the administration stated that only fertile lands, meaning monte-land, should be distributed among the landless; on the other hand, it also ordered that under no circumstances should henequen plantations suffer from land reform measures that deprived them of monte.[63] Thus, a conflict ensued in the rural sector as many planters refused to give up their uncultivated lands. Hacendados justified evading the responsibility of providing lands to campesinos on the grounds that, first, their landholdings were needed as sources of fuel to run the rasping machines and to produce timber for railroad ties; and second, that the plantations had only enough land to divide among their resident workers.[64]

Many planters also complained to the government that the distribution of monte-land might lower henequen production and result in financial losses to the state. Fearful of such an eventuality, the Alvarado regime modified its land policy to safeguard the state's economic interests. Where official investigations confirmed the planters' charges of a shortage of monte, the government permitted them to make arrangements with land recipients whereby the hacendados could obtain sufficient fuel from the lands they had subdivided. Manuel Rodríguez Acosta, for example, proprietor of Hacienda San Diego, agreed to cede two thousand mecates of land to the residents of nearby Citilcúm on the condition that they, in turn, sell to him wood collected in the process of clearing their plots. Under the agreement concluded, residents who had received land delivered one thousand loads of firewood at a cost of 3.50 pesos per load. In other instances the government permitted planters to enter ejidos (which had recently received their lands provisionally) for the purpose of collecting wood.[65] Thus, in a communication to the local committee governing the ejido of Yaxcucul, Carlos Baz wrote: "In order not to obstruct the rasping of henequen at Hacienda Santa Cruz, property of Arcadio Escobedo, you should permit the employees of the plantation each day to cut approximately ten loads of kindling wood and eight loads of firewood to be used as fuel to run the hacienda's steam engines."[66]

Although, as an agrarian reform policy, the plan that allowed campesinos to sharecrop had limitations, it did generate social mobilization and improved their living conditions. The documents available do not reveal the amount of land distributed among jornaleros through this program. The sources do show, however, that throughout Yucatán during 1915–1918 thousands of workers requested plots of land, and the planters were compelled to provide them. While other efforts to establish a large-scale reform program had been interrupted by Carranza, these measures helped alleviate the land problem by providing provisional lands to hundreds of campesinos and by transforming thousands of others into sharecroppers.

Conclusion

Land monopolization in Yucatán was similar to that which transpired in other states. In Yucatán the henequen boom influenced many planters to extend their landholdings by encroaching on village lands. Moreover, the planters obtained additional lands through colonization laws.

The governments that succeeded the ousted aristocracy in 1911–1914 failed to address land reform. However, with the arrival of Salvador Alvarado in 1915, Yucatán, especially during the first year of his administration, appeared ready to take measures to establish a full-scale land reform plan. These efforts were obstructed by President Carranza, who refused to permit states to implement their own agrarian reform programs until the enforcement of federal constitutional policy. Furthermore, Carranza, for ideological reasons, opposed the kind of land redistribution that Alvarado sought to promote in Yucatán; consequently, he forced the governor to discontinue important aspects of his agrarian reform policy.

Several factors explain Alvarado's decision to establish a state agrarian reform plan: (1) the January 6 agrarian law lacked the necessary provisions to distribute land to many of the dispossessed; (2) the Carranza regime failed to provide guidelines to the governors and state agrarian commissions that would explain how the federal agrarian law should be enforced; and (3) Alvarado realized that the first chief had no intention of implementing a full-scale agrarian plan. Government officials in Yucatán recognized that Carranza opposed wholesale land distribution and that he was not particularly entranced with effecting land reform through the medium of the ejido. Hence, as late as 1918, Carranza's agrarian program lacked direction and can be described as lethargic and indifferent. The president, for example, had not yet established enabling legislation to regulate Article 27 of the 1917 Constitution.

Yucatán's response to the land question reveals the problem that develops when a governor promotes reforms that are not favored by the chief executive. Further research on the relationship between governors and presidents of the nation, especially during the 1910–1920 period, would certainly reveal many interesting features of the revolution that have thus far been overlooked. For example, to what extent did Carranza's conservative stance on social reforms slow down the pace of agrarian reform at the national level? How much did Carranza's policies obstruct agrarian reform measures in other states? In his classic 1933 synthesis, *Peace by Revolution*, Frank Tannenbaum stated that from 1916 to 1920 Carranza "practically [brought] land distribution to a standstill."[67] Perhaps Tannenbaum was correct; at any rate, future regional studies will provide a more nuanced account of Mexico City's impact on local agrarian initiatives.

Finally, it is important to note that Alvarado governed Yucatán during a period of political change. His personalistic, populist regime represented a transition in the political order following the defeat of the traditional oligarchy. Under Alvarado's direction, the state not only shifted its economy from laissez-faire to state-controlled capitalism in order to benefit workers, but also established new political alliances with the working classes and initiated socioeconomic reforms in their behalf. Alvarado's land reform must be understood as a principal component of a caudillo-led, populist program undertaken at a time when the Mexican revolutionary state was just beginning its transition to a more institutionalized system.

8 The Rise and Fall of the Planter Class in Espita, 1900–1924

ROSEMARY L. BATT

Much of traditional anthropological research has studied peasants in isolation, in the tradition of Robert Redfield. On the other hand, research on the history of the Spanish conquest and later development of the Mexican state has tended to focus on the metropolis of Mérida and the growth of the hacienda and, later, henequen-plantation economy in the west. Few writers have given more than passing attention to the nonhenequen zones.[1] Whereas the state's economy rose or fell on the basis of henequen, the east was considered a "backwater"—isolated, "unproductive," and controlled by Mayan Indians after the Caste War.

Microhistorical studies—presented in the context of regional, national, and international political economy, from the perspective of the periphery of a dependent capitalist economy—round out our understanding of the social formation as a whole. The rise and fall of a local faction of the planter class in eastern Yucatán during the Porfiriato and the revolutionary period provide an opportunity to analyze the limits on capitalist development imposed by ecology, demography, and local culture, as well as the different adaptations that occur.

Antecedents

Espita lies 172 kilometers northeast of Mérida and 14 kilometers north of Valladolid. Like many other towns in Mexico during the Porfiriato, Espita was governed by a close network of families whose livelihood depended upon the control of land, labor, and production on their haciendas. By 1900, thirty sugar haciendas, spread over approximately one hundred thousand hectares of land, covered the Partido of Espita. The Peniche family and their extended kin were the dominant force in the community. Along with several other hacendados, the Peniches governed a population of nearly three thousand Maya living as debt peons on their estates.

How did this social arrangement develop? The roots of Spanish settlement in Espita date to the colonial period. Espita was granted in encomienda to Juan de Granados Baeza in 1549,[2] although the town itself was a Mayan community for a considerable period prior to the Spanish conquest.[3] The Mayan inhabitants paid tribute in maize, beans, chickens, cotton cloth, honey wax, and baskets, among other things, to the *encomendero* until the abolition of the system in 1785.[4] At that time there were 376 tributaries and an indigenous population of 1,298.[5] While the Maya paid tribute to the encomendero, they still lived in their traditional communities and farmed communal lands.

By the mid-eighteenth century, a number of additional Spanish settlers had moved to Espita. Foremost among them was Pedro Bernardino Peniche, a captain of the provincial militia. Included also were the Erosa, Patrón, López, and Rosado families. Unlike the western part of the state, where the wealthiest planters of the Porfiriato were direct descendants of the encomenderos, in Espita they traced their roots to these later settlers. By 1790, there were 306 "Spanish" residents in Espita.[6]

By the time the Caste War erupted little more than a half-century later, these Spanish residents had established thirty-seven sugar haciendas and 215 ranches in the area and were producing sugar and rum for the region's internal market.[7] The total population in Espita had grown to 18,691 by 1845.[8] Taken on a regional level, however, Espita was part of a secondary center for cane production. The east produced 22 percent of Yucatán's total, while the south grew 71 percent; Espita contributed 8 percent to the state's total.[9]

Espita was not as hard-hit by the Caste War as were other cane-producing areas such as Valladolid, Peto, and Tekax, perhaps because it had not expanded as rapidly as had its counterparts to the south.[10] While the town was twice occupied during the war and served as a center for arms, men, and refugees, it was not decimated at war's end. In 1850, twenty-five hundred hectares of maize and sixty hectares of cane were reported in cultivation.[11] By 1862, the number of haciendas had actually increased (to forty-one). And, while Espita's population dropped by one-third (to 12,055), the comparable demographic loss was 70 percent in Valladolid and 80 percent in Peto.[12]

After the war, Espita would be considered a post of strategic importance on the Mayan frontier, but it continued to have only minor economic significance for a number of reasons. First, having just fled from

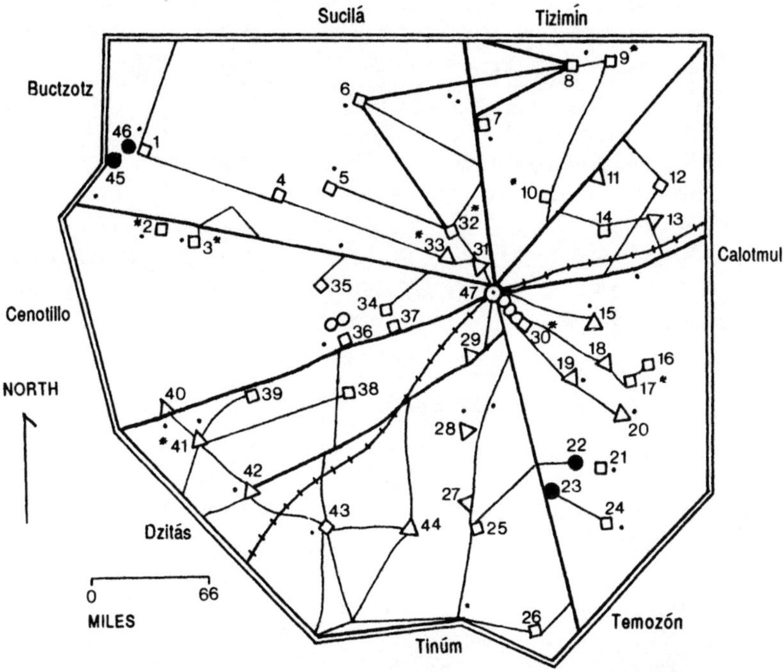

- ⊙ Municipal Seat
- ● Rancheria[4]
- □ Hacienda
- △ Rancho[5]
- Improved Road
- Road
- Railroad
- Tranvia
- Municipal Boundary
- • Cenote
- O Archaeological Mound

1. Humuch
2. Pom*
3. Chañ Pom*
4. Yohuáz
5. Makulán
6. Santo Domingo
7. Yokhóm
8. Santa Cruz
9. Holcah*
10. Chenkú*
11. Popep
12. Santa María
13. Tzitzilá
14. Chacabal
15. Yokdzonot
16. Tekóm
17. Santa Rita Yokhóm*
18. Tumbruchén
19. Halal
20. Dzitnup
21. Xuech
22. Nacuché
23. Kunche
24. Yaxché
25. Chan Xullúb
26. San Pedro Chenchelá
27. Yaxché
28. Tzabcanul
29. Dzulá
30. Actunkú*
31. Xyach
32. Kancabá*
33. San Andrés*
34. Nohoch Chioplé
35. Chan Chioplé
36. Xuencal
37. Nacantut
38. Mahalcáb*
39. Opná
40. Poxil
41. Tzabná*
42. Yokdzonot Norte
43. Xullúb
44. Paraiso
45. Xualtéz
46. Tusik
47. Espita

Map 8.1 Municipality of Espita, Yucatán, c. 1915

the war zone, many landowners would not return to, or reinvest in, the frontier. Second, cane producers in Yucatán were in an unfavorable competitive position vis-à-vis those in the Caribbean, who enjoyed more favorable soil and climate, cheaper transportation, and more-advanced technology. Steam power, for example, was not introduced into Yucatán until 1869. By comparison, the henequen market was wide open, and the thin limestone soil of Yucatán was well suited to this hardy plant. Third, the dramatic shift in population from the south and east to the northwest created a serious labor shortage on the frontier. Fourth, transportation of goods overland to Mérida and other parts of the northwest was time-consuming, difficult, and costly. These disadvantages also meant that henequen production on the frontier was not cost-effective during this period of time.

The growth of serious regional differences between members of the planter class developed in conjunction with the dramatic success of the henequen industry in the second half of the nineteenth century. Landowners in and around Mérida were in the best position to take advantage of the expanded U.S. market for fiber. Following the Caste War, they had undeveloped land on their cattle haciendas and a significantly larger potential labor pool to draw on. Mérida was already a regional financial center and was close to ports of trade. As more and more landowners converted their estates into commercial henequen operations and as the henequen market continued to grow, the henequeneros in the west became the major economic and political force in the state.

Regional economic differences increased in the second half of the nineteenth century as the western planters became increasingly tied to the international henequen market. Eastern planters in Espita supplied the smaller, Yucatecan market with sugar, rum, and other agricultural products because their weaker economic position required them to diversify production. The markedly different patterns of regional economic development fueled a significant debate, continuing into the next century. Henequen planters rapidly pursued a policy of monocrop cultivation and increasingly depended upon imported foodstuffs to meet basic needs. They were accused of creating a highly unstable economy dependent upon price fluctuations in the international henequen market.[13]

Economic differences caused political strains. The cane planters, for example, pressed unsuccessfully for protective legislation and rail transportation to the capital.[14] Planters from Espita had little political clout in Mérida. They continued to support political candidates from Valladolid and were not appointed to district or statewide office until the turn of the century.[15]

In the meantime, planters' control over local land and labor grew enormously between 1850 and 1900. After a century of occupation, the Peniche family was clearly dominant. They owned 35 percent of the urban properties and 50 percent of the landed estates in Espita by 1870.[16] The family benefited tremendously from land reform legislation such as La Ley de Desmortigación of 1856, which opened up vast areas of public land for private sale. Consistent with statewide patterns, public lands in Espita were rapidly converted to private ownership. Registered private holdings increased by 26 percent, for example, between the property tax assessments of 1869 and 1893.[17] Concentration of ownership also rose, with the Peniche family controlling 60 percent of the land by 1893. In addition, whereas twenty members of that family owned 50 percent of the land in 1869, ten members held title to 52 percent in 1893.[18]

This answer to the "land problem"—the conversion of public and communal land to private ownership—helped solve the "labor question." Maya from free pueblos, who lost access to public lands, had little choice but to become resident workers for planters who had bought the land. The dramatic increase in the population of debt peons in Espita was comparable to that on the statewide level. Whereas there were 763 debt peons on local haciendas in 1869, there were 967 in 1885,[19] and 2,897 in 1900.[20]

Sugar production, like the henequen industry, was capitalized during this period because of the introduction of steam-powered machinery. Productivity soared: In 1883, two and one-half times as much sugar was produced in the state as in 1844, but on 40 percent less land. Espita's share of statewide cane production rose from 8 to 12 percent. By 1900, Espita reported the highest number of steam-powered turbines of any locality in the state,[21] and was the site of fifteen registered distilleries.[22] The town had gained a reputation for its high-quality rum and other liquors.

Throughout the second half of the century, the economic control of the Peniche family was mirrored in their formal control of the governing council of the municipality. Tracing the descendants of Pedro Bernardino Peniche, the original settler of the family, provides a case in point. The two great grandchildren of Pedro Bernardino, Santiago and José Quirino Peniche Patrón, were the most powerful local planters at the turn of the century. Both expanded their estates by marrying into the López family, another major landowner. In 1869, Santiago operated two sugar haciendas—Santo Domingo and Holcah—and owned twenty landed estates, according to the property tax register of the time. José Quirino produced sugar on the haciendas of Yohuaz, Chenkú, and Tzitzilá, and held eleven other estates. Both headed the municipal council at various times. In

1879, they helped found La Sociedad Progreso y Recreo, which became a center of theater and social life recognized throughout the state.[23] In addition, they began publishing a newspaper, *El Demócrata*, which was a political voice for the regional cane growers and a vehicle for commercial advertising.

By the end of the century, the local elite, headed by the extended Peniche family, had consolidated its control over local land and labor. As will be shown, the haciendas functioned as plantation systems of production, albeit with some accommodations to the adverse conditions on the periphery. While their local control was complete, however, this faction of the agrarian-based capitalist class was in a dependent position vis-à-vis its metropolitan counterparts. The sugar haciendas in Espita were secondary developments, whose growth relied on the prosperity of henequen.

As henequen production grew, however, so did the espiteños, and the relationship between planters in the two regions became much stronger and more interdependent. Although initially selling only luxury items such as sugar and rum to the western market, eastern planters increasingly supplied corn and firewood, and, eventually, land to the expanding henequen economy. As monocrop cultivation swept the west, henequen planters became dependent on eastern growers for basic goods to maintain and further develop the western enterprises. This relationship of internal articulation (or economic interdependence) grew dramatically during the Porfiriato, and, with it, the political alliances between eastern and western factions of the planter class.[24]

Land, Labor, and Production on the Hacienda, 1900–1915

Economic interdependence did not always breed friendly relations. Henequen growers needed land, and the sugar haciendas were expendable. Given the unequal power of the two factions, planters in Espita had two options: Sell out or join the henequen interests.

In a policy apparently aimed at converting land from cane to henequen cultivation, then-Governor Olegario Molina dramatically raised taxes on sugar and rum between 1902 and 1906.[25] Taxes on distilleries alone tripled in 1906.[26] Reported production of rum dropped by three-quarters between 1901 and 1907.[27] By 1906, only thirteen of the thirty sugar haciendas that were functioning in 1901 were producing cane. Twelve of the original thirty had already planted henequen.[28] Henequen cultivation in Espita rose from seventeen hectares in 1883 to four thousand in 1910, with most of the increase occurring after 1900.[29] Olegario Molina purchased over eighteen thousand hectares and developed the largest, most highly mechanized plantation in Espita. By the time of the revolution, he controlled 20 percent of the local land and work force.

With the crisis in cane and the continuing development of monocrop agriculture in the west, the production and sale of maize took on greater significance in Espita. In 1912, Espita produced 17 percent of the state's maize, more than any other single district.

Landownership Patterns

Two dramatic changes occurred in local landownership patterns during the Porfiriato:[30] (1) as mentioned above, members of the elite strata of henequen growers from the west purchased huge tracts of land in Espita; and (2) local landowners consolidated their holdings into larger estates.

In the first instance, a number of henequen planters from the west purchased land in Espita beginning in the 1890s. By 1910, however, only two remained: Molina and his political ally, Santiago Espejo Medina. Together, they held 35 percent of the land. Another 60 percent was held by local families (80 percent by the Peniches). Eleven other proprietors owned 5 percent. In the second instance, while the number of private landholdings increased by 26 percent between 1869 and 1883, it decreased by over 65 percent between 1883 and 1910. Estates were consolidated through a combination of inheritance, purchase, and marriage (see Table 8.1 for the conformation of Espita's landholdings in 1910).

Production rose dramatically on the henequen estates with the introduction of larger-capacity, steam-powered equipment. Similarly, the number of debt peons living on the haciendas increased by 71 percent—from 2,897 in 1900 to 4,957 in 1910.[31] Symbolic of its incorporation into the henequen economy, Espita was finally linked by rail to Mérida in 1908. Molina had a tramway laid between his hacienda, Actunkú, and the railroad terminal. The henequen market was so good that it was finally profitable to invest in outlying areas such as Espita.

By analyzing the class of landholders and their kinship relations rather than landholdings per se, it is evident that the average hacienda (a combination of several landholdings) was larger than other studies have suggested.[32] Setting aside the extremes, the haciendas in Espita tended to range between twenty-five hundred and five thousand hectares in size. Much of this land lay fallow, allowing vegetation to grow, crops to be rotated, and firewood to be gathered to fuel the processing plants. The average hacienda had about thirty-five hundred hectares. Despite varia-

Table 8.1 Espita: Summary of Plantations by Size, Machinery, Value, and Population, 1910

	Percentage of Owners	Percentage of Holdings	Extension (in Hectares)	Percentage of Total Area	Machinery Steam	Machinery Manual	Declared (in US Dollars)	Estimated Value (in Pesos)	Declared Value[a] of Houses	Number Population[b]
Planters										
Regional[c]	2	19	36,631	34.7	7	5	935,080	1,800,000	174	1,422
Local										
Large	2	8	12,853	12.2	3	2	39,900	500,000	98	557
Medium	10	24	42,743	40.4	12	5	831,000	1,500,000	80	1,791
Small	6	14	7,461	7.1	2	4	101,000	300,000	38	165
Subtotal	20	65	99,688	94.4	24	16	1,906,980	4,100,000	390	3,935
Other Landowners										
Spanish	8	8	3,806	5.5	0	0	60,400	120,000	0	35
Mayan	3	3	210	0.1	0	0	5,200	10,400	0	0
Subtotal	11	11	4,016	5.6	0	0	65,600	130,400	0	35
Total	31	76	103,704	100.0	24	16	1,972,580	4,230,400	390	3,970

Sources: Yucatán, Property Tax Register (Mérida, 1903-1916); Secretaría de Agricultura y Fomento, División Territorial de los EUM, *Censo general de población* (Mexico City: Oficina Impresora de la Secretaría de Hacienda, 1910, 1921).

Notes:
a. Estimated value was arrived at by doubling the declared value.
b. Based on oral accounts.
c. Properties of Olegario Molina and S. Espejo Medina.

tions in size, haciendas employed similar systems of production and work organization.

Organization of Work and Production

Unlike haciendas in the monocrop henequen zone, those in the east maintained a diversified productive base; many times, both henequen and cane were cultivated and processed for regional and international markets and were the major sources of profits.[33] Maize, cattle, and yucca were also raised for sale in the region and for local consumption. Maize was grown according to the traditional milpa system of the Maya, interplanted with crops—chiles, different varieties of beans, squash, sesame seeds, and local crops such as *espelón*. Each hacienda had its own orchard (citrus fruits, bananas, papayas, mangos, and avocados, among other fruits) and yard and draft animals. Some landowners sold firewood to the railroad and to other haciendas, as well as precious woods for furniture and lumber for construction.[34]

While this description of landownership, diversified production, and self-reliance appears to resemble a hacienda (according to the Wolf-Mintz typology), the capitalization of production and organization of work in the haciendas in Espita more closely resembled plantation agriculture.[35] The processing plants for cane and henequen, located on the central hacienda, were run by free, skilled, wage laborers under a rigidly hierarchical organization of work. Both products required a relatively high division of labor, and coordination and supervision of tasks. Under the administrator, supervision was divided between the encargado, who assigned tasks, and the *mayocol,* or foreman, who kept quotas. In both henequen and sugar/molasses processing plants, there were eight to ten specialized jobs. Pay was set at between 1.25 and 1.50 pesos per day.[36]

Free artisans (carpenters, blacksmiths, masons, mechanics, and ropemakers, for example) lived in the town along with the skilled plantation workers and day wage laborers; the latter supplemented the labor of debt peons on a seasonal or "as needed" basis. Debt peons made up approximately 75 percent of the labor force.[37]

The work of the hacienda was divided into two parts: the *fagina* (unpaid work) and the task of the day.[38] The peons would awaken to a bell at 3:00 A.M. each day and would line up in the courtyard. Those who were late were whipped. The unpaid labor consisted of four to five hours of maintenance work for the hacienda—husking corn, feeding animals, cutting and hauling firewood, cleaning, and repairing tools. Paid work began at 9:00 A.M.: Peons would reassemble in the courtyard, the list of their names would be read again, and tasks assigned for the day. In some haciendas, pay was on a piece-rate basis; in others, on a flat rate. Peons earned between twelve and thirty-seven centavos per day in the Espita area. Work ended at 7:00 P.M. each day. Older and younger people were given less demanding chores and worked shorter hours.

In addition to daily pay, peons received a small plot of land to cultivate milpa for family consumption. Although this may be seen as remuneration for their unpaid work, the ex-peons did not link the two. Generally, the *patrón* would give "his" peons fifteen days each year to cut down vegetation to prepare the field. The ablest could cut approximately one hectare, which was sufficient to meet family subsistence needs for much of the year. Peons used their "free day," Sunday, to work their own fields.

Peons supplemented their production with purchases from the owner's store—either at the hacienda during the week or in town on Saturday (payday). Most planters had stores both on the estate and in town, or had a close relative who owned a store in town. Wages were issued in the hacienda's own currency (accepted at the owner's stores and, in some cases, other stores in town), in Mexican currency, or—while it was in circulation—Yucatecan currency. Some used all three, and payment varied according to the economic situation of the patrón, who frequently lacked circulating capital.

Town and hacienda were highly interdependent: In addition to supplying skilled workers and artisans, the town was a commercial center dominated by the planter class. They owned one-third of the commercial establishments generally, and one-half of the food stores registered in the tax lists of 1906 and 1909.[39] Their establishments were far larger than the others listed in the tax register, which included, for example, the meat and vegetable stands in the public market. Those stands were owned by a number of independent Mayan merchants.

The estates in Espita, similar to the traditional hacienda, were relatively self-reliant and based on diversified production. The hacendado used paternalism, accumulated debts of unskilled workers, and his control of undeveloped land to attract and maintain a stable labor force, and apparently suffered from insufficient liquid assets. On the other hand, like plantations (more capitalistic enterprises), Espita's estates were clearly articulated to the regional and international markets through the production of agroindustrial goods. These goods required a relatively high capitalization of production and division of labor. Moreover, the organization of work was similar to that of the plantations.

While a detailed discussion of these contradictions is not possible here, they may best be understood as a local adaptation to adverse conditions in a peripheral area.[40] The contradictions are similar to those found by Mintz in his study of Cañamelar, Puerto Rico:

> The limited contact between Cañamelar and the rest of Puerto Rico and the world required the local economy to be a substantially self-sufficient one, even though the enterprise was fundamentally capitalistic in its organization, its use of free landless labor, its reckoning of profits, and its market orientation. Thus, we are confronted with a capitalistic enterprise cloaked in a version of manorial tradition and isolation, a typical example of a remarkable nineteenth century plantation form which existed in Puerto Rico and many other locales.[41]

That these entrepreneurs in Espita did not follow model plantation behavior does not mean that they were not primarily capitalist in orientation. On the periphery, where severe limits were imposed on capitalist growth, they utilized a number of strategies to survive and make profits. These included substituting land as partial payment for work, binding workers to the hacienda through combined debts and paternalism, and maintaining diversified production for consumption and sale. Survival also required the planter to assume a variety of roles—landowner, administrator, merchant, lawyer, accountant, and politician.

The Local Planter Class: Politics, Kinship, and Culture

Over and above the economic relationships, the local faction of the planter class maintained its exclusive membership and its control over the local system of production by a variety of means:[42] Planters followed a clear ideology of paternalism in their relationship with "their" peons; they pursued various occupations, including professional ones; they extended their active involvement in politics to the statewide level; and they used their kinship network to consolidate and further their class position.

In the first instance, paternalistic behavior cemented economic relations. Peons were "sons and daughters" of the patrón, who made sure that they were baptized, married, and laid to rest in the Catholic church. He would call a doctor when they were sick and bring them presents at Christmas and on the feast of the patron saint of the hacienda. His acknowledged illegitimate children were raised with his own, and he was the godfather of all other children raised on his hacienda. This pattern of paternalism was reportedly followed even by absentee owner Olegario

Molina, who would periodically visit Actunkú—the wealthiest and most famous of Espita's haciendas.

Education was highly valued: Many planters held professional titles as doctors, lawyers, accountants, engineers, and teachers, which would later facilitate their absorption into the postrevolutionary state bureaucracy. The Peniche family had a reputation for its literary talent and made Espita somewhat of a regional center for theater and cultural events. The family christened the town "The Athens of Yucatán."

In local politics, while the Peniche family continued to dominate the municipal council, other, less-prestigious landowners and merchants were local officeholders during the first decade of the twentieth century. Some of the more powerful planters, particularly in the Peniche family, had either sold their haciendas (to Molina in most cases) and emigrated to Mérida, or had become absentee owners. In either case, several played important roles in state-level politics for the first time. Even less wealthy members of the family, such as Marcos Peniche Navarrete, owner of the small hacienda of Chacabal, had significant influence. A central local figure, he also became jefe político of the District of Espita in 1914 and treasurer general of the state in 1923.[43]

By this period, planters in Espita clearly were allied politically with Olegario Molina and the henequen oligarchy in Mérida. When Molina chose Múñoz Arístegui as his successor to the state governorship (1910–1914), it was the Peniche family that set up a local campaign office in Espita. By contrast, a decade earlier they had supported the regional candidate from Valladolid, Francisco Cantón. In opposition to the larger planters in Espita during the 1910 election, a group of small ranchers, merchants, and teachers formed a local support group for Delio Moreno Cantón, the nephew of Francisco Cantón, who was running against Múñoz Arístegui.[44]

As the economic interdependence of members of the planter class in the east and west grew, so did their political alliances. By 1910, the henequen boom had brought real prosperity to the eastern frontier. The west needed foodstuffs, firewood, and land from the east to expand the henequen economy. The east needed the western market and investment capital. The heightened internal articulation fostered political ties that would persist through the revolutionary period.

Kinship practices furthered politicoeconomic advantages. The general pattern of inheritance in Espita gave one child the major hacienda, with the other siblings receiving smaller properties. The land, however, was not fractionalized. The rest of the children assumed various roles and occupations that served the needs of the hacienda—as administrators or professionals, or as store-owners and merchants selling the hacienda's products. In addition, planters who were relatives often cooperated economically in a number of ways. Some jointly purchased land from those of their kin who wanted to emigrate to Mérida. Others cooperated in processing the harvest. Moreover, they often shared their peon work forces.

Since Espita was too small to support everyone, some siblings emigrated to Mérida. Whether it was a self-conscious policy, an unwritten rule, or simply voluntary, outmigration of family members grew after 1900. This practice enabled families in Espita to develop closer ties with members of their class in the west through intermarriage, as well as through their professional occupations and political activities.

A good case in point is the new generation of the Peniche López family (the offspring of Santiago and José Quirino Peniche, and the great, great grandchildren of Pedro Bernardino Peniche). By the 1890s, Santiago Peniche López had divided his estate among four children: José Isaac, José Caterino, Francisco, and Porfirio. Santiago's brother, José Quirino, left his haciendas to three children: Ignacia, Evaristo, and Josefa. By 1900, the seven Peniche López children owned the most productive haciendas in Espita, including Santa Cruz, Holcah, Kancabá, Santo Domingo, Tekóm, Pom, Yokhóm, and Humuch. For the first time, family members were appointed to district- and state-level political offices. They also, for the first time, married members of their class from the western part of the state. Both Evaristo and Ignacia, for example, married into the wealthy Sauri family from Mérida. Evaristo's son, Alfonso Peniche Sauri, went on to make Santa Cruz the most advanced sugar hacienda in the area, and among the most famous in the state. Alfonso also helped found La Unión Democrática in Espita, the local organization that supported Múñoz Arístegui in the elections of 1910, and he played a significant role in the Porfiriato and the revolutionary period. Ignacia's son, Juan López Peniche, became a lawyer, the administrator of Molina's Hacienda Actunkú, and secretary treasurer of the state under Molina. His own hacienda, Pom, was a major henequen plantation. José Isaac, a lawyer, owned a prosperous hacienda and was the head of the municipal council. In 1898 he was the first native son appointed as jefe político of the District of Espita. Francisco, likewise a planter and lawyer, became a deputy to the State Congress. José Caterino received a judicial appointment in the District of Mérida. Porfirio moved to Mérida to pursue a professional career and sold his land to Molina and Doctor Urbano Góngora, a relative newcomer also from Mérida.

These kinds of close economic, social, and political ties provided unity for the opposition to the revolution when General Alvarado came to Yucatán in 1915.

The Revolution in Espita, 1915–1924

Espiteños recall how "the revolution came to town": General Alvarado entered Espita with sixty soldiers, took a turn about the plaza, and departed, leaving some of his men behind. It was truly a "revolution from without."[45]

Upon hearing that Alvarado would arrive, the local planters had taken their families and hidden in their haciendas. When they later perceived that *El alvaradismo* was not socialism or bolshevism, that it did not destroy their henequen or expropriate their land, planters in Espita, and in the state generally, were forced to reevaluate their position. While the general's social reforms were sweeping and significant, his political and economic policies consistently attacked the elite strata of the planter class while inviting the majority of its members to join in and build a nationalist-oriented, capitalist economy.

In Espita, Alvarado came and went, and the landowners maintained control of the municipal council, their haciendas, and the local economy. Several planters, including Molina and members of the Peniche family, continued to buy land and expand production between 1915 and 1919, and some of the most distinguished of them were called on to join Alvarado's movement. For example, in a letter to Alfonso Peniche Sauri, Alvarado congratulated him on his "progressive attitude" with respect to intensive cultivation and the use of an irrigation system.[46] He then invited Peniche to contribute his knowledge to the recently established government School of Agriculture. The following December, Alvarado approved a license for Peniche to build a *tranvía*, or track, from his hacienda to the train station.[47] And, in February 1916, the government sponsored an agricultural conference in Espita with Hacienda Santa Cruz serving as a model for the application of modern techniques.[48] Similarly, Marcos Peniche Navarrete, a politically active member of the family, became president of the municipal council in 1915. He was assisted by a council of relatives and other local landowners.

Later, Alvarado would marry Laura Manzano Mendoza, daughter of the owner of another local hacienda, San Pedro Chenchilá. Clearly, Alvarado's strategy was to make alliances with members of the planter class to build a modern capitalist economy—one free of Molina's oligarchy. He was not, however, successful in Espita. Local members of the planter class were expedient politically and, when given the opportunity, worked to oust the new regime. They remained loyal to Molina and openly supported Abel Ortiz Argumedo, who led a rebellion against Alvarado in 1915. When that effort failed, they went on to help form the Liberal party, which would lead the political and military fight against the revolution.

Despite his friendly overtures, Alvarado's policies attacked the control of the planter class. He freed the debt peons and took control of the Henequen Market Regulatory Commission. Under Alvarado's new policies—aimed at breaking the control the financial brokers in Mérida exercised over the market—henequen planters had little choice but to sign five-year contracts to sell their crops through the commission.[49] He also heavily taxed henequen, changed the property tax system by placing the heaviest burden on the most affluent, and forced planters to loan large sums of money to the state to finance his reform program.[50] Finally, by enacting prohibition, the Alvarado administration further undermined the remaining cane producers in Espita, who relied in part on the sale of rum for their cash surplus.

Liberation

Freedom for the "slaves" came, apparently, without much fanfare. One ex-peon from a local hacienda recalled that thirty soldiers on horseback arrived at the estate and told the peons that they were free to go; they did not have to submit themselves to the patrón any more. The majority left with their possessions on their backs, headed for town.[51] On another hacienda, peons received the word of liberation from the patrón himself, who told them they were free to go, but that those who stayed would be paid what the government ordered (by military edict, pay had been raised to one and a half pesos per day). In addition, the owner assured them they could continue cultivating milpa on his land. In this instance, many peons stayed.[52]

Overall, however, most peons left. The hacienda population decreased by 72 percent between 1910 and 1921, and almost every hacienda suffered a substantial decline, according to census records.[53] Nevertheless, many planters withstood the impact of liberation, perhaps because most cultivated henequen; with the increased demand for natural fiber brought about by World War I, the market had never been better. However, Alvarado's prohibition policy, combined with liberation, undermined many sugar haciendas. By 1920, a large number had been abandoned, with cultivated fields, processing plants, and machinery left in place.

The threat of socialism became greater when Alvarado left and Yucatán's own Socialist party came to power. In 1917, Carlos Castro Morelos, Socialist party candidate, was elected governor of Yucatán. The Socialist party, reorganized under its militant new president, Felipe Carrillo Puerto, would make land reform a reality, at least for some. By 1918, party membership was estimated at twenty-six thousand. The party's organizing strategy was to found "resistance leagues" (Ligas de Resistencia) in towns and cities throughout the state in order to provide an alternative economic, social, and political institution at the local level, which ex-peons and workers could use as a base of support. This kind of structure was particularly needed as a focal point for ex-peons who descended from several generations and had lived their lives under the control of a patrón.

In Espita, the local league was formed when Alvarado came to the founding meeting in 1918.[54] Within a short time, membership reached one thousand and included ex-peons, workers, artisans, teachers, and small shop and property owners. Ex-members recall their "red card," with its organizational motto: Land and Liberty. To them, that was socialism. The league became the center of activity in town, a place where members could meet, discuss their problems, and find out what was going on throughout the state. It also was a place where members were taught about socialism. The first major task of the league was to apply for ejidos, land that would be given out by the state under the new Agrarian Reform Law. The ejido application was completed on August 7, 1918. Subsequently, the Agrarian Commission sent a representative to Espita to set up a local executive commission to survey land for the ejido. The commission was made up of three Maya: Fernando Tuz, Marcelino Yan, and José Pilar Puc.[55]

Local leadership of the league was primarily in the hands of members of the middle class, and two of the strongest leaders were descendants of the Peniche family. Gonzalo Peniche Osorio was the son of the former administrator of the haciendas of Opná and Poxil. His brother-in-law was Marcos Peniche Navarrete, local Liberal party leader. Gonzalo Peniche would become a personal friend of Carrillo Puerto and deputy to the State Legislature in 1918 and 1921 during the terms of the Socialist party administration. The second family member was José J. Peniche, an elementary school teacher who became a member of the First Directorate Board of the Socialist party.[56]

For their part, planters worked through two statewide organizations to oppose the Socialist party's government: the Association of Henequen Planters and the Liberal party. The first was founded in 1919 to stop the threat of land reform and to eliminate the Henequen Market Regulatory Commission. Henequen planters strongly opposed state control of the market and worked for deregulation. One member of the Peniche family, José Concepción Peniche López, became president of the association in 1919; during that same year, he was president of the Henequen Market Regulatory Commission. His relative, Juan López Peniche (former treasurer general under Molina), was the general treasurer for the regulatory commission at the same time.[57] It is unclear from available documents how they gained these positions, or what strategies they used to undermine the commission. However, by July 1919, the regulatory commission was derailed. Planters were allowed to cancel their contracts, and free trade was restored.[58]

At the same time, members of the Peniche family and other local landowners actively supported Mena Brito, Liberal party candidate for governor in 1919. When Mena Brito won, Marcos Peniche Navarrete became a representative to the state Congress and, in Espita, helped implement the "reign of terror," a statewide campaign of violence led by Colonel Zamarripa aimed at undermining support for socialism. Consistent with the new government's policies, Peniche ordered the closure of the league office and the seizure of all firearms. Every house was searched by federal soldiers, and those who refused to give up arms were jailed.[59]

The Liberal party ruled for less than one year, however. Although local landowners continued to obstruct the implementation of reforms, particularly land reform, by legal and extralegal means, almost one-fourth of their land was expropriated by 1921.[60]

Expropriation

The pattern of expropriation in Espita was calculated, but somewhat inconsistent. Five of the largest landowners were targeted (including Molina and Juan López Peniche), but not the five largest landowners nor the most active local leaders of the Liberal party. Marcos Peniche Navarrete, for example, was not affected, although his brother, Pablo, who owned a much larger hacienda, was. With respect to those landholdings that were affected by expropriation, some fundamental rules were followed: First, in each case, 83 percent of the landholding was expropriated (see Table 8.2); second, only land with high vegetation—that is, land that had not been cultivated for years—was taken for the ejido. This policy particu-

Table 8.2 Espita: Expropriation of Hacienda Land, 1921

Owner	Hacienda	Land (in Hectares)	Expropriated Land (in Hectares)	Percentage Affected
Molina	Acabchén	877	733	83.5
Molina	Holcah	3,511	2,933	83.5
Molina	Mahaicáb	4,266	3,565	83.6
Molina	Tamán	1,316	1,100	83.6
Molina	Yokhóm	1,725	1,441	83.6
Francisco Peniche López	Chenkú	1,081	903	83.6
Pablo Peniche	Labchén	426	355	83.4
Navarrete	Chioplé	4,589	3,667	80.0
Juan López	Pom	5,207	4,351	83.6
Peniche	San Andrés	658	550	83.6
Urbano Góngora	Kancabá	2,583	2,158	83.6
Total		26,239	21,760	
Overall Percentage				82.9

Source: Yucatán, Secretaría de la Reforma Agraria, Documents relating to the Acta de Posesión y deslinde del ejido de Espita (Mérida, August 27, 1921).

larly enraged the planters, who argued that they needed this vegetation for fuel and that their operations would fail without it. Third, land already cultivated in cane or henequen was left untouched; fourth, no hacienda buildings or processing plants were expropriated. Finally, all but one landowner was left with at least one thousand hectares of land (the exception retained over five hundred hectares). Molina was permitted to keep five thousand hectares in Espita.[61]

In 1923, Espita's planter class assisted in the last organized attempt to undermine the Socialist party's government by following the de la Huerta uprising. Liberal party members in Espita proclaimed in favor of the de la Huerta movement and supported Ricárdez Broca in the party's effort to reclaim the governorship.[62] While Carrillo Puerto and a small nucleus of supporters attempted to flee via the eastern port of Holbox, Ricárdez Broca assumed control of the state and installed supporters, including members of the Peniche family in Espita, in local and state government positions. On December 19, 1923, Ricárdez Broca sent his military commander to Espita to name Alfonso Peniche Sauri, Carlos Erosa Peniche, and Urbano Góngora to head the three-man municipal council. Once again the resistance league's office was closed, and the Socialists went underground.[63]

In the meantime, Carrillo Puerto and his supporters stopped in Espita on the way to the coast. While Carrillo continued on and was later captured and assassinated, some of his followers stayed behind and were successfully hidden in the hacienda of Marcos Peniche, their longtime enemy. His reward would come in April 1924, after the de la Huerta forces were driven from the state. When the Socialist party returned to power, Marcos Peniche Navarrete was named treasurer general of the state. Gonzalo Peniche Osorio became head of the municipal government. He reconstructed the local resistance league and proclaimed in favor of Alvaro Obregón.[64]

While the system of hacienda production declined in the 1920s, the ejido of Espita became the new productive base for ex-peons and town residents—21,760 hectares of land were granted to 1,088 ejidatarios. Espita's was the fourth-largest ejido in Yucatán; the three largest—Hunucmá, Maxcanú, and Muna—were all located in the western part of the state. These large ejidos contrasted sharply with the majority. Over 70 percent of Yucatán's ejidos were less than five thousand hectares in size, and over 90 percent were less than ten thousand.[65]

Under the terms of the Agrarian Reform Law, the nation retained ownership of the expropriated land. Landless peasants were then given plots with usufruct rights in perpetuity. In Yucatán, most of the land was given for communal, rather than individual, use, thereby providing all members of the ejido equitable access to land for water, firewood, construction materials, and hunting. This policy also made it easier for ejidatarios to continue the practice of slash-and-burn agriculture that was basic to traditional milpa cultivation.

During the decade of the 1920s, then, with the productive relations of the hacienda overturned, Espita's ex-peons generally spent their time cultivating their own milpas and worked on haciendas for wages to complement their subsistence. Local haciendas were regularly short of labor.[66] With an economic foundation based on the ejido, supplemented by hacienda wage work and backed by the resistance league, Espita's ex-peons looked forward to a better life.

By contrast, the combined effect of liberation and land reform dealt a critical blow to the planter class. The end of World War I caused the demand for henequen to return to prewar levels. By 1925, some of the most prosperous estates had ceased functioning. Others, such as Molina's hacienda of Actunkú, worked at half-capacity. By 1930, the grand old sugar hacienda of Espita, Santa Cruz, had discontinued production. The only local landowner who was still operating in the 1930s was Lázaro Peniche Navarrete, a brother of Marcos Peniche. He did so primarily because he had invested huge sums of money to develop the estate in 1920. Since henequen has a twenty-year growing cycle, with commercial harvesting only after the first six years, early abandonment would have meant a serious financial loss. By the mid-1930s, workers at this hacienda were under union contract. The end of the era was symbolized by the transfer of the electric generator from Santa Cruz to Espita in 1928. The people had lighted houses and streets for the first time. The owner, Alfonso Peniche Sauri, died in Espita a broken man.[67]

With the decline of the plantation economy, planters and their families fled to Mérida where they opened small shops or found work as professionals. They tended to congregate in one or two neighborhoods and maintained close family ties. Members of the Peniche López and Peniche Navarrete families, for example, followed this course. After 1920, only 10 percent of the descendants of planters would return to the land even though most held on to their properties through the 1940s and even later. Thirty percent established their own businesses in Mérida, the most successful of which were lumber and furniture stores supplied from their land in Espita. Fifty percent became professionals. Of these, two-thirds were self-employed; another third worked for the government as teachers. As a group, the overwhelming majority were employed by the government in bureaucracies such as the Property Tax Register, CORDEMEX (the state-owned cordage mills), the Banco Agrario, and various secretariats—Agrarian Reform, Public Works, Agriculture, and Education.[68] Thus, while plantation life was destroyed, members of the planter class used their varied skills and education to adapt to the new order.

Conclusion

The case of Espita demonstrates how, in the course of the nineteenth century, a local faction of the ruling class was able to monopolize land and labor sufficiently to extract wealth, accumulate capital, and build a network of profitable agroindustrial enterprises—despite the adverse conditions existing on the Caste War frontier. Proprietors were able to do so by adapting to local conditions and building relatively self-sufficient operations. Development beyond self-sufficiency depended on their ability to harness local land and labor for production in the context of swings in the international political economy of sugar and, later, henequen. In response to the growth of the wheat industry in the United States and, later, to the demand for ropes and cables during World War I, the market for henequen during the late Porfiriato was strong enough that expanding production to such marginal areas as Espita was profitable. Capitalists invested in hitherto-untouched areas, even though in some places the returns might be relatively low. However, unlike hacendados in the monocrop region of the west, eastern producers maintained a diversified productive base and continued to supply basic goods to the monocrop region. Yet, while benefiting from the henequen boom, it was clear that less-profitable estates would be the first to go when the market turned down or when other negative factors intervened.

These "other factors" came unexpectedly. With an imported revolution, there were few early-warning signals of unrest on the estates. The history of Espita is striking for the amount of economic, political, and social change that occurred in the absence of a popular revolt. Why was there no popular revolt? And why did planters not prevent peons from leaving the haciendas or at least put up a better fight? Their actions seem mild compared with the violence that wracked other parts of Mexico and still savages other Latin American countries in this century. Did they see that the elimination of debt peonage was inevitable and foresee a profitable accommodation to a free wage-labor system? This explanation appears likely. In Espita, landowners adjusted to the liberation of the peons, as has been shown, and continued expanding henequen production until 1920 or so. The strength of the market apparently allowed them to make the transition to free wage labor without undermining the system of plantation agriculture. Ex-peons were still dependent on the haciendas for work because the planters still monopolized the land.

The real disruption in the system, and hence in the power of the local planters, came with the 1921 expropriation of land and the formation of the ejido. The planters argued that the plantations would be destroyed if land was expropriated because the system was delicately balanced—they needed large extensions of uncultivated land to allow for the rotation of crops and the collection of firewood. The Socialists expropriated some of the land and the plantations failed.

Yet, more crucial to the planters' demise was the labor question. Even after expropriation, the landowners retained their investments in buildings, equipment, and 150 (later three hundred) hectares of cultivated plants, as well as one thousand hectares of uncultivated land. But, when the haciendas were partitioned, proprietors simultaneously lost control of their dependent work force. This lesser faction of the agroindustrial planter class lacked the capital to pay wages high enough to attract and keep workers. By contrast, Olegario Molina had this capacity and maintained a permanent, free wage-labor force. His hacienda continued production through the 1920s, until the collapse of the henequen market that came with the Great Depression and the introduction of synthetic fibers in the 1930s.

The question arises as to whether or not the Socialists realized that their combination of liberation and land reform would destroy plantation agriculture, at least in this peripheral zone. Would they have gone ahead with the same agrarian program if they had foreseen the consequences? Or, conversely, was it their intention to destroy the plantation economy?

Espita was in many ways the exception to the norm: Reforms worked much better than even the Socialists had envisioned and undermined the private economy more than they had anticipated. If the Socialists had planned to destroy the planter class, the most direct route would have been to confiscate the haciendas outright or, alternatively, seize production of the plantations and turn them into cooperative enterprises. But the Socialists did not attack directly nor seek revenge on the planter class per se. Their land reform policy in Espita was designed essentially to leave the plantations' central operations intact, redistributing only vacant land. In other words, reform sought only to redistribute unused land, giving the majority of the rural population its fair share. As it was, landowners were left with at least five hundred hectares, and in most cases a thousand. Ejidatarios, by contrast, had twenty hectares each. The agrarian reform established a solid base for, on the one hand, the growth of a productive peasantry cultivating the ejido, and, on the other, the emergence of a propertied rural middle class on the remains of old plantations.

A propertied rural middle class, however, did not emerge in the 1920s and 1930s. Espita's planter class fled to Mérida where they became part of the urban middle class. Why did they not stay? From their point of view, they could not rebuild enterprises in any way comparable to the haciendas of the past. The henequen and sugar markets were not as strong as they had been. Moreover, the haciendas relied on a large labor force. Even if the landowners had the money to pay them, few ejidatarios were interested in full-time wage labor. They had their own land and their freedom, and they were organized. Planters such as Lázaro Peniche Navarrete, who stayed in Espita until the mid-1930s, faced labor disputes with a work force that had learned the benefits of collective action.

In addition, after expropriation private land was somewhat splintered, and this pattern of ownership set inherent limits on production. Landowners could have stayed and developed self-sufficient farms or ranches, but they did not. The revolution had a profound psychological effect on both sides. While ejidatarios gained a sense of freedom and control over their future, the planter class was defeated; it had lost its way of life and its base of power. Most planters feared that if they stayed in Espita they would face not only a hostile social and political climate, but further expropriation.[69]

Whatever the outcome for particular actors, in Espita the revolution succeeded in destroying a system of landownership, production, and class relations that had developed over two centuries. It laid the base for a new economic order, but the remains of haciendas left a promise unfulfilled. The emergence of a propertied rural middle class would not begin until the 1940s when the state targeted private land in the east for development of a cattle industry. Today's mixed economy of subsistence corn producers on ejidos and independent ranchers on private estates is an outgrowth of the decisions made in the revolutionary period. From the new economic order a new social and political one has emerged, but one clearly not without its conflicts. The apparent calm belies relations that pit subsistence agriculturalists against ranchers, beef exporters, and the state in an ongoing struggle for control over land, labor, and production in rural Mexico.

9 *Workers Against Socialism? Reassessing the Role of Urban Labor in Yucatecan Revolutionary Politics*

DANIELA SPENSER

In June 1922, some of Yucatán's organized railway workers went on strike. The striking workers belonged to the Liga Obrera de Ferrocarrileros (LOF) and were protesting against their union's underrepresentation in the state-owned United Railways of Yucatán, and its discrimination against them. These workers felt that they were not being treated in the same way as were the workers who belonged to another labor organization, the Liga de Ferrocarrileros Torres y Acosta (LFTA). Indeed, unlike the LOF, LFTA supported the radically reformist government of Felipe Carrillo Puerto and therefore enjoyed better treatment at the hands of Carrillo's administration.

What appeared at first to be a local conflict grew into a major regional one, involving the states of Yucatán, Campeche, and Veracruz. The stevedores and dockworkers from the port of Progreso and the tramway workers from Campeche left their jobs in solidarity with the Yucatecan railwaymen. The Veracruzan workers similarly brought activity to a halt in support of the Yucatecans, causing havoc in Mexico's most important port. The strike lasted ten days and ended with most of labor's grievances seemingly satisfied. The men went back to work.

In December 1923, over half of the Mexican army, led by a cabinet minister, Adolfo de la Huerta, a Sonoran, rebelled against President Obregón. The rebellion rapidly spread throughout the country. In Yucatán, the army, backed by the henequeneros, overthrew Carrillo Puerto's radical government. The same workers, who a year earlier had struck the state-owned railway company, now helped to finance and provision the rebel army.

Labor's role in Yucatecan revolutionary politics raises a series of perplexing questions: Why did the workers rebel against a radically reformist government that was presumably their ally? Why did the conflict reach such proportions that it led to the workers' alliance with their class opponents? What caused the urban workers to engage in a fratricidal battle among themselves? And, finally, why did the urban working class never ally itself with the rural working population? The causes and consequences of the workers' actions may be reconstructed from available, albeit fragmentary, sources.

The favorable position of urban workers in Yucatán's export-oriented economy had two interrelated consequences: First, skilled workers in the two major cities—Mérida and Progreso—were in great demand and thus were able to muster their class organizations to negotiate the conditions of employment on their own terms; second, in view of the dramatically expanding volume of henequen exports and imports of foodstuffs, agricultural implements, and luxury goods throughout the Porfiriato, Yucatecan henequen producers and merchants found it in their best interests to establish a viable relationship with the workers. The response of employers to workers' organized actions was generally to meet their demands. Urban workers' strategic position within the henequen industry, the need for their skills and cooperation in ensuring the smooth handling of goods leaving and entering the peninsula, their freedom to quit a job and go elsewhere, gave them confidence and leverage vis-à-vis their employers. Skilled labor leaders emerged who proved themselves capable of representing the workers' interests, long before the state began encouraging the creation of unions.

The labor laws enforced by Salvador Alvarado in Yucatán after 1915 acknowledged the existing labor unions, generally strengthened the labor movement, and created new unions. However, as the state assumed increasingly monopolistic control of the henequen industry, it also extended its domination over the labor movement. The old unions resented this encroachment on their independence, and the labor movement split. One group was willing to accept patronage by the state in return for participation in the administration, while another clung tenaciously to its hard-earned independence.

Finally, the postwar price of henequen plummeted and new producers began to compete with Yucatán in the world market. The Socialist party government led by Carrillo Puerto required workers and peasants to cooperate, even at the cost of economic sacrifice, in order to get the party's radical reform program under way and to defend the revolution against growing opposition. But, while the campesinos were willing to back Felipe Carrillo Puerto, who offered them land, urban labor refused to bear the brunt of the economic crisis. In the end, the discontented workers arrived at an alliance with the army and the capitalists, against their fellow workers, Carrillo's government, and, indirectly, against the peasant resistance leagues.

Urban Labor in the Henequen Economy

As Allen Wells shows in Chapter 5 of this book, henequen had come to dominate the northwestern fields of the Yucatán Peninsula. Land that previously had been producing corn or serving as livestock pasture was now covered uniformly with the grayish agave. The Yucatecan elite had suitable land and experience in cultivating and processing henequen but lacked the capital to cultivate it in the quantities demanded by the North American market. North American interests—most notably International Harvester Company—soon found it expedient to advance the producers the necessary capital. Loans were funneled to planters through local casas exportadoras. In return, these local houses apparently saw to it that the producers delivered their fiber at prices stipulated by the North American companies. Nevertheless, such indirect foreign control left certain key means of production in the hands of Yucatecans—the henequen plantations, railroads, shipping lines, warehouses, and dock works.[1]

The region's monocrop economy soared throughout the Porfiriato. From forty thousand bales in 1875 (one bale equals 350 pounds), by 1914 production had reached six hundred thousand bales.[2] No doubt in part owing to manipulation by North American interests and Yucatecan export houses, henequen prices were subject to severe fluctuations.[3] Nevertheless, large planters still made a tidy profit, and travelers to Yucatán at the turn of the century described the wealth and modernity they saw there.

One consequence of the henequen boom was the expansion of the regional communications and transportation network. By 1890 the region had the most extensive railway network in the country. Eight hundred kilometers of main lines, which were connected to another six hundred kilometers of secondary ones, linked plantations with Mérida and the port of Progreso. In addition, over a thousand kilometers of movable Decauville tram tracks served transportation needs within individual haciendas. However, geared as it was for export production, this network failed to provide a comprehensive system of internal communication among the various pueblos and haciendas, which remained isolated from the economic centers and from each other.[4]

As distinct from the rest of the state, Mérida and Progreso prospered. To the casual visitor, Mérida made a majestic impression: Its streets were paved and lit by night, and it was said that their surface was "as smooth as glass, as clean as marble." The palatial houses of the planter oligarchs also dazzled passersby. Yet, although henequen profits went into the building of private mansions, capital was also invested in schools and other public works. Modern tramways, for example, provided the city's transport. The port of Progreso also flourished, becoming the hub of the region's commercial transactions, second only in volume of shipments to the more-established, national port of Veracruz. Wealthy meridanos built resort houses in Progreso. Henequeneros also invested in the building of warehouses, a new wharf, a customs building, and a variety of commission, brokerage, and trading houses.[5]

Of course, this prosperity did not extend to all; the vast majority of the population still lived in poverty. Moreover, there was an increasing gap between the urban and the rural working population. In contrast to the lot of hacienda laborers, the integration of railway, tramway, and port workers into the henequen economy generally represented an improvement in their occupation and well-being. Town-based artisans became skilled workers in cities that had some urban amenities, such as schools and electricity, and where life in the barrios lent itself to the creation of mutual-help societies.[6]

Our knowledge of the urban worker's origins and his life in Mérida and Progreso at the turn of the century is incomplete. We do not know the proportions of workers who were born in the cities or who migrated there from the Yucatecan countryside or from other parts of the nation (or abroad). It is likely that many of the workers came from other towns in the Yucatán Peninsula and that some immigrated from Cuba. For migrants, life in the cities would have represented a new start: a salary for some; improvement in a career as a tinsmith, mechanic, or engine-driver for others. For Cubans, Yucatán also would have been a haven from the turbulence that the 1898 war for independence from Spain created in their homeland.[7] All in all, by 1900 the urban work force was about two thousand strong.

We know next to nothing about the workers' family life or about the labor processes on the railways and the docks. Further, we can only speculate about laborers' ideological makeup. But, we can get an idea of workers' mentalities from their participation in state politics, their labor organizations, and the strikes and actions these organizations mounted in the period following the formation of urban labor as a class.

Broadly speaking, two trends of scholarship can be distinguished in the study of the history of workers' ideology prior to the outbreak of the Mexican Revolution. One emphasizes the importance of anarchism and anarchosyndicalism in the formation of the Mexican labor movement, and the influence of foreign, anarchist militants in the movement's earliest stages, particularly the Spanish and the North American Industrial Workers of the World. This trend also underscores the workers' anticapitalist and patriotic sentiments, which would later become part of the Mexican Revolution.[8]

The other trend plays down anarchist influence. Instead, it elaborates the idea—by and large—that, before the revolution, Mexican workers tended to endorse the capitalist principle that production should be lucrative and expansive. According to this argument, workers shared the bourgeoisie's confidence in material progress, liberty, constitutional democracy, universal education, and moral uplift. Workers' susceptibility to the positive aspects of Mexico's nascent capitalism ultimately tempered their rebelliousness.[9]

Current research on Yucatecan labor fails to provide evidence that would conclusively support one position to the exclusion of the other. For the moment, it can be said that both tendencies were present: Patron-client dynamics did often characterize relations between Yucatecan capitalists and workers; nevertheless, anarchism also seems to have influenced the labor movement.

There is little evidence of the presence of anarchists in Yucatán, but it is reasonable to assume that Progreso, like the other gulf cities of Veracruz and Tamaulipas, was also a port of entry and venue of anarchist militancy in the early years of the century. In 1907, for instance, the Yucatecan government informed Porfirio Díaz that it had deported two anarchist journalists. According to Marjorie Ruth Clark, Yucatán's intellectually vibrant milieu and the embryonic opposition that was forming against the oligarchy on the eve of the Mexican Revolution attracted the Spanish anarchist José Zaldívar.[10]

It is difficult to gauge the intensity and scope of the anarchists' influence in the region. But, it is a fact that Yucatecan artisans, railway and port workers were actively founding unions between 1907 and 1911, the period that coincided with the greatest alleged anarchist presence in the peninsula. Once organized, these unions pressed the workers' demands of higher wages and shorter working hours. Usually, they succeeded in achieving their goals. In 1907 the different railway companies, founded originally by several henequen magnates, merged into the United Railways of Yucatán, possibly to reduce costs. The three hundred affected workers formed a union, the Unión Obrera de los Ferrocarriles de Yucatán, in order to oppose a wage cut that management was trying to impose. The railway workers staged a strike—the classic anarchist tactic—in pursuit of higher wages, an eight-hour workday, and a collective agreement. The company satisfied the first demand but refused to grant the other two.

In addition, in 1909 the Unión Obrera, together with other urban syndicates that had come into existence, organized the Casa del Trabajo, a labor center that sought to educate workers in methods of union organization and labor disputes. The deal the railway workers struck with the company impressed white collar workers, who followed their example and founded the Alianza Mutualista de Empleados de Ferrocarril in 1909. The white collar workers demanded the same working conditions that the company had granted to manual workers. Moreover, by 1909 the port workers from Progreso had organized their own dockworkers' union, the Unión de Obreros Marítimos. This organizing activity was popularized and supported by labor as well as by liberal newspapers.[11]

If, as seems likely, anarchism sank roots into Yucatecan soil, how was labor activity reconciled with management control? In other parts of Mexico, labor militancy came up against bloody repressions,[12] yet, as far as we know, force was not used against the workers in Yucatán. Does this mean that Yucatecan bosses and trading-firm managers were benevolent employers, or does it point to the workers' bargaining strength and capacity to negotiate labor conditions with their employers?

There are indications of patron-client relationships between urban workers and their employers in Yucatán. Research on the workers' favorite pastime, baseball, suggests that the oligarchy regarded the sponsorship of baseball teams as a tactic for "co-opting or diffusing dissent in Yucatán's factories, railroad yards, and hacienda communities."[13] However, stronger than the case for a patron-client relationship between the workers and the oligarchy is the argument that can be made for an incipient alliance between labor and the expanding middle strata of Yucatecan society. Simply put, the economic, social, and, eventually, political divisions in late Porfirian Yucatán cut less across rigid capitalist-anticapitalist, labor-capital lines than across the expanding divide that separated the oligarchy and its international partners from the remainder of local society. The alliance that labor struck with the middle classes may have exerted some influence on the treatment the workers received as employees. On the other hand, the labor market favored skilled urban workers, which enhanced their bargaining power and autonomy in the workplace.[14]

Fragmentary as available data are, it is not clear how deeply the workers were affected by the decline in fiber prices after International Harvester began to collaborate in earnest with Olegario Molina in 1902. Nor can we easily assess the relationship between the subsequent deterioration in the workers' economic conditions and unionization activities. During the first decade of the twentieth century, inflation exacerbated workers' poor living conditions. They reacted by defending their wages, but it was the property-owning middle classes, gradually losing out to the planter oligarchy, who became most vociferous in their opposition. By 1909 groups of workers had begun to join them in a loosely organized antioligarchical campaign.

That same year, *antirreeleccionismo*, the opposition to President Porfirio Díaz's bid for reelection, became a nationwide phenomenon. The dictator's political longevity meant the perpetual reappointment of his henchmen as government ministers and state governors. Notwithstanding the generalized dissatisfaction with Díaz and his governing clique, opposing groups disagreed on who should replace them. Some believed that by replacing the aging president, the political system would be rejuvenated; others upheld the necessity of profound political and social change.

The national dilemma was replicated in Yucatán. There, the opposition to the Porfirian *molinista* faction was divided between those favoring José María Pino Suárez, a liberal candidate for the post of governor, and those supporting Delio Moreno Cantón, the conservatives' choice. Both candidates rallied worker, peasant, and middle-class support.[15]

Pino Suárez was a close associate of Francisco I. Madero, a liberal landowner from northern Mexico. Madero's family belonged to that segment of the Mexican elite that had not been admitted to the inner circles of Porfirian power. In spite of the fact that his original rallying cry was "Sufragio libre, no reelección" (a free vote, no reelection), Madero recognized the explosive popular mood and broadened his program to recognize the validity of such popular demands as land reform and the rights of urban workers. It was not surprising, therefore, that Madero counted on broad popular support.[16] In Mexico as a whole, and in Yucatán in particular, urban workers were by and large *maderistas*.

Unlike Pino Suárez, who was born in Tabasco, Moreno Cantón belonged to an old and established Yucatecan family with good social repute. Because of his regional roots, Moreno Cantón attracted a number of local popular leaders from the interior of the peninsula, including Felipe Carrillo Puerto from Motul, Pedro Crespo and Juan Campos from Temax, Elías Rivero from Peto, and Feliciano Canul Reyes from Hunucmá.[17]

Nevertheless, Yucatán's rather loose maderista coalition proved too weak to prevent the molinistas from imposing their candidate, Enrique Múñoz Arístegui, as governor. That, and the harassment of the opposition leaders that followed, radicalized peasant leaders in the countryside and broadened the urban labor movement. By 1913 Yucatecan railway and port workers were maintaining important political connections with powerful labor unions in Veracruz. The assassination of President Francisco I. Madero and his vice-president, Pino Suárez, by General Victoriano Huerta, and the subsequent imposition of military rule in Yucatán postponed the arrival of the revolution until Salvador Alvarado introduced it from without in March 1915. In the process, Alvarado would fan the existing regional discontents.[18]

Salvador Alvarado's Labor Program: Alliances and Discords

Alvarado's nationalist, antioligarchical stance prompted him to implement far-reaching economic and social reforms that had a real bearing on Yucatán's political structure. He eliminated the marketing arrangements that had sustained International Harvester's empire in Yucatán. From then on, the Yucatecan government, through its Henequen Market Regulating Commission, was the sole arbiter of price and export quotas for henequen. The government also took over United Railways and acquired a fleet of cargo ships to free Yucatecan exports and imports from foreign, monopolistic control. Alvarado could take such bold steps thanks to the increased demand for henequen during World War I. The price of fiber almost quadrupled, rising from 13.2 cents per kilogram in 1915 to 50.6 cents in 1918.[19]

The profit derived from the seller's market for henequen allowed Alvarado to distribute the "green ore's" wealth more equitably among the population: Money was funneled into fiber production and improved wages for hacienda peons and workers in urban shops, as well as into Alvarado's enlarged bureaucracy. Meanwhile, schools and libraries were built across the state, and labor, educational, and feminist congresses were organized.[20]

One of Alvarado's major social reforms was the promulgation of a radical labor law that heralded Article 123 of the 1917 Mexican Constitution. The Yucatecan labor law responded to the workers' traditional demands regarding wages and hours, working conditions, child labor, accident compensation, and collective bargaining agreements. It also granted the right to strike, created a Department of Labor and labor tribunals, and supported societies of mutual help and workers' unions. Under Alvarado's protection, "urban workers successfully began to press wage demands on employers, utilizing the new tribunals as well as their right to strike."[21]

In order to carry out such radical economic and social programs, Alvarado sought to create a coalition with the military, the middle strata, the henequen bourgeoisie, and a variety of rural and urban labor leaders. If this multiclass coalition were to endure, the general recognized, it would have to be institutionalized.[22]

Even though Alvarado endorsed the creation of new labor unions and recognized the old ones, he expected their leaders to collaborate with his government and tie their organizations to his administration. Alvarado rewarded their loyalty by entrusting important positions and tasks to Yucatecan labor leaders. For instance, a longtime railway worker, Carlos Castro Morales, who had distinguished himself as a union leader, became the director of the state railway company. The general recognized Felipe Carrillo Puerto's leadership of the rural Mayan population in and around his native Motul. Like other local chiefs, Carrillo Puerto became a "propaganda agent" and was dispatched into the countryside to organize the rural population under the banner of the revolution.[23]

Alvarado also invited labor leaders from Mexico City to Yucatán to help organize a new type of labor movement. These leaders belonged to the Casa del Obrero Mundial (COM), which had been founded in 1912 by Mexican and Spanish anarchists as a meeting place where workers might exchange organizational ideas and experiences. Originally, the COM avoided participation in national political life, in part out of anarchist conviction and in part for fear of repression. In May 1914 Victoriano Huerta closed the COM and persecuted its leaders as part of a general crackdown on the labor movement, but when Huerta was ousted from power later that year the COM was revived. Venustiano Carranza stood at the helm of the revolutionary movement, and his inclination to sanction social reforms impressed the previously defeated workers. In February 1915 COM leaders signed a pact with Carranza and the Constitutionalists to defend the revolution. As a result, Carranza recognized the COM as the representative body of the national labor movement.[24]

This was the COM Alvarado brought to Yucatán. The reforms the COM stood for were incorporated into the state labor law. Further, through the COM Alvarado expected the workers to recognize the expanded role of the state as the supreme arbiter of social and political matters, and as an impartial mediator between the forces of labor and capital. The Department of Labor and the tribunals of conciliation were to institutionalize this policy.[25]

Not all Yucatecan workers joined the COM. The new labor unions were created under its umbrella; the old ones, however, were reluctant to accept the state's authority over them and its arbitration in labor matters. After all, these unions had proved their capacity successfully to look after their own needs without the state's patronage. Alvarado saw things differently and barred labor leaders who did not join the COM from participating in decision-making that concerned the workers. This was the case for the Unión Obrera de Ferrocarriles. Because it refused to join the COM, the COM representative committee excluded it from the convention at which candidates for the labor tribunals were to be selected.[26]

In April 1916 Alvarado decided to close the Yucatecan branch of the COM. According to the available evidence, from which, unfortunately, we are not able to reconstruct the full story, several unions threatened to stage a strike. Alvarado considered such an independent step next to sedition, and he retaliated. Although Alvarado had sanctioned strikes, he nevertheless favored mutual-help and cooperative labor associations and viewed strikes as the ultimate weapon, to be used only when arbitration failed. It seems clear that Alvarado did not see a good reason for workers to strike when the state-directed economy was making progress. However, the workers considered closing the COM an arbitrary measure. It was at this point that some workers from the railway and port labor unions turned their backs on Alvarado.[27]

There is no doubt that the social reforms Alvarado implemented made a radical change in the lives of many Yucatecans. The general's agenda of modernization and "bourgeois reform" registered some impressive triumphs. Alvarado freed the peons from bondage and oppression, canceling their debts. Indeed, campesinos remember Alvarado to this day as the man who brought them *liberación*.[28] The dissenting urban workers, on the other hand, represented a small minority among Yucatecan laborers. However, because of their strategic position within the henequen production process and the support they could summon from labor organizations beyond the state's boundaries, they were able to influence Alvarado's reform project. He tried to integrate their organizations into his master plan but in a manner that usurped the workers' autonomy; one such organization was the Partido Socialista Obrero (PSO).

Until now, the literature dealing with this period has suggested that Alvarado was responsible for creating the PSO.[29] Little attention has been given to a different explanation of the party's origin, documented by one of its founders, Ramón Espadas y Aguilar.[30] According to this insider account, the PSO was established by a group of workers, artisans, and teachers at the time of Mérida's 1916 mayoral election. Originally, the group emerged from the rank and file who had sworn allegiance to Pino Suárez, the candidate for governor in 1909. According to Espadas y Aguilar, its members shared a common ideological platform: "We liked to read and study books that came from Spain; the majority were translations that dealt with anarchist, syndicalist and anarchosyndicalist doctrines. Our struggle was inspired by Spaniards who had emigrated from Spain because of their persecutions by the dominant authorities. Several of the Spaniards settled down as book-dealers; they had started as traveling salesmen [who] imported books such as Karl Marx's *Capital*. This book in particular attracted us: it consisted of three volumes."[31]

Espadas y Aguilar calls our attention to the fact that he and his colleagues were "true socialists," as distinct from leaders such as Carlos Castro Morales or Felipe Carrillo Puerto, who in 1909 had backed the conservative Delio Moreno Cantón. In 1916, the political differences that in 1909 had pitted one group of workers against another had been altered. All endorsed Alvarado's reforms, but some feared that his multiclass coalition might shift too far to the right and jeopardize the future of the revolution. To strengthen their position and influence, these socialists galvanized their meager forces into what they called a workers' party.

Among the PSO executive committee members was Rafael Gamboa, a barber, who was also known as "Ravachol," an allusion to the bold French anarchist who had had five murders to his credit, had blown up the homes of magistrates, and, in 1892, had been sent to the guillotine.[32] Also on the executive committee were railway worker Gonzalo Luis Heredia, journalist Alvaro Rivera, José Catalá, a pharmacist originally from Spain, and José Jesús Peniche and Espadas y Aguilar, who were teachers.[33]

The PSO seemed to have had no formal platform, other than to endorse most of the government's reforms. Therefore, it was easy for Alvarado and his closest labor associates to give the fledgling organization a program and gradually use it as a political arm of the state administration. Espadas y Aguilar later wrote that he was aware of changes, with which he did not agree, taking place in the orientation and leadership of the party, but he was unable to prevent them. For instance, in 1917 Carlos Castro Morales became the PSO president and a year later was replaced by Felipe Carrillo Puerto. Castro Morales, an Alvarado protégé, held the high administrative post of director of the United Railways of Yucatán. He later became the general's handpicked successor as governor. Felipe Carrillo Puerto, we have seen, distinguished himself as a peasant leader and propaganda agent for Alvarado. When he became the party's president, he changed its name to the Socialist Party of Yucatán.[34] The change of name reflected the change in the composition of its membership; under the new leadership, the party was broadened to include the rural population, which was organized in resistance leagues.

As in the case of the closing of the COM, these changes in the leadership and orientation of the Socialist party were seen as conspiracies by Alvarado and his closest allies against the original objective of the party: to support but also to remain critical of state policy.[35] The ease with which Alvarado was able to incorporate the Socialist party into his administration—to the extent that it has even gone down in history as his creation—demonstrates that at its founding the party lacked an independent program and a leadership strong enough to withstand the interference of a state that claimed, with good reason, to represent the popular masses.

Between its founding in 1916 and Felipe Carrillo Puerto's convening in 1918 of a statewide Socialist congress in his hometown of Motul, the party increased its membership as well as its sphere of influence. Only the recalcitrant LOF and the Federación Obrera del Puerto de Progreso remained outside the state coalition and party membership.

From Economic Crisis to Political Catastrophe

After three years of unprecedented boom, the price of henequen plummeted at the end of the war in 1918. The world market was glutted, fiber exports came to a temporary halt, and state revenues began a steady decline. In 1919 Yucatán received $37,581,495 from 141,414 tons of exported henequen; by 1922 income had fallen to $6,192,557, and henequen exports to 63,979 tons.[36]

The entire Yucatecan economy suffered as a result of the henequen crisis. As demand for henequen diminished, the state government lost control over the market. Yucatán had accumulated enormous stocks (623,576 bales in 1918), which it now was unable to sell.[37] Railway transport was paralyzed, as three-quarters of the freight cars, loaded with henequen, were held up in Progreso. The state government's inability to deal with the chaos triggered increases in the prices of consumer goods. The Henequen Market Regulating Commission quickly became superfluous. The Ministry of the Treasury dissolved it, confiscated the fleet of freighters that Alvarado had acquired, and applied pressure on Castro Morales's government to free the market of all state control. When Alvaro Obregón became the president of Mexico at the end of 1920, the federal government took the henequen business into its own hands.[38]

The poor economic situation played havoc with the labor market. A number of henequen haciendas ceased production or greatly reduced their output, which increased unemployment. To make matters worse, Alvarado had brought some twenty-one thousand field hands from other parts of the country to Yucatán during the height of the boom. Now, while local peons were desperate to find a piece of land to eke out a living, the imported contract workers were anxious to leave the peninsula. Many drifted into the cities, expecting to find a job while waiting for a steamship. From the letters exchanged between the migrant workers and the authorities in Progreso, Veracruz, and Mexico City, it is not clear how many of these enganchados were able to find their way back home. No institution was prepared to assume responsibility for the transportation expenses of the contract workers,[39] and, as a result, many stayed in Yucatán, creating something of an unskilled, reserve labor army.

The rural population reacted to the economic crisis by demanding land; wages from work on the henequen plantations proved insufficient and many plantations were idle. Transport labor and dockworkers, on the other hand, defended their wages, even though the local economy was suffering from a deep recession. In June 1918, for instance, the hauling firms in Progreso wanted to lower transport costs and employ the nonunion workers roaming the port in search of odd jobs. The organized workers (*carretilleros*) would have none of this, and the haulers were forced to pay the rates the workers demanded. This provoked an outcry from business. The Yucatecan Chamber of Commerce argued that, in view of the depressed economic situation, the workers' demand for high rates was unreasonable. The henequeneros, in turn, threatened that they would transfer the transport costs to their field laborers through lower wages, while retailers threatened to raise the price of consumer goods. Further discontent reached the central government from eight thousand nonunionized workers: They complained against the Unión Obrera de Ferrocarriles for not permitting them to work.[40]

The economic crisis was accompanied by political uncertainty. In 1918 Salvador Alvarado left Yucatán on President Carranza's orders. As the economy was collapsing Alvarado's governing coalition crumbled. Carlos Castro Morales remained Yucatán's governor, but he was under heavy pressure from the henequeneros and the central government to abandon the government's "socialist" policies. The planters lobbied Mexico City to make the Yucatecan government relinquish all control over the henequen market; they succeeded but matters did not stop there. They also demanded the removal of prominent Socialist party members from the government and the extinction of the entire popular movement. In Yucatán as well as in other parts of Mexico, terror and persecution was rampant throughout most of 1919. In March, Emiliano Zapata was assassinated; Felipe Ángeles, the most able of Villa's generals, was killed by Carranza's troops in November.[41] To avoid a similar fate, Felipe Carrillo Puerto left Yucatán and temporarily joined the zapatistas in Morelos. The popular movement in Yucatán, although in a state of disarray, was never extinguished; when Felipe Carrillo Puerto returned to the peninsula in the middle of 1920, he was able to revive the dormant resistance leagues. Venustiano Carranza was assassinated in March 1920 and was succeeded by Alvaro Obregón. Carrillo Puerto pledged his support to the triumphant faction of the Mexican "revolutionary family" and set about restoring a vigorous popular movement that might promote a variety of radical social reforms.[42]

Carrillo Puerto belonged to a different political culture than did Salvador Alvarado: Yucatán was his homeland and Maya his second language. Whereas Alvarado was inspired by the writings of utopian socialists and moral reformers, Carrillo Puerto met the envoy of the Communist International during his forced exile in Mexico City in 1919. Indeed, for a few months that year, Carrillo was regarded as a member of the Latin American Bureau of the Third International.[43] His brief stay among the zapatistas, who fought relentlessly for the restoration of lands that peasants had lost to the sugar planters, also made a deep impression on him.

On his return to Yucatán, Carrillo Puerto plunged himself into the political struggle to wrest the state government from the Liberal party of the hacendados. Once this had been achieved in the 1921 elections, Carrillo Puerto set out to reorganize his administration along much the same lines as those of his predecessor. Yet, unlike Alvarado, Carrillo Puerto had to navigate the shoals of a stricken Yucatecan economy.

At the end of 1920 the Yucatecan government admitted that it had lost the capacity to deal with the state's bleak economic situation; it let the federal government take charge of financing henequen production and of doing business with its foreign buyers and creditors. The federal government did not succeed in selling significant amounts of henequen, nor did it make available new credits for producers. Finally, all parties agreed to let the yucatecos resume responsibility for the henequen industry.[44]

Shortly after they had gained the upper hand in the state administration in 1921, Carrillo and other radical reformers in the Socialist party sought to reorganize the henequen export agency that Alvarado had created and Carranza had shut down. After being in business for a year, Carrillo's Commission for Henequen Export reported a modest recovery in the price of fiber and the acquisition of new lines of credit from North American banks. The commission also managed to reduce the stocks that it had inherited from its predecessor, which had depressed the price below production costs.[45]

Once the economic and political turmoil of the previous years had subsided, Carrillo Puerto and his aides attempted to incorporate the ligas de resistencia and the labor unions into the government's radical reform program. Carrillo Puerto's major goal was land reform: Land lost to the henequen barons was to be restored to the villages, and properties of abandoned or unproductive haciendas might eventually be expropriated. Distributing henequen land would not be sufficient; the economically strapped government could not guarantee campesinos the needed agricultural implements and working capital. Consequently, much of the distributed land was monte, which was planted in corn to feed the population or, in the southeast, in sugarcane, which was cultivated cooperatively.[46] By national standards, Carrillo Puerto's land reform was impressive. During 1922–1923 his administration distributed 438,866 hectares to 22,525 peasants.[47]

Even though land was distributed, life and production in the countryside were bedeviled by numerous conflicts between campesinos and landowners, and between neighboring villages. These conflicts were due to a shortage of resources for cultivation and often to a lack of experience in the management of cooperatives. Simply put, in such a short time, land distribution could not be accompanied by a restructuring of political and socioeconomic relationships. Instead, "the programs of the revolutionary regime and the formal administrative apparatus created to implement them often used and were used by local power brokers to consolidate and legitimize informal control."[48] Carrillo Puerto was often obliged to ally himself with these traditional brokers and caciques, many of whom joined the Socialist party bandwagon to seek new opportunities denied them by previous regimes. Unfortunately, Carrillo Puerto could not assume responsibility for the state administration and also supervise the political education of the masses that he himself espoused.[49] The power brokers on whom he relied for political control were not the most appropriate vehicles for conveying the socialist ideology that Carrillo Puerto wanted disseminated in resistance leagues in the farthest corners of the state, and beyond. Indeed, Carrillo Puerto attempted to enlist the support of the masses in neighboring states by extending his party's area of influence to Campeche, Tabasco, and Chiapas. In 1921 the party was renamed the Socialist Party of the Southeast to reflect this goal. However, in most parts of the peninsula, with the exception of Mérida and its neighboring towns, revolutionary fervor remained shallow.[50]

Thus, in spite of the economic crisis of the early 1920s, Carrillo Puerto's government had something to offer to the peasants and largely satisfied their craving for land. What did it have to offer to the urban workers? Did they perceive the land reform and the state's policy to stimulate corn production at the expense of henequen as a threat to their jobs? Higher production and exportation of henequen was in the workers' interest. On the other hand, Carrillo Puerto understood the dangers of monocrop production. To promote diversification, he encouraged the cultivation of corn and sugarcane rather than henequen on the land distributed to the peasants. Could this have caused the workers to realize that their interests were on a collision course with those of the peasants?

During the early part of 1921, the government sought to reduce the state-owned railway employees' wages and hours in order to be able to lower freight and transport costs. Workers from the Unión Obrera de Ferrocarrileros rejected the wage cuts. Carrillo Puerto criticized them for not seeing the larger implications of the sacrifice asked of them, for setting their "bread-and-butter" interests above those of the state. Then, as part of his political campaign to enlist the support of the working population for the forthcoming gubernatorial elections, Carrillo Puerto sponsored the creation of a parallel labor union, the LFTA. This rival union was made up of both blue and white collar workers who had accepted the company's cuts in wages and working hours. In short order, the United Railways of Yucatán signed a collective agreement with the new union.[51] Some of its workers had belonged to the Unión Obrera, which changed its name to the Liga Obrera de Ferrocarrileros (LOF).

What were the workers' motivations for leaving one union and joining another? What was the substance of the workers' split within the old railway union? Did the new union offer job opportunities, however limited, to unemployed workers? We do not have sufficient internal data to answer these questions definitely, but we do know from the agreement between the LFTA and the railway company that the formation of another union benefited one group of workers to the detriment of the other. Moreover, the collective agreement made the workers of the LOF feel that they had been grievously wronged.

The development of the conflict among the workers, and between the LOF and the state, can be examined using the contemporary account of

Juan Rico.[52] Rico was not an impartial observer: A labor leader himself, he belonged to the central government–sponsored Confederación Regional de Obreros Mexicanos (CROM), the most important national labor organization. As a member of CROM, Rico favored the Yucatecan government, which was a staunch supporter of the national regime, and he was critical of "black sheep" within the labor movement, as independent unions were regarded by the CROM. Juan Rico was sent to Yucatán at the beginning of 1922 to report on the evolution of the conflict and to prevent the outbreak of a strike, which the CROM feared would spread beyond the state's boundaries.[53]

Rico interviewed leaders from both unions, as well as state officials. He then reported to CROM headquarters in the capital that the LOF, the old union that consisted of about three hundred workers, was campaigning for the same working conditions the railway company had offered to the LFTA, which by then had become the majority union.[54] The LOF also had become vulnerable because it had lost important labor leaders: Some had joined Alvarado's coalition in 1915 and, subsequently, his Socialist Party of Mexico; others had become members of Carrillo Puerto's Socialist party.

According to Juan Rico, the LOF derived strength not so much from its rank and file as from its alliance with the powerful, well-organized Federación Obrera del Puerto de Progreso. He reported that the federation was "a complete organization, which has shown vigor on a number of occasions. As an instrument of the workers it has reached the summit; it cannot go any higher." No company had been able to force the federation to its knees; its workers had never been defeated. In order to cushion the impact of the fall in the price of fiber, all of the union's workers and employees—ferrymen, seamen, stokers, watchmen, fishermen, inspectors, dockworkers, wheelbarrow pushers, customs employees, carpenters, baggage crews—rotated shifts to keep everyone employed. Nonunionized workers were kept out. Yucatán's volume of production and exportation realistically provided enough work for no more than five hundred laborers, yet two thousand workers were employed in Progreso and the wages were distributed among all of them. "No wholesaler, with any quantity of goods to sell, discusses the price of hauling packages. He pays up without saying a word, for if he says anything [there is] a boycott." Resigned to the situation, the wholesalers typically did not protest but added the sums that the federation charged to the price of the goods they sold to retailers.[55] This is precisely what the government was trying to prevent in railway transport when it created the LFTA.

It was from this perspective that the powerful Progreso federation alerted other labor organizations in Campeche, Veracruz, and the entire gulf region about the plight of its aggrieved ally, the LOF: Railwaymen were being sacked without justification; stokers from the illegitimate LFTA were allowed to drive passenger trains, which was against the company's rules; the railway company made the workers "tighten their belts," yet some employees received high salaries. When the CROM leaders in Mexico City got wind of what was happening in Yucatán, they immediately feared that if the railway workers went on strike, the ports of Progreso and Veracruz would close down in a show of solidarity. "Remember," they wrote to Juan Rico, "that Progreso has declared sympathy strikes in favor of Veracruz, so Veracruz owes them, and the day they ask for help they will no doubt receive it for 'to give is to receive.' " And, bear in mind, the letter concluded, workers from Veracruz know how to conduct strikes in earnest.[56]

Responding to simultaneous pressure from the Progreso federation, the CROM, and the railroad workers themselves, the railway company's management began negotiations with the LOF. The workers petitioned the company to sign a collective agreement with both organizations and to adopt the same rotating labor system that existed in Progreso. Even then, to equalize the number of workers from both unions, two hundred workers from the LFTA would have to be laid off. The LFTA rejected this and instead proposed that the LOF merge with the LFTA; after all, their leaders argued, they had sacrificed themselves for the company. The LOF rejected the proposal because it meant subordinating itself to the LFTA, and its blue collar workers to white collar workers, foremen, and office clerks.[57]

With no settlement in sight, the CROM proposed that United Railways sign collective agreements with both labor organizations. The company agreed to examine the proposition, and negotiations were postponed for two days. Emotions remained pent up in the workshops. On the day talks were to resume, the parties involved, and Yucatecans in general, were stunned by the news that a group of workers from the LOF had assassinated two foremen—leaders of the LFTA—in their workshops. The two men, Claudio Sacramento of the carpenters' shop and Gregorio Misset of the electrical shop, had previously belonged to the LOF. We do not know whether a specific incident motivated their assassination or whether the two men, because of their previously prominent role in the LOF and in the workshops, had fallen victims of the workers' anger and frustration. The workers took further revenge on the company by overturning three engines. The following night, Pomposo de la Fuente, a worker who had stayed on in the LOF but remained a close friend of Claudio Sacramento, was shot in the dark streets of Mérida. De la Fuente was murdered on his way home after expressing his condolences to Sacramento's family, as well as his dismay at the workers' brutality.[58]

The perpetrators of the violence were sacked by the company and jailed, but, soon after, by order of General Francisco Serrano, the secretary of war, all except eight were reinstated to their jobs. Not only was the federal government eager to resolve the conflict, but it also seems that powerful labor leaders from Veracruz had arrived and insisted on the reinstatement of the railwaymen.[59] There is no available evidence of Carrillo Puerto's reaction to the central government's reinstatement of the workers his administration had dismissed. Yet, in view of the recent events, it seems that Carrillo Puerto was little disposed to continue the negotiations between the rival labor unions. In the meantime, encouraged by the central government's intervention, which weakened the authority of the state government, as well as by signs of solidarity from workers in Progreso and Veracruz, the LOF declared a strike. Workers in Progreso, Campeche, and Veracruz announced a solidarity strike in support of the Yucatecans. Thus, in the early days of June, all gulf ports, except Tamaulipas, ground to a standstill.[60]

The liberal press in Yucatán and the anarchist press in Veracruz and Mexico City declared Carrillo Puerto responsible for the labor dispute and strike because of his intransigence in dealing with the problem.[61] Even though Carrillo Puerto regarded the strike as utterly unjustified, he could have broken it only if the mass of the population had demanded it. We do not know whether the strike caused the rural population economic hardship; the fact is that it did not arouse the kind of generalized popular discontent that would have justified the Yucatecan government's intervention. To the contrary, the involvement of the central government in the dispute tied Carrillo Puerto's hands and prevented him from acting in the way he saw fit. The governor's low profile during the strike was also dictated by his awareness that had he confronted the central government, the workers, and the capitalists all at once, he might have put his entire reform agenda at risk.[62]

It was again the CROM that stepped in to mediate between the conflicting parties. After stormy talks among the company, the workers, and the CROM (which represented the point of view of the central government), it was decided that all of the LOF workers would be employed, except those awaiting trial. To accomplish this, United Railways had to dismiss 150 workers from the LFTA. On June 15 the strike ended in Yucatán and expired two days later in Veracruz and Campeche.[63]

Thus backed by their powerful allies in Progreso and Veracruz and aided by the federal government's desperation to end the costly national walkout, the workers from the LOF won the strike as well as the labor dispute with the railway company. Had they also come to the conclusion that they would be better off without Carrillo Puerto? Juan Rico thought so, reflecting bitterly that while the LOF's dissident workers had prevailed in the strike, they had lost what, in fact, had become a fight to destabilize Carrillo Puerto's government.[64] Further events confirm that the workers from the LOF remained at odds with Carrillo Puerto until the end.

In December 1923 over half of the generals in the federal army revolted against the government of Alvaro Obregón. Treasury Minister Adolfo de la Huerta headed the rebellion, which quickly spread to most of the states in the country. The Yucatecan henequeneros welcomed the rebels and supported them financially. Carrillo Puerto's government came under attack, and the governor, together with his closest collaborators, was forced to flee Mérida. They were subsequently captured by the insurgent federales and brought back to the state capital. On January 4, 1924, Felipe Carrillo Puerto and his closest collaborators were executed by the delahuertistas.[65]

The ligas de resistencia, the cornerstone of Carrillo Puerto's political edifice, were unprepared for such a swift military invasion and powerless to mount an effective opposition to the well-equipped, insurgent federal troops. Moreover, many of the resistance leagues were headed by local caciques who proved unreliable defenders of the embattled Socialist party regime. A number of them expediently chose to ally themselves with the insurgent federales to protect their gains and capitalize on the losses of their rivals.[66]

During the reorganization of the Yucatecan government, the delahuertistas sacked more workers belonging to the carrillista LFTA in favor of those belonging to the LOF. Anatolio B. y Buenfil, a veteran labor leader who had joined Alvarado's ranks, was appointed director of the United Railways of Yucatán. The workers of the LOF, supporting the delahuertistas, handed their "Jefe de la Revolución" ten thousand pesos and paid the cost of one day's provisions for his troops.[67]

Conclusion

In his recent study, Charles Bergquist drew the attention of students of Latin American labor history to the central role of workers in export-led economies.[68] Bergquist argued that putting these workers at the center of historical inquiry provides clues for understanding broader political and economic trajectories that otherwise remain difficult to fathom. The reason lies in the fact that since the end of the nineteenth century the growth and development of Latin American societies depended on the success or failure of their export sectors. Thus, correlating the development of a specific export sector to the characteristics of a particular working class formed in a particular export environment and to demographic factors such as trends in migration, as well as to larger, national economic and political developments, Bergquist attempts to create a model of the Latin American working class, its labor movement and organizations. This model seeks to explain the labor movement's strengths and weaknesses as it was influenced by the export economy and the dynamics of the social classes linked to it.

Drawing upon this explanatory model, as well as an emerging historiography treating the Mexican labor movement, this chapter has attempted to explain a case of opposition by dockworkers and transport workers to a radically reformist government in the henequen-exporting region of Yucatán. The history of this labor movement is insufficiently documented, and conclusions must therefore be tentative. Nevertheless, by incorporating the role of urban workers into the analysis of the overthrow of the Yucatecan Socialist party government, we gain an important insight into the workers' political culture and add yet another dimension to Yucatecan social history. Moreover, putting workers in the henequen economy at the center of events takes some of the weight of responsibility for the split within the labor movement (and for the weaknesses of the Socialist party government) off the shoulders of the human actors involved by allowing us to grasp the *structural* parameters of the case.

Even though we have not been able to document working-class life in the Yucatecan cities in any detail, we know from the rich comparative literature on urban labor history that once they settled down in their new environment, workers were quick to develop mutual-aid societies and barrio culture.[69] Moreover, the Yucatecan experience underscores that soon after becoming urban dwellers, workers were able to create their own labor organizations. This was due to a variety of interrelated factors, most notably the fact that in the Yucatecan henequen industry the demand for skilled workers exceeded supply. The leverage that skilled workers had in the labor market gave them a degree of bargaining power that they successfully tested once the private railway companies merged into the United Railways of Yucatán in 1907. Then, too, anarchist labor leaders also played a role in labor organization, introducing the Yucatecans to syndicalist ideas and practices.

Based on the evidence at our disposal, we can concur with Alan Knight that urban workers tended to endorse the capitalistic notion of business expansion—as long as it also benefited the workers. Capitalist expansion did not necessarily clash with the anarchist concept of justice, as long as capitalists recognized worker participation in the profits of enterprise. More often than not, however, capitalists did not accept this and sought to protect their interests by stymieing the workers' defensive tactics. In Yucatán, although the means of production remained in local hands, foreign capital controlled the henequen market through local intermediaries. The social and political contradictions this economic relationship generated created opposition not between the workers and the owners of the means of production, but between the oligarchy and the rest of the population, which suffered the effects of monopoly control of the monocrop. Between 1902 and 1911, henequen prices dropped while prices of consumer goods rose. These events motivated the workers and the middle sectors of society to adopt an antioligarchical position that became manifest during the state elections in 1909. Although initially defeated, the antioligarchical cause remained latent until 1915, when the arrival of the revolution made it possible to alter the regional political economy and give Yucatecans more control over the henequen export base.

The reformist regime of Salvador Alvarado took full charge of the economy and the state government, thanks largely to favorable wartime market conditions and to the military power that underwrote Alvarado's regime. But while the state became the supreme arbiter of economic and political matters, it also tended to usurp workers' control over their own organizations. Those labor unions that had proved their efficacy in the prerevolutionary period were particularly reluctant to accept the state's patronage. The Yucatecan labor movement split as new unions and some old labor leaders joined Alvarado's coalition.

Carrillo Puerto's Socialist party regime, by contrast, had to cope with an extremely difficult economic situation in the postwar period. Moreover, Carrillo Puerto had a more ambitious and revolutionary project for Yucatán than had Alvarado. While he wanted the state to resume the control over the henequen market that it had lost during the 1918–1919 political crisis, Carrillo also projected a much more far-reaching agrarian reform than Alvarado ever intended. In order to be able to carry it out, Felipe Carrillo Puerto needed the transport workers to cooperate by accepting lower wages and shorter working hours. Those workers who agreed to do so received better treatment from the United Railways of Yucatán than did the members of the union that refused to cooperate.

Subsequently, the difficult economic situation, the sense of injustice that the dissident workers harbored for being discriminated against by the company for which they had been working most of their adult lives, created a frustration and anger that, ironically, the workers directed against their fellow workers and against their employer, the Socialist state.

10 Conclusion: Yucatecan Political Economy in Broader Perspective

JEFFERY T. BRANNON

This book chronicles two hundred years of struggle for possession of a region's human and nonhuman resources. This period coincides roughly with the birth of the modern nation-state, the consolidating and internationalizing of capitalist processes and institutions, and the humanist reaction—socialism—to the alienated and brutalized production relations that the industrial revolution seemed to portend.

As the introductory chapter by Joseph points out, too much has been made of the isolation of the Yucatán Peninsula from these historical processes and, consequently, of its allegedly unique economic and social development. Our contributors' microhistorical research seems to suggest the contrary: The process of development in Yucatán was firmly and inextricably linked to national and global forces of change during these tumultuous two centuries. The capitalist paradigm and the structure of production relations that it rationalized were accepted by the regional elite almost coincidentally with the publication of Adam Smith's *Wealth of Nations* in the late eighteenth century. The development of sugar, logwood, and henequen activities during the nineteenth century was a direct response to the demands of markets in the United States and Europe, as well as to nascent technological change. Consequently, local production and social relations were profoundly altered to reflect the requirements of a larger system that was driven by profits and capital accumulation.

Nowhere in the peninsula is the influence of the emerging system of interrelated world markets on local institutions and processes seen in bolder relief than in Yucatán's henequen zone. In less than fifty years, the hacienda system described by Güémez and Patch had disappeared. Production of basic foodstuffs was progressively relegated to a minor role, and the status that land bestowed became firmly linked to its owner's control over financial and physical capital, rather than to ownership per se. By the end of the nineteenth century, peasant modes of subsistence production had all but vanished from the henequen zone, and the patron-client relationship between the Maya and their white patrones had become one of de facto slavery on many haciendas because of state-enforced debt peonage laws. Yucatecan elites owned the great henequen estates and built the railways that linked their plantations to foreign markets. However, their very existence depended upon the vicissitudes of markets that served a handful of countries in the throes of the industrial revolution and on the accumulation of financial capital that accompanied that process.

The Mexican Revolution introduced a new variable into Yucatecan development. Yucatán became, however reluctantly, part of a new Mexican nation. Prior to the revolution, Mexico was not a nation in the current meaning of the word. It possessed little control over its own territory and was held together, not by common assent or rule of law, but by the ancient and time-tested mechanism of *caudillismo*. The revolution both obeyed and dictated in Yucatán. The Alvarado and Carrillo Puerto regimes were limited in their efforts to promote reform by the constraints imposed by the international markets for natural fiber. Reforms required resources. In the absence, at that time, of a strong federal commitment to radical change in Mexico's agricultural sector, neither leader deemed it prudent to mount a frontal assault on the region's prevailing economic order, fearing that, in the process, export earnings from henequen might be disrupted.

Alvarado and Carrillo Puerto did, however, promote the interests of the emerging revolutionary state in Yucatán, and they succeeded briefly in driving a wedge between the economic elite and political power in the region. Both men were strongly influenced by utopian socialist and Marxist thought. And, they understood that a realignment of production relations and political power in favor of the exploited agricultural population revolved critically around agrarian reform and state intervention into what had heretofore been private sector economic transactions. Neither man was able to realize his vision, but the actions of both drew Yucatán irrevocably into the state-building process that was evolving in the rest of Mexico.

More than ten years after the assassination of Carrillo Puerto, at a time when the revolution was largely dormant in Yucatán, a national administration came to power that was bent on finishing the political consolidation and centralization begun by its predecessors. General Lázaro Cárdenas, president of the republic from 1934 to 1940, recognized more clearly than other postrevolutionary leaders that the country's long-term political stability and the survival of the official party as Mexico's legitimate leader depended upon popular support. In Mexico, where 80 percent of the population still depended upon agriculture for its subsistence, swift and mass-based agrarian reform offered the greatest promise for achieving this objective. Cárdenas was influenced by the Soviet experiments in collectivization, and he viewed the reconstitution of the ejido as the key element in the future development of Mexico's agricultural sector. During his administration, more land was distributed to peasant groups than had been distributed by all of his predecessors combined. Cárdenas's actions not only fulfilled the revolutionary promise of social justice to the landless campesinos who had been the cannon fodder of the revolution but also served political ends: First, land reform weakened the political and economic status of the Mexican landowning elite, who, for the most part, opposed the revolution; second, the distribution of property to landless peasants created a large, durable, and manipulable base of support for the official party. Cárdenas's genius helped create a political structure that would be highly resistant to effective opposition until the late 1980s.

As Chacón, Batt, and Spenser demonstrate, Lázaro Cárdenas did not initiate agrarian reform in Yucatán; between 1915 and 1933, about one-fifth of all cropland in the state was distributed to landless campesinos.[1] However, the economic and political significance of these early measures was limited because most of the land was located outside the henequen zone.[2] Private fiber-producing interests were largely unaffected. After the death of Carrillo Puerto, the regional elite managed to reestablish political control and forestall further changes in the status quo.

Unlike the agrarian programs of Alvarado and Carrillo Puerto, that of the Cárdenas administration was national in scope and thoroughgoing in its implementation. Importantly, the popular president had access to federal resources to ensure enforcement of the sweeping changes in land tenure arrangements that he decreed. He also had the will and the popular support needed to resist the pressures of entrenched agricultural interests. The henequen plantations played a key role in Cárdenas's plans for the Mexican agricultural sector. Henequen would be one of the model projects in the administration's collective ejido program; by 1940 the Ejido Credit Bank (Banco Nacional de Crédito Ejidal, or BNCE) had helped organize more than five thousand collectives throughout the country.[3] The president's early efforts to expropriate henequen fields were strongly resisted by their owners. But, a determined Cárdenas came to Mérida in 1937 to expedite the process. After two frantic weeks of expropriation and surveying, 276 newly formed ejidos found themselves in possession of 61 percent of all land sown in henequen.[4]

Unfortunately, agrarian reform in Yucatán's henequen zone was hastily conceived and implemented. Many of the new ejidos did not receive lands that were properly proportioned between fields in the productive and unproductive stages. Nor were they allowed to take possession of the equipment needed to transform the leaves into fiber. Lacking managerial expertise as well as adequate financial and physical capital, the income-generating potential and value of the lands acquired by the collectives were modest. The depressed state of the world market for hard fibers and the continued hostility of the former plantation owners made it even more unlikely that the new production units would survive. To insure the survival of the Cárdenas reforms in Yucatán, the federal government was forced to assume, through the BNCE, many of the responsibilities for henequen production in the ejidal sector. However, the government's efforts proved to be short-lived. The infelicitous combination of low fiber prices, uneconomic production organization, and a lack of expertise and capital on the part of the BNCE caused the government to reverse direction in the henequen zone shortly after land redistribution took place. In early 1938, the BNCE, unable to cope with the organizational and financial problems of the ejidos, turned their administration over to the governor of Yucatán, who in turn made them the responsibility of a reorganized Henequeneros de Yucatán.[5]

The increased demand for natural fiber that accompanied World War II caused prices again to rise to profitable levels after almost two decades of depression. During the war, Henequeneros de Yucatán ran the ejido sector as if it were one large plantation. Ejidatarios were paid a fixed wage. Yucatecans, including some ex-hacendados, came to dominate the organization, and the ejidatarios, although they had legal right to the land, fared little better than they had prior to agrarian reform. During the war the henequen ejidos, which supported almost forty thousand workers and their families, received 48 percent of the price paid by Henequeneros for raw fiber; by contrast, the few hundred owners of processing equipment were given the remaining 52 percent. As this price was less than the world market price, the state organization was able to divert an estimated 42 percent of total sales revenue for its own use.[6] Rumors of corruption in Henequeneros and the ejidos were rife by the end of the war. In 1955 President Adolfo Ruiz Cortines, concerned about both the corruption and the industrial depression following the end of the Korean War, dissolved Henequeneros and reasserted the federal presence in the ejidal sector. The administration of the ejidos was turned over to a new federal credit agency.

Cárdenas's efforts to bring about thoroughgoing agrarian reform in Yucatán failed. His greatest error was in not giving the collectives progressive control over the exploitation of their own land. By permitting the ex-hacendados to retain possession of the processing equipment, the federal government sanctioned the continued exploitation of the ejidatarios by their former masters. The renewed presence of the federal government after 1955 was an effort to bring some order and stability to the industry and to counter the rejuvenated regional bourgeoisie. However, the new bank that was charged with the task of providing credit and technical assistance to the ejidos rapidly became a cynical, corrupt, and predatory bureaucracy that was hated and feared by most ejidatarios. The control exercised by the bank and the owners of processing equipment essentially eliminated the ejidatarios' disposition of their own land and labor. They were treated and came to perceive themselves as wage laborers rather than property owners. Their status was made worse by the gross mismanagement of the henequen bureaucracy, which more often than not took actions in its own interests or those of Mexico City. By the 1960s not a single henequen collective could have survived without subsidies provided by the federal government. The ejidatarios had become wards of the state and an increasingly burdensome drain on the federal treasury.

The problems that the ejidos experienced did not chasten the federal government. In the early 1960s, it increased its involvement in Yucatán's henequen industry through the purchase of forty private cordage mills. The official objective was to streamline and modernize the production of finished products from henequen so that Mexico would be more competitive in world markets for natural fiber. In practice, the creation of CORDEMEX, a parastatal firm that was granted a monopoly over both the purchase of raw fiber and the production and sale of cordage products, only deepened the federal government's involvement in the regional economy and hastened the demise of henequen as a viable, large-scale economic activity. CORDEMEX's efforts to become more competitive in world markets were hampered by a secular decline in the demand for natural fibers and by the organization's inefficiency, which was related to the firm's political functions in Yucatán.[7]

Despite CORDEMEX's modernization program, Mexico and other natural fiber–producing nations confronted increasing competition from synthetics in the 1960s and 1970s. World production and consumption of sisal and henequen declined steadily throughout both decades. CORDEMEX's situation was worsened by the steady decline in Mexico's share of the natural fiber market to sisal-producing countries such as Brazil and Tanzania, which had lower production costs. Because of the political and social functions with which CORDEMEX was charged, it literally lost control of its costs. By 1980 it was losing tens of millions of dollars a year, adding to the federal government's huge subsidies to the henequen ejidos.

From the inception of its operations, CORDEMEX wielded enormous economic and political power in Yucatán. Its director and the director of BANRURAL—the federal credit bank that financed the ejidal sector—were, along with the governor, the most important representatives of the federal government and the Partido Revolucionario Institucional (PRI) in Yucatán. The economic objectives of both CORDEMEX and BANRURAL were, as often as not, subordinated to political exigencies in the state. Yucatán, which before the revolution had been isolated and often alienated from Mexico's central government, posed a political problem for Cárdenas's successors. By the late 1960s, elements of the private sector and the old henequen elite had joined with the Catholic church and a disaffected middle class in Mérida to forge a formidable electoral opposition to the PRI in state elections. The PRI managed to win the state governorship in 1970 only by vote fraud. Throughout the 1970s, in an effort to strengthen its political base with urban and rural labor, the central government funneled millions of dollars to those sectors through CORDEMEX and BANRURAL, with seeming disregard for the financial condition of the two entities.

The Cárdenas reforms marked the beginning of a process through which the federal government firmly established its political and economic dominance of Yucatán. In 1980, federal entities, including BANRURAL and CORDEMEX, had budgeted expenditures in excess of a billion pesos for the state. This was more than five times the budget of the state government. Further, almost 80 percent of the state budget consisted of revenue-sharing funds from Mexico City.[8] Few of Mexico's other thirty-one states' well-being is so tightly linked to federal coffers. Significantly, this extreme degree of dependency is shared by Quintana Roo, which became a state in the 1970s. Prior to construction of the resort of Cancún in that same decade, the state had fewer than twenty thousand inhabitants. Federal investment in infrastructure and tourist facilities has been the critical element in the pattern of development over the past two decades that has attracted thousands of Yucatecans and other Mexicans to Quintana Roo. This is an interesting turnabout when one considers that less than one hundred years ago the central government's role in the peninsula was negligible, and, as documented by Cal, Konrad, and Wells, commercial activity depended upon private entrepreneurs' assessment of the risk and return of the siren call of foreign markets.

Thus, in the decades following the outbreak of the Mexican Revolution, the state has supplanted private capital, both foreign and domestic, and become the prime shaper of economic activity in Yucatán. Nevertheless, the benefits of this substitution are lost for most Yucatecans, who continue to labor in near-subsistence agricultural activities or poorly remunerated urban jobs. The peninsula remains a backward, low-income area, heavily dependent on the largesse of Mexico City. The once-proud henequen industry has reached its lowest ebb and is an embarrassment to the central government both for the documented corruption associated with its fifty-year stewardship and the poverty of the designated beneficiaries of agrarian reform.

The state-building process has been costly for the federal government, but what were the alternatives for Mexico's postrevolutionary leaders? Yucatecan campesinos had been, since independence, locked into an exploitive labor regime that left them without rights and was unresponsive to the demands of a modern Mexico. The agrarian reform of the 1930s was essentially a political exchange in which the henequen worker gave up his right of effective suffrage for a new and less-onerous system of patronage. Ironically, the future well-being of Yucatán's rural dwellers probably will have much less to do with their relationship to the land, because most will leave it. It is the city, where the new master—technology—resides, that represents opportunity and freedom. The struggles over land and labor that have been recounted in this book will be replaced by the struggle for knowledge and a place in an urban society that is rapidly changing.

Notes

Abbreviations

Short titles have generally been used for repeated citations of works in the notes. Archival sources and titles of journals frequently cited have been identified by the following abbreviations:

AB	Archives of Belize
AB/B	Archives of Belize, *Bluebooks*
AB/CR	Archives of Belize, Colonial Records
ABH	Archives of British Honduras
AGEY	Archivo General del Estado de Yucatán
AGEY/C	Archivo General del Estado de Yucatán, Colonial
AGEY/F	Archivo General del Estado de Yucatán, Fomento
AGEY/J	Archivo General del Estado de Yucatán, Justicia
AGEY/PE	Archivo General del Estado de Yucatán, Poder Ejecutivo
AGN	Archivo General de la Nación
AGN/FP/OC	Archivo General de la Nación, Fondo Presidente, Obregón/Calles
AGN/G	Archivo General de la Nación, Gobernación
AGN/G/SS	Archivo General de la Nación, Gobernación, Sin Sección
AGN/T	Archivo General de la Nación, Trabajo
ANEY	Archivo Notarial del Estado de Yucatán
GRB	General Registry of Belize
HAHR	*Hispanic American Historical Review*
LARR	*Latin American Research Review*

1. The New Regional Historiography

1. Luis González, *Invitación a la microhistoria* (Mexico City: SepSetentas, 1973).

2. Luis González, "Microhistory, *Terruño*, and the Social Sciences: A Prefatory Note," in *Regional Impacts of U.S.-Mexican Relations*, ed. Ina Rosenthal-Urey (La Jolla, Calif.: Center for U.S.-Mexican Studies, 1986), p. ix.

3. Eric Van Young, "Mexican Rural History Since Chevalier: The Historiography of the Colonial Hacienda," *LARR* 18, no. 3 (1983): 34.

4. Enrique Krauze, "Chihuahua, ida y vuelta," in his *Por una democracia sin adjetivos* (Mexico City: Joaquín Mortiz Planeta, 1986), p. 113.

5. González, *Invitación*, pp. 8–72.

6. See, for example, the papers presented at the colloquium Modernization and Postmodernity in Mexico, in February 1988 at the Center for U.S.-Mexican Studies, La Jolla, California. The quotation is from Alberto Aziz Nassif, "Modernización y vacío." In another of the colloquium's papers, "La mueca de la postmodernidad," Roger Bartra also accentuated the significance of subnational fragmentation in Mexico's new postmodern era—which Bartra rather sardonically characterizes as "des*mothern*ista"!

7. See, for example, Francisco J. Paoli and Enrique Montalvo, *El socialismo olvidado de Yucatán: Elementos para una reinterpretación de la Revolución Mexicana* (Mexico City: Siglo XXI, 1977); and Daniela G. O. Spenser, *Partido Socialista Chiapaneco: Rescate y reconstrucción de su historia* (Mexico City: La Casa Chata, 1988); cf. Barry Carr, "Recent Regional Studies of the Mexican Revolution," *LARR* 15, no. 1 (1980): 3–14.

8. Wigberto Jiménez Moreno, cited in Thomas Benjamin, "Provinces of the Revolution: Provincial, Regional and Local History in Revolutionary Historiography," in *Mexican Revolutions: Essays on Regional Mexican History, 1910–1929*, ed. Thomas Benjamin and Mark Wasserman (Albuquerque: University of New Mexico Press, 1990).

9. For the importance of regional and local approaches to the larger enterprise of social history, see the essays by Charles Tilly and Olivier Zunz, in *Reliving the Past: The Worlds of Social History*, ed. Olivier Zunz (Chapel Hill: University of North Carolina Press, 1985); and Benjamin, "Provinces."

10. See, for example, Sergio Ortega Noriega, "Archivos históricos regionales y locales," *Boletín del Archivo General de la Nación*, 3d. ser., no. 1 (July–September 1977); and Gilbert M. Joseph, *Rediscovering the Past at Mexico's Periphery: Essays on the History of Modern Yucatán* (University: University of Alabama Press, 1986), Ch. 1.

11. The salient literature is reviewed in a variety of places. See, for example, Thomas Benjamin and William McNellie, eds., *Other Mexicos: Essays on Regional Mexican History, 1876–1911* (Albuquerque: University of New Mexico Press, 1984); Benjamin and Wasserman, *Mexican Revolutions*; and Van Young, "Mexican Rural History."

12. See, for example, the rather flexible conceptual framework employed in Joseph L. Love, "An Approach to Regionalism," in *New Approaches to Latin American History*, ed. Richard Graham and Peter H. Smith (Austin: University of Texas Press, 1974), pp. 137–55.

13. Eric Van Young, "Mexican Regions: Comparative History and Development," Manuscript, proposal for a research workshop, 1988.

14. Ibid.; cf. Eric Van Young, "Doing Regional History: Methodological and Theoretical Considerations," in *City, Country, and Frontier in Mexican History*, ed. Eric Van Young and Roberto Moreno de los Arcos (Mexico City: UNAM, forthcoming); Benjamin, "Provinces"; and Joseph, *Rediscovering the Past*, esp. pp. 134–35, 177.

15. Gilbert M. Joseph and Allen Wells, "Yucatán: Elite Politics and Rural Insurgency in a Period of Transition, 1897–1913," in Benjamin and Wasserman, *Mexican Revolutions*; Alma García, "Recent Studies in Nineteenth- and Early Twentieth-Cen-

tury Regional Mexican History," *LARR* 22, no. 2 (1987): 255–66. A group of Mexican regional historians and political economists, led by Mario Cerutti of the Universidad Autónoma de Nuevo León, has been particularly successful in conceptualizing regional problems in national and global terms. In 1980, Cerutti organized the first of several national conferences on La Formación del Capitalismo en México desde la Perspectiva Regional. In short order, these events gave rise to a newsletter and, ultimately, to a fine journal, *Siglo XIX*. For a partial survey of the group's research agenda prior to 1986, see Cerutti, "Contribuciones recientes y relevancia de la investigación regional sobre la segunda parte del siglo XIX," Manuscript, 1986.

16. Joseph and Wells, "Yucatán"; and Joseph, *Rediscovering the Past*, pp. 23–24.

17. In this regard, see Paul J. Vanderwood's insightful critique, "Building Blocks but Yet No Building: Regional History and the Mexican Revolution," *Mexican Studies* 3, no. 2 (Summer 1987): 421–32; cf. Gilbert M. Joseph, "Preface to the Paperback Edition," *Revolution from Without: Yucatán, Mexico, and the United States, 1880–1924* (Durham, N.C.: Duke University Press, 1988), pp. xxiii–xxv; and Magnus Mörner, "Research on Latin American History Today: New Challenges," *Boletín de Estudios Latino-americanos y del Caribe* 37 (December 1984): 9–18, esp. 17–18.

18. To be sure, Latin Americans have been slower to embrace this "professionalized regional approach" to the past, no doubt in part because of the prevailing North American orientation. See Mörner, "Research on Latin American History Today," p. 17.

19. For an appreciation of the genre, see Luis González, *Invitación* and *Nueva invitación a la microhistoria* (Mexico City: Sep/80, 1982); Benjamin, "Provinces"; and Joseph, *Rediscovering the Past*. Luis González's *Pueblo en vilo: Microhistoria de San José de Gracia* (Mexico City: El Colegio de México, 1972) and Colombian historian Orlando Fals Borda's *Historia doble de la costa*, 3 vols. (Bogotá: Carlos Valencia Editores, 1981) represent innovative professional treatments of their rustic *terruños* that are deeply indebted to local narrative and oral traditions. The methodological and ideological difficulties that elite amateur chronicles often present for professional scholars are skillfully analyzed by Belizean historian Peter Ashdown in "The Problem of Creole Historiography," in *Readings in Belizean History*, 2d ed., ed. Lita Hunter-Krohn (Belize City: St. John's College, 1987), pp. 142–52.

20. See, for example, Manuel Moreno Fraginals et al., eds., *Between Slavery and Free Labor: The Spanish-Speaking Caribbean in the Nineteenth Century* (Baltimore: Johns Hopkins University Press, 1985); and Allen Wells, "The Terrible Green Monster: Recent Literature on Sugar, Coffee, and Coerced Labor in the Caribbean," *LARR* 23, no. 2 (1988): 189–205.

21. The field of Andean social and agrarian history has also benefited from close, structured collaboration. See, most recently, Steve J. Stern, ed., *Resistance, Rebellion, and Consciousness in the Andean Peasant World, 18th to 20th Centuries* (Madison: University of Wisconsin Press, 1987).

22. For a detailed examination of modern Yucatecan historiography, see Joseph, *Rediscovering the Past*, and his "From Caste War to Class War: The Historiography of Modern Yucatán (c. 1750–1940)," *Hispanic American Historical Review* 65, no. 1 (February 1985): 111–34.

23. Yucatecan regionalism is examined in some detail in Joseph, *Rediscovering the Past*, which also references the relevant literature. Not surprisingly, many social anthropologists of Mexico have privileged ethnic and cultural factors in their understanding of region. For example, see Guillermo de la Peña, "Los estudios regionales y la antropología social en México," *Relaciones* 2, no. 8 (Fall 1981): 43–93.

24. For the critique of regionality based on politicoadministrative structure, see Van Young, "Doing Regional History," and Claudio Stern, *Las regiones de México y sus niveles de desarrollo socio-económico* (Mexico City: El Colegio de México, 1973), esp. pp. 13–19.

25. Van Young, "Doing Regional History" and "Mexican Regions," underscores the importance of working toward an a priori definition of region and suggests that economic criteria—principally market and exchange relationships—may well provide the most useful integrating theme for comparative regional studies. Students of Brazilian regionalism, on the other hand, have thus far resisted a priori definitions, favoring more flexible, multivalent understandings of regionality. In addition to Love, "Approach to Regionalism," see Ciro Flamarión Cardoso, "Regional History," *Biblioteca Americana* 1, no. 1 (September 1982): 1–8 (which draws upon the perspective on regional history of the French Annales school); and Barbara Weinstein, "Brazilian Regionalism," *LARR* 17, no. 2 (1982): 262–76. Van Young is organizing a research workshop, Mexican Regions: Comparative History and Development, in an effort to inject greater rigor into the definition of regions, regionality, and regionalism.

26. Edward H. Moseley and Edward D. Terry, eds., *Yucatan: A World Apart* (University: University of Alabama Press, 1980); Antonio Mediz Bolio, "Prólogo," in Salvador Alvarado, *Actuación revolucionaria del Gral. Salvador Alvarado en Yucatán* (Mexico City: Costa-Amic Editor, 1965), p. 14.

27. Cf. the new regional history of the United States, which plays down "American exceptionalism" and examines the U.S. agrarian experience comparatively, in the light of long-term developments in world capitalism. See Steven Hahn and Jonathan Prude, eds., *The Countryside in the Age of Capitalist Transformation: Essays in the Social History of Rural America* (Chapel Hill: University of North Carolina Press, 1985).

28. The architectural consequences of Yucatán's evolving political economy are examined in a well-illustrated collection of essays published by the local Facultad de Arquitectura of the Universidad Autónoma de Yucatán. See Pedro Echeverria, ed., *Cuadernos de arquitectura de Yucatán* (Mérida: Universidad Autónoma de Yucatán, 1987).

29. A preoccupation with similar themes over the longue durée has characterized the regional historiography of Chiapas, Guatemala, and southern Peru. See the special issue, "Approaches to the Regional History of Nineteenth- and Twentieth-Century Chiapas," in *Mesoamérica* (forthcoming); W. George Lovell, "Surveying Conquest: The Maya of Guatemala in Historical Perspective," *LARR* 23, no. 2 (1988): 25–57; and Carlos Monge, "El sur del Perú en perspectiva regional," Paper presented at the 34th Annual Meeting of the Southeastern Council on Latin American Studies (SECOLAS), Mérida, Yucatán, April 1987.

30. Joseph, *Rediscovering the Past*, pp. 23–24, and his "Caste War to Class War," pp. 113–14.

31. Historians working on other regions of Mexico and Latin America have also underscored the significance of the larger period running from about 1750 to 1940. Indeed, scholars have begun to speak of a pivotal "middle period" of Latin American history—an extended corridor of transition that illustrates the persistence of colonial patterns and traces the contours of modern Latin American life. Thus, the new regional historiography not only challenges traditional Mexican periodizations, but also calls into question the customary bipartite division of Latin American history into "colonial" and "national" or "modern" eras. Stuart Voss, a scholar of Sonora and the Mexican northwest, is currently at work on a book titled *Latin America: The Middle Period from Imperial Reform to World Depression*. Also see Mark D. Szuchman, ed., *The Middle Period in Latin America History: Values and Attitudes in the 18th–19th Centuries* (Boulder: Lynne Rienner Publishers, 1989).

32. Nancy Farriss, *Maya Society under Colonial Rule: The Collective Enterprise of Survival* (Princeton, N.J.: Princeton University Press, 1984).

33. Inga Clendinnen, *Ambivalent Conquests: Maya and Spaniard in Yucatán, 1517–1570* (Cambridge: Cambridge University Press, 1987).

34. Victoria Reifler Bricker, *The Indian Christ, The Indian King: The Historical Substrate of Maya Myth and Ritual* (Austin: University of Texas Press, 1981).

35. Gilbert M. Joseph and Allen Wells, *Summer of Discontent, Seasons of Upheaval: Elite Politics and Rural Protest in Yucatan, 1890–1915* (Albuquerque: University of New Mexico Press, forthcoming). These themes have recently received sophisticated treatment for the Andean region, most notably in Stern, *Resistance*.

36. For a survey of recent advances, see Joseph, *Rediscovering the Past*, esp. Ch. 2 and "Epilogue"; Herman W. Konrad, "Anthropological Studies in Yucatán and the Historical Dimension," *Mexican Studies* 3, no. 1 (Winter 1987): 163–80; and Grant D. Jones, ed., *Anthropology and History in Yucatan* (Austin: University of Texas Press, 1977).

37. See Joseph, *Rediscovering the Past*, pp. 12–15.

38. See Edward D. Terry et al., "Analyzing a Region: The Interaction of the University of Alabama and the Yucatan," *SECOLAS Annals* 13 (1982): 32–47.

39. Universidad de Yucatán, *Memorias de la Primera Semana de la Historia* (Mérida: Universidad de Yucatán, 1980).

40. These regional events are examined in Joseph, *Rediscovering the Past*, Ch. 1.

41. Othón Baños Ramírez, ed., *Sociedad, estructura agraria y estado en Yucatán* (Mérida: Universidad Autónoma de Yucatán, 1990).

Introduction to Part I

1. Pedro Bracamonte y Sosa's paper, "Hacienda y ganado en el noroeste de Yucatán (primera mitad del siglo XIX)," appears in Baños Ramírez, *Sociedad*. Bracamonte acknowledges an intellectual debt to the earlier agrarian research of Howard Cline and Robert Patch. Citations and a discussion of their contributions appear in Joseph, *Rediscovering the Past*, Ch. 3.

2. For example, see Eric J. Hobsbawm, *Bandits*, rev. ed. (New York: Pantheon, 1981); E. P. Thompson et al., *Albion's Fatal Tree: Crime and Society in Eighteenth-Century England* (New York: Pantheon, 1975); and Eric J. Hobsbawm and George Rudé, *Cap-*

tain Swing (New York: Pantheon, 1968). These and other works are discussed in the context of Latin American "social crime" in Gilbert M. Joseph, "On the Trail of Latin American Bandits: A Reexamination of Peasant Resistance," *LARR* 25, no. 3 (1990): 7–53.

3. For example, see James C. Scott, *Weapons of the Weak: Everyday Forms of Peasant Resistance* (New Haven: Yale University Press, 1985); the special issue devoted to "Everyday Forms of Peasant Resistance" in the *Journal of Peasant Studies* 13, no. 2 (January 1986); and Joseph, "Latin American Bandits."

4. See, for example, Gilbert M. Joseph and Allen Wells, "El monocultivo de henequén y sus contradicciones: Estructura de dominación y formas de resistencia en haciendas yucatecas a fines del Porfiriato," *Siglo XIX* 3, no. 6 (July–December 1988): 215–77.

5. The classic treatment of the rebellion remains Nelson Reed, *The Caste War of Yucatan* (Stanford: Stanford University Press, 1964). For a discussion of recent contributions on the insurrection, which places it in historical perspective and examines the appropriateness of the term "Caste War," see Joseph, *Rediscovering the Past*, Ch. 3.

6. Eric Wolf, *Europe and the People Without History* (Berkeley: University of California Press, 1982), Ch. 3.

7. Also see Catherine LeGrand, *Frontier Expansion and Peasant Protest in Colombia, 1850–1936* (Albuquerque: University of New Mexico Press, 1986).

8. Woodrow Borah, *Justice by Insurance: The General Indian Court of Colonial Mexico and the Legal Aides of the Half-Real* (Berkeley: University of California Press, 1983); Charles Gibson, *The Aztecs under Spanish Rule* (Stanford: Stanford University Press, 1964); William Taylor, *Landlord and Peasant in Colonial Oaxaca* (Stanford: Stanford University Press, 1972); Steve J. Stern, *Peru's Indian Peoples and the Challenge of Conquest* (Madison: University of Wisconsin Press, 1982); Farriss, *Maya Society*.

9. A brief but valuable recent contribution is Marco Bellingeri, "El tributo y los indios y el estado de los criollos: Las obvenciones eclesiásticas en Yucatán en el siglo XIX," Manuscript, 1987.

2. Everyday Forms of Mayan Resistance

Translated by Knut Walter and Gilbert M. Joseph. The author wishes to thank Sergio Quezada, who directed the thesis on which this chapter is based; Heriberto Moreno García for his suggestions on an earlier draft; and Gilbert M. Joseph for his encouragement of the project and the insights he offered regarding the comparative history of social crime.

1. See, for example, Scott, *Weapons of the Weak*; Michael Adas, "From Avoidance to Confrontation: Peasant Protest in Precolonial and Colonial Southeast Asia," *Comparative Studies in Society and History* 23, no. 2 (April 1981): 217–47; and the special issue "Everyday Forms of Peasant Resistance" in the *Journal of Peasant Studies*.

2. Scott, *Weapons of the Weak*; also see James C. Scott, "Resistance without Protest and without Organization: Peasant Opposition to the Islamic *Zakat* and the Christian Tithe," *Comparative Studies in Society and History* 29, no. 3 (July 1987): 417–52. Here, the more characteristically Mexican/Latin American term *campesino* is used—instead of

peasant—to refer to the poor, overwhelmingly Mayan cultivators who lived in the village and hacienda communities in northwestern Yucatán during the first half of the nineteenth century. Peon or sirviente is used to refer more specifically to those campesinos who resided on haciendas and were increasingly tied to them through the mechanism of debt.

3. See, for example, Robert Patch's chapter in this book, and Farriss, *Maya Society*, Ch. 9.

4. Broadly speaking, two categories of documents pertaining to the Mayan response to creole agricultural expansion between 1821 and 1847 can be distinguished in AGEY/J and AGEY/PE: (1) Those files revealing the extent of Mayan litigation against individuals or institutions affiliated with the creole ruling group, as in cases of land usurpation, abuses of authority, unwarranted tax collections, and seizures of persons and property; and (2) those files in which Mayan campesinos appear as transgressors of the interests of the creole elite, as in cases of land invasions, disrespect for authorities, tax evasions, conspiracies and civil disorders, cattle rustling and other thefts, and vagrancy.

5. For an appreciation of quieter forms of Mayan resistance in northwestern Yucatán following the Caste War, during the late-century henequen boom, see Joseph and Wells, "Monocultivo de henequén."

6. Scott, *Weapons of the Weak*, p. 300, and "Resistance without Protest," p. 452.

7. Yucatán, *Memoria leída ante el augusto Congreso Extraordinario de Yucatán, por el Secretario General de Gobierno, el día 18 de septiembre de 1846* (Mérida: Imprenta de Castilla, 1846), docs. 1–18.

8. José María Regil and Alonso M. Peón, *Estadística de Yucatán publicada por acuerdo de la Sociedad de Geografía y Estadística* (Mexico City: n.p., 1853), vol. 1, pp. 174–76, 281.

9. José Tiburcio Cervera, "Apuntes sobre la industria pecuaria en Yucatán," *Boletín de la Sociedad Mexicana de Geografía y Estadística* 4 (1872): 399–400; cf. Pedro Bracamonte y Sosa, "Seis características de las haciendas yucatecas entre 1821–1847," Manuscript, n.d.

10. Yucatán, *Memoria leída*, docs. 34–41.

11. Tomás Aznar Barbachano, ed., *Las mejoras materiales* (Campeche: Imprenta de la Sociedad Tipográfica, 1859), vol. 1, p. 39.

12. Nancy M. Farriss, "Propiedades territoriales en Yucatán en la época colonial," *Revista de la Universidad de Yucatán* 146 (1983): 55–61.

13. AGEY/PE, Ramo Tierras, vol. 1, exp. 30, July 1837.

14. Ibid., exp. 20, July 1831.

15. José María Peón and Isidro Gondra, eds., *Colección de leyes, decretos y órdenes del augusto Congreso del Estado Libre de Yucatán*, 2 vols. (Mérida: Lorenzo Seguí, 1832), vol. 1, pp. 225–26.

16. Alonso Aznar Pérez and Rafael Pedrera, eds., *Colección de leyes, decretos, órdenes o acuerdos de tendencia general del poder legislativo del Estado Libre y Soberano de Yucatán*, 3 vols. (Mérida: Imprenta del Editor, 1849–51), vol. 2, pp. 275–79.

17. Robert Patch, "La formación de estancias y haciendas en Yucatán durante la colonia," in Universidad de Yucatán, *Cuatro ensayos antropológicos* (Mérida: Ediciones de la Universidad de Yucatán, 1979), pp. 28–30.

18. AGEY/J, Ramo Penal, case 11-A, vol. 16, exp. 74, 1841.

19. Ibid., case 13-C, vol. 18, exp. 93, 1843.

20. Regil and Peón, *Estadística de Yucatán*, vol. 1, pp. 199–200. Numbers in the source are used incorrectly: They include only those prisoners defined as castas. The real totals gleaned from the same set of data (bracketed in the quotation) bring together both Indian and casta prisoners. In addition, the number of castas involved in rustling should be 39, not 41, and the number of castas involved in other theft should be 31 instead of 35. Thus, of the 73 individuals imprisoned for rustling, 34 were Indians, while of the 50 imprisoned for other kinds of theft, 19 were Indians.

21. AGEY/PE, Ramo Decretos y Leyes, vol. 3, exp. 3, 1836.

22. AGEY/J, Ramo Penal, case 1, vol. 3, exp. 16, 1832.

23. Ibid., 1835.

24. AGEY/PE, Ramo Tierras, vol. 1, exp. 13, 1827.

25. Ibid.

26. AGEY/J, Ramo Penal, case 10, vol. 14, exp. 62, 1838.

27. Ibid., case 9, vol. 14, exp. 11, 1838; case 33, 1845.

28. Ibid., case 8, vol. 12, exp. 9, 1836.

29. Ibid., exp. 11, 1836.

30. Ibid., case 10, vol. 14, exp. 62, 1838.

31. Ibid., case 2, vol. 3, exp. 2, 1824.

32. Ibid., case 7, vol. 11, exp. 38, 1835.

33. Ibid., case 9, vol. 14, exp. 31, 1837.

34. Ibid., case 6, vol. 10, exp. 27, 1834.

35. Ibid., case 8, vol. 12, exp. 73, 1836.

36. Peón and Gondra, *Colección de leyes*, vol. 1, p. 240.

37. Ibid., vol. 2, pp. 66–72.

38. Ibid., vol. 1, pp. 239–40.

39. AGEY/J, Ramo Penal, case 2, vol. 3, exp. 28, 1825.

40. Peón and Gondra, *Colección de leyes*, vol. 1, pp. 101–102.

41. Ibid., p. 77.

42. Miguel Castro y Araoz, *Edicto contra ladrones de ganado* (Mérida: n.p., 1819), pp. 1–3.

43. Ibid., p. 15.

44. Ibid., pp. 5–11.

45. Ibid., p. 11.

46. Ibid., p. 12.

47. Ibid., p. 14.

48. José María Peón and Isidro Gondra, eds., *Projecto de Presidio Correccional para dar ocupación a los presos aprobado y mandado observar por la honorable Junta Provisional de decreto de 18 de julio de 1823* (Mérida: Oficina Republicana del Sol, 1823), pp. 1–6; AGEY/PE, Ramo Ayuntamientos, vol. 1, exp. 28, 1825.

49. "Representación del síndico primero de esta capital sobre estinción del Presidio Correccional y su junta de caridad" (1825), Manuscript in the Biblioteca Crescencio Carrillo y Ancona, Mérida.

50. Peón and Gondra, *Presidio Correcional*, p. 6.

51. Ibid., pp. 8–9.

52. "Representación del síndico primero."

53. AGEY/PE, Ramo Ayuntamientos, vol. 1, exp. 28, 1825.

54. "Representación del síndico primero."

55. Ramón Osorio Carbajal, "Historia de la medicina alopática en la época independiente," in *Enciclopedia Yucatanense* (Mexico City: Gobierno del Estado de Yucatán, 1977), vol. 4, pp. 326–28.

56. AGEY/PE, Decretos y Leyes, vol. 3, exp. 3, 1836.

57. Ibid.

58. Ibid.

59. Ibid.

60. Ibid.

61. Ibid.

62. Ibid.

63. Ibid.

64. Ibid.; also see Aznar Pérez, *Colección de leyes*, vol. 1, p. 257.

65. Real Academia de la Historia, *Las siete partidas del Rey Don Alfonso el Sabio, cotejadas con varios códices antiguos*, 2 vols. (Paris: Lasserre Editor, 1847), vol. 2, p. 358.

66. AGEY/J, Ramo Penal, case 3, vol. 4, exp. 1, 1826.

67. Ibid., case 4, vol. 7, exp. 18, 1829.

68. Yucatán, *Memoria presentada por el Congreso del Estado de Yucatán por el Secretario de Gobierno en 29 y 30 de septiembre de 1841* (Mérida: Imprenta de José Dolores Espinosa, 1841), p. 9.

69. AGEY, Congreso, Sessiones 1841–43, vol. 10, exp. 1, pp. 121–23.

70. Aznar Pérez, *Colección de leyes*, vol. 2, pp. 146–47.

71. AGEY/J, Ramo Penal, case 12, vol. 17, exp. 87, 1842; case 13-B, vol. 18, exp. 29, 1843.

72. Ibid., case 33, 1844; case 29, 1845.

73. AGEY/PE, Ramo Gobernación, case 10, 1844.

74. Ibid.

75. Eric J. Hobsbawm, "Peasants and Politics," *Journal of Peasant Studies* 1, no. 1 (1973): 12.

3. Origins of the Caste War, 1812–1847

1. For the negotiations at Tzucacab, see Serapio Baqueiro, *Ensayo histórico sobre las revoluciones de Yucatán desde el año de 1840 hasta 1864*, 3 vols. (Mérida: Manuel Heredia Argüelles, 1878–87), vol. 1, pp. 416–21; and Eligio Ancona, *Historia de Yucatán*, 4 vols. (Mérida: Manuel Heredia Argüelles, 1878–80), vol. 4, pp. 110–19.

2. See the series of articles that he wrote for his newspaper, *El Fénix*, in 1848 and 1849. See also Justo Sierra O'Reilly, *Los indios de Yucatán: Consideraciones históricas sobre la influencia del elemento indígena en la organización social del país*, 2 vols. (Mérida: Tipográfica Yucateca, 1954–57), which is a collection of some of Sierra's writings compiled and published by Carlos R. Menéndez (it does not, however, include all of Sierra's articles from *El Fénix*).

3. See especially Ancona, *Historia de Yucatán*, vol. 4, pp. 5–16.

4. Howard F. Cline, "Regionalism and Society in Yucatan: 'Progressivism' and the Origins of the Caste War, 1825–1847" (Ph.D. diss., Harvard University, 1947). Parts of Cline's thesis were published in article form and thus are more readily accessible. See esp. Howard F. Cline, "The Sugar Episode in Yucatan, 1825–1850," *Inter-American Economic Affairs* 1 (1948): 79–100.

5. Reed, *Caste War*.

6. Moisés González Navarro, *Raza y tierra: La Guerra de Castas y el henequén* (Mexico City: El Colegio de México, 1970); Bricker, *Indian Christ, Indian King*, pp. 92–95; and Marie Lapointe, *Los mayas rebeldes de Yucatán* (Zamora: El Colegio de Michoacán, 1983), pp. 25–72. González Navarro follows Cline only indirectly, for though he did not consult Cline's thesis, he did include Reed's book in his bibliography. On the other hand, he also goes somewhat beyond Reed's summary of Cline's interpretation by giving more importance to the problem of clerical exactions as a cause of the Caste War.

7. Fidelio Quintal Martín, *Yucatán: Carácter de la Guerra Campesina de 1847: Una síntesis interpretativa* (Mérida: Ediciones de la Universidad de Yucatán, 1976).

8. For a general overview of colonial land policy, see José M. Ots Capdequí, *El régimen de la tierra en la América española durante el período colonial* (Ciudad Trujillo: Universidad de Santo Domingo, 1946); Lucio Mendieta y Núñez, *El problema agrario de México* (México: Editorial Porrúa, 1982 [originally published 1923]), pp. 33–96.

9. In addition to Ots Capdequí and Mendieta y Núñez, see François Chevalier, *La Formation des grands domaines au Mexique* (Paris: Institut d'Ethnologie, Travaux et Mémoires, 1952), pp. 57–145.

10. Ibid., pp. 301–44.

11. For a discussion of the Constitution of Cádiz and Yucatán, see Jorge Isidro Castillo Canché and Roger Alonso Domínguez Saldívar, "La Constitución de Cádiz en Yucatán, 1812–1814" (Graduate thesis, Universidad Autónoma de Yucatán, 1986).

12. Jean Sarrailh, *L'Espagne éclairée de la seconde moitié du XVIIIe siècle* (Paris: Imprimerie Nationale, 1954), pp. 543–71, 613–61; and Richard Herr, *The Eighteenth-Century Revolution in Spain* (Princeton: Princeton University Press, 1958), pp. 376–80, 384–87, 400–407.

13. See J. Ignacio Rubio Mañé, *Los sanjuanistas de Yucatán: Manuel Jiménez Solís, el padre Justis* (Mexico City: n.p., 1971).

14. "Acuerdos y Sesiones de la Excelentísima Diputación Provincial de la Península de Yucatán, 1812–1820," Manuscript in Biblioteca Crescencio Carrillo y Ancona, Mérida.

15. Peón and Gondra, *Colección de leyes* (1896 edition), vol. 2, pp. 86–89.

16. Cline, "Regionalism and Society," Ch. 7, esp. pp. 562–72.

17. Peón and Gondra, *Colección de leyes*, vol. 2, pp. 215–18, 222–23, 507–10; Aznar Pérez and Pedrera, *Colección de leyes*, vol. 1, pp. 94–95, 100–101, 155–57, 259–60.

18. Aznar Pérez and Pedrera, *Colección de leyes*, vol. 2, pp. 116–19.

19. Ibid., pp. 215–16.

20. Ibid., p. 288.

21. Ibid., pp. 352–53.

22. The best treatment thus far of the intellectual environment, economy, and society of postindependence Yucatán is Cline, "Regionalism and Society."

23. Sierra, *Indios*, vol. 1, pp. 31–32. Cf. John Lloyd Stephens, *Incidents of Travel in Yucatan*, 2 vols. (New York: Harper and Brothers, 1843), esp. vol. 1, pp. 165–70.

24. Sierra, *Indios*, vol. 1, pp. 79–83.

25. Ibid., p. 83.

26. R. M. Nettings, "Maya Subsistence: Mythologies, Analogies, Possibilities," in *The Origins of Maya Civilization*, ed. R. E. W. Adams (Albuquerque: University of New Mexico Press, 1977), pp. 299–333. See also the various articles in Mary Pohl, ed., *Prehistoric Lowland Maya Environment and Subsistence Economy* (Boston: Peabody Museum of Archaeology and Ethnology, 1985); Kent V. Flannery, ed., *Maya Subsistence: Studies in Memory of Dennis E. Puleston* (New York: Academic Press, 1982); and Peter D. Harrison and B. L. Turner, eds., *Pre-Hispanic Maya Agriculture* (Albuquerque: University of New Mexico Press, 1978).

27. Nancy Farriss, "Nucleation versus Dispersal: The Dynamics of Population Movement in Colonial Yucatan," *HAHR* 58, no. 2 (1978): 187–216. Much of what follows is based in part on this article.

28. Ibid., pp. 205–13; and Farriss, *Maya Society*, pp. 199–223, 355–88.

29. Farriss, *Maya Society*, pp. 359–65; Robert Patch, "A Colonial Regime: Maya and Spaniard in Yucatán" (Ph.D. diss., Princeton University, 1979), pp. 361–63, 383–87, 403–409, 417–21, 451–69.

30. Cline, "Regionalism and Society," pp. 592–611; González Navarro, *Raza y tierra*, pp. 63–65.

31. Cited verbatim in AGEY/PE, Informe del Prefecto de Tekax al Secretario General de Gobierno, April 28, 1838.

32. Ibid.

33. AGEY/PE, Oficio del Jefe político subalterno de Bacalar al Jefe Superior político de Tekax, December 14, 1841; cited verbatim in Oficio de la Gefatura Superior política del Departamento de Tekax al Srio. Gral. de Gob., December 29, 1841.

34. AGEY/PE, Oficio de la Autoridad 1a. Municipal de Maní al Srio. Gral. de Gob., October 10, 1844.

35. AGEY/PE, Oficio del Jefe político de Peto al Srio. Gral. de Gob., July 16, 1844.

36. AGEY/PE, Circular de la Junta Departamental de Yucatán al Gobernador, April 11, 1837.

37. AGEY/PE, Carta del Subprefecto de Temax al Jefe político de Izamal, July 12, 1837, cited verbatim in Carta del Jefe político de Izamal al Srio. Gral. de Gob., July 18, 1837. The discussion that follows is based on this and a slightly later report by Castellanos, in Carta del Subprefecto de Temax al Prefecto de Izamal, November 6, 1838.

38. See for example AGEY/PE, exp. del *Cacique* y *República de Indígenas* de Seyé, July 27, 1835.

39. AGEY/PE, Oficio del Jefe político Subalterno accidental de Bolonchenticul al Srio. Gral. de Gob., October 13, 1842.

40. AGEY/PE, exp. de Matías Estévez, March 10, 1840.

41. AGEY/PE, exp. de Francisco Vázquez, n.d. (c. March 1840).

42. AGEY/PE, exp. de Francisco Buenfil, May 11, 1837.

43. AGEY/PE, exp. de Pablo José Arceo, March 25, 1845.

44. AGEY/PE, Plano orográfico de las seis leguas de tierras vendidas por el Supremo Govierno a D. Jeorge Fischer [*sic*] por si y como apoderado de otros dos Señores, January 31, 1842.

45. AGEY/PE, Oficio del Jefe político de Bacalar al Srio. Gral. de Gob., August 12, 1845.

46. AGEY/PE, Oficio del Subprefecto de Sotuta al Prefecto de Izamal, October 30, 1838.

47. AGEY/PE, Oficio del Subprefecto de Motul al Prefecto de Izamal, October 18, 1838.

48. AGEY/PE, Oficio del Subprefecto de Temax al Prefecto de Izamal, November 6, 1838.

49. AGEY/PE, Oficio del Juez de 1a. Instancia de Beneficios Altos al Srio. Gral. de Gob., December 7, 1840.

50. AGEY/PE, Ramo de Tierras, exp. del Ayuntamiento de Hampolol, June 10, 1822.

51. AGEY/C, Ramo de Ayuntamientos, vol. 1, exp. 6, Representación del Ayuntamiento de Champotón, April 24, 1813; AGEY/PE, Oficio del Jefe político de Hopelchén al Srio. Gral. de Gob., March 2, 1846.

52. AGEY/PE, Dictámenes de las Comisiones del Exmo. Consejo de Estado, Dictamen de Don Juan de Dios Cosgaya, January 9, 1844; Oficio del Jefe político Subalterno de Tecoh al Jefe político de Mérida, August 16, 1845; Oficio del Jefe político de Izamal al Srio. Gral. de Gob., August 13, 1845; Expediente del Juzgado del Alcalde 10. de Tixcacalcupul al Gobernador, October 22, 1844.

53. AGEY/PE, Solicitud del Juez de Paz del Rancho Nohcacab al R. Ayuntamiento de Peto, October 25, 1845. See also Oficio de la Asamblea Departamental al Goberna-

dor, July 31, 1844, for the elevation of the Rancho Cholul to pueblo status with the name of Libre Unión.

54. See, for example, AGEY/PE, exp. de los vecinos de Muna, November 13, 1837; Oficio de la Municipalidad de Halachó al Gobernador, February 20, 1841; Oficio del Jefe político Superior de Valladolid al Srio. Gral. de Gob., March 8, 1842; Oficio del Jefe político de Valladolid al Srio. Gral. de Gob., February 19, 1844; exp. del Cacique y República de Indígenas de Nunkiní, August 28, 1845; Circular de la Junta Departamental de Yucatán al Gobernador, December 13, 1836; exp. de Sebastián Avila, September 10, 1836; Oficio de la Asamblea Departamental al Gobernador, November 13, 1844.

55. See, for example, AGEY/PE, Oficio de la Subdelegación y Juzgado de 1a. Instancia de Sierra Baja al Gobernador, June 28, 1837; exp. del Cura Don Raymundo Pérez, May 24, 1837; exp. de Doña Magdalena Mendicuti, April 4, 1837.

56. AGEY/PE, exp. de Don José Teodoro Rodríguez, December 24, 1837. See also ibid., Dictámenes de las Comisiones del Exmo. Consejo de Estado, Dictamen de Don Juan de Dios Cosgaya, January 9, 1844, cited above in n. 52.

57. AGEY/PE, exp. de la República de Indígenas del Pueblo de Kinchil, November 15, 1837.

58. AGEY/PE, exp. del Alcalde de Huhí, June 23, 1845.

59. AGEY/PE, Oficio del Jefe político de Izamal al Srio. Gral. de Gob., April 28, 1845.

60. AGEY/PE, Oficio del Jefe político de Campeche al Srio. Gral. de Gob., April 29, 1845.

61. AGEY/PE, Plan de Arbitrios de este Pueblo de Kinchil que este municipio dirijió al Sr. Jefe Superior Político de este distrito . . . , June 20, 1845.

62. AGEY/PE, Oficio del Jefe político de Motul al Jefe político de Izamal, April 26, 1845, cited verbatim in Oficio del Jefe político de Izamal al Srio. Gral. de Gob., April 28, 1845; Oficio del Jefe político de Izamal al Srio. Gral. de Gob., June 3, 1845.

63. AGEY/PE, Oficio del Jefe político de Tekax al Srio. Gral. de Gob., April 30, 1845.

64. AGEY/PE, Oficio del Jefe político de Izamal al Srio. Gral. de Gob., June 1, 1845.

65. ANEY, Notarías de Manuel Barbosa, Francisco del Río, Pedro José Canto, José Dolores Roche, Antonio Patrón, Joaquín María Mendoza, and Manuel Gonzáles, 1843–47.

66. "Registro de anotaciones de las denuncias de terrenos baldíos, consecuente del Art^{o}. 1°. del acuerdo de la Exma. Asamblea Departamental de 5 de Diciembre de 1844," Manuscript formerly belonging to the now defunct Instituto Yucateco de Antropología e Historia, now in the special collection of manuscripts of the Biblioteca Crescencio Carrillo y Ancona, Mérida.

67. This was probably because the state government did not pay much attention to accurate record-keeping and therefore did not bother to ensure that a systematic registry was kept. At the same time, a claim filed in the registry, while aiding in a legal

dispute if someone else should claim the same land, did not signify legal title to the claim, while a notarial document did.

68. The political jurisdictions used in Tables 3.1, 3.2, and 3.3 are those in effect in the 1840s, with the exceptions of Izamal and Temax. The latter was a subprefecture in 1837 but was added shortly thereafter to the prefecture of Izamal. However, an extraordinarily large number of premios de campaña were granted in the area east of Dzilam, part of the former subprefecture of Temax and a region quite different from that of Izamal. Therefore, I chose to differentiate the two by maintaining the existence of the Temax subprefecture—detaching all of its former jurisdiction from that of Izamal. In other words, in the 1840s these two jurisdictions were in fact unified, but I have chosen to separate them for purposes of analysis. Also, it should be pointed out that the concept of political jurisdiction or territorial organization differed somewhat from similar concepts in English-speaking countries. The Spanish system stressed jurisdiction over people, not territory, and this continues to a certain extent in Mexico today, especially at the level of the municipio. In practice, this meant that unpopulated areas were virtually ignored by government officials, who were concerned only with the people under their jurisdiction.

69. Adjudicated terrenos baldíos in eighty-one notarial entries might also be included in the Registry of Claims, and therefore these cases have been left out in Table 3.3 to avoid possible double counting.

70. ANEY, Joaquín María Mendoza and Manuel Barbosa, January 13 and 14, 1847.

71. The data derived from the notarial records are as follows: Of 523 individuals who received terrenos baldíos, 286 were registered as ciudadanos and 237 as dones; they acquired 87.36 leagues and 174.48 leagues respectively. Of the 249 individuals who received premios de campaña, 198 were registered as ciudadanos and 51 as dones; they received 54.09 and 19.70 leagues respectively. Finally, of 319 people who purchased terrenos baldíos, 82 were ciudadanos and 237 were dones; they bought 33.271 and 154.79 leagues respectively. There is some overlap in the case of the data on the recipients, because 45 individuals purchased terrenos baldíos and received premios de campaña at the same time. These people had to be counted among both the purchasers and the veterans, but they were not double counted in the total.

72. "Registro de anotaciones . . . ," p. 49.

73. See Borah, *Justice by Insurance*.

74. AGEY/PE, Oficio del Jefe político de Izamal al Srio. Gral. de Gob., October 31, 1843.

75. AGEY/PE, Dictámenes de las Comisiones del Exmo. Consejo de Estado, Dictamen de Justo Sierra, January 19, 1844.

76. AGEY/PE, Oficio del Jefe político de Mérida al Srio. Gral. de Gob., July 9, 1844; Oficio del Jefe político de Hecelchakán al Srio. Gral. de Gob., November 30, 1844.

77. For cases of villages laying claim to terrenos baldíos, see AGEY/PE, Oficio de la Jefatura Superior política de Mérida al Srio. Gral. de Gob., November 24, 1846 (claim made by the pueblo of Kinchil); Oficio de la Asamblea Departamental al Gobernador, November 13, 1844 (Bécal); exp. del Cacique y República de Indígenas de Nunkiní, August 28, 1845 (Nunkiní); Oficio del Jefe político de Izamal al Srio. Gral. de Gob., Au-

gust 13, 1845 (which refers simply to claims being put forth by "various pueblos" of the prefecture); and in the Registry of Claims, see "Registro de anotaciones . . . ," pp. 13 (Tecoh), 17 (Nunkiní), 26 (Peto), 36 (Kinchil), 40 (Sitilpech), 51 (Rancho Santa Ursula), 52 (Rancho Tekao), and 55 (Tixcancal).

78. AGEY/PE, exp. de la República de Indígenas del Pueblo de Kinchil, November 15, 1837.

79. AGEY/PE, Oficio del Juzado 1o. Municipal de Dzoncauich al Srio. Gral. de Gob., July 18, 1843; Dictámenes de las Comisiones del Exmo. Consejo de Estado, Dictamen de Don Juan de Dios Cosgaya, January 9, 1844.

80. AGEY/PE, exp. de Pablo José Reyes, April 14, 1845.

81. AGEY/PE, exp. de Cristóbal Espínola, April 15, 1845.

82. In an 1836 dispute between the villages of Muna and Opichén, the former pueblo also attempted to justify its case by introducing old documents as evidence. However, the villagers of Opichén objected to Muna's efforts to base its claim "on papers from the conquest and other ridiculous documents," which suggests that Muna's procedures were not very common. See AGEY/PE, exp. de Sebastián Avila, September 10, 1836.

83. AGEY/PE, exp. de Felipe Gil, July 11, 1837.

84. For examples, see AGEY/PE, exp. de Da. Francisca Mena, April 10, 1840, and de Marcelino Peniche, October 21, 1841; Dictámenes de las Comisiones del Consejo de Estado, Dictamen de José Tiburcio López, December 26, 1843; Oficios del Jefe político de Yaxcabá al Srio. Gral. de Gob., July 30, October 6 and 23, 1844; Oficio del Jefe político de Izamal al Srio. Gral. de Gob., August 13, 1845; exp. de José Anastasio Pérez, August 29, 1845, and de Pedro José Campos, July 27, 1844.

85. For example, see AGEY/PE, exp. de Santiago Chan, June 2, 1840; Inventario de los bienes de Don Clemente Uc, expediente de octubre 20, 1844; Oficio de la Asamblea Departamental al Gobernador, November 20, 1844; Oficio del Jefe político de Campeche al Srio. Gral. de Gob., August 26, 1845.

86. AGEY/PE, Oficio de la Asamblea Departamental al Gobernador, November 30, 1844.

87. AGEY/PE, Oficio del Ynspector de Caminos de Acanceh al Sr. Ynspector de Caminos, March 5, 1841.

88. AGEY/PE, Oficio del Jefe político de Tecoh al Srio. Gral. de Gob., April 27, 1843.

89. AGEY/PE, exp. del Alcalde Municipal de Huhí, June 23, 1845.

90. AGEY/PE, Oficio de la Jefatura política accidental de Ticul al Srio. Gral. de Gob., April 21, 1843.

4. Capital-Labor Relations

1. Hubert H. Bancroft, *History of Central America 1801–1887* (San Francisco: History Company Publishers, 1887), vol. 3, p. 702.

2. Reed, *Caste War.*

3. Robert F. Chamberlain, *The Conquest and Colonization of Yucatan* (Washington, D.C.: Carnegie Institution of Washington, 1948).

4. See, for example, Alfonso Villa Rojas, *Los eligidos de Dios: Etnografía de los mayas de Quintana Roo* (Mexico City: Instituto Nacional Indigenista, 1978), pp. 80–81.

5. Philip Ainsworth Means, "History of the Spanish Conquest of Yucatan and of the Itzas," *Papers of the Peabody Museum* 7 (1917): 54–83.

6. Quoted in Eric Thompson, *The Maya of Belize: Historical Chapters since Columbus* (Belize City: Benex Press, 1972), p. 15.

7. France Scholes and Eric Thompson, "The Francisco Pérez Probanza of 1654–56 and the Matrícula of Tipu (Belize)," in *Anthropology and History in Yucatan*, ed. Grant D. Jones (Austin: University of Texas Press, 1977), pp. 43–68.

8. H. Whitney, *The Honduras Almanack for 1839* (Belize City: n.p., 1839).

9. Lawrence Feldman, "Belize and Its Neighbors: A Preliminary Report on the Spanish Colonial Records of the Audiencia of Guatemala," in *Archaeology at Colha, Belize: The 1981 Interim Report*, ed. T. H. Hester et al. (San Antonio: University of Texas Press, 1982), pp. 251–60.

10. José Calderón Quijano, Belice, *1663[?]–1821: Historia de los establecimientos británicos del Río Valis hasta la independencia de Hispanoamérica* (Seville: Escuela de Estudios Hispanoamericanos de la Universidad de Sevilla, 1944).

11. Lindsay W. Bristowe and Philip B. Wright, *The Handbook of British Honduras for 1888–1889* (Edinburgh and London: William Blackwood and Sons, 1890).

12. David Pendergast, "Under Spanish Rule: The Final Chapter in Lamanai's Maya History," Manuscript, 1985; see also Grant Jones, "The Last Maya Frontiers of Colonial Yucatan," in *Spanish and Indians in Southeastern Mesoamerica*, ed. Murdo MacLeod and R. Wasserstrom (Lincoln: University of Nebraska Press, 1983), pp. 64–91.

13. Gilbert Joseph, "The Logwood Trade and its Settlements," in *Readings in Belizean History*, vol. 1, ed. John Mahler (Belize City: BISRA, 1978), pp. 7–22.

14. George Henderson, *An Account of the British Settlement of Honduras* (London: C. & R. Baldwin, 1809), pp. 12–13; see also ABH, Note from an inhabitant to the Magistrates, February 19, 1807, p. 101.

15. Henderson, *British Settlement*, p. 13.

16. AB, Report on Yellow Fever Epidemics from earliest times to 1922, by Thomas Gann, Public Medical Practitioner, Minute Paper, pp. 260–62.

17. AB, Report R. 25, [n.d.], p. 244.

18. AB, Supt. Macdonald to Sec. of State, R. 14a, August 25, 1837, pp. 22–26.

19. AB, John Hodge to Lt. Gov., November 30, 1865, pp. 8–29.

20. Ibid., p. 83.

21. Ibid., pp. 8–29.

22. ABH, General Meeting at Kay Casine, April 10, 1765, p. 107.

23. See, for example, GRB, Will of Robert Perry, Book 1a, October 15, 1787, pp. 187–89. The superintendent was the highest-ranking British official in the settlement. His immediate superior was the governor of Jamaica.

24. ABH, Supt. Marcus Despard to Lord Sydney, March 4, 1787, p. 161.

25. Nigel Bolland, "Slavery in Belize," *BISRA*, Occasional Publication 7 (1979), p. 7.

26. Ministry of Lands and Survey, Belmopan, Belize, Map Collection, Map no. 419, 1867[?].

27. AB, George Arthur to Earl Bathurst, Shofield Papers 188, October 7, 1820. After declaring martial law, Superintendent Arthur toured the mahogany camps to find out the cause of the revolt. He reported that "the Negroes who had first deserted and had excited others to join them, had been treated with very unnecessary harshness by their Owner, and had certainly good grounds for complaint."

28. Narda Dobson, *A History of Belize* (Kingston, Jamaica: Longman Caribbean, 1973), p. 151.

29. GRB. Mentioned in Registrar's Reason for Decision in Vega vs. Carmichael, 1862–63.

30. AB, Supt. Frederick Seymour to J. Faber, R. 72, August 2, 1862, pp. 135–36.

31. AB, Supt. F. Fancourt to Gov. of Jamaica, R. 25, March 13, 1848, pp. 305–307.

32. AB, Supt. to Authorities in Bacalar, R. 16, 1839[?].

33. M. Mazarrelli, "Continuity in Change: Settlement in the Upper Belize Valley" (M. A. thesis, no university given, n.d.).

34. See, for example, AB, Supt. to Gov. of Jamaica, R. 52, July 14, 1857, p. 275.

35. AB, Magistrate Salmon to Fancourt, R. 36, December 30, 1850, pp. 122–32.

36. See, for example, AB, G. Escobar to Supt., R. 33, July 9, 1850, pp. 232–35.

37. AB, Fancourt to Gov. Grey, R. 31, January 11, 1850, p. 50.

38. GRB, Vega vs. Carmichael, Testimony of P. Orío, August 25, 1863.

39. AB, F. E. Gabb, "Notes on Villages in the Orange Walk District," R. 118, August 30, 1884, p. 250.

40. GRB, Vega vs. Carmichael, Testimony on John Faber, October 20, 1863.

41. AB, John Young to Sir F. Rogers, R. 70, August 2, 1860, pp. 265–320.

42. GRB, Application for land title registration, July 1861.

43. AB, An Analysis . . . of Colonial Timber, R. 116, August 1878, pp. 402–24; for 1860 land concentration figures, see Chief Justice Robert Temple's notes, R. 76, February 4, 1860, pp. 219–38.

44. Oral informant, village of Yo Creek, August 3, 1982; AB, Shofield Papers, Recapitulation of Returns respecting the Estate of John Carmichael, September 21, 1873.

45. See G. A. Menéndez Reyes, *Quintana Roo album monográfico* (Chetumal: Editorial del Estado de Quintana Roo, 1979).

46. Thomas Gann, *The Maya Indians of Southern Yucatan and Northern British Honduras* (Washington, D.C.: U.S. Government Printing Office, 1918).

47. For example, most of the Maya were monolingual, which reduced the facility of making business arrangements with managers of local British firms, generally equally monolingual in English.

48. Oral informant, village of Yo Creek.

49. Oral informant, village of San Antonio, Río Hondo, August 5, 1982.

50. AB, Edmund Burke to Basilio Grajales, R. 84, May 26, 1864, p. 315.

51. AB, Laws of British Honduras, vol. 31, Vic. Cap. 4, 1868.

52. Ibid., vol. 18, Vic. Cap. 18, 1855.

53. Ibid., vol. 25, Vic. Cap. 16, 1862.

54. AB, Attorney General to Lt. Gov., R. 113, March 14, 1873, pp. 34–35.

55. Cline, "Sugar Episode."

56. AB, Burke to Seymour, R. 74, January 8, 1862, pp. 353–58.

57. AB, James Hume Blake to Seymour, R. 79, March 20, 1863, pp. 526–30.

58. AB, Seymour to Rhys, R. 72, October 4, 1862, pp. 171–75.

59. AB, Statement of James Haylock, R. 89, December 24, 1866, pp. 583–88.

60. Oral informant, village of San Antonio.

61. AB, Supt. to Gov. of Jamaica, R. 38, March 1, 1852, pp. 43–46.

62. Oral informant, village of Yo Creek.

63. AB, Edward Kreft to Acting Supt., R. 71, July 9, 1860, p. 55.

64. AB, Shofield Papers, Recapitulations of Returns Respecting the Estate of John Carmichael, September 21, 1873.

65. AB, Florencio de la Vega to Supt., R. 29, August 17, 1850, pp. 545–46.

66. AB, Lt. Gov. to Gov. of Jamaica, R. 81, March 11, 1865, pp. 458–60; Immigration Agent to Lt. Gov., R. 89, July 4, 1865, pp. 102–103.

67. See, for example, AB, Petition of William Carter, R. 77, [n.d.], pp. 155–56.

68. GRB, Probate and Administration Records, Micaila Mai of Cocos, Affidavit of John Travis, March 28, 1854.

69. AB, Statement of Cultivation of Br. Hond. Co. lands, Rio Hondo, R. 86, 1865, p. 372.

70. AB, Petitioners to Supt., R. 54, August 15, 1856, pp. 499–50.

71. AB, John Carmichael to Brig. Gen. Harley, R. 109, October 30, 1871, p. 245.

72. See, for example, GRB, Probate and Administration Records, Estate of Román Acosta, April 8, 1859.

73. AB, José María Tzuc to Supt., R. 78, October 27, 1853, pp. 240–41.

74. AB, Marcos Canul and Rafael Chan to Lt. Gov., R. 106, May 4, 1870, pp. 137–39; Lt. Gov to Gov. of Jamaica, R. 92, December 28, 1866, pp. 390–92.

75. Ángel E. Cal, "The Corozal (Goshen) Estate," *Belcast Journal of Belizean Affairs* 1 (1984): 41–47.

76. Bill Albert and Adrian Graves, eds., *Crises and Change in the International Sugar Economy 1860–1914* (Edinburgh: I. S. C. Press, 1984), p. 1.

77. Roberta Delson, "Sugar Production for the 19th Century British Market: Rethinking the Roles of Brazil and the British West Indies," in ibid., pp. 59–81.

Introduction to Part II

1. See, for example, William B. Taylor, "Between Global Process and Local Knowledge: An Inquiry into Early Latin American Social History, 1500–1900," in Zunz, *Reliving the Past*, Ch. 3, esp. p. 170.

2. See, for example, John M. Hart, *Revolutionary Mexico: The Coming and Process of the Mexican Revolution* (Berkeley: University of California Press, 1987); and Ramón E. Ruiz, *The People of Sonora and Yankee Capitalists* (Tucson: University of Arizona Press, 1988).

3. The substantial literature on the consequences of the rebellion and the rise of henequen is surveyed in Joseph, *Rediscovering the Past*, pp. 36–52.

4. See Wells et al., *Yucatán y la International Harvester* (Mérida: Maldonado Editores, 1986), a collection of writings originally published in English in *LARR* during 1982–83.

5. Joseph and Wells, "Monocultivo de henequén." The Mérida Specialists Conference in April 1987 introduced other valuable research on henequen monoculture's structure and ideology of domination. In "Mujeres, intercambios matrimoniales y esclavitud durante el Porfiriato, 1880–1910," anthropologist Piedad Peniche Rivero offered provocative findings from a long-term project on the role of women in the henequen zone during the fiber boom. Peniche suggested that large henequen planters may well have engaged in the commercial exchange of Mayan women to gain greater leverage over reproduction and ensure themselves a more stable labor force. Her quantitative study is still in its early stages. In "Hacia una nueva agricultura: Yucatán a mediados del siglo XIX," historian of science Alejandra García Quintanilla offered a fresh examination of how Yucatán's modernizing planter elite began to fashion a new positivistic understanding of agriculture and nature itself. Ironically, creole planter-intellectuals appropriated aspects of traditional Mayan agronomy, even as they labeled them regressive. Peniche's and García's essays appear in Baños Ramírez, *Sociedad*.

6. Farriss, *Maya Society*, makes the same point regarding the progressive erosion of northwestern Mayan society beginning in late colonial times.

7. For example, see Taylor, "Global Process and Local Knowledge"; and Carol A. Smith, "Local History in Global Context: Social and Economic Transitions in Western Guatemala," *Comparative Studies in Society and History* 26 (April 1984): 193–228; and see the discussion in Joseph, *Rediscovering the Past*, pp. 135–36, 177–78.

8. For example, Wells et al., *Yucatán y la International Harvester*; Joseph, *Revolution from Without*; and Farriss, *Maya Society*.

9. Cf. the excellent multilayered analysis of the prolongation of the Caste War by Canadian ethnohistorian Marie Lapointe, *Mayas rebeldes*, esp. Chs. 4, 6–8.

5. From Hacienda to Plantation

This chapter is a substantially revised version of Chapter 5 of *Yucatán's Gilded Age: Haciendas, Henequen, and International Harvester, 1860–1915* (Albuquerque: University of New Mexico Press, 1985). The author gratefully acknowledges the support of the National Endowment for the Humanities, the American Philosophical Society, and the University Research Committee of Appalachian State University.

1. Three excellent studies of the commercialization of agriculture during the late nineteenth century are Manuel Moreno Fraginals, *El ingenio: Complejo económico social cubano del azúcar*, 3 vols. (Havana: Editorial de Ciencias Sociales, 1978); Arnold Bauer, *Chilean Rural Society* (Cambridge: Cambridge University Press, 1975); and Arturo Warman, *Y venimos a contradecir: Los campesinos de Morelos y el estado nacional* (Mexico City: La Casa Chata, 1976).

2. Marx understood that the transition to agrarian capitalism would not be uniform: "The history of this expropriation (of the peasant from the soil) in different countries, assumes different aspects, and runs through its various phases in different orders of succession, and at different periods." Karl Marx, *Capital* (New York: International Publishers, 1967), Vol. 1, p. 716.

3. Eric R. Wolf and Sidney W. Mintz, "Haciendas and Plantations in Middle America and the Antilles," *Social and Economic Studies* 6 (1957): 380. An excellent overview of the literature on the traditional hacienda in Mexico is found in Van Young, "Mexican Rural History." For further discussion of the definition of a plantation, see Lloyd Best, "Outlines of a Model of a Pure Plantation Economy," *Social and Economic Studies* (September 1968); Edgar T. Thompson, "The Plantation as a Social System," in Pan American Union, *Plantation Systems of the New World* (Washington, D.C.: PAN, 1959); and George L. Beckford, *Persistent Poverty: Underdevelopment of Plantation Economies of the Third World* (New York: Oxford University Press, 1972), Ch. 1.

4. Magnus Mörner, "La hacienda hispanoamericana: Examen de las investigaciones y debates recientes," in *Haciendas, latifundios y plantaciones en América Latina*, ed. Enrique Florescano (Mexico City: Siglo XXI Editores, 1975), p. 17. Wolf and Mintz, "Haciendas and Plantations," p. 381, caution that the hacienda and plantation types are not the only systems found in Middle America nor are they polar concepts. Moreover, they insist that the hacienda and the plantation are not necessarily sequential stages in the development of modern commercial agriculture. Notwithstanding these caveats, the definitions themselves and Mörner's concept of a continuum that incorporates the plantation, hacienda, and ranch as variations of the same phenomenon help us to understand the evolution of the landed estate in Yucatán.

5. Wolf and Mintz based their analytical framework on field research in Puerto Rico, Jamaica, and Mexico.

6. On the transformation of the Caribbean sugar industry, see Manuel Moreno Fraginals, "Plantations in the Caribbean: Cuba, Puerto Rico, and the Dominican Republic in the Late Nineteenth Century," in Moreno Fraginals et al., *Slavery and Free Labor*, pp. 3–21; and Christian Schnakenbourg, "From the Sugar Estate to Central Factory: The Industrial Revolution in the Caribbean (1840–1905)," in Albert and Graves, *Crisis and Change*, pp. 83–93.

7. For an interesting discussion of Wolf and Mintz's definitions, see Kenneth Duncan and Ian Rutledge, eds., *Land and Labour in Latin America: Essays on the Development of Agrarian Capitalism in the Nineteenth and Twentieth Centuries* (Cambridge: Cambridge University Press, 1977), pp. 5–7.

8. Wolf and Mintz, "Haciendas and Plantations," p. 390.

9. Ibid., p. 401.

10. Duncan and Rutledge have created a fourfold typology for differentiating patterns of capitalist development in rural Latin America: (1) traditional hacienda to capitalist estate; (2) plantation with labor recruitment from highland peasant communities; (3) commercial agriculture using European immigrant labor; and (4) transition from slave plantation to capitalist plantation. Although Yucatán's henequen economy exhibits many characteristics of the first pattern, it evolved into a monocrop economy. See Duncan and Rutledge, *Land and Labour*, "Introduction."

11. Those who speak in the language of the "articulation of modes of production" would point to Yucatán as a perfect example of a rural society that was undergoing a transition in the nineteenth century from a precapitalist to a capitalist mode of production. But, beyond the notion that the characteristics pertaining to any given agrarian system depend to a large extent upon the manner in which it has developed out of the previous mode of production, such generalizations offer little insight regarding concrete instances of transition. For a sample of the literature on modes of production analysis, see John G. Taylor, *From Modernization to Modes of Production: A Critique of the Sociologies of Development and Underdevelopment* (London: Macmillan, 1979); David Goodman and Michael Redclift, *From Peasant to Proletarian: Capitalist Development and Agrarian Transitions* (New York: St. Martin's Press, 1982), Ch. 2; and Roger Bartra, "Peasants and Political Power in Mexico: A Theoretical Approach," *Latin American Perspectives* 5 (1975): 125–45.

12. For a thorough investigation of labor relations on Yucatecan henequen estates, see Joseph and Wells, "Monocultivo de henequén."

13. See Allen Wells, "Family Elites in a Boom and Bust Economy: The Molinas and Peóns of Porfirian Yucatán," *HAHR* 62, no. 2 (1982): 224–53. It is instructive that landowners referred to themselves as "hacendados" during the henequen boom, while catastral lists and press reports always called the henequen estates "haciendas," not plantations. The terms *hacendado* and *hacienda* meant something special to contemporaries, otherwise labels such as "plantations" and "corporate managers" would have found their way into the literature. It should be noted that *hacienda* had been a catchall term throughout the colonial period in Mexico, signifying the large estate. In fact, sugar plantations, ranches, and farms that grew cereals, all were labeled haciendas by contemporaries. See David Brading, "Hacienda Profits and Tenant Farming in the Mexican Bajío, 1700–1860," in Duncan and Rutledge, *Land and Labour*, p. 23.

14. I am deeply indebted to Juan Peón Ancona and Carlos Peniche Escalante for providing me with a wealth of private papers on the emergence of Santo Domingo Xcuyum and other haciendas.

15. The emergence of the hacienda in Yucatán was a delayed phenomenon. Unlike many regions of Latin America, Yucatán's harsh, forbidding physical environment, climate, and lack of precious metals retarded the development of the great estate until the eighteenth century. Until that time, the peripheral colony was characterized by small cattle *estancias* and semiautonomous Mayan Indian communities. For an insightful discussion of Yucatán's cattle and maize haciendas see Patch, "Colonial Regime"; and Farriss, *Maya Society*, Ch. 12.

16. Patch, "Formación de estancias"; and his "Agrarian Change in Eighteenth-Century Yucatán," *HAHR* 65, no. 1 (1985): 21–49. Farriss speaks to the devastating impact

of the encroaching hacienda on the twin principles of reciprocity and corporateness that had sheltered Mayan communities during the colonial period in *Maya Society*, Ch. 12.

17. As Farriss indicates, the hacienda's social organization was only "a deformed imitation of a pueblo," lacking its cohesive and semiautonomous character. The Maya were totally dependent on the amo and the mayordomo for food, land for milpa, famine relief, justice, protection, and other services. If the hacienda offered security, it did so at the expense of the Mayan community. See *Maya Society*, pp. 385–86.

18. Stanley J. Stein and Barbara H. Stein, *The Colonial Heritage of Latin America* (New York: Oxford University Press, 1970), pp. 137–38.

19. I am grateful to the late Alfredo Barrera Vázquez for furnishing me with the correct etymology of *Xcuyum*.

20. Personal papers of Juan Peón Ancona, "Títulos de Santo Domingo Xcuyum" (hereafter referred to as Peón Ancona papers).

21. Calderón sold the estate in 1769, and from that date until 1836 the property changed hands four times. Although the surface area of Xcuyum was recorded as one square league (1,755 hectares) during the colonial era, that was only a rough estimate since boundaries were far from precise. In addition, tax assessments were based in part on property size, so many hacendados took great pains to hide the true extent of their estates from Crown tax collectors. Although the boundaries of Xcuyum did undergo some modification during the sixty years from the Conde's sale to the purchase by Manuel Casares de las Llanes in 1836, the hacienda did not witness any significant development. Peón Ancona papers, passim.

22. Still, in 1830 local elites recognized the crop's potential and formed an economic society to promote, perfect, and increase the cultivation of the agave. Benito Aznar et al., *Reglamento de la Compañía para el cultivo y beneficio del henequén* (Mérida: n.p., 1830).

23. Peón Ancona papers, "Venta de la hacienda Xcuyum." On Casares family background, see José María Valdés Acosta, *A través de los siglos*, 3 vols. (Mérida: Talleres "Pluma y Lápiz," 1926–29), vol. 3, pp. 384–89. Manuel Casares de las Llanes opened the Liceo Yucateco in 1833, the first school offering English instruction in the peninsula. For health reasons, he closed the school three years later.

24. Patch, "Colonial Regime," chs. 4 and 5 esp.; and Farriss, *Maya Society*, Ch. 12.

25. Manuel bought nearby haciendas Xkantun and Chaczinkin, neither of which encompassed more than a quarter of a square league (approximately four hundred hectares). This added two hundred head of cattle to the Casares herd. Peón Ancona papers, passim.

26. Valdés Acosta, *A través de los siglos*, vol. 3, pp. 384–89.

27. AGEY/PE, Padrón General, Tixkokob partido, 1879.

28. Peón Ancona papers, Terrenos nacionales, Yaxkukul (Contreras), May 10, 1886.

29. On Conkal purchases, see personal papers of Carlos Peniche Escalante, Títulos de ejidos, Conkal, 1889–90.

30. See, for permutas with Leandro León Ayala, José Patrón Zavlegui, Oficio no. 5, vol. 58, October 28, 1890, pp. 1394–96; with Esteban Andrade, Patrón Zavlegui, vol. 58, October 3, 1890, pp. 1287–90; and with Hacienda Dzonot, Patrón Zavlegui, vol. 59, January 19, 1891, pp. 157–59.

31. A classic violent confrontation between ejidatarios and landowners took place in Cepeda, a town on the fringes of the Puuc region, in 1908. See Joseph and Wells, "Yucatán." For an excellent synthesis of agrarian unrest during the nineteenth and twentieth centuries in Mexico, see John Tutino, *From Insurrection to Revolution in Mexico: Social Bases of Agrarian Violence, 1750–1940* (Princeton: Princeton University Press, 1986).

32. Mayan villagers must have yearned for the days when semiautonomous communities, which had sufficient financial resources, not only petitioned the Crown against encroaching hacendados but filed suits in the courts to protect their properties. See Farriss, *Maya Society*, pp. 272–85.

33. For a discussion of these inefficient manual implements, see the *Cordage Trade Journal* 35, no. 2 (July 18, 1907): 24–26.

34. Frederick A. Ober, *Travels in Mexico and Life among the Mexicans* (Boston: Estes and Lauriat, 1884), p. 83.

35. A small yet profitable service industry did develop locally to service the needs of henequen machine houses. See Eric N. Baklanoff and Jeffery Brannon, "Forward and Backward Linkages in a Plantation Economy: Immigrant Entrepreneurship and Industrial Development in Yucatan, Mexico," *Journal of Developing Areas* 18, no. 1 (1984): 83–94.

36. *U.S. Consular Reports*, Commerce, Manufacturing, etc., 71, no. 271 (April 1903), p. 477.

37. AGEY/PE, Relación de todos las máquinas existentes en este cabecera y pueblos de su partido aplicables a la raspa de henequén con expresión de la fuerza de caballo de cada uno y ruedas que mueven, 1879, and Estado que manifesta . . . , 1884; and AGEY/J, Inventario de la Hacienda Santo Domingo Xcuyum, 1895.

38. AGEY/J, Inventario de la Hacienda Santo Domingo Xcuyum, 1895.

39. ANEY, Patrón Zavlegui, vol. 40, December 31, 1885, pp. 1122–34.

40. It is also instructive to note that many of the lenders, such as Casares, José María Ponce, José Font, and Pedro Leal Gamboa, were part of General Cantón's political *camarilla* or faction. See Joseph and Wells, "Yucatán."

41. ANEY, Patrón Zavlegui, vol. 40, December 31, 1885, pp. 1122–34.

42. AGEY/PE, Registro Público de Propiedad, Cancelaciones, 1897.

43. José I. Rivas Font, *Apuntes sobre el cultivo y la explotación del henequén* (Mérida: El Eco del Comercio, 1906), p. 12.

44. Also on henequen cultivation, see Roland Emanuel Paul Chardon, *Geographic Aspects of Plantation Agriculture in Yucatan* (Washington, D.C.: National Academy of Sciences, 1961); Rafael de Portas, *Tratado sobre el cultivo de la caña: Elaboración del azúcar y cultivo del henequén* (Mérida: Imprenta del Gobierno, 1872); and José A. Bolio, *Manual práctico del henequén* (Mérida: Imprenta de la Empresa Editorial Católica, 1914).

45. *El Agricultor* 1 (January 1, 1907): 12–13.

46. *La Razón del Pueblo* (Mérida), 1892–94, passim.

47. Ibid.

48. *El Henequén* (Mérida), January 15, 1916.

49. AGEY/J, Remate de la Hacienda Santo Domingo Xcuyum, 1895.

50. On 1879 data, see AGEY/PE, Padrón General, 1879. On 1895 data, see Peón Ancona papers, Inventario de la Hacienda Santo Domingo Xcuyum, 1895.

51. A thorough examination of the diverse work force found on the henequen estate is beyond the scope of this chapter. See Allen Wells, "Yucatán: Violence and Social Control on Henequen Plantations," in Benjamin and McNellie, *Other Mexicos*, pp. 213–41; Marco Bellingeri, "Proyecto de investigación: La hacienda y la sociedad yucateca en el siglo XIX," *Yucatán: Historia y Economía* 1 (November–December 1977): 3–13; and Alan Knight, "Mexican Peonage: What Was It and Why Was It?" *Journal of Latin American Studies* 18, no. 1 (1986): 41–74. For a discussion of the peonage laws adopted by Yucatecan state governments during the nineteenth century, see González Navarro, *Raza y Tierra*, pp. 54–64.

52. Allen Wells, *Yucatán's Gilded Age: Haciendas, Henequen, and International Harvester, 1860–1915* (Albuquerque: University of New Mexico Press, 1985), pp. 174–76. For a fascinating discussion of debts and wages on henequen and maize haciendas in Yucatán during the auge, see Christopher J. Gill, "Regional Variation and Patterns of Resistance: The Henequen Boom in Yucatan, 1880–1915" (Seniors Honors thesis, University of Michigan, 1987), Ch. 3.

53. Tutino argues that resident peons tied by debts still found security on Yucatecan henequen estates, thereby inhibiting mobilization during the last years of the Porfiriato; see *Insurrection to Revolution*, pp. 288–97. For a contrasting view, see Joseph and Wells, "Yucatán."

54. Wages varied depending on the task completed. I have used here Keith Hartman's figures, with which, on the average, I concur. Hartman, "The Henequen Empire in Yucatan: 1870–1910" (Master's thesis, University of Iowa, 1966), p. 118.

55. Friedrich Katz, "Labor Conditions on Haciendas in Porfirian Mexico: Some Trends and Tendencies," *HAHR* 54, no. 1 (1974): 1–47. Katz's figures are taken from *Estadísticas económicas del Porfiriato: Fuerza de trabajo y actividad económica por sectores* (Mexico City: El Colegio de México, 1964), pp. 147–48.

56. AGEY/PE, Circular de la Secretaría de Fomento, March 25, 1902.

57. The servants' wages were 37.50 centavos per thousand leaves cut; 25 centavos per mecate cleared and weeded; and 37.50 centavos for a lote of firewood. See ANEY, Maximiliano Canto, Cuarto Bimestre, November 29, 1901.

58. *El Eco del Comercio* (Mérida), March 20, 1902.

59. *Boletín de Estadística*, October 1 and 16, 1894.

60. *Mexican Herald* (Mexico City), June 16, 1908.

61. For a thorough discussion of cooperative societies and the reasons for their failure, see Gilbert M. Joseph and Allen Wells, "Summer of Discontent: Economic Rivalry among Elite Factions during the Late Porfiriato in Yucatán," *Journal of Latin American Studies* 18, no. 2 (1986): 261–66; and Gonzalo Cámara Zavala, *Reseña histórica de la industria henequenera de Yucatán* (Mérida: Imprenta del Oriente, 1936).

62. AGEY/J, Remate de la Hacienda Santo Domingo Xcuyum, 1895.

63. It is important to note that Casares threw this celebration just as the henequen economy was about to come unglued. No doubt the expense involved contributed to his financial difficulties.

64. *El Eco del Comercio*, February 18 and March 7, 1893.

65. Among the dignitaries who visited Xcuyum were Governor Francisco Cantón in 1898 and the archbishop of Yucatán in 1908.

66. Valdés Acosta, *A través de los siglos*, vol. 3, pp. 381–84.

67. For a detailed discussion of entrepreneurial activity in the face of hazardous economic conditions, see Wells, "Family Elites."

68. Juan Miguel Castro, *El henequén de Yucatán y el monopolio* (Mérida: Imprenta del Comercio de Nestor Rubio Alpuche, 1876).

69. *Testimonio de escritura de transacción celebrada entre el síndico de la quiebra de los Sres. M. Dondé y Cía y el Sr. D. Manual Dondé Cámara* (Mérida: Imprenta Gamboa Guzmán, 1895); *Notable dictamen de varios distinguidos jurisconsultos sobre Manuel Dondé Cámara* (Mérida: Imprenta Gamboa Guzmán, 1897).

70. See Gilbert M. Joseph and Allen Wells, "Collaboration and Informal Empire in Yucatán: The Case for Political Economy," *LARR* 18, no. 3 (1983): 208, n. 4, for a complete discussion of the National Cordage Company's attempted corner on the market in 1889/90.

71. Derived from AGEY/J, Remate de la Hacienda Santo Domingo Xcuyum, 1895.

72. ANEY, Maximiliano Canto, 3d Trimestre, October 13, 1897; and Manuel Avila Maldonado, December 30, 1893, vol. 55, pp. 628–33, 637.

73. AGEY/J, Remate de la Hacienda Santo Domingo Xcuyum, 1895.

74. Ibid.

75. Ibid.

76. *El Crédito del Estado* (Mérida) 12, July 15, 1895, in the Biblioteca Carlos R. Menéndez, Mérida.

77. AGEY/J, Incidente promovido por el apoderado de D. Dolores Guerra de Mendoza pidiendo la suspensión del remate de la hacienda Xcuyum, 1895.

78. Ibid.

79. *El Crédito del Estado* (Mérida) 12, July 15, 1895.

80. ANEY, Avelino López, Oficio no. 10, vol. 27, February 27, 1899, pp. 254–61.

81. *La Razón del Pueblo*, January 7, 1895.

82. *El Henequén*, January 15, 1916.

83. For a thorough discussion of the ailing henequen industry, see Jeffery Brannon and Eric N. Baklanoff, *Agrarian Reform and Public Enterprise in Mexico: The Political Economy of Yucatán's Henequen Industry* (University: University of Alabama Press, 1987).

6. Capitalism on the Tropical-Forest Frontier

1. The concept of *frontier* in both the North and Latin American historical tradition has taken the colonizer's point of view. This might be seen as a variant of metropole-hinterland perceptions and experiences within a context of conquest, expansion, and integration of peoples and territories. For a discussion of the idea of frontier and its usage, see Ray A. Billington, *The American Frontier Thesis: Attack and Defense* (Washington, D.C.: American Historical Association, 1973); Alistair Hennessey, *The Frontier in Latin American History* (Albuquerque: University of New Mexico Press, 1978); José H. Rodríguez, "Webb's Great Frontier and the Interpretation of Modern History," in *The New World Looks at its History*, ed. A. Lewis and T. McGann (Austin: University of Texas Press, 1963), pp. 155–64; George R. Taylor, *The Turner Thesis Concerning the Role of the Frontier in American History*, 3d ed. (Boston: Heath, 1956); Walter P. Webb, *The Great Frontier* (Cambridge: Harvard University Press, 1952); Silvio Zavala, "The Frontiers of Hispanic America," in *The Frontier in Perspective*, ed. W. D. Wyman and C. G. Kroeber (Madison: University of Wisconsin Press, 1957), pp. 35–58.

2. For British interactions with the Maya, see Lapointe, *Mayas rebeldes*. For views from Mérida, see Antonio Canto López, *El Territorio de Quintana Roo y Yucatán* (Mérida: Estado de Yucatán, 1954); Carlos A. Echánove Trujillo, *Una tierra en disputa: Belice ante la historia* (Mérida: Universidad de Yucatán, 1951); Bernardino Mena Brito, *Historia de las desmembraciones del Estado de Yucatán efectuados por el gobierno nacional: El Petén, Belice, Campeche, Quintana Roo* (Mexico City: Ediciones Bota, 1962). For the reaction to Bravo's capture of Chan Santa Cruz, see *Diario Oficial* (Yucatán) (1901); for the separation of Quintana Roo, see *Diario Oficial de la Nación* (1902), and AGN/G, exp. 902 (3) 9, 1902.

3. Sylvanus Morley, *The Ancient Maya*, 3d ed. (Stanford: Stanford University Press, 1956); and J. Eric Thompson, *Maya History and Religion* (Norman: University of Oklahoma Press, 1970).

4. Farriss, *Maya Society*.

5. D. E. Dumond, "Independent Maya of the Late Nineteenth Century: Chiefdoms and Power Politics," in Jones, *Anthropology and History*, pp. 103–38; Grant D. Jones, "La estructura política de los Mayas de Chan Santa Cruz: El papel del respaldo Inglés," *América Indígena* 31, no. 2 (1971): 415–28; and Lapointe, *Mayas rebeldes*.

6. Anthony P. Andrews, "Puertos costeros del postclásico temprano en el norte de Yucatán," *Estudios de Cultura Maya* 11 (1978): 75–93, and his *Maya Salt Production and Trade* (Tucson: University of Arizona Press, 1983); Frans Blom, "Commerce, Trade, and Monetary Units of the Maya," *Middle American Papers* no. 4 (1932), pp. 531–56; Jeremy Sabloff and Willima L. Rathje, *A Study of Changing Pre-Colombian Commercial Systems: The 1972–1973 Seasons at Cozumel, Mexico*, Monographs of the Peabody Museum no. 3 (Cambridge: Harvard University Press, 1975).

7. Chamberlain, *Conquest and Colonization*.

8. For an overview of such projects, see Lapointe, *Mayas rebeldes*; and AGN/FP/OC, Informe . . . Territorio Federal de Quintana Roo, exp. 241-A-Q-2, 1925.

9. Herman W. Konrad, "Fallout of the War of the Chacs: The Impact of Hurricanes and Implications for Prehispanic Quintana Roo Maya Processes," in *Status,*

Structure, and Stratification: Current Archaeological Reconstructions, ed. M. T. Garcia and M. Thompson (Calgary: Calgary Archaeology Association, 1985), pp. 321–30.

10. Andrews, "Puertos costeros"; and Joseph W. Ball and Jack D. Eaton, "Marine Resources and the Prehistoric Lowland Maya: A Comment," *American Anthropologist* 74, no. 3 (1972): 772–76.

11. Rosemary L. Lee, "The Tourist Industry in Yucatan: A Case Study in the Interaction Between Class Structure and Economic Development" (Ph.D. diss., University of California, Irvine, 1977).

12. See Ramón Beteta, *Tierra del chicle*, 3d ed. (Mexico City: Editorial Ilustrada, 1951); and Enrique Vásquez Islas, *Chicle: Ensayo de novela del trópico mexicano* (Mexico City: Cicerón, 1951).

13. This was recognized in the reports of early governors of Quintana Roo, as in a 1903 report of General José M. de la Vega, AGN/G/SS, case 767, exp. 1, and in a 1925 report by General Amado Aguirre, AGN/FP/OC, exp. 241-A-Q-2. It is confirmed by the countless chiclero trails used in the past by contractors and by my own field work in the forests of Quintana Roo, 1975–86.

14. Chamberlain, *Conquest and Colonization*; Ralph L. Roys, *The Political Geography of the Yucatán Maya* (Washington, D.C.: Carnegie Institution of Washington, 1957); Helmuth O. Wagner, "Subsistence Potential and Population Density of the Maya on the Yucatan Peninsula and the Causes for the Decline of Population in the Fifteenth Century," *Verhandlungen des 38 Internationalen Americanistenkongressen, Stuttgart-München* 1 (1970): 185–91.

15. Arthur Miller and Nancy Farriss, "Religious Syncreticism in Colonial Yucatan: The Archaeological and Ethnohistorical Evidence from Tancah, Quintana Roo," in *Maya Archaeology and Ethnohistory*, ed. N. Hammond and G. Willey (Austin: University of Texas Press, 1979), pp. 223–40; Roys, *Political Geography*; Ralph Roys et al., "Report and Census of the Indians of Cozumel, 1570," *Contributions to American Anthropology and History* 6 (1940): 1–30.

16. Farriss, *Maya Society*.

17. Ibid., pp. 199–223.

18. *Estadística de Yucatán* (Mexico City: Imprenta de Ignacio Cumplido, 1953).

19. Ibid., p. 243.

20. Lapointe, *Mayas rebeldes*, p. 75.

21. Ibid., p. 81.

22. Ibid.

23. Nigel Bolland and Assad Shoman, *Land in Belize, 1765–1871* (Mona, Jamaica: University of the West Indies, 1977).

24. AB/B, 1890–91.

25. Ibid.

26. AB/B, 1886–1900.

27. Ibid.

28. For example, data in AB/B and the other main source of similar data, the AB/CR, 1898–1935, are not consistent in reporting on the same items, and the Belizean statistics seldom coincide with those from Mexican sources.

29. AB/B and AB/CR.

30. Lapointe, *Mayas rebeldes.*

31. Ibid.

32. R. A. Humphreys, *Diplomatic History of British Honduras* (Oxford: Oxford University Press, 1961); D. C. M. Platt, "Economic Imperialism and the Businessman: Britain and Latin America before 1914," in *Studies in the Theory of Imperialism*, ed. Roger Owen and Bob Sutcliffe (London: Longman, 1976), pp. 295–311.

33. Ibid.; for railroad development in Mexico, see Matías Romero, *Coffee and India-Rubber Culture in Mexico: Preceded by Geographical and Statistical Notes on Mexico* (New York and London: Putnam's Sons, 1898).

34. Lapointe, *Mayas rebeldes*, p. 207.

35. Ibid., pp. 148, 240.

36. Víctor Suárez Molina, *La evolución económica de Yucatán a través del siglo XIX* (Mérida: Universidad de Yucatán, 1977), vol. 1, pp. 215–18.

37. Carlos Hoy, *Breve historia de Quintana Roo*, 2d ed. (Chetumal: Impresora México, 1983), pp. 29–39; Lapointe, *Mayas rebeldes*, pp. 151–53; Romero, *Coffee and India-Rubber*, pp. 1–7.

38. Hoy, *Quintana Roo*, pp. 41–72; Lapointe, *Mayas rebeldes*, pp. 201–16.

39. Lapointe, *Mayas rebeldes*, pp. 201–16; Reed, *Caste War*, pp. 185–228.

40. Lapointe, *Mayas rebeldes*; Reed, *Caste War*.

41. For lists of railroad construction contract dates, see Romero, *Coffee and India-Rubber*, pp. 193–95. For overviews of building, see Suárez Molina, *Evolución económica*, vol. 2, pp. 171–88, and Wells, *Yucatan's Gilded Age*, pp. 89–111.

42. Suárez Molina, *Evolución económica*, vol. 2, pp. 174–82; Wells, *Yucatán's Gilded Age*, pp. 89–111.

43. *Revista de Yucatán*, November 9, 1898; Suárez Molina, *Evolución económica*, vol. 2, pp. 183–84.

44. Suárez Molina, *Evolución económica*, vol. 2, pp. 183–84; *Revista de Yucatán*; and Wells, *Yucatán's Gilded Age*, pp. 96–100.

45. Wells, *Yucatan's Gilded Age*, p. 107.

46. An unpublished professional evaluation of these properties, by V. Sánchez Gavito, "El Cuyo y Anexas," for the Bank of London and Mexico (1911) provides many details. See also *Revista de Mérida* 33 (November 18, 1898), and Suárez Molina, *Evolución económica*, vol. 1, pp. 212–15.

47. Sánchez Gavito, "Cuyo."

48. Ibid.

49. Suárez Molina, *Evolución económica*, vol. 1, p. 215.

50. Sánchez Gavito, "Cuyo."

51. Romero, *Coffee and India-Rubber*, represents this trend; see also Carlos Días Dufoo, *México y los capitales extranjeros* (Mexico City: Bouret, 1918).

52. Romero, *Coffee and India-Rubber*; Días Dufoo, *México*.

53. Francisco P. Troncoso, *Las guerras con las tribus yaquis y mayos* (Mexico City: INI, 1977).

54. Reed, *Caste War*, pp. 229ff; Mena Brito, *Historia*, pp. 48–49.

55. That international, national, and regional capital interests were involved is clearly indicated in AGEY/F, Serie Colonización (Ferrocarriles, Telégrafos, Industria y Comercio, Estadística y Obras Publicas), 1898.

56. Cuauhtémoc González Pacheco, *Capital extranjero en las selvas de Chiapas, 1883–1982* (Mexico City: Universidad Autónoma de México, 1983).

57. There was a 300 percent increase in demand for chicle between the 1885/86 and 1895/96 seasons in the lower gulf coastal regions; see Romero, *Coffee and India-Rubber*, pp. 53–54.

58. *Diario Oficial de la Nación*, 1894.

59. Cf. Jorge González Durán, *La rebelión de los mayas y el Quintana Roo chiclero* (Mérida: Editorial Dosis, 1974), pp. 61–64; Hoy, *Quintana Roo*, pp. 55–56; Villa Rojas, *Eligidos de Dios*, pp. 117–18.

60. See Hoy, *Quintana Roo*, pp. 41–50; Menéndez Reyes, *Quintana Roo*, pp. 40ff; Reed, *Caste War*, pp. 235–38; Villa Rojas, *Eligidos de Dios*, pp. 116–17.

61. Hoy, *Quintana Roo*, pp. 41–50; Menéndez Reyes, *Quintana Roo*, p. 40ff; Reed, *Caste War*, pp. 235–38; Villa Rojas, *Eligidos de Dios*, pp. 116–17.

62. For regular campaign reports, see *Revista de Mérida*, 1899–1901.

63. Ibid.

64. Reed, *Caste War*, p. 240, suggests that a measles epidemic shattered the resistance. The campaign reports filed by General Bravo were published in *Diario oficial* (Yucatán) (January 1899–May 1901) and make numerous mention of smallpox. General de la Vega placed importance upon the disease factor as well; see AGN/G/SS, case 767, exp. 1 (January 26, 1903). John K. Turner, *México Bárbaro* (Mérida: Gobierno del Estado, 1979), pp. 126–28, popularized the disease-ridden conditions of Bravo's campaign.

65. A close reading of Mérida's publications (*Diario de Yucatán, Diario Oficial* [Yucatán], *Diario Yucateco, Revista de Yucatán*, and *La Voz de la Revolución*) in the first quarter of the twentieth century reveals continuing military encounters between the Maya and federal forces.

66. Reed, *Caste War*, pp. 270–80, discovered this when visiting the region in 1959, and the author has witnessed the same during the 1970s and 1980s.

67. De la Vega, AGN/G/SS, case 767, exp. 1 (1903) indicates the railroad was already being constructed as well as a system of communications, via roads and telegraph.

68. AGN/G/SS, case 751, exp. 1 (1901).

69. Ibid., September 23, 1901.

70. The Yucatecan views are seen in Canto López, *Quintana Roo*; Mena Brito, *Historia*; and Echánove Trujillo, *Vida Prócer.*

71. See the reports of Quintana Roo's governors, AGN/G, 1902–20.

72. Campeche and Yucatán continued lobbying the federal government to return Quintana Roo to them. President Ortiz Rubio did so on December 14, 1931, a step that President Lázaro Cárdenas reversed on January 10, 1934; see Hoy, *Quintana Roo*, pp. 107–39.

73. *Revista de Yucatán*, June 1901; AGEY, Guerra y Marina, case 151, June 10, 1901.

74. As of July 7, 1902, the territory was declared a duty-free zone and special concessions were offered to colonists; see *Revista de Yucatán*, June 3, 1903.

75. AGN/G/SS, case 767, exp. 1.

76. James C. Carey, *The Mexican Revolution in Yucatan, 1915–1924* (Boulder and London: Westview Press, 1984); Reed, *Caste War*, pp. 245–46.

77. Turner, *México Bárbaro*, pp. 126–28.

78. Reed, *Caste War*, p. 246.

79. AGN/G/SS, case 767, exp. 1, January 26, 1903.

80. Wells, *Yucatán's Gilded Age*, p. 107, Table 5.

81. AGN/G, exp. 905 (3) 10, January 4, 1904.

82. Secretaría de Relaciones Exteriores, Archivo Historico (15–15–9), Belize, 1905.

83. AGN/G, exp. 904 (3) 5, 1905.

84. Ibid.

85. Suárez Molina, *Evolución económica*, vol. 1, pp. 212–15.

86. Sánchez Gavito, "Cuyo."

87. Suárez Molina, *Evolución económica*, vol. 1, p. 215.

88. Sánchez Gavito, "Cuyo."

89. Ibid.

90. A small fishing village still exists here today.

91. AGN/G, Período Revolucionario, case 22, exp. 31.

92. *Revista de Mérida* 33 (November 18, 1898); Suárez Molina, *Evolución económica*, vol. 1, pp. 215–18.

93. *Revista de Mérida* 33; Suárez Molina, *Evolución económica*, vol. 1, pp. 215–18.

94. See n. 92 above.

95. The federal government anticipated substantial costs in occupying the area and creating the territory; see AGN/G/SS, case 767, exp. 1.

96. Mena Brito, *Historia*, pp. 56–58, claims that more than fifty thousand "troops, prisoners, and political enemies" of Porfirio Díaz died in Quintana Roo. Reed, *Caste War*, p. 246, and Villa Rojas, *Eligidos de Dios*, p. 120, refer to very high casualty rates. None of these statements is documented from primary sources, however. This question remains to be studied in greater detail from data in the AGN and the archives of

the Mexican Secretariate of Defense. The *Revista de Yucatán* (June 24, 1911) refers to Bravo as a "true feudal lord who exploits every class of business."

97. Carey, *Mexican Revolution*, p. 7; Reed, *Caste War*, pp. 243–48.

98. This is clearly indicated from newspaper reports from Mérida in the first decade of the twentieth century; see *Diario de Yucatán, Diario Yucateco, Revista de Yucatán*, and *Razón del Pueblo*.

99. The Alvarado period is extensively covered in Carey, *Mexican Revolution*, and Joseph, *Revolution from Without*.

100. See *Revista de Yucatán*, September to December 1912.

101. Ibid., December 4, 1912.

102. Ibid., November 18, 1912.

103. Ibid. for 1913 (September 30 to December 20) and 1914 (January 6, 9, and 14; March 3, 5, and 7; June 3; August 25; November 11).

104. Hoy, *Quintana Roo*, pp. 82–83; *Revista de Yucatán*, March 3, 1916.

105. Thomas W. Gann, *In an Unknown Land* (New York: Scribner's, 1924), pp. 23–27, provides a description of damage along the Quintana Rooan coasts. See also AGN/G, Período Revolucionario, case 82, exp. 6.

106. Miguel A. Bartolomé and Alicia M. Barabas, *La resistencia maya: Relaciones interétnicas en el oriente de la península de Yucatán* (Mexico City: INAH, 1977), p. 46; Hoy, *Quintana Roo*, p. 84; Villa Rojas, *Eligidos de Dios*, p. 122.

107. Carey, *Mexican Revolution*; Joseph, *Revolution from Without*; Wells, *Yucatán's Gilded Age*.

108. AGN/FP/OC, exp. 241-A-Q-2; AGN/G, Período Revolucionario, case 4, exp. 37, and case 10, exp. 23.

109. AGN/FP/OC, exp. 245-C1-Q-1.

110. *La Voz de la Revolución*, August 26, 1917.

111. AGN/G, Período Revolucionario, case 82, exp. 6; Gann, *Unknown Land*, pp. 23–27.

112. *La Voz de la Revolución*, July 15, 1916.

113. AGN/FP/OC, exp. 241-A-Q-2; AGN/G, Período Revolucionario, case 57, exp. 10 and case 133, exp. 22.

114. AGN/G, Período Revolucionario, case 67, exp. 16.

115. Herman W. Konrad, "Una población chiclera: Contexto histórico-económico y un perfil demográfico," *Boletín de la Escuela de Ciencias Antropológicas de la Universidad de Yucatán* 8, no. 45 (1980): 2–39, and his "Plantation Labor Systems in the Tropical Forests: The Case of the Chewing Gum Tappers," in *Plantations Around the World*, ed. Sue Eakin and John Tarver (Baton Rouge: Louisiana State University, 1986), pp. 82–113.

116. Konrad, "Población chiclera" and "Plantation Labor Systems."

117. González Pacheco, *Capital extranjero*.

118. AGN/G, Período Revolucionario, case 90, exp. 1.

119. AGN/G, Período Revolucionario, case 133, exp. 22.

120. AGN/FP/OC, exp. 241-A-Q-2, p. 35.

121. Ibid.

122. Ibid.; Luis G. Jiménez M., *El chicle: Su explotación forestal e industrial* (Mexico City: Imprenta Manuel Casas, 1951), p. 78.

123. Felipe N. Avila Zapata, *El General May, último jefe de las tribus mayas* (Mérida: Gobierno del Estado, 1974).

124. *Revista de Yucatán*, 1919 (January 16, April 11–12).

125. Avila Zapata, *General May*; *Diario Yucateco*, November 30, 1928.

126. Observation during author's field work; and Herman W. Konrad, "De la subsistencia forestal tropical a la producción para la exportación: La industria chiclera y la transformación de la economía maya de Quintana Roo, de 1890 a 1935," Paper presented at the 45th Congreso Internacional de Americanistas, Bogotá, Colombia.

127. Discussions of such projects are to be found in virtually every annual report of the Quintana Rooan governors, from 1903 onward; see AGN/G, Período Revolucionario; AGN/G/SS; AGN/FP/OC.

128. Konrad, "Subsistencia forestal tropical."

129. Ibid.; Correspondence of General Francisco May.

130. *Diario Yucateco*, December 13, 1929; see also Bartolomé and Barabas, *Resistencia Maya*; Thomas W. Gann, *Maya Indians*, and *Maya Cities: A Record of Exploration and Adventure in Middle America* (London: Duckworth, 1927); González Navarro, *Raza y Tierra*; Santiago Pacheco Cruz, *Estudio etnográfico de los mayas del exterritorio de Quintana Roo: Su incorporación de la vida nacional* (Mérida: Imprenta Oriental, 1934); Juventino Poot Canul, *Le Cha'a Yeetel le Maya'ob Way Ti' Quintana Roo/El Chicle y los mayas de Quintana Roo* (Mexico City: SEP/INI, 1982); George C. Shattuck et al., *The Peninsula of Yucatan: Medical, Biological, Meteorological and Sociological Studies* (Washington, D.C.: Carnegie Institution of Washington, 1933).

131. AGN/FP/OC, exp. 241-A-Q-2.

132. AGN/G/OC, exp. 427-Q-1.

133. AGN/FP/OC, exp. 241-A-Q-2.

134. Jiménez, *Chicle*, pp. 78–89.

135. Konrad, "Subsistencia forestal tropical."

136. AGN/G, Dirección General del Gobierno, case 48, exp. 2-127-4.

137. AGN/FP/OC, exp. 241-A-Q-2.

138. Ibid.

139. AGN/G, Dirección General del Gobierno, case 48, exp. 2-127-4.

140. Ibid.

141. Ibid.

142. Ibid.

143. Ibid.

144. AGN/G, Dirección General del Gobierno, case 101, exp. 9 and 10.

145. AGN/G/OC, exp. 427-Q-1.

Introduction to Part III

1. The field is surveyed in Joseph, *Rediscovering the Past*, Ch. 5.

2. For example, see Francisco J. Paoli, *Yucatán y los orígenes del nuevo estado mexicano: Gobierno de Salvador Alvarado, 1915–1918* (Mexico City: Ediciones Era, 1984); and Joseph, *Revolution from Without*, esp. Chs. 4 and 5.

3. For the literature on the cardenista reform, see Joseph, *Rediscovering the Past*, pp. 124–27; and Brannon and Baklanoff, *Agrarian Reform*, esp. Ch. 3.

4. Paoli and Montalvo, *Socialismo olvidado*; Joseph, *Revolution from Without*.

5. Charles Bergquist, *Labor in Latin America: Comparative Essays on Chile, Argentina, Venezuela, and Colombia* (Stanford: Stanford University Press, 1986).

6. Paoli and Montalvo, *Socialismo olvidado*.

7. Joseph, *Revolution from Without*, Chs. 7–9.

7. Salvador Alvarado and Agrarian Reform

1. Helen Phipps, *Some Aspects of the Agrarian Question in Mexico: A Historical Study* (Austin: University of Texas Bulletin, 1925), p. 77.

2. Paul Friedrich, *Agrarian Revolt in a Mexican Village* (Englewood Cliffs, N.J.: Prentice-Hall, 1970), p. 3.

3. Daniel Cosío Villegas, ed., *Historia moderna de México*, 9 vols. (Mexico City: Editorial Hermes, 1948–72), vol. 4, p. 197.

4. Antonio Betancourt Pérez, *Revoluciones y crisis en la economía de Yucatán* (Mérida: Talleres Gráficos del Sudeste, 1953), p. 52.

5. Ramón D. Chacón, "Yucatán and the Mexican Revolution: The Pre-Constitutional Years, 1910–1918" (Ph.D. diss., Stanford University, 1982), pp. 25–26, 37.

6. Betancourt Pérez, *Revoluciones y crisis*, p. 52.

7. *Diario Oficial* (Yucatán), June 26, 1915, pp. 2006–2007.

8. AGEY, Informe del Inspector Administrativo del Departamento de Temax, Capitán E. González, al Gobernador Salvador Alvarado, July 4, 1917.

9. AGEY, Informe del Inspector Administrativo del Departamento de Temax, José A. Erosa, al Gobernador Salvador Alvarado, September 15, 1917.

10. AGEY, Informe del Abogado Consultor de la Comisión Local Agraria, Patricio Sabido, al Director de la Oficina de Información y Propaganda, July 29, 1915.

11. Fernando González Roa, *El aspecto agrario de la revolución mexicana* (Mexico City: Poder Ejecutivo Federal, 1919), pp. 77–83.

12. Yucatán was divided into seventeen political partidos or districts. The jefe político served as the political boss of a specific district and, especially during the Porfiriato, was equated with political bossism and repression.

13. González Navarro, *Raza y tierra*, pp. 193–95. The Territory of Quintana Roo, the Islas de las Mujeres, and the Island of Cozumel offer examples of national lands

that fell into the hands of a small group of influential men. In November 1902, the Díaz regime carved 50,844 square kilometers out of the State of Yucatán and created the federal Territory of Quintana Roo. The territory was divided into three districts and distributed among a few Díaz favorites in the form of concessions. Faustino Martínez received the northern section; the central district was divided among Ángel Rivas, Benjamín Barrios, A. Terrazas, Olegario Molina y Cía, and Faustino Martínez; and Rodolfo Reyes, Rafael Peón, Faustino Martínez, and the foreign companies of E. Plummer and Stanfords obtained the southern region. Cozumel was divided between Manuel Sierra Méndez and José Dolores Pérez, while one person received the Islas de las Mujeres concession. The companies headed by these men were authorized to exploit the forest and export valuable lumber. See Antonio Bustillos Carrillo, *Yucatán al servicio de la patria y la revolución* (Mexico City: Casa Ramírez Editores, 1959), pp. 52–53.

14. González Navarro, *Raza y tierra*, p. 210.

15. Cosío Villegas, *Historia moderna*, vol. 4, p. 210; George M. McBride, *The Land Systems of Mexico* (New York: American Geographical Society, 1923), p. 155.

16. McBride, *Land Systems*, p. 154; González Navarro, *Raza y tierra*, p. 209.

17. Carranza's political movement, as well as his armed forces, was termed Constitutionalist.

18. Adolfo de la Huerta, *Memorias de Don Adolfo de la Huerta según su propio dictado* (Mexico City: Ediciones Guzmán, 1958), pp. 70–71, 286; Alberto Morales Jiménez, *Hombres de la revolución mexicana: 50 semblanzas biográficas* (Mexico City: Instituto Nacional de Estudios Históricos de la Revolución Mexicana, 1960), pp. 223–25.

19. Frank Tannenbaum, *Peace by Revolution: An Interpretation of Mexico* (New York: Columbia University Press, 1933), p. 117.

20. Mary Kay Vaughan, *The State, Education, and Social Class in Mexico, 1880–1928* (DeKalb: Northern Illinois University Press, 1982), p. 103.

21. Víctor Manuel Villaseñor, "Salvador Alvarado," *Revista de la Universidad de Yucatán* 6 (July–August 1964): 125; Salvador Alvarado, *La reconstrucción de México: Un mensaje a los pueblos de América*, 3 vols. (Mexico City: J. Ballesca, 1919), vol. 1, p. 22.

22. Chacón, "Yucatán and Revolution," pp. 234, 379–80.

23. Renán Irigoyen, *Salvador Alvarado: Extraordinario estadista de la revolución* (Mérida: Ediciones del Gobierno del Estado, 1973), p. 36.

24. Michael L. Conniff, "Introduction: Toward a Comparative Definition of Populism," in *Latin American Populism in Comparative Perspective*, ed. Michael L. Conniff (Albuquerque: University of New Mexico Press, 1982), pp. 3–30; Steven Stein, *Populism in Peru: The Emergence of the Masses and the Politics of Social Control* (Madison: University of Wisconsin Press, 1982), pp. 3–17.

25. Paoli, *Yucatán y orígenes*, p. 153. For additional works on Alvarado and his role as a populist caudillo in the formation of the Yucatecan state, see Enrique Montalvo, "Caudillismo y estado en la revolución mexicana: El gobierno de Alvarado en Yucatán," *Nova Americana* 2 (1979): 13–36 and Paoli and Montalvo, *Socialismo olvidado*, Ch. 2.

26. Martín Luis Guzmán, *The Eagle and the Serpent*, tr. Harriet de Onis, reprint ed. (Gloucester, Mass.: Peter Smith, 1969), pp. 73–74.

27. James Linn Rodgers to Secretary of State, December 30, 1915, 812.61326/197, in U.S. National Archives, Records of the [U.S.] Department of State Relating to the Internal Affairs of Mexico, 1910–1929, Microfilm Copy 274, 1959.

28. AGEY, Alvarado to Carranza, May 20, 1915.

29. José C. Valadés, the Mexican historian, wrote that until the Battle of Celaya there existed no central control over the various carrancista armies. Generals Alvaro Obregón, Manuel Diéguez, Pablo González, and Alvarado had considerable autonomy in their respective military districts: "General Jesús Agustín Castro, in Chiapas, and also General Salvador Alvarado, in Yucatán, did not have specific instructions from the first chief, and they decreed civilly what they believed to be convenient without following or obeying a central or principal idea of the revolution, in the same manner that they recruited and mobilized their troops at their whim and fancy." See Valadés, *Historia general de la revolución mexicana*, 10 vols. (Mexico City: Manuel Quesada Brandi Editor, 1963–67), vol. 5, pp. 96–97.

30. In a report to Carranza, Alvarado wrote that military chiefs padded their payrolls in excess of the actual number of men under their control. Alvarado pointed out that he made enemies in the military because of his honesty and stated that many officers were not interested in serving under his command since they could not engage in corrupt practices, concluding with a statement that left no doubt as to his fear of the revolutionary armies: "Since all the chiefs want to pad the rolls, . . . their forces are a real source of prostitution. Frankly, I tremble to think what might happen to our nation with two hundred thousand armed men with such an unrestrained hunger and an unsatisfied appetite." See AGEY, Alvarado to Carranza, May 20, 1915.

31. *La Voz de la Revolución* (Mérida), May 6, 1915, pp. 1, 2; *Diario Oficial*, May 7, 1915, pp. 1159–61.

32. Salvador Alvarado, *Carta al pueblo de Yucatán* (Mérida: La Voz de la Revolución, 1916); Alvarado, *Mi sueño: El primer dividendo de la Comisión Reguladora del Mercado de Henequén* (Mérida: Imprenta del Gobierno Constitucionalista, 1917).

33. See, for example, Jesús Silva Herzog, *Breve historia de la revolución mexicana: La etapa constitucional y la lucha de facciones* (Mexico City: Fondo de Cultura Económica, 1960); Marjorie Ruth Clark, *Organized Labor in Mexico* (Chapel Hill: University of North Carolina Press, 1934); Tannenbaum, *Peace by Revolution*; Valadés, *Historia general*, vol. 5, pp. 90–100.

34. Silva Herzog, *Historia de la revolución*, p. 196.

35. There were several states, among them Coahuila, Sonora, San Luis Potosí, Michoacán, and Oaxaca, that were impressed with Alvarado's revolutionary achievements in Yucatán and requested information pertaining to reforms established under his administration. See, for instance, AGEY, Alvarado to General Jesús A. Castro, Oaxaca, January 13, 1916.

36. Eyler N. Simpson, *The Ejido: Mexico's Way Out* (Chapel Hill: University of North Carolina Press, 1937), pp. 58–60.

37. Article 27 established the process by which land reform would be carried out in Mexico. It called for the destruction of latifundios and the redistribution of land among the rural populace. Charles C. Cumberland described the article as, "in a word, the very heart of the Constitution and a perfect expression of the actionists' phi-

losophy of nationalism and function of government." See Cumberland, *Mexico: The Struggle for Modernity* (New York: Oxford University Press, 1968), p. 266.

38. Simpson, *Ejido*, pp. 60–61; Nathan L. Whetten, *Rural Mexico* (Chicago: University of Chicago Press, 1948), pp. 114–15.

39. Clarence Senior, *Land Reform and Democracy* (Gainesville: University of Florida Press, 1958), p. 25.

40. Alvarado, *Reconstrucción*, vol. 1, p. 128.

41. *Breves apuntes acerca de la administración del General Salvador Alvarado como gobernador de Yucatán* (Mérida: Imprenta del Gobierno Constitucionalista, 1917), p. 6.

42. AGEY, Patricio Sabido, Legal Adviser to the State Agrarian Commission, to Alvarado, July 29, 1915.

43. *Diario Oficial*, June 11, 1915, pp. 1708–10; October 24, 1915, p. 4039.

44. AGEY, Copy of the action carried out in the village of Umán in order to nullify the breaking up of that village, July 23, 1915.

45. Alvarado's land law is published in Alvaro Gamboa Ricalde, *Yucatán desde 1910*, 3 vols. (Veracruz: Imprenta Standard, 1943–55), vol. 2, p. 504.

46. Rolland's report is included in AGEY, Alvarado to the Secretaría de Gobernación, January 11, 1916.

47. AGEY, Carranza to Alvarado, January 19, 1916; see also Pastor Rouaix, president of the National Agrarian Commission, to Alvarado, January 25, 1916.

48. AGEY, Carranza to Alvarado, January 19, 1916; and Rouaix to Alvarado, January 25, 1916.

49. AGEY, Alvarado to Carranza, January 25, 1916.

50. Ibid.

51. Ibid.

52. Alvarado, *Actuación revolucionaria*, p. 87.

53. Francisco Bulnes, *The Whole Truth About Mexico: President Wilson's Responsibility* (New York: Mr. Bulnes Book Company, 1916), pp. 355–56.

54. Douglas Richmond's study of Carranza, perhaps the major work on the first chief, fails to provide new information on the idea that U.S. pressure forced Carranza to obstruct Yucatán's land reform program. Richmond contends that poor food harvests became the Carranza government's central concern and that the first chief curtailed land reform in order not to obstruct agricultural production. See Douglas W. Richmond, *Venustiano Carranza's Nationalist Struggle, 1893–1920* (Lincoln: University of Nebraska Press, 1983), pp. 114–15.

55. AGEY, Carlos Baz, director of the State Agrarian Commission, to Alvarado, April 3, 1917.

56. AGEY, Edmundo Torres, secretary general to President Carranza, to Alvarado, April 30, 1917.

57. AGEY, Baz to Alvarado, May 23, 1917.

58. AGEY, Baz to Alvarado, September 27, 1917; Severiano Barea of Kancabchen, to Alvarado, September 24, 1917. The government realized that the amounts distrib-

uted were insufficient for campesinos to turn to subsistence farming on a full-time basis. That was not the regime's intention. As noted above, the government's plan called for the distribution of small plots among the rural working class to help workers economically. See AGEY, Baz to Alvarado, September 11, 1917; *Diario Oficial* (Yucatán), August 29, 1917, pp. 4237–38; *La Voz de la Revolución*, March 16, 1916, p. 1.

59. *Diario Oficial* (Yucatán), August 29, 1917, pp. 4237–38.

60. AGEY, Report from the military commander of Ticul to Alvarado, October 29, 1916.

61. AGEY, Alvaro Torre Díaz, secretary general to Alvarado, to Luis D. Molina, August 21, 1917; Director of the Department of Labor to Liga de Agricultores de Chilam Balam, n.d.

62. AGEY, Torre Díaz to Luis D. Molina, August 21, 1917.

63. *Diario Oficial* (Yucatán), August 29, 1917, pp. 4237–38.

64. AGEY, Director of the Department of Labor to the municipal president of Hunucmá, October 31, 1917. Génaro Rodríguez, the municipal president of Kanasín, wrote that in his district, landowners "refuse to distribute lands, maintaining that they need them for their rasping machines." See AGEY, Rodríguez to Alvarado, September 8, 1917.

65. AGEY, Baz to the president of the committee administering the Ejido of Chicxulub, July 23, 1917.

66. AGEY, Baz to the president of the committee administering the Ejido of Yaxkukul, July 5, 1917.

67. Tannenbaum, *Peace by Revolution*, pp. 202–203. Governor Francisco Múgica of Tabasco was another serious agrarian reformer that Carranza restrained during the preconstitutional years. See Alan Knight, *The Mexican Revolution*, 2 vols. (New York: Cambridge University Press, 1986), vol. 2, pp. 466–67.

8. The Planter Class in Espita

Data for this study were gathered in two field seasons in 1977 and 1978 under the direction of Arturo Warman. Financial support came from the Universidad Autónoma Metropolitana and the Centro de Investigaciones Superiores del Instituto Nacional de Antropología e Historía (CISINAH). The most vital archival sources included the public tax register, the census, the Henequen Commission, the Agrarian Reform Commission, and contemporary periodicals. The most important informants included Don José Concepción Sansor Díaz, Don Francisco Sánchez, and members of the Peniche, Rosado, and Patrón families, all of whom gave generously of their time. I also conducted a genealogical study of one thousand members of three interrelated families across five generations. Oral accounts were consistently cross-checked against the public record.

1. Important exceptions include Cline, "Sugar Episode," and his *Related Studies in Early Nineteenth Century Yucatecan Social History* (1950), Microfilm Collection of Manuscripts on Middle American Cultural Anthropology no. 32, University of Chicago Library; and Suárez Molina, *Evolución económica*.

2. Oswaldo de Baqueiro, *La ciudad heroica: Historia de Valladolid* (Mérida: Imprenta Oriente, 1943), p. 210. It is unclear whether the encomendero actually resided in Espita at this time or not.

3. Ralph Roys, *The Indian Background of Colonial Yucatan* (Washington, D.C.: Carnegie Institution of Washington, 1943).

4. Baqueiro, *Cuidad heroica*.

5. Prudencio Patrón Peniche, *Espita: Su historia desde los tiempos más remotos* (Mérida: n.p., 1959), p. 217; Census of 1790 (Mérida: n.p.).

6. Census of 1790.

7. Suárez Molina, *Evolución económica*, vol. 1, pp. 118–19.

8. Ibid., pp. 49–50. With independence from Spain in 1823, colonial restrictions that had protected Spanish producers from competition were lifted. The Yucatecan Legislature passed a series of protective laws in 1823, 1826, 1837, and 1841 to foster cane cultivation. See Cline, "Sugar Episode," p. 85.

9. Suárez Molina, *Evolución económica*, vol. 1, pp. 169–71. Suárez Molina's subregionalization of the Yucatán into four economic zones is useful. Traditional cattle haciendas and, later, henequen dominated the northwest (Mérida-Progreso) and central (Motul-Izamal) zones. Cane covered the southern (Ticul-Peto) and eastern (Valladolid-Espita-Tizimín) fronts. Political and social differences accompanied economic ones.

10. Significant research has clearly identified the rapid expansion of sugar plantations into traditional Mayan "free pueblo" areas as the major cause of the Mayan revolt. See, for example, González Navarro, *Raza y tierra*; and Patch, "Formación de estancias."

11. Patrón Peniche, *Espita*, p. 90.

12. Suárez Molina, *Evolución económica*, vol. 1, pp. 49–50.

13. At the agricultural fair of 1879, for example, products from Espita's haciendas included rum, an anise liquor, a variety of grades of sugar, *almidón* (a type of adhesive material made from the yucca), maize, beans, achiote (a kind of spice), sesame seeds, peanuts, coffee, tobacco, and espelón and *ibes*, two other vegetables. Patrón Peniche, *Espita*, pp. 134–35. By the end of the century, the heated debate on the issue filled the pages of regional periodicals, including *La Revista de Yucatán* and *El Boletín de Estadística*.

14. *El Demócrata* (Espita), 1886–88.

15. Municipal Archives of Espita, Register of Political Officials; Patrón Peniche, *Espita*.

16. Property Tax Register, 1869, Mérida; *Libro de fincas rústicas del partido de Espita, 1871–1874*, Library of La Sociedad Progreso y Recreo, Espita.

17. Property Tax Register, 1869, 1893.

18. Ibid.

19. González Navarro, *Raza y tierra*, p. 20.

20. Suárez Molina, *Evolución económica*, vol. 1, p. 161. Statewide, the number of debt peons rose from twenty thousand to eighty thousand between 1880 and 1900.

21. Ibid., pp. 285, 289.

22. *El Demócrata*, August 20, 1906. Hacendados' wealth clearly depended on the production of rum rather than sugar. Espita supplied 3 percent of the state's sugar and 11 percent of its rum. *Boletín de Estadística*, 1907, Mérida.

23. Documents on file at the library of La Sociedad Progreso y Recreo, Espita; *El Demócrata*, 1886–88.

24. For a fuller elaboration of the concept of "internal articulation," see Ángel Palermo, *Modos de producción y formaciones socioeconómicas* (Mexico City: Ediciones Edicol, 1976).

25. It was Molina who headed the small clique of financiers in Mérida who controlled the henequen export market through ties with U.S. importers. He signed a secret contract with International Harvester in October 1902 to monopolize the export market. See, for example, Joseph, *Revolution from Without*, Chs. 1–3; and Wells, *Yucatán's Gilded Age*.

26. *El Demócrata*, August 20, 1906.

27. Production dropped from 375,962 liters in 1901 to 81,591 liters in 1907. *El Demócrata*, May 24, 1908.

28. *El Demócrata*, August 20, 1906.

29. Prudencio Patrón Peniche, *Geografía del Departamento de Espita* (Mérida: n.p., 1919), p. 4.

30. This section is based on an analysis of approximately 105,000 hectares of land in Espita and adjacent areas (where owners in Espita had land in adjacent municipalities). Landownership data are derived from Property Tax Registers of 1869, 1883, and 1903–16 (Mérida), and were corroborated by key informants.

31. Census, 1900 and 1910 (Mérida).

32. Other studies have set the average hacienda size at between one thousand and two thousand hectares and one hundred debt peons. See Frank Tannenbaum, *The Mexican Agrarian Revolution* (New York: Macmillan, 1929), pp. 98–101; Lee, "Tourist Industry," p. 125; and Nathaniel Raymond, "The Impact of Land Reform in the Monocrop Region of Yucatan, Mexico" (Ph.D. diss., Brandeis University, Waltham, Mass., 1971), p. 100.

33. This section is based on accounts from ex-peons, independent workers from Espita, and descendants of hacendados. Two of the most important and helpful informants were Don José Concepción Sansor Díaz and Don Francisco Sánchez, both of whom worked independently for many of the hacendados before and after the revolution. See also the detailed description of the life of workers on Espita's haciendas in Luis Aboites, *La revolución mexicana en Espita: 1910–1940: Microhistoria de la formación del estado de la revolución* (Mexico City: Cuadernos de La Casa Chata, 1982), pp. 29–40.

34. Interviews with Don José C. S. Díaz, Don Frank Peniche, Doña Jacinta Peniche Dzul, and Don Francisco Sánchez.

35. See Wolf and Mintz, "Haciendas and Plantations."

36. Interviews with Don Frank Peniche and Don Francisco Sánchez. At this time, one peso equaled U.S. $1.00.

37. Comparison of tax register with census records and with oral accounts, particularly with Don José C. S. Díaz.

38. The following narrative about life on a hacienda is based on interviews with Don Francisco Sánchez, and ex-peons Don Cayetano Noh Canul of Chahkaba, Don Laureano Balam of Sahcaba, and Don Pablo of Chuhka.

39. AGEY/PE, Leg. Dept. Ag., 1916.

40. See R[osemary] Laura Batt, "Capitalist Class Formation in Dependent Economies: The Case of Espita, Yucatan, Mexico" (Master's thesis, University of Kentucky, 1981), pp. 104–14.

41. Sidney Mintz, *Caribbean Transformations* (Chicago: Aldine, 1974), p. 114.

42. This section is based on interviews with descendants of hacendados in the course of a genealogical investigation. Included were the Patrón, Rosado, Peniche, and López families.

43. Patrón Peniche, *Espita*, pp. 138–141; *El Boletín Estadística*, organ of the state's director general (Mérida, 1894–1914).

44. *El Demócrata*, August 11 and 25, 1909.

45. See Joseph, *Revolution from Without*.

46. Published in *La Voz de la Revolución*, September 30, 1915.

47. *Diario Oficial* (Yucatán), December 11, 1915.

48. AGEY/PE, Leg. Dept. Ag., 1916.

49. By April 1916, only forty-nine of the approximately one thousand henequen planters had failed to sign. See David Franz, "Bullets and Bolshevists: A History of the Mexican Revolution and Reform in Yucatan, 1910–1924" (Ph.D. diss., University of New Mexico, 1973), p. 121.

50. Ibid. Franz provides an excellent, detailed account of Alvarado's political and economic agenda.

51. Interview with ex-peon, hacienda of Dzitás.

52. Interview with Don José C. S. Díaz.

53. Secretaría de Agricultura y Fomento, *División territorial de los EUM correspondiente al censo de 1910* (Mexico City: Impresora de la Secretaría de Hacienda, 1912). Significantly, the census listed population by hacienda, rancho, and pueblo so that changes in population patterns can be traced. The pattern of population loss was consistent from hacienda to hacienda.

54. Information on the founding and early development of the league in Espita was provided by Don Francisco Sánchez in conjunction with documents from the Secretariat of Agrarian Reform.

55. Secretaría de la Reforma Agraria, Mérida.

56. Paoli and Montalvo, *Socialismo olvidado*, p. 5.

57. *Revista de Yucatán*, October 26, 1919.

58. Paoli and Montalvo, *Socialismo olvidado*, p. 11.

59. One hundred forty-one arms were confiscated in Espita. Anastacio Chávez and José Arias, president and treasurer respectively of the local resistance league, were jailed until they turned in their firearms. See *La Revista de Yucatán*, November 30, 1919.

60. Marcos Peniche Navarette and Urbano Góngora, among other planters, wrote letters and refused to cooperate with the government officials who came to survey land for the ejido. Yucatán, Secretaría de la Reforma Agraria, *Acta de posesión y deslinde del ejido de Espita*, Mérida, August 27, 1921.

61. Ibid.

62. *La Revista de Yucatán*, December 1920.

63. Ibid., December 1923.

64. Ibid., April 19, 1924.

65. Secretaría de la Reforma Agraria, Mérida.

66. Interview with Don José C. S. Díaz.

67. Interview with Don José C. S. Díaz; and Patrón Peniche, *Espita*.

68. This information is based on the genealogical survey of one thousand members of the Peniche and Rosado families.

69. In fact, under Cárdenas, eight additional ejidos were formed in the municipality of Espita, and the ejido of Espita was enlarged by 9,156 hectares in 1941. Secretaría de la Reforma Agraria, Mérida.

9. Workers Against Socialism?

1. Joseph, *Revolution from Without*, pp. 46–54.

2. Ibid., pp. 30–53.

3. Ibid., pp. 57–58.

4. Ibid., pp. 34–35; Wells, *Yucatán's Gilded Age*, pp. 29–34.

5. Joseph, *Revolution from Without*, pp. 35–36.

6. See, for example, Michael M. Hall and Hobart A. Spalding, "The Urban Working Class and Early Latin American Labour Movements, 1880–1930," in *The Cambridge History of Latin America*, ed. Leslie Bethell, vol. 4, c. 1870–1930 (Cambridge: Cambridge University Press, 1986), pp. 325–66; and Bergquist, *Labor*. The best, but incomplete, source on the lives of Yucatecan workers is Juan Rico, *La huelga de junio*, 2 vols. (Mérida: n.p., 1922).

7. Rico, *Huelga*, vol. 1, pp. 139–58; Gilbert M. Joseph, "Documenting a Regional Pastime: Baseball in Yucatán," in *Windows on Latin America: Understanding Society Through Photographs*, ed. Robert M. Levine (a special issue of *South Eastern Latin Americanist* [June–September 1987]), p. 79.

8. John M. Hart, *Anarchism and the Mexican Working Class, 1860–1931* (Austin: University of Texas Press, 1978), pp. ix and 103.

9. Alan Knight, "The Working Class and the Mexican Revolution, 1900–1920," *Journal of Latin American Studies* 16, no. 1 (May 1984): 52–57.

10. Elena Azaola Garrido, *Rebelión y derrota del magonismo agrario* (Mexico City: Fondo de Cultura Económica/Sep-80, 1982); Rodney D. Anderson, *Outcasts in Their Own Land: Mexican Industrial Workers, 1906–1911* (DeKalb: Northern Illinois University Press, 1976), p. 314; Clark, *Organized Labor*, p. 6.

11. José Luis Sierra Villarreal, "Prensa y lucha política en Yucatán, 1895–1925," Manuscript, n.d., pp. 38–39; Carlos Loveira, *El socialismo en Yucatán* (Havana: El Siglo XX, 1923); Gamboa Ricalde, *Yucatán*, vol. 3, p. 40; Fidelio Quintal Martín, "Breve historia de Yucatán durante la última década del porfiriato," *Boletín E.C.A.U.D.Y.* 2, no. 65 (1984): 55.

12. Río Blanco, Puebla, and Cananea, Sonora, are the most notorious, yet not isolated, cases of labor repression by management; cf. Ciro Cardoso et al., *De la dictadura porfirista a los tiempos libertarios* (Mexico City: Siglo XXI, 1980).

13. Joseph, "Regional Pastime," p. 81.

14. This is, of course, inferred from similar cases of successful unionization early in the century in other Latin American countries with dynamic economies that experienced a demand for skilled labor. See, for example, Thomas Skidmore, "Workers and Soldiers: Urban Labor Movements and Elite Responses in Twentieth-Century Latin America," in *Elites, Masses, and Modernization in Latin America, 1850–1930*, ed. Virginia Bernhard (Austin: University of Texas Press, 1979), pp. 79–155.

15. Joseph, *Revolution from Without*, p. 191; José Luis Sierra, "La lucha antirreeleccionista en Yucatán," Manuscript, n.d.; Carey, *Mexican Revolution*, pp. 14–15.

16. Friedrich Katz, *The Secret War in Mexico: Europe, the United States and the Mexican Revolution* (Chicago: University of Chicago Press, 1981), p. 128; Anderson, *Outcasts*, pp. 257, 312.

17. Joseph, *Revolution from Without*, p. 191; Knight, *Mexican Revolution*, vol. 1, p. 52; Gilbert Joseph and Allen Wells, "The Rough-and-Tumble Career of Pedro Crespo," in *The Human Tradition in Latin America: The Twentieth Century*, ed. William H. Beezley and Judith Ewell (Wilmington, Del.: Scholarly Resources, 1987), pp. 29–30; José Luis Sierra, "Las luchas antirreleccionistas y la emergencia popular," Manuscript, n.d.

18. Joseph and Wells, "Pedro Crespo," p. 30; *Luz* (Mérida) 1, no. 3, June 20, 1920; Joseph, *Revolution from Without*, pp. 2–3.

19. Joseph, *Revolution from Without*, p. 141.

20. Ibid.

21. Ibid., p. 110.

22. Ibid., p. 112.

23. Ibid., p. 108; Alvarado, *Actuación revolucionaria*.

24. Hart, *Anarchism*, pp. 126–27; Barry Carr, "The Casa del Obrero Mundial, Constitutionalism and the Pact of February 1915," in *El trabajo y los trabajadores en la historia de México*, ed. Elsa Cecilia Frost et al. (Mexico City: El Colegio de México and Tucson: University of Arizona Press, 1979), pp. 605–12; Clark, *Organized Labor*, p. 31; Jean Meyer, "Los obreros en la revolución mexicana: Los batallones rojos," *Historia Mexicana* 20 (July–September 1971).

25. Joseph, *Revolution from Without*, p. 110; Loveira, *Socialismo*. Loveira was a Cuban socialist who was the head of the Labor Department during Alvarado's governorship in Yucatán.

26. *La Voz de la Revolución*, January 2 and 3, 1916.

27. Joseph, *Revolution from Without*, p. 111; Knight, *Mexican Revolution*, vol. 2, p. 432; *La Voz de la Revolución*, November 22 and December 1, 1916.

28. Cf. Eric Villanueva Mukul, *Así tomamos las tierras* (Mérida: Maldonado Editores, 1984).

29. Cf. Paoli and Montalvo, *Socialismo olvidado*, pp. 51–52; Joseph, *Revolution from Without*, p. 112.

30. Ramón Espadas y Aguilar, *Fundación del Partido Socialista Obrero: Junio de 1916* (Mérida: n.p., 1972).

31. Ibid., p. 3.

32. Roger Shattuck, *The Banquet Years: The Origins of the Avant Garde in France, 1885 to World War I* (New York: Vintage Books, 1968), pp. 20–21.

33. Espadas y Aguilar, *Fundación del Partido*, p. 10.

34. Ibid., pp. 12–16.

35. Ibid.

36. Joseph, *Revolution from Without*, p. 250.

37. Enrique Montalvo, "Imperialismo y henequén: Estudio de las clases sociales en Yucatán, 1900–1919" (Thesis, Universidad Iberoamericana, Mexico City, 1976), pp. 108–19, 134–38.

38. AGN/FP/OC, 241-P4-Y-1, Felipe Carrillo Puerto from Mérida, Yucatán, to Obregón, January 19, 1921; AGN/FP/OC, 707-Z-2, Delfino Cano from Mérida to Obregón, May 21, 1921; AGN/FP/OC, 802-Y-4, Obregón from Mexico City to José Vales Castillo, president of the Yucatán Chamber of Agriculture, February 14, 1921.

39. *La Voz de la Revolución*, July 1, 1918. The correspondence concerning the plight of numerous workers who were stuck in Yucatán without finding employment, yet could not leave because no one wanted to assume the cost of their transport and maintenance during the journey, is to be found in AGN/T, 1918–20.

40. AGN/T, 216-16-76, Yucatán Chamber of Commerce from Mérida to Alvaro Obregón, December 1, 1920.

41. Joseph, *Revolution from Without*, pp. 165–68; Katz, *Secret War*, pp. 533–40; *Tierra* (Mérida), August 21, and October 1, 1919. *Tierra* was the weekly, sometimes irregularly published, organ of the Socialist party.

42. Paco Ignacio Taibo II and Rogelio Viscaino, "Informe sobre los rojos: Mayo 1918–Febrero 1921," in *Historia y crónicas de la clase obrera en México* (Mexico City: Editorial Instituto Nacional de Antropología e Historia and Escuela Nacional de Antropología e Historia, 1981), pp. 61–71, 86–87.

43. Ibid., p. 66.

44. Correspondence cited; see n. 38.

45. AGN/FP/OC, 424-H-21, Felipe Carrillo Puerto from Mérida to Obregón, Reseña de la acción de la Exportadora en su primer año de existencia.

46. Armando Bartra, "Movimientos campesinos, 1920–1976," Manuscript, n.d., pp. 138–39.

47. AGN/FP/OC, 818-Y-4, Manuel Berzunza from Mérida to Obregón, September 16, 1921; Joseph, *Revolution from Without*, pp. 239–40.

48. Joseph, *Revolution from Without*, pp. 207–208.

49. In letters to his sister, who was in the United States at the time, Felipe Carrillo Puerto expressed his dismay at the monumental task that his popular government faced in attempting to educate politically ignorant peasants. The model that Carrillo Puerto wanted to follow was that of the Russian Soviet, a self-governing social and political entity, responsible but not subordinate to the socialist state. Carrillo Puerto to Dora Carrillo, October 12, 1919, and March 22, 1920. Letters in the Museo Felipe Carrillo Puerto, Motul.

50. The Mérida-based Liga Carlos Marx was critical of the inadequately "socialist" behavior of leaders who took advantage of their positions at the expense of the leagues; cf. *El Popular* (Mérida), February 7, 1922, August 21 and 23, 1923; also, *El Diario del Sureste* (Mérida), July 4, 1922.

51. AGN/FP/OC, 818-Y-4, Manuel Berzunza from Mérida to Obregón, September 16, 1921.

52. Rico, *Huelga.*

53. Ibid., p. 28.

54. Ibid., pp. 5–6.

55. Ibid., pp. 8–9, 55.

56. Ibid., pp. 28–31.

57. Ibid., pp. 50–51.

58. Ibid., pp. 78–83, 143.

59. AGN/FP/OC, 407-Y-1, Francisco Serrano from Mérida to Obregón, June 5, 1922; the U.S. chargé d'affaires to the secretary of state, Mexico, May 31, 1922; U.S. National Archives, Washington, D.C., Record Group 59, Reel 163, File 200.

60. U.S. National Archives, Record Group 59, Consul Foster from Veracruz to the State Department, June 12, 1922; Rico, *Huelga.*

61. *El Frente Único* (Veracruz), June 6, 1922; *La Plebe* (Mexico City), June 9, 1922; Rico, *Huelga*, pp. 99, 103; Rico, p. 276, tried to alert public opinion to the fact that capitalist support of the strikers had no other goal than the eventual overthrow of Carrillo's Socialist party government. Thus, he believed that the strike's origins were more politically inspired than labor related.

62. AGN/FP/OC, 407-Y-1, Carrillo Puerto from Mérida to Obregón, June 7 and 13, 1922.

63. Rico, *Huelga*, pp. 168, 213–17; Gamboa Ricalde, *Yucatán*, vol. 3, p. 273.

64. Rico, *Huelga*, pp. 276–77.

65. Joseph, *Revolution from Without*, pp. 264–68.

66. Ibid., pp. 270–73.

67. *La Revista de Yucatán*, December 13, 18, and 28, 1923.

68. Bergquist, *Labor*, Ch. 1.

69. An excellent example of this is Peter DeShazo, *Urban Workers and Labor Unions in Chile, 1902–1927* (Madison: University of Wisconsin Press, 1983).

10. Political Economy in Broader Perspective

1. Simpson, *Ejido*, pp. 611, 625.

2. Raymond, "Land Reform," p. 7; Simpson, *Ejido*, p. 607.

3. John Mogab, "The Mexican Experience in Peasant Agricultural Credit," *Development and Change* 15, no. 2 (1984): 205–207.

4. Armour Research Foundation of Illinois Institute of Technology, *Technological Audit of Selected Mexican Industries with Industrial Research Recommendations* (Ann Arbor: Edward Brothers, 1946), p. 86; Jorge Tomás Vera Pren, "La industria henequenera en la perspectiva histórica," *Yucatán: Historia y Economía* 35 (January–February 1983): 30.

5. The first Heneqeneros de Yucatán was organized under orders of President Plutarco Calles in 1925 and charged with establishing an orderly market in the chaotic economic conditions that preceded World War II.

6. Antonio Rodríguez, *El henequén: Una planta calumniada* (Mexico City: Costa Amic, 1966), pp. 280, 283.

7. Brannon and Baklanoff, *Agrarian Reform*, Ch. 5.

8. *Informe económico* (Mérida: Gobierno del Estado de Yucatán, 1980), pp. 70–76.

Glossary

agave. Any of various plants of the genus *Agave* in the Amaryllis family; the plants have spiny-margined, fleshy leaves and bear flowers in tall, spreading panicles. There are eight varieties of agave that are native to the Yucatán Peninsula. Of these, *sacci* or white henequen (*Agave fourcroydes*) was the fibrous plant cultivated during the henequen boom.

alcalde. City councilman and magistrate.

almud. A dry measure equal to one-twelfth *carga*.

amo. The master or patrón of an estate; the term suggests the paternalistic relationship between masters and servants on henequen estates.

anexa. A tract of land adjoining a large estate and annexed to it.

ara. A metric unit of area equal to one hundred square meters, or one-tenth of a hectare.

Asamblea Departamental. The State Congress of Yucatán during the period when all Mexican states were called departments, after the French model.

ayuntamiento. The municipal government of a city, town, or village.

Banco Agrario. The Agrarian Bank of Mexico.

Belizean creoles. Belizeans of African descent.

cabecera. A settlement that, because of its size, location, or other considerations, became the administrative center of a district.

cacique. The Indian leader of a village during colonial times and the nineteenth century.

campesino. A rural dweller or cultivator; the term includes agricultural workers as well as independent farmers.

carga. A corn measure that in the early part of the colonial period was equal to one-half *fanega* (about 0.75 bushels).

Carrancistas. Followers of Venustiano Carranza.

casas exportadoras. Import-export houses that dealt primarily in the henequen trade. They also served as moneylenders to the henequen estates during the boom period of the late nineteenth and early twentieth centuries.

casco. The center or heart of a henequen estate. Usually, the casco contained the landowner's residence, the machine house, and the workers' dwellings.

categoría política. A legal term used to identify the classes of communities that were recognized as having the requisite political or legal status to benefit under the agrarian reform: villages (*congregaciones* and *comunidades*); pueblos (towns); and *rancherías* (settlements).

caudillo. An autocratic chief or strongman.

centiaras. A metric unit of area equal to a square meter, or one-hundreth of a hectare.

chiclero. A laborer who tapped the gum of the chicozapote tree.

científicos. Literally, "scientists": the liberal, modernizing elites who constituted the inner circle of Porfirio Díaz's government.

Comisión Local Agraria. State Agrarian Commission, established to enforce, at the state level, the decrees of the federal government's National Agrarian Commission.

confradías. Religious brotherhoods; sodalities.

contribución patriótica. A tax levied after Mexican independence.

creoles. People of Hispanic culture born in America. (*See also* Belizean creoles.)

cruzob. The Mayanized plural of the word *cross.* The term was used to refer to the "people of the cross," the rebel Mayan group that refused to surrender in the Caste War and maintained an independent chiefdom in Quintana Roo until 1901.

cuatrero. Thief of cattle, horses, and other livestock; rustler.

ejidos. In the nineteenth century, communal village lands; in the twentieth century, land restored or granted to Mexican villages (*pueblo ejidos*) or the populations of former haciendas (*acasillado ejidos*) under the aegis of the Constitution of 1917 and subsequent agrarian reform legislation.

encomendero. The recipient of an encomienda from the Spanish Crown.

encomienda. An arrangement whereby Indians were entrusted to an encomendero, who, until 1549, received tribute and/or personal service from them. In return, the encomendero was required to Christianize and protect his charges.

enganchados. Literally, "hooked ones": contract workers from central Mexico who were coaxed or coerced into signing agreements with labor contractors to work specified periods of time on henequen estates.

entradas. Expeditions into largely unknown or hostile areas.

estancia. A cattle ranch.

finca. A rural estate.

gente decente. "Genteel people": this term identified local elites as a cultured and refined group within Yucatecan society.

hacendado. The owner of an hacienda, or great estate.

henequenal. A henequen field.

henequenero. A Yucatecan landowner who primarily cultivated henequen.

jabí. An American hardwood tree that is a member of the Papilionaceous family.

jefe político. The official in charge of a political unit embracing a district or a group of villages; same as a prefect.

jornaleros. Agricultural workers who worked on haciendas. They were not always resident peons.

juez de paz. Justice of the peace, a judicial official at the local level.

juicio de oposición. A judgment filed by plaintiffs who objected to a decision made by a court.

latifundio/latifundismo. A pattern of large-scale land ownership in which land is monopolized by a small elite at the expense of other rural dwellers.

latifundistas. Hacendados with extensive landholdings.

Ley Lerdo of 1856. The legislation that prohibited ecclesiastical and civil institutions from administering and owning real property not directly used in day-to-day operations. This law worked to the detriment of Indian villages, forcing them to sell off their communal landholdings.

lote. A small parcel of land distributed to each head of household. As a result of the Ley Lerdo, the federal government gradually surveyed the common public lands of corporate villages and distributed the lotes.

luneros. Residents of an agricultural estate who paid their rent in labor.

mayordomo. The resident manager of an estate.

mecate. A unit of land measurement used in Yucatán, equal to approximately 0.04 hectares, or 0.098 acres.

milpa rosa. A term used to describe the first year's corn crop, produced after clearing a piece of land using slash and burn techniques. The second year's crop is called *milpa caña.*

milpas. Cultivated fields; land planted in corn and other crops.

milpero. An agriculturalist who tends a milpa.

monte. Woodland; rural landholdings preserved by Yucatecan hacendados primarily to produce timber, which was needed to fuel the operation of the henequen rasping machines.

moscavado sugar. An unrefined brown sugar with high molasses content.

mozos. Peons; servants involved in a patron-client relationship with, and, more often than not, heavily indebted to, the master of an estate.

municipio. A local political unit embracing one to four villages.

partido. A political unit embracing a district or a group of villages.

patrón. Landlord.

pequeñas propiedades. Small landholdings.

pequeños propietarios. Small landholders.

Porfiriato. The dictatorship of Porfirio Díaz, who ruled Mexico 1876–1911.

ramón. A flowering tree that is indigenous to Yucatán.

rancherías. Settlements founded without legal authorization.

ranchero. The owner of a small to medium-sized farm or ranch. In the former case, rancheros almost always produced a cash crop. In Belize, most were tenant farmers.

ranchos. In the late eighteenth and nineteenth centuries, farms or landholdings dedicated to agriculture; also, settlements founded without legal authorization.

real. Monetary unit equal to one-eighth of a silver peso.

real merced. A royal land grant, given to an individual as private property or to a village in corporate ownership.

república de indígenas. Indian village government.

Secretaría de Gobernación. Ministry of the Interior.

síndico del concurso. A receiver assigned by the judge to oversee bankruptcy proceedings.

sirvientes. Resident workers tied to an estate by debt; peons; mozos.

subdelegado. Subprefect.

sublevados. Rebel Maya outside the direct control of the Yucatecan or Campechano governments.

terrenos baldíos. Uncultivated or unused lands. These lands had never been lawfully alienated by the nation or allocated for public use, and often included Indian village landholdings.

tienda de raya. A company store that sold goods on credit to resident workers on estates.

trapiche technology. A method of processing sugarcane into sugar that involved very simple techniques such as animal-powered mills and backyard boiling facilities.

vara. A variable unit of length of about 2.8 feet.

Villistas. Followers of the revolutionary chief, Pancho Villa.

visita village. A village without a resident priest, which received missionary clergy at periodic intervals.

Zapatistas. Followers of the revolutionary chief, Emiliano Zapata.

zona henequenera. The principal subregion given over to henequen production in Yucatán. This zone encompasses the area within a radius of seventy to eighty kilometers of Mérida.

Selected Bibliography

Aboites, Luis. *La revolución mexicana en Espita: 1910–1940: Microhistoria de la formación del estado de la revolución.* Mexico City: Cuadernos de La Casa Chata, 1982.

Adas, Michael. "From Avoidance to Confrontation: Peasant Protest in Precolonial and Colonial Southeast Asia." *Comparative Studies in Society and History* 23, no. 2 (April 1981): 217–47.

Albert, Bill, and Adrian Graves, eds. *Crises and Change in the International Sugar Economy 1860–1914.* Edinburgh: I. S. C. Press, 1984.

Alvarado, Salvador. *Actuación revolucionaria del General Salvador Alvarado en Yucatán.* Mexico City: Costa-Amic Editor, 1965.

———. *La reconstrucción de México: Un mensaje a los pueblos de América.* 3 vols. Mexico City: J. Ballesca, 1919.

———. *Mi sueño: El primer dividendo de la Comisión Reguladora del Mercado de Henequén.* Mérida: Imprenta del Gobierno Constitucionalista, 1917.

Ancona, Eligio. *Historia de Yucatán.* 4 vols. Mérida: Manuel Heredia Argüelles, 1878–80.

Anderson, Rodney D. *Outcasts in Their Own Land: Mexican Industrial Workers, 1906–1911.* DeKalb: Northern Illinois University Press, 1976.

Andrews, Anthony P. *Maya Salt Production and Trade.* Tucson: University of Arizona Press, 1983.

———. "Puertos costeros del postclásico temprano en el norte de Yucatán." *Estudios de Cultura Maya* 11 (1978): 75–93.

Armour Research Foundation of Illinois Institute of Technology. *Technological Audit of Selected Mexican Industries with Industrial Research Recommendations.* Ann Arbor: Edward Brothers, 1946.

Ashdown, Peter. "The Problem of Creole Historiography." In *Readings in Belizean History.* 2d ed. Ed. Lita Hunter-Krohn. Belize City: St. John's College, 1987.

Avila Zapata, Felipe N. *El General May, último jefe de las tribus mayas.* Mérida: Gobierno del Estado, 1974.

Azaola Garrido, Elena. *Rebelión y derrota del magonismo agrario.* Mexico City: Fondo de Cultura Económica/Sep-80, 1982.

Aznar Pérez, Alonzo, and Rafael Pedrera, eds. *Colección de leyes, decretos y órdenes o acuerdos de tendencia general del poder legislativo del Estado Libre y Soberano de Yucatán.* 3 vols. Mérida: Imprenta del Editor, 1849–51.

Baklanoff, Eric N., and Jeffery Brannon. "Forward and Backward Linkages in a Plantation Economy: Immigrant Entrepreneurship and Industrial Development in Yucatan, Mexico." *Journal of Developing Areas* 18, no. 1 (1984): 83–94.

Ball, Joseph W., and Jack D. Eaton. "Marine Resources and the Prehistoric Lowland Maya: A Comment." *American Anthropologist* 74, no. 3 (1972): 772–76.

Bancroft, Hubert H. *History of Central America 1801–1887*. Vol 3. San Francisco: History Company Publishers, 1887.

Baños Ramírez, Othón, ed. *Sociedad, estructura agraria y estado en Yucatán*. Mérida: Universidad Autónoma de Yucatán, 1990.

Baqueiro, Oswaldo de. *La ciudad heroica: Historia de Valladolid*. Mérida: Imprenta Oriente, 1943.

Baqueiro, Serapio. *Ensayo histórico sobre las revoluciones de Yucatán desde el año de 1840 hasta 1864*. 3 vols. Mérida: Manuel Heredia Argüelles, 1878–87.

Bartolomé, Miguel A., and Alicia M. Barabas. *La resistencia maya: Relaciones interétnicas en el oriente de la península de Yucatán*. Mexico City: INAH, 1977.

Bartra, Roger. "Peasants and Political Power in Mexico: A Theoretical Approach." *Latin American Perspectives* 5 (1975): 125–45.

Batt, R[osemary] Laura. "Capitalist Class Formation in Dependent Economies: The Case of Espita, Yucatan, Mexico." Master's thesis, University of Kentucky, 1981.

Bauer, Arnold. *Chilean Rural Society*. Cambridge: Cambridge University Press, 1975.

Beckford, George L. *Persistent Poverty: Underdevelopment of Plantation Economies of the Third World*. New York: Oxford University Press, 1972.

Benjamin, Thomas. "Provinces of the Revolution: Provincial, Regional and Local History in Revolutionary Historiography." In *Mexican Revolutions: Essays on Regional Mexican History, 1910–1929*. Ed. Thomas Benjamin and Mark Wasserman. Albuquerque: University of New Mexico Press, 1990.

Benjamin, Thomas, and William McNellie, eds. *Other Mexicos: Essays on Regional Mexican History, 1876–1911*. Albuquerque: University of New Mexico Press, 1984.

Bergquist, Charles. *Labor in Latin America: Comparative Essays on Chile, Argentina, Venezuela, and Colombia*. Stanford, Calif.: Stanford University Press, 1986.

Best, Lloyd. "Outlines of a Model of a Pure Plantation Economy." *Social and Economic Studies* (September 1968).

Betancourt Pérez, Antonio. *Revoluciones y crisis en la economía de Yucatán*. Mérida: Talleres Gráficos de Sudeste, 1953.

Beteta, Ramón. *Tierra del chicle*. 3d ed. Mexico City: Editorial Ilustrada, 1951.

Billington, Ray A. *The American Frontier Thesis: Attack and Defense*. Washington, D.C.: American Historical Association, 1973.

Bolio, José A. *Manual práctico del henequén*. Mérida: Imprenta de la Empresa Editorial Católica, 1914.

Bolland, Nigel. "Slavery in Belize." *BISRA*. Occasional Publication 7 (1979).

Bolland, Nigel, and Assad Shoman. *Land in Belize, 1765–1871*. Mona, Jamaica: University of the West Indies, 1977.

Borah, Woodrow. *Justice by Insurance: The General Indian Court of Colonial Mexico and the Legal Aides of the Half-Real.* Berkeley: University of California Press, 1983.

Brading, David. "Hacienda Profits and Tenant Farming in the Mexican Bajío, 1700–1860." In *Land and Labour in Latin America: Essays on the Development of Agrarian Capitalism in the Nineteenth and Twentieth Centuries.* Ed. Kenneth Duncan and Ian Rutledge. Cambridge: Cambridge University Press, 1977.

Brannon, Jeffery, and Eric N. Baklanoff. *Agrarian Reform and Public Enterprise in Mexico: The Political Economy of Yucatán's Henequen Industry.* University: University of Alabama Press, 1987.

Breves apuntes acerca de la administración del General Salvador Alvarado como gobernador de Yucatán. Mérida: Imprenta del Gobierno Constitucionalista, 1917.

Bricker, Victoria Reifler. *The Indian Christ, The Indian King: The Historical Substrate of Maya Myth and Ritual.* Austin: University of Texas Press, 1981.

Bristowe, Lindsay W., and Philip B. Wright. *The Handbook of British Honduras for 1888–1889.* Edinburgh and London: William Blackwood and Sons, 1890.

Bulnes, Francisco. *The Whole Truth About Mexico: President Wilson's Responsibility.* New York: Mr. Bulnes Book Company, 1916.

Bustillos Carrillo, Antonio. *Yucatán al servicio de la patria y la revolución.* Mexico City: Casa Ramírez Editores, 1959.

Cal, Ángel E. "The Corozal (Goshen) Estate." *Belcast Journal of Belizean Affairs* 1 (1984): 41–47.

Calderón Quijano, José. 1663[?]–1824: *Historia de los establecimientos británicos del Río Valis hasta la independencia de Hispanoamérica.* Seville: Escuela de Estudios Hispanoamericanos de la Universidad de Sevilla, 1944.

Cámara Zavala, Gonzalo. *Reseña histórica de la industria henequenera de Yucatán.* Mérida: Imprenta del Oriente, 1936.

Canto López, Antonio. *El Territorio de Quintana Roo y Yucatán.* Mérida: Estado de Yucatán, 1954.

Cardoso, Ciro, et al. *De la dictadura porfirista a los tiempos libertarios.* Mexico City: Siglo XXI, 1980.

Carey, James C. *The Mexican Revolution in Yucatan, 1915–1924.* Boulder and London: Westview Press, 1984.

Carr, Barry. "Recent Regional Studies of the Mexican Revolution." *Latin American Research Review* 15, no. 1 (1980): 3–14.

———. "The Casa del Obrero Mundial, Constitutionalism and the Pact of February 1915." In *El trabajo y los trabajadores en la historia de México.* Ed. Elsa Cecilia Frost et al. Mexico City: El Colegio de México and Tucson: University of Arizona Press, 1979.

Castillo Canché, Jorge Isidro, and Roger Alonso Domínguez Saldívar. "La Constitución de Cádiz en Yucatán, 1812–1814." Graduate thesis, Universidad Autónoma de Yucatán, Mérida, 1986.

Castro, Juan Miguel. *El henequén de Yucatán y el monopolio.* Mérida: Imprenta del Comercio de Nestor Rubio Alpuche, 1876.

Chacón, Ramón D. "Yucatán and the Mexican Revolution: The Pre-Constitutional Years, 1910–1918." Ph.D. diss., Stanford University, Stanford, Calif., 1982.

Chamberlain, Robert F. *The Conquest and Colonization of Yucatan*. Washington, D.C.: Carnegie Institution of Washington, 1948.

Chardon, Roland Emanuel Paul. *Geographic Aspects of Plantation Agriculture in Yucatan*. Washington D.C.: National Academy of Sciences, 1961.

Chevalier, François. *La Formation des grands domaines au Mexique*. Paris: Institut d'Ethnologie, Travaux et Mémoires, 1952.

Clark, Marjorie Ruth. *Organized Labor in Mexico*. Chapel Hill: University of North Carolina Press, 1934.

Clendinnen, Inga. *Ambivalent Conquests: Maya and Spaniard in Yucatán, 1517–1570*. Cambridge: Cambridge University Press, 1987.

Cline, Howard. "The Sugar Episode in Yucatan, 1825–1850." *Inter-American Economic Affairs* 1 (1948): 79–100.

———. *Related Studies in Early Nineteenth Century Yucatecan Social History*. Pts. 1–3. Chicago: University of Chicago Library, Microfilm Collection of Manuscripts on Middle American Cultural Anthropology no. 32, 1950.

———. "Regionalism and Society in Yucatan: 'Progressivism' and the Origins of the Caste War, 1825–1847." Ph.D. diss., Harvard University, Cambridge, 1947.

Conniff, Michael L. "Introduction: Toward a Comparative Definition of Populism." In *Latin American Populism in Comparative Perspective*. Ed. Michael L. Conniff. Albuquerque: University of New Mexico Press, 1982.

Cosío Villegas, Daniel. *Historia moderna de México*. 9 vols. México: Editorial Hermes, 1948–72.

Cumberland, Charles C. *Mexico: The Struggle for Modernity*. New York: Oxford University Press, 1968.

De la Huerta, Adolfo. *Memorias de Don Adolfo de la Huerta según su propio dictado*. México: Ediciones Guzmán, 1958.

De la Peña, Guillermo. "Los estudios regionales y la antropología social en México." *Relaciones* 2, no. 8 (Fall 1981): 43–93.

De Portas, Rafael. *Tratado sobre el cultivo de la caña: Elaboración del azúcar y cultivo del henequén*. Mérida: Imprenta del Gobierno, 1872.

DeShazo, Peter. *Urban Workers and Labor Unions in Chile, 1902–1927*. Madison: University of Wisconsin Press, 1983.

Días Dufoo, Carlos. *México y los capitales extranjeros*. Mexico City: Bouret, 1918.

Dobson, Narda. *History of Belize*. Kingston, Jamaica: Longman Caribbean, 1973.

Dumond, D. E. "Independent Maya of the Late Nineteenth Century: Chiefdoms and Power Politics." In *Anthropology and History in Yucatan*. Ed. Grant Jones. Austin: University of Texas Press, 1977.

Duncan, Kenneth, and Ian Rutledge, eds. *Land and Labour in Latin America: Essays on the Development of Agrarian Capitalism in the Nineteenth and Twentieth Centuries*. Cambridge: Cambridge University Press, 1977.

Echánove Trujillo, Carlos A. *La vida prócer de Quintana Roo*. Mérida: Gobierno del Estado, 1962.

———. *Una tierra en disputa: Belice ante la historia*. Mérida: Universidad de Yucatán, 1951.

Espadas y Aguilar, Ramón. *Fundación del Partido Socialista Obrero: Junio de 1916*. Mérida: n.p., 1972.

Fals Borda, Orlando. *Historia doble de la costa*. 3 vols. Bogotá: Carlos Valencia Editores, 1981.

Farriss, Nancy. *Maya Society under Colonial Rule: The Collective Enterprise of Survival*. Princeton: Princeton University Press, 1984.

———. "Nucleation versus Dispersal: The Dynamics of Population Movement in Colonial Yucatan." *Hispanic American Historical Review* 58, no. 2 (1978): 187–216.

———. "Propiedades territoriales en Yucatán en la época colonial." *Revista de la Universidad de Yucatán* 146 (1983): 55–61.

Feldman, L. "Belize and Its Neighbors: A Preliminary Report on the Spanish Colonial Records of the Audiencia of Guatemala." In *Archaeology at Colha, Belize: The 1981 Interim Report*. Ed. T. H. Hester et al. Austin: University of Texas Press, 1982.

Flamarión Cardoso, Ciro. "Regional History." *Biblioteca Americana* 1, no. 1 (September 1982): 1–8.

Flannery, Kent V., ed. *Maya Subsistence: Studies in Memory of Dennis E. Puleston*. New York: Academic Press, 1982.

Friedrich, Paul. *Agrarian Revolt in a Mexican Village*. Englewood Cliffs, N.J.: Prentice-Hall, 1970.

Gann, Thomas. *The Maya Indians of Southern Yucatan and Northern British Honduras*. Washington, D.C.: U.S. Government Printing Office, 1918.

García, Alma. "Recent Studies in Nineteenth- and Early Twentieth-Century Regional Mexican History." *Latin American Research Review* 22, no. 2 (1987): 255–66.

Gill, Christopher J. "Regional Variation and Patterns of Resistance: The Henequen Boom in Yucatan, 1880–1915." Seniors Honors thesis, University of Michigan, Ann Arbor, 1987.

González, Luis. *Nueva invitación a la microhistoria*. Mexico City: Sep/80, 1982.

———. *Invitación a la microhistoria*. Mexico City: SepSetentas, 1973.

———. *Pueblo en vilo: Microhistoria de San José de Gracia*. Mexico City: El Colegio de México, 1972.

———. "Microhistory, *Terruño*, and the Social Sciences: A Prefatory Note." In *Regional Impacts of U.S.-Mexican Relations*. Ed. Ina Rosenthal-Urey. La Jolla, Calif.: Center for U.S.-Mexican Studies, 1986.

González Durán, Jorge. *La rebelión de los mayas y el Quintana Roo chiclero*. Mérida: Editorial Dosis, 1974.

González Navarro, Moisés. *Raza y tierra: La Guerra de Castas y el henequén*. Mexico City: El Colegio de México, 1970.

González Pacheco, Cuauhtémoc. *Capital extranjero en las selvas de Chiapas, 1883–1982*. Mexico City: Universidad Autónoma de México, 1983.

González Roa, Fernando. *El aspecto agrario de la revolución mexicana.* Mexico City: Poder Ejecutivo Federal, 1919.

Goodman, David, and Michael Redclift. *From Peasant to Proletarian: Capitalist Development and Agrarian Transitions.* New York: St. Martin's Press, 1982.

Guzmán, Martín Luis. *The Eagle and the Serpent.* Tr. Harriet de Onis. Reprint ed. Gloucester, Mass.: Peter Smith, 1969.

Harrison, Peter D., and B. L. Turner, eds. *Pre-Hispanic Maya Agriculture.* Albuquerque: University of New Mexico Press, 1978.

Hart, John M. *Anarchism and the Mexican Working Class, 1860–1931.* Austin: University of Texas Press, 1978.

———. *Revolutionary Mexico: The Coming and Process of the Mexican Revolution.* Berkeley: University of California Press, 1987.

Hartman, Keith. "The Henequen Empire in Yucatan: 1870–1910." Master's thesis, University of Iowa, Iowa City, 1966.

Henderson, George. *An Account of the British Settlement of Honduras.* London: C. & R. Baldwin, 1809.

Hennessey, Alistair. *The Frontier in Latin American History.* Albuquerque: University of New Mexico Press, 1978.

Herr, Richard. *The Eighteenth-Century Revolution in Spain.* Princeton: Princeton University Press, 1958.

Hobsbawm, Eric J. "Peasants and Politics." *Journal of Peasant Studies* 1, no. 1 (1973): 12.

Hoy, Carlos. *Breve historia de Quintana Roo.* 2d ed. Chetumal: Impresora México, 1983.

Humphreys, R. A. *Diplomatic History of British Honduras.* Oxford: Oxford University Press, 1961.

Hunt, Marta Espejo-Ponce. "Colonial Yucatan: Town and Region in the Seventeenth Century." Ann Arbor: University Microfilms, 1974.

Irigoyen, Renán. *Salvador Alvarado: Extraordinario estadista de la revolución.* Mérida: Ediciones del Gobierno del Estado, 1973.

Jiménez M., Luis G. *El Chicle: Su explotación forestal e industrial.* Mexico City: Imprenta Manuel Casas, 1951.

Jones, Grant D., ed. *Anthropology and History in Yucatan.* Austin: University of Texas Press, 1977.

———. "La estructura política de los Mayas de Chan Santa Cruz: El papel del respaldo Inglés." *América Indígena* 31, no. 2 (1971): 415–28.

———. "The Last Maya Frontiers of Colonial Yucatan." In *Spanish and Indians in Southeastern Mesoamerica.* Ed. Murdo MacLeod and R. Wasserstrom. Lincoln: University of Nebraska Press, 1983.

Joseph, Gilbert M. "Documenting a Regional Pastime: Baseball in Yucatán." In *Windows on Latin America: Understanding Society Through Photographs.* Ed. Robert M. Levine. A special issue of *South Eastern Latin Americanist* (June–September 1987).

———. "From Caste War to Class War: The Historiography of Modern Yucatán (c. 1750–1940)." *Hispanic American Historical Review* 65, no. 1 (February 1985): 111–34.

———. "The Logwood Trade and its Settlements." *Readings in Belizean History*. Vol. 1. Ed. John Mahler. Belize City: BISRA, 1978.

———. *Rediscovering the Past at Mexico's Periphery: Essays on the History of Modern Yucatán*. University: University of Alabama Press, 1986.

———. *Revolution from Without: Yucatán, Mexico, and the United States, 1880–1924*. Cambridge: Cambridge University Press, 1982; Durham, N.C.: Duke University Press, 1988.

Joseph, Gilbert, and Allen Wells. "El monocultivo de henequén y sus contradicciones: Estructura de dominación y formas de resistencia en haciendas yucatecas a fines del Porfiriato." *Siglo XIX* 3, no. 6 (July–December 1988): 215–77.

———. "Summer of Discontent: Economic Rivalry among Elite Factions during the Late Porfiriato in Yucatán." *Journal of Latin American Studies* 18, no. 2 (1986).

———. *Summer of Discontent, Seasons of Upheaval: Elite Politics and Rural Protest in Yucatán, 1890–1915*. Albuquerque: University of New Mexico Press, forthcoming.

———. "Yucatán: Elite Politics and Rural Insurgency in a Period of Transition, 1897–1913." In *Mexican Revolutions: Essays on Regional Mexican History, 1910–1929*. Ed. Thomas Benjamin and Mark Wasserman. Albuquerque: University of New Mexico Press, 1990.

———. "The Rough-and-Tumble Career of Pedro Crespo." In *The Human Tradition in Latin America: The Twentieth Century*. Ed. William H. Beezley and Judith Ewell. Wilmington, Del.: Scholarly Resources, 1987.

Katz, Friedrich. "Labor Conditions on Haciendas in Porfirian Mexico: Some Trends and Tendencies." *Hispanic American Historical Review* 54, no. 1 (1974): 1–47.

———. *The Secret War in Mexico: Europe, the United States and the Mexican Revolution*. Chicago: University of Chicago Press, 1981.

Knight, Alan. *The Mexican Revolution*. 2 vols. New York: Cambridge University Press, 1986.

———. "Mexican Peonage: What Was It and Why Was It?" *Journal of Latin American Studies* 18, no. 1 (1986): 41–74.

———. "The Working Class and the Mexican Revolution, 1900–1920." *Journal of Latin American Studies* 16, no. 1 (May 1984): 52–57.

Konrad, Herman W. "Anthropological Studies in Yucatán and the Historical Dimension." *Mexican Studies* 3, no. 1 (Winter 1987): 163–80.

———. "Fallout of the War of the Chacs: The Impact of Hurricanes and Implications for Prehispanic Quintana Roo Maya Processes." In *Status, Structure, and Stratification: Current Archaeological Reconstructions*. Ed. M. T. Garcia and M. Thompson. Calgary: Calgary Archaeology Association, 1985.

———. "Una población chiclera: Contexto histórico-económico y un perfil demográfico." *Boletín de la Escuela de Ciencias Antropológicas de la Universidad de Yucatán* 8, no. 45 (1980): 2–39.

Krauze, Enrique. "Chihuahua, ida y vuelta." In *Por una democracia sin adjetivos*. Mexico City: Joaquín Mortiz Planeta, 1986.

Lapointe, Marie. *Los mayas rebeldes de Yucatán*. Zamora: El Colegio de Michoacán, 1983.

Lee, Rosemary L. "The Tourist Industry in Yucatan: A Case Study in the Interaction Between Class Structure and Economic Development." Ph.D. diss., University of California, Irvine, 1977.

Love, Joseph L. "An Approach to Regionalism." In *New Approaches to Latin American History*. Ed. Richard Graham and Peter H. Smith. Austin: University of Texas Press, 1974.

Loveira, Carlos. *El socialismo en Yucatán*. Havana: El Siglo XX, 1923.

Lovell, W. George. "Surveying Conquest: The Maya of Guatemala in Historical Perspective." *Latin American Research Review* 23, no. 2 (1988): 25–57.

McBride, George M. *The Land Systems of Mexico*. New York: American Geographical Society, 1923.

Means, Philip Ainsworth. "History of the Spanish Conquest of Yucatan and of the Itzas." *Papers of the Peabody Museum* 7 (1917): 54–83.

Mediz Bolio, Antonio. "Prólogo." In Salvador Alvarado, *Actuación revolucionaria del Gral. Salvador Alvarado en Yucatán*. Mexico City: Costa-Amic Editor, 1965.

Mena Brito, Bernardino. *Historia de las desmembraciones del Estado de Yucatán efectuados por el gobierno nacional: El Petén, Belice, Campeche, Quintana Roo*. Mexico City: Ediciones Bota, 1962.

Menéndez Reyes, G. A. *Quintana Roo album monográfico*. Chetumal: Editorial del Estado de Quintana Roo, 1979.

Meyer, Jean. "Los obreros en la revolución mexicana: Los batallones rojos." *Historia Mexicana* 20 (July–September, 1971).

Miller, Authur, and Nancy Farriss. "Religious Syncreticism in Colonial Yucatan: The Archaeological and Ethnohistorical Evidence from Tancah, Quintana Roo." In *Maya Archaeology and Ethnohistory*. Ed. N. Hammond and G. Willey. Austin: University of Texas Press, 1979.

Mintz, Sidney. *Caribbean Transformations*. Chicago: Aldine, 1974.

Mogab, John. "The Mexican Experience in Peasant Agricultural Credit." *Development and Change* 15, no. 2 (1984): 203–21.

Monge, Carlos. "El sur del Perú en perspectiva regional." Paper presented at the 34th Annual Meeting of the Southeastern Council on Latin American Studies, Mérida, Yucatán, April 1987.

Montalvo, Enrique. "Imperialismo y henequén: Estudio de las clases sociales en Yucatán, 1900–1919." Thesis, Universidad Iberoamericana, Mexico City, 1976.

Morales Jiménez, Alberto. *Hombres de la revolución mexicana: 50 semblanzas biográficas*. Mexico City: Instituto Nacional de Estudios Históricos de la Revolución Mexicana, 1960.

Moreno Fraginals, Manuel. *El ingenio: Complejo económico social cubano del azúcar*. 3 vols. Havana: Editorial de Ciencias Sociales, 1978.

———. "Plantations in the Caribbean: Cuba, Puerto Rico, and the Dominican Republic in the Late Nineteenth Century." In *Between Slavery and Free Labor*. Ed. Manuel Moreno Fraginals et al.

——— et al., eds. *Between Slavery and Free Labor: The Spanish-Speaking Caribbean in the Nineteenth Century*. Baltimore: Johns Hopkins University Press, 1985.

Mörner, Magnus. "Research on Latin American History Today: New Challenges." *Boletín de Estudios Latino-americanos y del Caribe* 37 (December 1984): 9–18.

Moseley, Edward H., and Edward D. Terry, eds. *Yucatan: A World Apart*. University: University of Alabama Press, 1980.

Nettings, R. M. "Maya Subsistence: Mythologies, Analogies, Possibilities." In *The Origins of Maya Civilization*. Ed. R. E. W. Adams. Albuquerque: University of New Mexico Press, 1977.

Ober, Frederick A. *Travels in Mexico and Life Among the Mexicans*. Boston: Estes and Lauriat, 1884.

Ortega Noriega, Sergio. "Archivos históricos regionales y locales." *Boletín del Archivo General de la Nación*, 3d. ser., no. 1 (July–September 1977).

Osorio Carbajal, Ramón. "Historia de la medicina alopática en la época independiente." In *Enciclopedia Yucatanense*. Mexico City: Gobierno del Estado de Yucatán, 1977.

Ots Capdequí, José M. *El régimen de la tierra en la América española durante el período colonial*. Ciudad Trujillo: Universidad de Santo Domingo, 1946.

Palermo, Ángel. *Modos de producción y formaciones socioeconómicas*. Mexico City: Ediciones Edicol, 1976.

Paoli, Francisco José. *Yucatán y los orígenes del nuevo estado mexicano: Gobierno de Salvador Alvarado, 1915–1918*. Mexico City: Ediciones Era, 1984.

Paoli, Francisco J., and Enrique Montalvo. *El socialismo olvidado de Yucatán: Elementos para una reinterpretación de la Revolución Mexicana*. Mexico City: Siglo XXI, 1977.

Patch, Robert. "Agrarian Change in Eighteenth-Century Yucatán." *Hispanic American Historical Review* 65, no. 1 (1985): 21–49.

———. "A Colonial Regime: Maya and Spaniard in Yucatán." Ph.D. diss., Princeton University, Princeton, N.J., 1979.

———. "La formación de estancias y haciendas en Yucatán durante la colonia." *Boletín de la Escuela de Ciencias Antropológicas de la Universidad de Yucatán* 4, no. 19 (1976): 21–61. Reprinted in Universidad de Yucatán. *Cuatro ensayos antropológicos*. Mérida: Ediciones de la Universidad de Yucatán, 1979.

Patrón Peniche, Prudencio. *Geografía del Departamento de Espita*. Mérida: n.p., 1919.

———. *Historia de Espita de los tiempos más remotos*. Mérida: n.p., 1959.

Peón, José María, and Isidro Gondra, eds. *Colección de leyes, decretos y órdenes del augusto Congreso del Estado Libre de Yucatán*. 2 vols. Mérida: Lorenzo Seguí, 1832; Mérida: Tipógrafo de G. Canto, 1896, in 3 vols.

Phipps, Helen. *Some Aspects of the Agrarian Question in Mexico: A Historical Study*. Austin: University of Texas Bulletin, 1925.

Platt, D. C. M. "Economic Imperialism and the Businessman: Britain and Latin America before 1914." In *Studies in the Theory of Imperialism*. Ed. Roger Owen and Bob Sutcliffe. London: Longman, 1976.

Pohl, Mary, ed. *Prehistoric Lowland Maya Environment and Subsistence Economy.* Cambridge, Mass.: Peabody Museum of Archaeology and Ethnology, 1985.

Poot Canul, Juventino. *Le Cha'a Yeetel le Maya'ob Way Ti' Quintana Roo/El chicle y los mayas de Quintana Roo.* Mexico City: SEP/INI, 1982.

Quintal Martín, Fidelio. "Breve historia de Yucatán durante la última década del porfiriato." *Boletín E.C.A.U.D.Y.* 2, no. 65 (1984): 55.

———. *Yucatán: Carácter de la Guerra Campesina de 1847: Una síntesis interpretativa.* Mérida: Ediciones de la Universidad de Yucatán, 1976.

Raymond, Nathaniel. "The Impact of Land Reform in the Monocrop Region of Yucatan, Mexico." Ph.D. diss., Brandeis University, Waltham, Mass., 1971.

Reed, Nelson. *The Caste War of Yucatan.* Stanford, Calif.: Stanford University Press, 1964.

Regil, José María, and Alonso M. Peón. *Estadística de Yucatán publicada por acuerdo de la Sociedad de Geografía y Estadística.* Mexico City: n.p., 1853.

Richmond, Douglas W. *Venustiano Carranza's Nationalist Struggle, 1893–1920.* Lincoln: University of Nebraska Press, 1983.

Rico, Juan. *La huelga de junio.* 2 vols. Mérida: n.p., 1922.

Rivas Font, José I. *Apuntes sobre el cultivo y la explotación del henequén.* Mérida: El Eco del Comercio, 1906.

Rodríguez, Antonio. *El henequén: Una planta calumniada.* Mexico City: Costa-Amic, 1966.

Rodríguez, José H. "Webb's Great Frontier and the Interpretation of Modern History." In *The New World Looks at its History.* Ed. A. Lewis and T. McGann. Austin: University of Texas Press, 1963.

Roys, Ralph. *The Indian Background of Colonial Yucatan.* Washington, D.C.: Carnegie Institution of Washington, 1943.

Rubio Mañé, J. Ignacio. *Los sanjuanistas de Yucatán: Manuel Jiménez Solís, el padre Justis.* Mexico City: 1971.

Sabloff, Jeremy, and Willima L. Rathje. *A Study of Changing Pre-Colombian Commercial Systems: The 1972–1973 Seasons at Cozumel, Mexico.* Monographs of the Peabody Museum no. 3. Cambridge, Mass.: Harvard University Press, 1975.

Sarrailh, Jean. *L'Espagne éclairée de la seconde moitié du XVIII*[e] *siècle.* Paris: Imprimerie Nationale, 1954.

Schnakenbourg, Christian. "From the Sugar Estate to Central Factory: The Industrial Revolution in the Caribbean (1840–1905)." In *Crisis and Change in the International Sugar Economy, 1860–1914.* Ed. Bill Albert and Adrian Graves. Norwich and Edinburgh: ISC Press, 1984.

Scholes, France, and Eric Thompson. "The Francisco Pérez Probanza of 1654–56 and Matrícula of Tipu (Belize)." In *Anthropology and History in Yucatan.* Ed. Grant D. Jones. Austin: University of Texas Press, 1977.

Scott, James C. "Resistance without Protest and without Organization: Peasant Opposition to the Islamic *Zakat* and the Christian Tithe." *Comparative Studies in Society and History* 29, no. 3 (July 1987): 417–52.

———. *Weapons of the Weak: Everyday Forms of Peasant Resistance*. New Haven: Yale University Press, 1985.

Senior, Clarence. *Land Reform and Democracy*. Gainesville: University of Florida Press, 1958.

Sierra O'Reilly, Justo. *Los indios de Yucatán: Consideraciones históricas sobre la influencia del elemento indígena en la organización social del país*. 2 vols. Mérida: Tipográfica Yucateca, 1954–57.

Silva Herzog, Jesús. *Breve historia de la revolución mexicana: La etapa constitucional y la lucha de facciones*. Mexico City: Fondo de Cultura Económica, 1960.

Simpson, Eyler N. *The Ejido: Mexico's Way Out*. Chapel Hill: University of North Carolina Press, 1937.

Skidmore, Thomas. "Workers and Soldiers: Urban Labor Movements and Elite Responses in Twentieth-Century Latin America." In *Elites, Masses, and Modernization in Latin America, 1850–1930*. Ed. Virginia Bernhard. Austin: University of Texas Press, 1979.

Spenser, Daniela G. O. *Partido Socialista Chiapaneco: Rescate y reconstrucción de su historia*. Mexico City: La Casa Chata, 1988.

Stein, Stanley J., and Barbara H. Stein. *The Colonial Heritage of Latin America*. New York: Oxford University Press, 1970.

Stein, Steven. *Populism in Peru: The Emergence of the Masses and the Politics of Social Control*. Madison: University of Wisconsin Press, 1982.

Stephens, John Lloyd. *Incidents of Travel in Yucatan*. 2 vols. New York: Harper and Brothers, 1843.

Stern, Claudio. *Las regiones de México y sus niveles de desarrollo socio-económico*. Mexico City: El Colegio de México, 1973.

Stern, Steve J., ed. *Resistance, Rebellion, and Consciousness in the Andean Peasant World, 18th to 20th Centuries*. Madison: University of Wisconsin Press, 1987.

Suárez Molina, Víctor. *La evolución económica de Yucatán a través del siglo XIX*. Vols. 1–2. Mérida: Ediciones de la Universidad de Yucatán, 1977.

Tannenbaum, Frank. *Peace by Revolution: An Interpretation of Mexico*. New York: Columbia University Press, 1933.

———. *The Mexican Agrarian Revolution*. New York: Macmillan, 1929.

Taylor, John G. *From Modernization to Modes of Production: A Critique of the Sociologies of Development and Underdevelopment*. London: Macmillan, 1979.

Terry, Edward D. et al. "Analyzing a Region: The Interaction of the University of Alabama and the Yucatan." *SECOLAS Annals* 13 (1982): 32–47.

Thompson, Edgar T. "The Plantation as a Social System." In Pan American Union, *Plantation Systems of the New World*. Washington, D.C.: Pan American Union, 1959.

Thompson, Eric. *Maya History and Religion*. Norman: University of Oklahoma Press, 1970.

———. *The Maya of Belize: Historical Chapters since Columbus*. Belize City: Benex Press, 1972.

Tiburcio Cervera, José. "Apuntes sobre la industria pecuaria en Yucatán." *Boletín de la Sociedad Mexicana de Geografía y Estadística* 4 (1872): 399–400.

Troncoso, Francisco P. *Las guerras con las tribus yaquis y mayos*. Mexico City: INI, 1977.

Tutino, John. *From Insurrection to Revolution in Mexico: Social Bases of Agrarian Violence, 1750–1940*. Princeton, N.J.: Princeton University Press, 1986.

Universidad de Yucatán. *Memorias de la Primera Semana de la Historia*. Mérida: Universidad de Yucatán, 1980.

Valadés, José C. *Historia general de la revolución mexicana*. 10 vols. Mexico City: Manuel Quesada Brandi Editor, 1963–67.

Valdés Acosta, José María. *A través de los siglos*. 3 vols. Mérida: Talleres "Pluma y Lápiz," 1926–29.

Vanderwood, Paul J. "Building Blocks but Yet No Building: Regional History and the Mexican Revolution." *Mexican Studies* 3, no. 2 (Summer 1987): 421–32.

Van Young, Eric. "Doing Regional History: Methodological and Theoretical Considerations." In *City, Country, and Frontier in Mexican History*. Ed. Eric Van Young and Roberto Moreno de los Arcos. Mexico City: Universidad Autónoma de México, forthcoming.

———. "Mexican Rural History since Chevalier: The Historiography of the Colonial Hacienda." *Latin American Research Review* 18, no. 3 (1983): 5–62.

Vásquez Islas, Enrique. *Chicle: Ensayo de novela del trópico mexicano*. Mexico City: Cicerón, 1951.

Vaughan, Mary Kay. *The State, Education, and Social Class in Mexico, 1880–1928*. DeKalb: Northern Illinois University Press, 1982.

Vera Pren, Jorge Tomás. "La industria henequenera en la perspectiva histórica." *Yucatán: Historia y Economía* 35 (January–February 1983): 21–42.

Villanueva Mukul, Eric. *Así tomamos las tierras*. Mérida: Maldonado Editores, 1984.

Villa Rojas, Alfonso. *Los eligidos de Dios: Etnografía de los mayas de Quintana Roo*. Mexico City: Instituto Nacional Indigenista, 1978.

Villaseñor, Víctor Manuel. "Salvador Alvarado." *Revista de la Universidad de Yucatán* 6 (July–August 1964): 125.

Wagner, Helmuth O. "Subsistence Potential and Population Density of the Maya on the Yucatan Peninsula and the Causes for the Decline of Population in the Fifteenth Century." *Verhandlungen des 38 Internationalen Americanistenkongressen, Stuttgart-München* 1 (1970): 185–91.

Warman, Arturo. *Y venimos a contradecir: Los campesinos de Morelos y el estado nacional*. Mexico City: La Casa Chata, 1976.

Weinstein, Barbara. "Brazilian Regionalism." *Latin American Research Review* 17, no. 2 (1982): 262–76.

Wells, Allen. "Family Elites in a Boom and Bust Economy: The Molinas and Peóns of Porfirian Yucatán." *Hispanic American Historical Review* 62, no. 2 (1982): 224–53.

———. "The Terrible Green Monster: Recent Literature on Sugar, Coffee, and Coerced Labor in the Caribbean." *Latin American Research Review* 23, no. 2 (1988): 189–205.

———. *Yucatán's Gilded Age: Haciendas, Henequen, and International Harvester, 1860–1915*. Albuquerque: University of New Mexico Press, 1985.

Whetten, Nathan L. *Rural Mexico*. Chicago: University of Chicago Press, 1948.

Whitney, H. *The Honduras Almanack for 1839*. Belize City: n.p., 1839.

Wolf, Eric R., and Sidney W. Mintz. "Haciendas and Plantations in Middle America and the Antilles." *Social and Economic Studies* 6 (1957): 380–412.

Zunz, Olivier, ed. *Reliving the Past: The Worlds of Social History*. Chapel Hill: University of North Carolina Press, 1985.

Contributors

ROSEMARY L. BATT is currently a Ph.D. candidate in the Department of Urban Studies at the Massachusetts Institute of Technology. She has done extensive field research in Yucatán and Michoacán, Mexico, and holds a masters degree in anthropology from the University of Kentucky.

JEFFERY T. BRANNON is Associate Professor of Economics at the University of Texas at El Paso. He is the co-author of *Agrarian Reform and Public Enterprise in Mexico: The Political Economy of Yucatán's Henequen Industry* (1987) and has published numerous articles on Mexico in scholarly journals that include *World Development, Journal of Developing Areas,* and *Latin American Research Review.* He is presently doing research on poverty along the U.S.-Mexico border.

ÁNGEL E. CAL is a doctoral candidate in history at the University of Arizona. He is writing a dissertation on British capital investment in the eastern coast of Central America during the nineteenth century. He is also Lecturer in History and Acting Academic Dean at the University College of Belize in Central America.

RAMÓN D. CHACÓN is Associate Professor of History and Director of Ethnic Studies at Santa Clara University. He is a specialist in Mexican history and Chicano studies. His articles have been published in anthologies and in journals such as *Peasant Studies, Journal of Church and State, The Americas, Social Science Quarterly,* and *Journalism History.* He is currently working on two manuscripts, one on the Salvador Alvarado era in Yucatán, and the other a cross-cultural community study of Fresno, California.

JOSÉ ARTURO GÜÉMEZ PINEDA is Research Fellow at the Centro de Investigaciones Regionales of the Universidad Autónoma de Yucatán. A specialist in nineteenth-century social and ethnohistory, he has done extensive research on Indian-white relations in Yucatán and is the author of several works on Mayan rustling and other forms of resistance and accommodation prior to the Caste War.

GILBERT M. JOSEPH is Professor of History at the University of North Carolina at Chapel Hill. He is the author of *Revolution from Without: Yucatán, Mexico, and the United States, 1880–1924* (1982) and *Rediscovering the Past at Mexico's Periphery* (1986), and (with Allen Wells) is the co-editor of *Yucatán y La International Harvester* (1986). In addition, he has published numerous articles on the Mexican Revolution and the social history of rural crime and protest.

HERMAN W. KONRAD is Professor of Anthropology and History at the University of Calgary. His interest in Yucatecan society began while he was director of the Instituto Interuniversitario para Investigaciones en Ciencias Sociales in Mérida, Yucatán. His book, *A Jesuit Hacienda in Colonial Mexico: Santa Lucia, 1576–1767* (1980), won the Bolton Prize, which is awarded annually to the best book in Latin American history. For the past dozen years, he has been conducting a long-term, extensive study of the transformation of the tropical forest habitat of the Yucatán peninsula.

ROBERT W. PATCH is Assistant Professor of History at the University of California at Riverside. He also taught at the Universidad Autónoma de Yucatán, where he was one of the founders of the Masters Program in Ethnohistory. He has written numerous articles on the history of Yucatán and is the author of *Maya and Spaniard in Yucatán: A Colonial Regime, 1648–1808* (forthcoming).

DANIELA SPENSER is Research Fellow at the Centro de Investigaciones y Estudios Superiores en Antropología Social (CIESAS) in Mexico City and a doctoral candidate in history at the University of North Carolina at Chapel Hill. Her book, *Partido Socialista Chiapaneco: Rescate y reconstrucción de su historia* (1988), won the Instituto Nacional de Antropología e Historia's Francisco Javier Clavijero Prize. In addition to publishing various articles on the political economy of coffee in the Chiapanecan Soconusco, she is the co-author of *Los Empresarios Alemanes, El Tercer Reich y La Oposición de Derecha a Cárdenas* (1988).

ALLEN WELLS is Associate Professor of History at Bowdoin College. He is the author of *Yucatán's Gilded Age: Haciendas, Henequen, and International Harvester, 1860–1915* (1985) and co-editor of *Yucatán y La International Harvester* (1986). He also has published articles in the *Latin American Research Review* and the *Journal of Latin American Studies*. He and Gilbert M. Joseph are completing a book titled *Summer of Discontent, Seasons of Upheaval: Elite Politics and Rural Rebellion in Yucatán, 1890–1915*, which will be published by the University of New Mexico Press.

Index